Steve —
You have all t...
and conquer the ...
have fun and s...
Risks! [signature]



# Air Force Officer's Guide

Stephen:
Congratulations and Best of Luck
on your new Career
Col Perkins, May 95

Steve, Congrats and best
wishes in your career and
marriage. Never fear trying
new ideas and new
methods!
Capt Hall

Steve! Good luck! You've
made a good start and
built a solid foundation
here for a great career!
Enjoy it!
[signature]

# AIR FORCE OFFICER'S GUIDE

## 30th Edition

LT. COL. JOHN HAWKINS NAPIER III,
USAF (RET.)

STACKPOLE BOOKS

Published by
STACKPOLE BOOKS
5067 Ritter Road
Mechanicsburg, PA 17055

Continuously published and copyrighted since 1948 by The Military Service Publishing Company, Harrisburg, Pa. (1948-57), and Stackpole Books, Harrisburg, Pa. (1959-93), and Mechanicsburg, Pa. (1993-).

Thirtieth Edition.



*Color photographs of medals by Ken Smith; most photos courtesy USAF*

*Cover design by Mark B. Olszewski*

Printed in the U.S.A.

10 9 8 7 6 5 4 3 2 1

**Library of Congress has cataloged this serial publication as follows:**

Air Force officer's guide/by John H. Napier III.— —Harrisburg, Pa.: Stackpole Books.

v.: ill.; 23 cm.

Began with: 23rd ed.
Description based on: 26th ed.
Continues: Air officer's guide.
ISSN 0739-635X = Air Force officer's guide.

1. United States. Air Force—Officers' handbooks.

UG633.A1A49 358.4'00973—dc19 83-644873
AACR 2 MARC-S

# Contents

*THE United States Air Force is an instrument available to the people of this Republic for their common defense and for the advancement of the interests of the United States throughout the World. Insofar as this Air Force—this instrument—is strong, sharp, and ready, its existence tends to deter the potential aggressor, giving warning of swift punishment for the lawless. A great and historic interest of the American people lies in their desire for a world of peace and justice. The U.S. Air Force, through prompt and efficient completion of its assigned missions, can ensure the arrival of that long-hoped-for day when all human beings may walk in freedom and in fear of none save their God . . . or, by slipshod and indifferent performance of its part, the Air Force can cause the American people to lose what Abraham Lincoln called the last, best hope of earth. The issue is in the balance. You, as a member of the U.S. Air Force, will tip the scales for better or for worse.*

The U.S. Air Force is symbolized by the American bald eagle with wings elevated and displayed in front of a puff cloud.

The striking power of the Air Force is from above the clouds and is represented by the winged thunderbolt taken from Mars's shield, which is placed above the cloudlike base represented by the nebular partition line and white background.

Thirteen stars surround the coat of arms, and the Roman numerals "MCMXLVII" translate "1947."

The eagle is looking to the right, the field of honor.

Part One • You, the USAF Officer

# 1

# Appointments and Assignments

*The Air Force needs you, and the nation needs you, as much as ever before.*
—General David C. Jones, USAF, former Chairman, Joint Chiefs of Staff

**OATH OF OFFICE**

I, ________(name)________, having been appointed a ________(grade)________, United States Air Force, do solemnly swear (or affirm) that I will support and defend the Constitution of the United States against all enemies, foreign and domestic; that I will bear true faith and allegiance to the same; that I take this obligation freely, without any mental reservation or purpose of evasion; and that I will well and faithfully discharge the duties of the office upon which I am about to enter, SO HELP ME GOD.

Congratulations on the honor of receiving your commission! The oath you have taken, printed here for you to reread and remember, is essentially the same as that taken by American officers since George Washington. Rudyard Kipling once wrote, "He became an officer *and* a gentleman, which is an enviable thing," to which we should add the alternative words "she" and "lady." You have joined a long line of dedicated and talented officers in khaki, olive drab, and blue who have gone before you in upholding our nation's security. Their watchword, as ours, does not belong to West Point alone: Duty, Honor, Country.

*Air Force Officer's Guide* is designed to help you begin your Air Force career. The guide dates back to 1948, after the U.S. Air Force became independent of the U.S. Army. Its genesis, however, lies in the parent *Officer's Guide* (now *Army Officer's Guide,* in its 46th edition), which first appeared in 1930, and which during World War II was an indispensable source of reference for hundreds of thousands of wartime officers. Our hope is that this 30th edition of *Air Force Officer's Guide* will be the same for you. Good luck to you.

## THE PROFESSION OF ARMS

Congratulations! You have just joined the profession of arms. Perhaps you may need to know what sets professionals apart from people in some other kind of employment and what sets you as a professional officer apart from your civilian colleagues.

According to Samuel P. Huntington, corporateness, expertise, and responsibility distinguish a profession from some other kind of employment. The profession of arms is similar to other professions in that it, too, requires corporateness, expertise, and responsibility.

Just as any other profession, the profession of arms has corporateness, a sense of unity, and consciousness as a group apart. It is a body of men and women bound together by warm ties of camaraderie, feeling themselves a corporate entity, holding to similar values and ideals, set apart from the commonalty by distinct traditions and usages, undergoing common experiences and concerns, and using a distinctive vocabulary. Part of what sets each traditional profession apart from other employment and from other professions and makes its members feel the corporateness of their profession includes the lengthy preparation needed for professional competence, the common bond of high calling, and distinctive ceremonial garb, such as the priest's vestments, the judge's robes, the professor's academic regalia, or the officer's uniform and insignia. Customs, traditions, schools, journals, and associations also strengthen the corporate bond, perhaps especially in the military.

Besides corporateness, professions require expertise. The profession of arms also requires expertise, not only in any one of various specialties within the military, such as medicine, law, computer science, aviation science, or engineering, but also in military affairs. Just as other professions do, the profession of arms requires higher education, a college degree or degrees, specific professional preparation, continuing education, technical training, and professional military education in at least three levels of schools.

In addition to corporateness and expertise, professions have as their motive a responsibility to society. The profession of arms also requires responsibility, a charge to measure up to demanding criteria, to be accountable for other people and accountable to authority and to oneself, and to defend one's country with one's life, if need be. Professions often express that responsibility in a set of moral norms, a code of ethics, such as the priest's vows, the physician's Hippocratic oath, the standard of bar and bench, and the officer's code of honor. Also, a profession admits its practitioners to assume this responsibility itself, such as by the ordination of the priest, the licensing of the physician, the admission of the attorney to the bar, the award of the doctorate to the professor, and the commissioning of the officer.

## SOURCES OF OFFICERS

The Air Force has a variety of sources for meeting its active duty officer requirements (projections of numbers commissioned are for fiscal year 1995).

**The Service Academies.** The Air Force Academy produces about 950 graduates a year. In addition, the Air Force appoints a limited number of Naval Academy and Military Academy graduates.

**Air Force ROTC (AFROTC).** The Air Force conducts an ROTC program at more than 138 colleges and universities throughout the nation. This source supplies about 1,450 second lieutenants to the Air Force each year. The AFROTC four-year program requires four academic years of ROTC studies and four weeks of field training. The AFROTC two-year program requires two academic years of aerospace studies plus six weeks of field training.

**Officer Training School (OTS).** The Air Force conducts an intensive three-month training course at Maxwell Air Force Base, Alabama, for college graduates who are not ROTC graduates. The Air Force selects OTS candidates whose academic majors fill Air Force needs. Successful applicants train in the pay grade of staff sergeant and enter active duty in the grade of second lieutenant immediately upon completion of the course. This program is a valuable supplement to the Air Force ROTC program and provides an avenue of commissioning each year for about 350 people who, for various reasons, are not ROTC graduates.

**Direct Commissions.** The Air Force commissions annually about 1,100 medical personnel, judge advocates, and chaplains, plus a few Air Force reservists. These receive officer orientation at their respective schools at Maxwell Air Force Base, Alabama.

**About Your Fellow Officers.** You are joining about 85,000 Air Force officers on active service, ranging from 11 four-star generals down, nearly all of whom once sported the newest gold bars on base. About 12 percent are Air Force Academy graduates, 40 percent are from AFROTC, 34 percent are from OTS or the former OCS (Officer Candidate School), and 14 percent fall into the "other" category, which includes graduates of West Point and Annapolis, aviation cadets, and direct appointments. They fly 7,100 aircraft. About 11 percent are black or belong to other racial minorities. About 14 percent are women, who, since they began flying training in 1977, include several hundred pilots and navigators among them. The average age of Air Force officers is 35. In the officer corps, 51 percent have bachelor's degrees; 47 percent, master's; and 1.37 percent, doctorates. Your fellow officers also include about 50,000 who are active in Air Force Reserve or Air National Guard units, flying another 2,250 aircraft. Furthermore, about 150,000 retired Air Force officers are also your comrades in arms who passed your way a little bit ahead of you.

**The Military in Public Esteem.** Gallup polls show consistently that the public institutions in which the American public have the greatest confidence remain the military and the church (about 57 percent each), followed by the Supreme Court, banks, public schools, newspapers, television, and labor. It is up to you to see that the military continues to merit that special trust and confidence.

## APPOINTMENT OF OFFICERS

**Regular Air Force Appointment.** All reserve line officers entering active duty receive many opportunities to achieve regular status. Active duty reserve line officers receive consideration upon promotion to the temporary grades of captain, major, lieutenant colonel, and colonel and also upon completion of five and seven years' active commissioned service. The Air Force automatically considers eligible officers and neither requires nor accepts applications for regular status. Under present law, officers selected are appointed in their current active-duty grade.

An annual central appointment board selects nonline officers, such as chaplains,

*To all who shall see these presents, greeting:*

*Know ye, that reposing special trust and confidence in the patriotism, valor, fidelity and abilities of* **JOHN E. DOE** *, I do appoint* **HIM** **SECOND LIEUTENANT** **RESERVE** *in the*

# United States Air Force

*to* **DATE** *as such from the* **THIRTY-FIRST** *day of* **MAY** *, nineteen hundred and* **NINETY-FIVE** *. This officer will therefore carefully and diligently discharge the duties of the office to which appointed by doing and performing all manner of things thereunto belonging.*

*And I do strictly charge and require those officers and other personnel of lesser rank to render such obedience as is due an officer of this grade and position. And this officer is to observe and follow such orders and directions, from time to time, as may be given by the President of the United States of America, or other superior officers acting in accordance with the laws of the United States of America.*

*This commission is to continue in force during the pleasure of the President of the United States of America, under the provisions of those public laws relating to Officers of the* Armed Forces of the United States of America *and the component thereof in which this appointment is made.*

*Done at the City of Washington, this* **THIRTY-FIRST** *day of* **MAY** *in the year of our Lord, one thousand nine hundred and* **NINETY-FIVE** *, and of the Independence of the United States of America, the* **TWO HUNDRED AND NINETEENTH YEAR**

*By the President:*

Lieutenant General, USAF
Deputy Chief of Staff, Manpower and Personnel

Secretary of the Air Force

OFFICER APPOINTMENT, AIR FORCE RESERVE.

judge advocates, nurses, and so on. The year groups considered for appointment vary each year according to vacancies in the regular structure. Under this program, the board automatically considers all eligible officers in the announced year groups. Physicians and dentists may also submit application for appointment.

**Appointment in the Air National Guard.** The Air National Guard has authority to appoint officers in required specialties under state appointment criteria. Normally, the federal government also recognizes such officers and concurrently awards them appointments as Reserve of the Air Force in the same grade. The adjutant general of the state National Guard handles requests for information or applications for appointment.

**Direct Appointments in the Air Force Reserve.** At present, the Air Force Reserve limits direct appointments to chaplains, legal officers, and medical specialists.

## INITIAL ACTIVE-DUTY ASSIGNMENT

As an officer newly appointed in the Air Force Reserve or other Air Force component, you will receive from Headquarters USAF a letter of notification with an oath of office and other pertinent papers attached. You should execute the oath of office and any other documents associated with your commission and return these papers to Headquarters USAF as directed. Then wait for orders to active duty. When you receive these orders to an initial tour of active duty, you probably will find that you have at least thirty days to prepare for your initial assignment.

**Military Sponsor Program.** The Air Force operates a "sponsor" program to assist new officers in getting settled into their assignments. The organization that is to receive the new officer appoints a sponsor—usually an officer of about the same age and grade—to advise and assist the newcomer. Normal procedure is for the sponsor to get in touch with the incoming officer by telephone or letter to give the newcomer information regarding the organization to which he or she is being assigned, the housing situation, the climatic conditions, and other pertinent facts. If you have not received a contact from a sponsor shortly after receiving your orders, you should telephone the organization, ask the name of your assigned sponsor, and then get in touch with your sponsor directly. Conditions differ considerably among the various Air Force stations, and nothing is better than getting the word from someone who is already wherever you're heading.

**Records and Orders.** You should carry in a briefcase or other handy place copies of all orders received, all personnel records, and all other pertinent documents that bear upon your military service or appointment as a commissioned officer. As a matter of fact, any time you receive orders, you should immediately make about ten copies. Put one copy into your wallet, and keep the other copies handy because several offices at your new duty station, such as finance, transportation, and housing, will need copies of your orders for inprocessing. You should also carry any other papers, such as insurance records, automobile titles, and income tax records, that you may need to conduct your personal affairs in the immediate future.

**Uniforms and Equipment.** Chapter 5 explains Air Force uniforms and equipment officers use. Before departing for an initial tour of active duty, you should get and plan to have with you at all times at least the minimum required equipment: one complete service uniform, all-season, with all necessary associated components such as shirts, socks, ties, and insignia; an authorized all-weather coat; and necessary underwear.

You can get additions to the military wardrobe at most bases, but the best policy is to come prepared. If you do not already have these minimums, you should make sure you get only regulation articles, which you can get at Air Force base exchanges (the BX).

**Reporting for Duty.** The orders that assign you to a base for duty include a date for reporting. You should make every effort to report between 0900 and 1200 of the date required so that you can complete many important arrangements on the day you report.

In those cases in which a large number of officers report within a short period, as at a training center or port of embarkation, a receiving committee may handle the reception of arriving officers. In such a case, the formality of reporting consists only of presenting yourself at the proper office, which is usually indicated by signs, presenting your orders, signing the register, and receiving instructions. A member of this committee usually handles quartering and messing arrangements and provides, often in a photocopied order, any information newcomers may need. At a later meeting, the commander or his representative may address the group for purposes of organization or orientation. In such mass inprocessing situations, make sure that you have received all of the instructions you should have and that you understand them thoroughly.

Normally, your sponsor should help you get settled into your new environment and assist you in every way possible during your initial period at your new assignment. Your sponsor should arrange a time to call upon the commander and arrange for you to meet your immediate commander. Your sponsor should also tell you your quarters assignment or whom to see to get this information or advise you where to get information regarding available civilian housing. The sponsor may also arrange for delivery of your baggage to your quarters and provide you a copy of the local base regulations and a map of the base.

**Officer's Identification Card.** Upon coming to active duty as a commissioned officer, you will receive an identification card (DD Form 2 AF) printed in bleeding ink on watermarked safety paper compressed between laminated plastic sheets. It will bear your photograph, signature, and other essential data. Carry it at all times. It will establish your identity and will help you get the rights and privileges to which active duty entitles you. In the event of its loss (which should never occur), report the fact promptly to Pass and ID Section of the military personnel flight (MPF).

Upon promotion, you will receive a new card.

Retired officers, officers on inactive service, and dependents receive identification cards with their status clearly shown.

**Getting Established in Quarters.** After reporting at the headquarters and to the subordinate commander under whom you are to serve, find your quarters, have your baggage moved in, and get established at once. On a permanent base, the housing office may assign you a set of quarters or an apartment in the bachelors' building, or you may need to make temporary arrangements off the base, pending the assignment of quarters. Custom dictates that, as a newly joined officer, you will have sufficient time to get settled and to establish yourself before undertaking your duties.

**Messing Arrangements.** Unless you get quarters with kitchen privileges and facilities where you can provide your own meals, you may eat at the officers' open mess, commonly termed the officers' club. The mess officer will give you complete information concerning dues rates, prices, and operating hours. The officers' mess provides the social setting to widen your acquaintance with your fellow officers. Its atmosphere is warm and friendly, and it is a privilege to enjoy its facilities. For further information, see AFR 215-11.

**Local Regulations.** Carefully study the local base regulations, and comply with them fully. They usually contain much useful information on local conditions, facilities, conveniences, and requirements. Because these regulations answer many questions, they will assist you in making adjustments to the new environment and may save you embarrassment. If the regulations don't make sense, ask old-timers in your organization what they mean.

**The Quarters Situation.** Officers' quarters vary widely from one base to the next. Many bases have only limited housing for families of officers. Private housing in civilian communities near bases is sometimes scarce, and rents are high in some areas of the country and the rest of the world. Officers should thoroughly research the exact family housing conditions that confront them before moving members of their families from a comfortable place. As for the bachelor officer, the usual quarters assignment is a bachelor officers' quarters (BOQ) room.

**Learn Your Way Around.** Study a map of the base, and find the important buildings, roads, training areas, and recreational facilities.

**The Base Exchange.** Visit the base exchange (BX) soon after you arrive. Operated under the supervision of the commander, it is a community store under the Defense Department Exchange System. At most stations, the exchange consists of a general store, a tailor shop, a shoe repair shop, and a barber shop. It also supplies other services for the benefit of officers and airmen of the base. Newly joined officers can satisfy most of their immediate needs at the exchange, and because the BX is closely supervised, they can know that their purchases will meet local conditions and requirements.

OFFICER RE-UPPING AN AIRMAN IN SAUDI ARABIA.

**Getting Set with the Accounting and Finance Office.** As soon as possible after arrival at the base, you should visit the base accounting and finance office. Here you should arrange to collect travel allowances and to receive monthly pay and allowances. At this time, also initiate any allotments desired. In all of these matters, personnel at the finance office will help you figure out which forms to use and how to fill them out.

**Starting to Work.** As a new officer arriving on active duty for a first tour, you will find that no one expects you to be expert in performing your duties or in knowing about the Air Force. You will also find, however, that seniors and contemporaries will expect you to go about bettering your technical capabilities and expanding your knowledge. Practically everyone on the base from the airman to the commander and even civilian personnel will be ready to assist you in any way he or she can. As a new officer, you should neither bluff nor exercise false pride that could prevent you from seeking information and assistance. Simply proceed in a reasonable manner to learn your job and your way around.

## CHANGE OF STATION

When you as an officer already assigned on active duty to a base or other station receive orders reassigning you to a different station, you must perform certain duties before you leave. Although the most important of these duties relates to securing release from responsibility for unit property and funds (see chapter 10), you must also take care of certain *personal* responsibilities when departing a station.

**Be Prepared.** In the Air Force, reassignments to new stations, including stations overseas, are routine and frequent events. Quite often, such shifts from one base to another, or even from one continent to another, occur with little warning, if any. In such cases, the needs of the Air Force outweigh the convenience of the individual officer. Your duty, therefore, is to keep ready for departure from your current assignment at any time. The Air Force has even had to recall officers from leave to depart immediately for oversea stations. Accordingly, you must maintain your personal affairs and your personal equipment to permit sudden departure from your base.

**Reassignment to a New Station.** (For information concerning transfer to an oversea station, see chapter 22. Also see chapter 20.) Upon receipt of orders for a change of station, you should proceed to the base headquarters, where you can obtain a clearance form. This form will require you to obtain the initials of a large number of custodial and administrative officials, such as the club officer, the finance officer, the flight surgeon, and many others, to show that you have cleared up any unfinished business with them before you leave the base. For example, you must pay all outstanding bills owed to the officers' mess or to the officers' club, turn in all equipment drawn from the base supply officer, and discharge many other such requirements. Generally, you can clear the base from one central location.

You must also remember to prepare and submit any required performance reports on other officers before you leave a station.

If you have outstanding debts or bills in the local community near the base you are

---

*Note:* The Armed Forces Hostess Association will provide on request considerable information on your new base, whether CONUS or overseas. The address is Room 1A736, The Pentagon, Washington, DC 20310-3133. Call (703) 697-3180/6857.

Also see *Guide to Military Installations,* 4th ed., by Dan Cragg, Stackpole Books, 1994.

departing, you should either pay these obligations or make satisfactory arrangements with your creditors to pay them.

Before leaving, also make sure that you have copies of all the following kinds of paperwork: all official orders, records of immunizations, eyeglass prescriptions, orders terminating assignment of quarters, military pay records, and personnel records. If you plan to travel by personal transportation, make sure your orders authorize both this action and the time necessary to complete such travel. If you don't plan to use personal transportation to go to your new assignment, secure transportation requests. If you don't know what to do about orders and transportation requests, ask your administrative noncommissioned officer (admin NCO) for advice and help with the forms.

Before leaving for your first duty station—and, for that matter, every time you change duty stations—find these records and use this checklist to make sure you don't forget any of them:

- Copies of orders.
- Automobile insurance policy.
- Automobile registration or title.
- Bank books.
- Copy of birth certificate.
- Driver's license.
- Immunization records.
- Insurance policies or numbers thereof.
- Social Security card.
- University transcripts.

If married, also take copies of your marriage license and your spouse's and children's birth certificates, immunization records, and Social Security cards.

The staff judge advocate's office at your duty station can draw up a power of attorney and a will.*

## ASSUMPTION OF A NEW ASSIGNMENT

Although many of the rapidly occurring changes in the lives and careers of Air Force officers involve physical movement from one air base to another, quite often the change confronting an Air Force officer is in the nature of the assumption of a new duty. Command is a very infrequent duty assignment. By far the majority of the officers of the Air Force are engaged in duties that do not involve exercising command over units of the Air Force. Such work is extremely important in many cases. Every officer must be determined to perform it in an outstanding manner, despite the absence of the advantages of a command position.

**Assuming a Staff Position.** Upon reporting for duty on staff assignments, officers should report first to the executive of the staff agency to which assigned and thereafter to the chiefs of subbranches or sections as directed by the executive. Usually, a well-administered headquarters will have published a manual for staff officers that sets forth the organization and the particular staff procedures desired by the commander of the headquarters. On joining a staff, you should find one of these manuals and study it with care.

---

* Also see chapter 9, "Your Legal Survival Kit," *The Servicemember's Legal Guide,* 2nd ed., by Jonathan P. Tomes, Stackpole Books, 1992.

The next step is to become acquainted with the other members of the staff, especially with those members of staff sections closely allied to your own.

Having mastered the organization and the procedures and having become acquainted with the members of the staff to which you are assigned, you should go meet and get acquainted with officers in staffs senior and junior to your own. For example, as an officer assigned to the operations section of a group headquarters, you should become acquainted with the operations personnel in the wing headquarters and also in each of the squadron headquarters within your own group. These personal relationships often go far in mitigating misunderstanding among staffs of various levels.

As a staff officer, you must constantly bear in mind that you are not a commander and have no power of command. Frequently, however, you may act for the commander in matters of considerable importance. In doing so, you must strictly adhere to the policies of the commander. On the other hand, you certainly should not evade your own responsibilities by seeking to discover the views of the commander in every specific instance. You must act within the scope of the commander's authority and policies, and you must act as if you yourself bore the sole responsibility for your actions. Consider these questions whenever you have to make decisions for or in other ways act for your commander: (1) Would I be willing to undertake the execution of the decision I recommend were I a subordinate element commander receiving orders of this staff? (2) Would I be willing to accept the full responsibility for the effect of this decision were I the chief of this staff?

**Assuming an Assignment with the Air Reserve Forces.** The size and importance of the Air National Guard, the Air Force Reserve, and the Air Force ROTC make an assignment with one of these components both an opportunity and a challenge. Duty with these elements imposes upon the officer perhaps the maximum requirement for tact and diplomacy. In assuming an assignment with the Air Reserve forces, just as if you were assuming a staff position, you should become thoroughly familiar with the organization and the procedures of the element to which assigned. You should also become acquainted with the members of the Air Reserve unit with which you will be associated.

Duty with the Air Force ROTC involves the special situation of dealing with students who are not members of the military forces and with civilian college and university administrators, staff, and faculty whose principal interest lies in conducting civilian education. The Department of Aerospace Studies is an integral part of the college or university and must conform to the academic standards of the institution. Most host institutions give constructive credit toward degree requirements for AFROTC courses, and others grant nominal credit counting only toward the grade-point average.

## ASSUMPTION OF A COMMAND POSITION

Each Air Force officer must anticipate being assigned without warning to assume command of an Air Force unit. This opportunity may arise as a result of combat or less dramatically as the result of a sudden need to shift personnel. As an Air Force officer in such a situation, you may find that the command position given is a larger one than normally associated with your grade. Therefore, you should develop the habit of getting to know the problems of command of the next higher unit whenever you assume any new assignment.

**Assumption of Command in Combat.** During operations against an enemy, your next higher superior may become wounded. If you are the next junior officer down the chain of command, your immediate duty is to take over the responsibility of your senior. This need could result, for example, from any one of several situations, such as a flight leader shot down in aerial combat, the commander of a security police squadron struck by enemy gunfire on the ground, or the commander of a maintenance squadron becoming ill. In any case, you, as the junior, must act at once to ensure that the unit continues to perform its mission. Although such assumption of command under conditions of combat may prove to be only a temporary expedient, you must never allow a break in the continuity of command during combat. Like every other officer, you must be prepared to step in and take over when necessary.

**Assumption of Command under Conditions Other than Combat.** Whenever the commander of an Air Force unit is detached from command of the organization for any reason, the next senior officer present for duty automatically assumes command, pending orders from higher authority. In such a situation, the officer assuming command shoulders all the responsibility and the authority previously held by the officer replaced. If you assume command during such a sensitive situation, act slowly and cautiously. For example, you may want to defer promotion or demotion of airmen until after the new commander has been officially announced.

**Transfer of Responsibilities.** Other than under conditions of combat, officers assuming command take over all standing orders, the unit fund, all public property pertaining to the unit, and the organization's records. The transfer of these responsibilities, especially for property and funds, should proceed in a careful and thorough manner with the outgoing and the incoming commanders reaching jointly acceptable conclusions. As the new commander, you should decline to accept responsibility until you have satisfied yourself that the property, the funds, and the records of the unit are in understandable and proper order.

**Do Not Hasten to Change Things.** Sometimes, officers assuming command of an Air Force unit are overly quick to disrupt standing operating procedures (SOPs), to modify radically policies the unit personnel have become familiar with, and generally to create confusion. As the new commander, you should allow a reasonable period of time to study the organization, the personnel, and the practices that preceded your period of command before launching into major changes.

# 2

# Military Courtesy

*In dealing with others be courteous, sir; the courtesy affirms both your own good breeding and your attitude of respect toward your fellow man.*

—General R. E. Lee

A very fine line distinguishes military courtesies from military customs. Both categories owe their existence to a common source: the respect for one another that is the proper attitude among military personnel. Military courtesies, however, are mandatory. Omission of them can and most likely will bring immediate disciplinary action. They are a part of an officer's duty; they are a strong strand in the mesh of discipline that holds a military organization together. Whoever ignores military customs will be privately censured. Whoever ignores military courtesies, however, will be officially clobbered.

Even though an officer has no choice as to whether to pay required military courtesies, a little thought would make this requirement no burden at all. Almost all the specifics of military courtesy parallel or are identical to those acts of civility, good breeding, and thoughtfulness observed among polite people everywhere. Such courtesies improve relations between people, ease the conduct of business affairs, and add smoothness to otherwise awkward and undesirable situations. For example, people commonly address an elderly gentleman in civilian life as "Sir" or with his full title, such as "Mister Smith." Few, if any, people of younger age would say to such a man of distinguished years, "Hey, you," or "Say, Mac . . ." Why? No discipline in civilian life requires it, but people have learned through experience that to pay certain courtesies in certain situations is a better idea than not to do so. The Air Force and other military services have codified for you such lessons learned through experience and made them mandatory so that you need not blunder along until experience teaches the proper reactions to all the many situations you may meet.

## CORRECT USE OF TITLES

**Titles of Officers.** Officially address lieutenants as "Lieutenant." Use the adjectives "First" and "Second" only in written communications.

Address or refer to other officers by their titles. In conversation and in nonofficial correspondence, refer to and address brigadier generals, major generals, and lieutenant generals as "General" and lieutenant colonels and colonels as "Colonel."

Senior officers frequently address juniors as "Smith" or "Jones," but this practice does not give juniors the privilege of addressing seniors in any way other than by their proper titles. If airmen are present, senior officers should address junior officers by their titles. Officers of the same grade, when among themselves, may address one another by their given names.

Address chaplains as "Chaplain" regardless of their grades. Address as "Father" Roman Catholic chaplains and Episcopal chaplains who prefer it.

**Titles of Cadets.** Address cadets of the United States Air Force Academy and the United States Military Academy as "Cadet" officially and in written communications.

Members of the brigade at the Naval Academy have the title of "Midshipman." Address them by the title of "Mister" or "Miss."

**Titles of USAF Enlisted Personnel.** In official communications, address enlisted personnel by their full titles. In conversation and in nonofficial correspondence, refer to and address enlisted personnel as follows:

| | |
|---|---|
| Chief master sergeants | "Chief" |
| Senior master sergeants | "Sergeant" |
| Master sergeants | "Sergeant" |
| Technical sergeants | "Sergeant" |
| Staff sergeants | "Sergeant" |
| Sergeants | "Sergeant" |
| Senior Airmen | "Airman" |
| Airmen first class | "Airman" |
| Airmen | "Airman" |
| Airmen basic | "Airman" |

**Identification and Titles of Officers of Other Services.** You must also meticulously observe military courtesies in contacts with officers of the Army, the Navy, the Marine Corps, and the Coast Guard in the same manner as for officers of the Air Force.

The corresponding grades of commissioned officers in the Air Force, the Army, and the Navy are in the illustrations in chapter 5. The grades of commissioned officers in the Marine Corps are the same as those of the Army and the Air Force. In the Coast Guard, the grades correspond to those of the Navy. Respective dates of commission determine relative rank within grades.

## MILITARY SALUTES

**History of the Military Salute.** Men of arms have used some form of the military salute as an exchange of greeting since the earliest times. All modern armed forces that inherited their military traditions from the Age of Chivalry have preserved the military salute and continued its use. The method of giving the salute has varied through the ages, as it still varies in form among the armed forces of today. Whatever form it has taken, it has always pertained to military personnel.

PASSING IN REVIEW.

Although the genesis of the military salute is shrouded in the mysteries of the ages, historians do have some idea how it began. In the Age of Chivalry, for example, the knights were all mounted and wore steel armor that covered the body completely, including the head and the face. When two friendly knights met, their custom was for each to raise the visor and expose his face to the view of the other. They always raised the visor with the right hand and held the reins with the left. It was a significant gesture of friendship and confidence because it exposed the features and also removed the right hand—the sword hand—from the vicinity of the weapon. Also, in ancient times, the freemen (soldiers) of Europe could carry arms; when two freemen met, each would raise his right hand to show that he held no weapon in it and that the meeting was a friendly one. Slaves could not carry arms, and they passed freemen without the exchange of a greeting. The knightly gesture of raising the hand to the visor came to be recognized as the proper greeting between soldiers. Its use continued even after modern firearms had made steel armor a thing of the past. The military salute is today, as it seems always to have been, a unique form of exchange of greeting between military people, between comrades in the honorable profession of arms. Military prisoners, however, are not permitted to salute.

**The Different Forms of the Salute.** Although in this chapter, unless otherwise stated, salute means the hand salute, prescribed salutes can take several forms. The officer uses the hand salute and the salute by removing the civilian headdress; airmen use each of these methods and the several methods of saluting with arms, such as the salute by a sentinel armed with a carbine.

When a salute is prescribed (except in formation), the military member either faces toward the person or colors saluted or turns the head so as to observe the person or color saluted.

Covered or uncovered, military members exchange salutes in the same manner.

People who are running come to a walk before saluting.

The smartness with which officers and airmen give the salute indicates the degree of pride they have in their profession. A careless or half-hearted salute is discourteous.

One custom in the Army and the Air Force is that newly commissioned officers give a dollar to the first enlisted member who salutes them.

Other means of saluting besides the hand salute include Present Arms, Eyes Right, Present Saber or Sword (in the three other services), Present Guidons, dipping unit colors, Ruffles and Flourishes, the president's and vice president's marches, gun salutes, three rifle volleys at graveside, dipping airplane wings, and the ceremonial flyover.

**Methods of Saluting Used by Officers.** Officers salute by using the hand salute and the salute by placing the civilian headdress over the left breast.

The hand salute is the usual method. While in most instances officers give the hand salute while standing or marching at attention, they may also give it while seated, such as when an officer seated at a desk acknowledges the salute of an officer or an airman who is making a report.

Officers use the salute by placing the headdress, held in the right hand, over the left breast under three conditions. At a military funeral, all military personnel dressed in civilian clothes use this form of the salute as a courtesy to the deceased. Members of the military service dressed in civilian clothes and covered (wearing headdress) use the method to salute the National Anthem or "To the Color (Standard)." While in the same dress, they also use this salute to pay homage to the national flag or color. Members in civilian clothing and uncovered (without headdress) stand at attention, holding the hand over the heart, as a courtesy to the National Anthem or the national flag or color.

**Execution of the Hand Salute.** Salute within saluting distance, the distance within which recognition is easy and usually less than thirty paces. Begin the salute when you are about six paces from the person or the colors you are saluting or, in case the approach is outside that distance, six paces from the point of nearest approach. Before the instant arrives to give the salute, stand or walk erectly, hold your head up, tuck your chin in, and pull in on your stomach muscles. Look squarely and frankly at the person to be saluted.

To execute the hand salute correctly, raise the right hand smartly until the tip of the forefinger touches the lower part of the headdress or forehead above and slightly to the right of the right eye, thumb and fingers extended and joined, palm to the left, upper arm horizontal, forearm inclined at a 45° angle, hand and wrist straight; at the same time, turn the head toward the person saluted. To complete the salute, drop the arm to its normal position by the side in one motion, at the same time turning the head and eyes to the front.

If you are returning the salute of an airman or of an officer junior to yourself, execute the two movements of the salute in the cadence of marching, ONE, TWO. If you are saluting a superior officer, execute the first movement and HOLD the position until the salute is acknowledged, and then complete your salute by dropping the hand smartly to your side.

Do these things correctly and you will derive many rewards. Your airmen will be quick to notice your salute, and they will vie with you in efforts to outdo their officer—a particularly healthy reaction. Thus, you may set the example that may then extend to other matters. At the time of exchanging salutes, you may also certainly say, "Good morning" or "Good afternoon."

Try to avoid making these frequently observed errors in saluting: failure to hold the position of the salute until it is returned, failure to look at the person or color saluted, failure to assume the position of attention while saluting, failure to have the thumb and finger extended and joined (a protruding thumb is especially objectionable), a bent wrist (the hand and wrist should be in the same plane), and failure to have the upper arm horizontal. By all means, avoid these gross errors: saluting with a cigarette in the right hand or in the mouth, saluting with the left hand in a pocket, or returning a salute in a casual or perfunctory manner.

**Uncovering.** As a general rule, officers and airmen under arms do not uncover. They do uncover, however, in these circumstances:

- When they are seated as members of or in attendance at courts or boards. (Sentinels over prisoners do not uncover.)
- When they enter places of divine worship.
- When they are indoors not on duty and want to remain informal.
- When they attend official receptions.

Members in uniform may salute civilians when appropriate, but they will not raise the uniform hat or cap as a form of salutation.

**Interpretation of Outdoors and Indoors.** In the application of military courtesies, the military considers as "outdoors" structures such as hangars, gymnasiums, and other roofed structures when used for drill or exercise of troops.

"Indoors" means offices, hallways, dining halls, kitchens, orderly rooms, recreation rooms, libraries, and quarters or other places of abode.

**Meaning of Under Arms.** The expression "under arms" means with arms in hand or having attached to the person a hand arm or the equipment pertaining directly to the arm, such as a cartridge belt, a pistol holster, or an automatic rifle belt.

## COURTESIES AIRMEN GIVE TO OFFICERS

**Occasions.** Airmen must give the hand salute outdoors both on and off military installations whether on or off duty, except when the salute would be manifestly inappropriate or impractical. They must also give the hand salute in all official greetings in the line of duty, for ceremonial occasions, and when the National Anthem is played or the colors pass by.

Those entitled to the salute are commissioned officers of the Air Force, the Army, the Navy, the Marine Corps, and the Coast Guard. Saluting officers of friendly foreign countries, such as officers of the armed forces of NATO, when they are in uniform is also customary.

The Air Force urges its members to be meticulous in giving salutes to and returning salutes from personnel of the sister services. Such courtesy increases the feeling of respect that all members should feel toward comrades in arms.

Covered or uncovered, military members exchange salutes in the same manner.

Members salute only once if the senior remains in the immediate vicinity and no conversation takes place.

Among a group of airmen on a military base and not in formation, the first person noticing the approach of an officer calls the group to attention. If the group of airmen is in formation, the one in charge calls the group to attention. If outdoors and not in formation, they all salute; in formation, the airman in charge salutes. If indoors and not under arms, they uncover and come to attention.

Drivers of vehicles salute only when the vehicle is halted. Any other military person in the vehicle salutes whether the vehicle is halted or in motion. A noncommissioned officer (or officer) in charge of a detail riding in a vehicle salutes for the entire detail.

An airman in charge of a detachment salutes officers by bringing the organization or detachment to attention before saluting.

**Courtesies Exchanged When an Officer Addresses an Airman.** In general, when a conversation takes place between an officer and an airman, the following procedure is correct: They exchange salutes; they complete the conversation; they exchange salutes again. *Exceptions:* An airman in ranks comes to attention and does not salute. Indoors, they do not exchange salutes except when an airman reports to an officer.

**When NOT to Salute.** The following cases require no salutes:

An airman in ranks and not at attention comes to attention when addressed by an officer but does not salute.

Details (and individuals) at work do not salute. The officer or noncommissioned officer in charge, if not actively engaged at the time, salutes or acknowledges salutes for the entire detail.

When actively engaged at games, such as baseball, tennis, or golf, one does not salute.

When in churches, theaters, or other public places or when using public transportation, military members do not exchange salutes.

When carrying articles with both hands, or when otherwise so occupied as to make saluting impracticable, a military member does not salute. A nod and a greeting are, however, always courteous.

A member of the guard who is engaged in the performance of a specific duty, the proper execution of which would prevent saluting, does not salute.

A sentinel armed with a pistol does not salute after challenging. He stands at *raise pistol* until the challenged party has passed.

The driver of a vehicle in motion does not salute.

**Reporting to Officers in Their Offices.** When reporting to officers in their offices, airmen (unless under arms) uncover, knock, and enter when told to do so. Upon entering, they march up to within about two paces of the officer's desk, halt, salute, and report in this manner, for example: "Sir, Airman Jones reports to Captain Smith" or "Sir, Airman Jones reports to the squadron commander." After the report, the officer and the airman carry on the conversation in the first or second person. When the business is complete, the airman salutes, executes about face, and withdraws. An airman uncovers (unless under arms) on entering a room where an officer is present.

**Procedure When an Officer Enters a Dining Hall or Mess Tent.** When an officer enters the dining hall or mess tent, airmen seated at meals remain seated at ease and continue eating unless the officer directs otherwise. *Exception:* An airman addressed ceases eating and sits at attention until completion of the conversation.

**Procedure When an Officer Enters a Barracks or Tent.** In a barracks or tent, airmen rise, uncover (if unarmed), and stand at attention when an officer enters. If more than one person is present, the first to perceive the officer calls, "Attention." On suitable occasions, the officer commands, "Rest" or "At ease," when he expects to remain in the room and does not want them to remain at attention. It is not strictly correct to call officers to attention when the commander enters a room. Instead, the person nearest the door should warn of the commander's approach by calling, "Ladies and gentlemen, the commander!" Officers will then come to attention.

**Personal Courtesies.** When accompanying a senior, a junior walks or rides on the left.

**Entering Automobiles and Small Boats.** Military persons enter automobiles and small boats in inverse order of rank; that is, the senior enters an automobile or a small boat last and leaves first. Juniors, although entering the automobile first, take their appropriate seats in the car. The senior is always on the right. In the case of aircraft, the senior usually boards first and departs first. Officers sit in the back seat of passenger cars driven by airmen unless the car is full.

## COURTESIES AN OFFICER GIVES TO A SENIOR OFFICER

**General.** The courtesies exchanged between officers are those prescribed in Air Force Regulation (AFR) 50-14 and, in addition, those observed through the force of custom as discussed in chapter 3, "Customs of the Service." Of course, officers should return correctly the salutes of airmen and their junior officers.

Many of the courtesies airmen must extend to officers apply with equal force and in identical manner to officers in relations with seniors. The junior salutes first. In making reports at formations, however, the person making the report salutes first regardless of rank. A squadron commander, for example, reporting to the adjutant at a ceremony salutes first.

Several courtesies airmen must extend to officers are not required between officers. The prescribed formalities airmen must observe in a dining hall or mess tent while at meals, for example, do not apply to officers. Also, in an officer's quarters, courtesies prescribed when an officer enters a barracks or tent occupied by one or more airmen are not necessary.

**Specific Courtesies Observed between Officers.** An individual officer outdoors must salute when meeting a person entitled to the salute or when addressed by a senior entitled to the salute.

When reporting in an office to an officer senior in rank, the junior follows the same procedure as described for airmen.

An officer (or a noncommissioned officer) in charge of a detail riding in a vehicle salutes for the entire detail.

Organization or detachment commanders salute officers of higher grades by bringing the organization or detachment to attention before saluting.

The officer (or the noncommissioned officer) in charge of a detail at work, if not actively engaged at the time, salutes for the entire detail.

The officer uncovers (unless under arms) on entering a room where a senior is present.

## HONORS AND CEREMONIES ACCORDED DISTINGUISHED VISITORS (DVs)

The honors and ceremonies prescribed are designed for greeting all distinguished visitors on arrival and are accorded to some on departure. None of the following minimum requirements prevent additional or subsequent ceremonies, such as reviews or parades. The table of honors lists persons entitled to honors by precedence. The intent of honors is to extend a mark of courtesy to a distinguished visitor. The military accords honors to individuals rather than to groups and honors committees and delegations in the person of the senior or ranking member. Overseas, refer unusual questions of precedence to the nearest embassy. Generally, keeping in mind that the intent is to honor a distinguished guest of the Air Force will readily resolve most situations (AFR 50-14).

**Occasions.** Unless directed otherwise, any Air Force installation will accord full honors to the president of the United States on arrival and departure regardless of the day or the hour.

The Air Force accords honors to officials of the same level as or higher than the chief of staff, USAF, during hours between reveille and retreat on work days. The chief of staff, USAF, or commander of a major continental or oversea command may direct or request exceptions to this policy.

The Air Force accords honors to officials from the grade or equivalent of full general through brigadier general on arrival at any Air Force installation for their first visit in a calendar year during hours between reveille and retreat on work days. The chief of staff, USAF, or commander of a major continental or oversea air command may direct exceptions to this policy.

Persons entitled to honors may themselves prescribe the omission of any ceremonies otherwise due.

The Air Force does not ordinarily accord honors to other commissioned officers of the U.S. armed forces unless specifically directed by the chief of staff, USAF. Foreign officers regardless of rank should receive honors on appropriate occasions.

When travel is by air, the airplane commander will include the pertinent part of a prescribed code in the teletype message filed with flight service at the departure point.

**Location.** The ceremonies may take place at any assembly area, but the arrangement of distances and timing must reflect dignity and a sense of protocol. The same ceremonies apply when the visitor's transportation is by means other than airplane. Where facilities are limited, installations will accord such honors as are possible and will control the site to avoid disturbance during the ceremony by the intrusion of spectators.

**Formation.** The receiving party consists of the installation commander, the appointed aide, and, if necessary, the minimum number of staff personnel to properly attend high-ranking members of the distinguished visitor's party. The receiving party participates in the ceremony, but is not part of the honor formation. The aide and staff personnel may act as guides or escort and will provide any necessary assistance throughout the visit.

The honor formation consists of these elements:

- Honor flight commander.
- Color guard.
- Honor flight as prescribed.
- Band, if available. If not, substitute recorded music of the Air Force Band.
- Additional flights in line with band. (The installation commander may use these additional flights on other special occasions.)

The commander will select members of the honor formation for their alertness, dress, and military bearing. Airmen in the honor flight are arranged according to size. The members of the honor formation will wear ribbons denoting decorations and awards on coats. Uniform will be service with white-covered service cap and (except for the members of the band) white gloves, plus special-issue white aiguillettes and white scarves, when available. Color bearers' slings will be white. Color guards will be the only armed members of the honor formation and will carry pistols in holsters. Pistol belts and lanyards will be white.

Where appropriate, the installation commander may invite local civilian officials to join in welcoming the distinguished visitor.

**Arrival of a Distinguished Visitor.** The installation commander with his receiving party will take a post convenient to the designated point of arrival of the dignitary. Relative distances depend upon the location of the ceremony and the visitor's means of transportation. The honor flight will form two lines of airmen in the prescribed number, at normal interval, facing one another so as to form an aisle five paces wide. This aisle will begin at and extend behind and away from the line on which the installation commander and his receiving party take their posts. The honor flight commander will center himself five paces beyond the end of the aisle of airmen. The colors and color guard will form at normal interval centered four paces behind him. The band, if available, will center itself four paces to the rear of the colors and color guard. Additional flights of airmen for a presidential ceremony or other special occasions will form on line with and on each flank of the band. Each flight will consist of not more than 30 airmen. All members of the formation except the aisle of airmen will face the designated point of arrival of the visitor's transportation.

The dignitary's transportation will go to a selected position so that the distinguished visitor will exit from it toward the formation. The honor flight commander will call the formation to attention as the installation commander and receiving party come forward and salute the visitor. The installation commander will welcome the visitor to the base. Unless the visitor desires that certain members of his party share honors, none will participate.

The installation commander will then escort the person to receive honors to a central position facing the colors two paces from the line at which the aisle of airmen begins and stand on the visitor's left. Members of the party sharing honors, if numerous, will form a line or lines behind the visitor and the installation commander. The honor flight commander, upon signal from the installation commander, will order, "Present arms." The band or music will play ruffles and flourishes and the honors march, during which all present, except the national color, salute. (A flourish is a brief trumpet fanfare; a ruffle is a roll of the drums given as the flourish sounds.) The person receiving honors acknowledges them throughout the music by personal salute. Personnel in uniform witnessing the ceremony salute facing toward the person honored. Male personnel in civilian clothes face and salute by placing the hat held in the right hand over the heart. Female personnel in civilian clothes and persons not wearing headgear salute by standing at attention. When the music stops, the honor flight commander will command, "Order arms," which all present will execute.

As the installation commander escorts the visitor forward to enter the staff car, which has moved from the left to a point in front of the honor flight commander and between him and the aisle of airmen, the flight commander will command, "Flight, present arms." (Only the honor formation will salute.) On this command, the band will play inspection music or a march. The aide will escort members of the visiting dignitary's party receiving honors with him through the aisle of airmen, and they will enter their staff cars. After the last of the staff cars departs from the vicinity, the formation will return to the order upon command by the flight commander when the music has stopped. The flight commander will then issue necessary orders to dismiss the formation.

**Departure of a Distinguished Visitor.** The ceremony on departure of distinguished visitors entitled to such honors is substantially the same as that on arrival, but in reverse. The formation is identical. The ceremony may change if visitors depart from the installation in a type of transportation different from that in which they arrived.

The ceremony described hereafter is one for departure by aircraft. The visitor's car moves to a point as before in front of the honor flight commander, who brings the formation to attention and salutes. The band plays inspection music or a march. The visitor, either accompanied or met there by the installation commander, proceeds to the same place as for honors on arrival, and both take the same positions facing the colors. The aide will meanwhile escort members of the visitor's party from their cars to the aircraft by a route outside the aisle of honor airmen. The honor flight commander then comes to the order as the music stops and commands, "Present arms." All salute as before while the music sounds ruffles and flourishes and the honors march. When the music stops, the flight commander will command, "Order arms." The installation commander escorts the visitor to the aircraft and says good-bye. After all have embarked, the receiving party will withdraw to their posts at the beginning of the aisle of honor airmen as before. When space does not permit the honor formation to remain in position as outlined above, the flight commander should issue necessary orders to re-form the honor flight at a safe distance from point of departure of the aircraft. In most instances, closing ranks by the honor airmen will be sufficient. The installation commander, alone, salutes as the visitor's aircraft moves away. If a distinguished person departs by automobile, the commander may adapt the ceremony according to the location by substituting the car for the aircraft. Drivers of staff cars for the visitor and party will not salute during the ceremony. They will remain in their vehicles alert to move forward. The positions of the vehicles depend upon the location of the ceremony.

## TABLE OF HONORS

In place of gun salutes, the number of aircraft in a memorial flyover or the number of persons in the honor cordon indicates the type of honors accorded. The numbers in the "honor cordon" column include the honor cordon commander and airmen, but do not include additional flights for presidential ceremonies or for special occasions the installation commander considers appropriate.

| Distinguished Persons | Honor Cordon [1] | Ruffles & Flourishes | Music | Flags [10] |
|---|---|---|---|---|
| President | 21 | 4 | National Anthem [2]<br>Hail to the Chief [2,3] | United States and Presidential |
| Ex-President | 21 | 4 | National Anthem | United States |
| Heads of state of foreign countries and reigning royalty | 21 | 4 | Foreign Anthem | United States and Foreign |
| Vice President | 19 | 4 | Hail Columbia | United States and command |
| Governor of a state of the United States in jurisdiction | 19 | 4 | Honors March [5] | United States and command |

| Distinguished Persons | Honor Cordon [1] | Ruffles & Flourishes | Music | Flags [10] |
|---|---|---|---|---|
| The Chief Justice of the United States | 19 | 4 | Honors March [5] | United States and command |
| Foreign prime minister or other cabinet officer, foreign ambassador, high commissioner, or special diplomatic representative whose credentials give authority equal to or greater than that of an ambassador | 19 | 4 | National or Foreign Anthem [4] | United States and command |
| Speaker of the House of Representatives | 19 | 4 | Honors March [5] | United States and command |
| Secretary of State | 19 | 4 | Honors March [5] | United States and command |
| The United States Representative to the United Nations | 19 | 4 | Honors March [5] | United States and command |
| Associate Justices of the Supreme Court of the United States | 19 | 4 | Honors March [5] | United States and command |
| Secretary of Defense | 19 [6] | 4 | Honors March [5] | United States and command |
| Cabinet members | 19 | 4 | Honors March [5] | United States and command |
| Governor of a state of the United States out of jurisdiction | 19 | 4 | Honors March [5] | United States and command |
| United States Senators | 19 | 4 | Honors March [5] | United States and command |
| Members of the House of Representatives of the United States | 19 | 4 | Honors March [5] | United States and command |
| Deputy Secretary of Defense; Secretaries of the Army, the Navy, and the Air Force | 19 [6] | 4 | Honors March [5] | United States and command |
| Director of Defense Research and Engineering | 19 [6] | 4 | Honors March [5] | United States and command |
| Chairman of the Joint Chiefs of Staff; Chief of Staff, United States Army; Chief of Naval Operations; Chief of Staff, USAF; Commandant of the Marine Corps | 19 [6] | 4 | Honors March [5] | United States and command |
| General of the Army; Fleet Admiral; General of the Air Force (five-star rank) | 19 [6] | 4 | Honors March [5] | United States and command |
| Undersecretaries of the Cabinet, Solicitor General | 17 | 4 | Honors March [5] | United States and command |
| Assistant Secretaries of the Cabinet; Assistant to the Attorney General | 17 | 4 | Honors March [5] | United States and command |
| Assistant Secretaries of Defense and the General Counsel of the DOD and Undersecretaries of the Army, the Navy, and the Air Force | 17 [6] | 4 | Honors March [5] | United States and command |
| Generals and Admirals (four-star rank) | 17 [6] | 4 | Honors March [5] | United States and command |
| Assistant Secretaries of the Army, the Navy, and the Air Force | 17 [6] | 4 | Honors March [5] | United States and command |
| Lieutenant Generals, Vice Admirals | 15 [6] | 3 | Honors March [5] | United States and command |
| Foreign ambassadors out of jurisdiction | 15 | 2 | Honors March [5] | United States and command |

| Distinguished Persons | Honor Cordon [1] | Ruffles & Flourishes | Music | Flags [10] |
|---|---|---|---|---|
| Major Generals, Rear Admirals (Upper half) | 13[6] | 2 | Honors March[5] | United States and command |
| Brigadier Generals, Rear Admirals (Lower half) | 11[6] | 1 | Honors March[5] | United States and command |
| Other commissioned officers | 9[6] | 1 | Honors March[5] | United States and command |

[1] Honor cordon has same number on departure as on arrival for all distinguished persons.

[2] The United States Navy Band's arrangements of the National Anthem and the United States Marine Corps Band's arrangements of "Hail to the Chief" are the official Department of Defense arrangements for all service bands to play on appropriate occasions.

[3] The traditional musical selection "Hail to the Chief" is a musical tribute to the president of the United States; as such, military musical organizations will not perform it as a tribute to other dignitaries. Performances of this selection is subject to these policies:

a. During "Hail to the Chief" by military musical organizations, military personnel in uniform, other than band personnel, will accord the same honor as they would for the National Anthem or "To the Color."

b. If, in the course of any ceremony, a band must perform honors more than once, the band may use "Hail to the Chief" interchangeably with the National Anthem as honors to the president of the United States.

c. When specified by the president, the secretary of state, the chief of the Secret Service, or their authorized representatives, commanders may use "Hail to the Chief" as an opportunity for the president and immediate party to move to or from their places while all others stand fast.

[4] When a band is to perform one or more foreign national anthems and the U.S. National Anthem, the band will play the U.S. National Anthem last, except in conjunction with morning colors.

[5] Army or Air Force generals receive the Generals March; admirals, commodores, or Marine generals receive the Admirals March; all others not specified receive the last 32-bar strain of "The Stars and Stripes Forever."

[6] Foreign civilian and military officials occupying positions comparable to these U.S. officials will receive equivalent honors. Foreign recipients of honors must be representatives of countries recognized by the United States.

[7] Appropriate background music is any music such as a national air or a folk song favorably associated with the distinguished person or that person's country. If no such music is available, any good music of universal appeal and propriety will do. The band will perform all background music appropriately subdued to the principal action.

[8] Appropriate inspection music may be in any meter, and the inspection party need not conform to its cadence.

[9] Commanders of Air Force installations may obtain recorded music for use in connection with honors and ceremonies by writing directly to the Audio Section, United States Air Force Band, Bolling AFB, DC 20332.

[10] In events honoring foreign dignitaries, the color guard should include the flag of the foreign country of the guest or guests honored, when available.

## COURTESIES TO THE NATIONAL FLAG AND NATIONAL ANTHEM

**The Flag of the United States.** The term "flag" applies regardless of size, relative proportions, or manner of display (see AFR 50-14). The national flag, in its various sizes and uses, is the base flag, the all-purpose flag, the ceremonial flag, and the interment flag.

Air Force bases fly the following flags from a staff:

- U.S. base flag: 10′ hoist by 19′ fly; used in pleasant weather.
- U.S. all-purpose flag: 5′ hoist by 9′6″ fly; used in stormy and windy weather and as prescribed by the commander.

A military unit carries these flags:

- Ceremonial flag: 4′4″ hoist by 5′6″ fly; carried when the Air Force ceremonial flag is appropriate.
- Organizational flag: 3′ hoist by 4′ fly; not a national but a unit flag; carried when the organizational flag is appropriate.

The interment flag used to cover a casket at a funeral has the same dimensions as the all-purpose flag.

*Special-Purpose Flags.* A guidon is a swallow-tailed organizational flag carried by smaller units, such as squadrons, batteries, companies, or troops. A pennant is a triangular flag used ashore primarily for parade markers and so on. Other special-purpose flags include Air Force Recruiting Service, chapel, chaplain, and Geneva Convention flags.

*Flag Appurtenances.* A silver spearhead tops the pike or staff of Air Force flags. Other flag appurtenances may include unit streamers and silver bands, cords and tassels, and flag slings (see AFR 50-14).

**Respect.** Members of the military service are meticulous in observing the courtesies the national flag or the National Anthem requires. Colors or standards of organizations receive the same courtesy as the national flag flown from a flagstaff. The trumpet call "To the Color (Standard)" receives the same courtesy as the National Anthem.

When the National Anthem sounds indoors, officers and airmen will stand at attention and face the music or the flag if one is present. They do not salute unless under arms.

Officers and airmen show the same marks of respect to the national anthem of any other country played upon official occasions.

**Courtesies at Retreat and Escort of the Color.** Retreat is a daily ceremony at bases or stations during which all personnel must pay homage or courtesy to the flag. The ceremony may include a retreat parade; if units on parade carry organization colors or standards, participants in the ceremony or spectators at the ceremony usually pay the courtesy to those colors or standards. The ceremony of retreat includes a trumpeter sounding the trumpet call "Retreat" and then, if present, the band playing the National Anthem; in the absence of the band, field music sounds the trumpet call "To the Color (Standard)." Personnel lower the flag slowly, as if reluctantly; whereas, in the morning at colors, they raise it smartly, as if eagerly. After they lower the flag, they fold it into a triangular shape, supposedly commemorative of the Revolutionary War soldier's cocked hat.

At the first note of the National Anthem, or its counterpart in field music, all officers and airmen present but not in formation face the color or flag and give the prescribed salute. They hold the salute until the last note of the music sounds. For all officers and airmen not in formation, the prescribed salute is the hand salute. The prescribed salute for military personnel dressed in civilian clothes and wearing headdress is to stand at attention, remove the headdress, and hold it over the left breast.

Vehicles in motion halt, and occupants remain seated in the vehicle.

Occupants of military vehicles other than passenger cars and motorcycles remain seated in the vehicle at attention, the person in charge of the vehicle dismounting and saluting.

**Salute to Passing Colors.** When passing or being passed by an uncased national color, personnel give honors in the same manner as described above. For purposes of protection, the colors may be furled and then covered with a canvas case of special manufacture. When so carried, they do not require honors.

**Courtesies to the National Anthem.** Whenever or wherever the National Anthem or "To the Color (Standard)" sounds, at the first note thereof, all officers and airmen

RETREAT CEREMONY.

present but not in formation will face the music, stand at attention, and give the prescribed salute. *Exception:* At the ceremony of retreat or escort of the color, they face the color or flag. They hold the position of salute until the last note of the music sounds. The prescribed salute is the same, in all cases, as those described for the ceremonies of retreat and escort of the color.

Remembering this obvious rule can help prevent embarrassment: If you are paying homage to the flag, face the flag and salute; if you are paying homage to the National Anthem or "To the Color (Standard)" played by field music, face the source of the music and salute.

AFM 50–14 prescribes the method and personnel required for raising and lowering the flag on a flagstaff.

**Dipping the Flag or Colors.** Do not dip the national flag by way of salute or compliment. Dip the organization color as a salute when the reviewing officer has the rank of a general officer: Lower the pike (as the staff of a color is called) to the front so that it makes a 45° angle with the ground.

The organization flag salutes in all military ceremonies while the National Anthem or "To the Color" sounds and when honoring its commander or a person of higher rank, but in no other case.

When not in use, unit flags are usually on display in the commander's office.

**Funerals.** The national flag covers the casket at the military funeral of members of the military service. The flag is lengthwise on the casket with the union at the head and over the left shoulder of the deceased. Personnel do not lower the flag into the grave and do not allow it to touch the ground.

HOW TO DISPLAY THE FLAG.

1. When displayed over the middle of the street, the flag should hang vertically with the union to the north in an east-and-west street or to the east in a north-and-south street.

2. When displayed with another flag from crossed staffs, the U.S. flag should be on the right (the flag's own right), and its staff should be in front of the staff of the other flag.

3. When flying the flag at half-staff, the flag detail should first hoist the flag to the peak and then lower it to the half-staff position, but before lowering the flag for the day, they should again raise it to the peak.

4. When flags of states or cities or pennants of societies fly on the same halyard with the U.S. flag, the U.S. flag should always be at the peak.

5. When the flag hangs over a sidewalk from a rope extending from house to pole at the edge of the sidewalk, the flag should go out from the building, toward the pole, union first.

6. When the flag is on display from a staff projecting horizontally or at any angle from the window sill, balcony, or front of a building, the union of the flag should go to the peak of the staff (unless the flag is to be at half-staff).

7. When the flag covers a casket, the union should be at the head and over the left shoulder of the deceased. The flag should not be lowered into the grave or allowed to touch the ground.

8. When the flag is on display other than by flying from a staff, it should be flat whether indoors or out. When displayed either horizontally or vertically against a wall, the union should be uppermost and to the flag's own right, that is, to the observer's left. When displayed in a window, it should appear the same way, that is, with the union or blue field to the left of the observer in the street.

9. When carried in a procession with another flag or flags, the U.S. flag should be either on the marching right or, when there is a line of other flags, in front of the center of that line.

10. When a number of flags of states or cities or pennants of societies are grouped on display from staffs with our national flag, the U.S. flag should be at the center or at the highest point of the group.

11. When the flags of two or more nations are on display, they should fly from separate staffs of the same height, and the flags should be of about equal size. International usage forbids displaying the flag of one nation above that of another nation in time of peace.

**Display and Use of the Flag.** International usage forbids the display of the flag of one nation above the flag of another in time of peace. When the flags of two or more nations are on display, they should fly from separate staffs or from separate halyards of equal size and on the same level.

The national flag, when not flown from a staff or mast, should always hang flat, whether indoors or out, neither festooned over doorways or arches nor tied in a bow-knot or fashioned into a rosette. When used on a rostrum, it should be above and behind the speaker's desk. It should never cover the speaker's desk or drape over the front platform. Bunting of the national colors, arranged with the blue above, the white in the middle, and the red below, serves such purposes well. Under no circumstances should anyone drape the flag over chairs or benches, place any object or emblem of any kind above or upon it, or hang it where something could easily contaminate or soil it. No lettering of any kind should ever appear on the flag. No one should ever use it for advertising purposes. When metal or cloth replicas of the national flag are decorations for civilian clothing (such as costume jewelry) or an identifying symbol, the positioning and treatment should be with the greatest possible respect. When carried with other flags, the national flag should always be on the right as color bearers are facing or in front. When a number of flags are grouped on display from staffs, the national flag should always be in the center or at the highest point of the group.

Public Law 623–77th Congress prescribes the display and use of the flag by civilians or civilian groups. See the accompanying illustration of how to display the flag.

## DISPLAY OF UNITED NATIONS FLAG

When the United States flag and the United Nations flag are on display together, the United States flag is on the right, best identified as "the marching right." The United States flag will be equal in size or larger, in the position of honor on the right (observer's left), and above the United Nations flag. Troops will carry the United Nations flag only on occasions honoring the United Nations or high dignitaries thereof. When so carried, the United Nations flag will be on the marching left and below the United States flag.

## COURTESIES TO THE MILITARY DEAD

**General.** The military dead receive a dignified and ceremonial funeral service in keeping with the military tradition, with the flag at half-staff and prescribed salutes to the deceased. At a military funeral, one salutes the caisson or hearse as it passes and the casket as it is carried. One also salutes during firing of volleys and playing of taps. If a unit or detail passes a burial procession or coffin, the officer or NCO in charge will give the command "Eyes Right" (or Left) and salute. When an officer dies, the commander details another officer from the unit to escort the remains to the place of burial.

Officers who must plan a military funeral should consult AFR 143-1, which covers in detail several types of funeral ceremonies.

**The Flag at Half-Staff.** When displaying the national flag at half-staff, the flag detail first hoists it to the top of the staff and then lowers it to the half-staff position. Before lowering the flag, they again raise it to the top of the staff. A flag in any position below the top of the staff is technically in the half-staff position. For an unguyed flagstaff of one piece, the middle point of the hoist of the flag should be midway between the top of the staff and the foot thereof (AFR 50-14).

A PRACTICE MILITARY FUNERAL.

**Occasions for the Flag at Half-Staff.** On Memorial Day at all Air Force bases and stations, the national flag flies at half-staff from reveille to retreat.

On the death of an officer at a base, the flag flies at half-staff and remains so between reveille and retreat or until completion of the burial service, after which the flag detail hoists it to the top, or, if burial is not at the base, until the remains depart the base.

Whenever regulations prescribe or proper authority orders military mourning for the death of any person entitled to personal honors, all flags are at half-staff, and the national and organizational colors are draped.

# 3

# Customs of the Service

*Well, the primary custom of the Air Force is to just get the damn job done.*
—General Carl Spaatz, First Chief of Staff, USAF

A custom is an established usage. Customs include positive actions—things to do—and taboos—things to avoid doing.

Customs are those reasonable, consistent, universally accepted practices that make for a more pleasant life or more orderly procedures. Continued without interruption for a long time, they become compulsory. Some customs may even have the force of law.

## AIR FORCE CUSTOMS

The Air Force has its own customs, some older than others. For instance, the dining-in, explained in chapter 19, is a relatively new Air Force custom. Another pleasant practice that seems to be growing into a custom is for an active Air Force wing to adopt a cadet wing of the Air Force Academy or of the AFROTC. Those customs that persist stand on their own merits and are unwritten in the sense that they do not appear in official orders or regulations. Many Air Force customs complement procedures required by military courtesy, while others merely add to the graciousness of life. The breach of some customs merely brands the offender as ignorant, careless, or ill bred, but the violation of others brings official censure or disciplinary action.

Unquestionably, most Air Force customs are derived from Army customs, as the Air Force descended from the Army. Therefore, most Air Force customs are almost identical to Army customs, but there is a difference. This difference manifests itself in a way so abstract that it defies concrete description. Some have said that the Air Force has adopted practically all of the Army's customs, but with a little more leaven of humor, a little less rigidity, a little more warmth. Perhaps this abstract difference between Army and Air Force customs goes with the saying that the Air Force cares a great deal more for the substance than for the form. For example, an Air Force officer arriving on a new station is likely to be far more impressed with the warmth of your welcome if you take positive action to help unpack, invite both officer and family to dinner, personally introduce the officer to your friends, or pass on solid tips on how to tackle the new job, than the same officer would be by a perfunctory, formal social visit executed with clocklike precision at the proper hour and lasting no more and no less than the prescribed time. The Air Force has no great amount of patience with mere rote. The officers of the Air Force do not, however, ignore custom. In truth, the great "custom" of the Air Force is to inject into old customs grown cold through unthinking, routine obedience to them a new glow, a new warmth, a new humor that says for itself: "I'm not doing this thing because I should, because I have to—I'm doing it because I want to."

The personalities of several of the top leaders directly influence the conduct and mannerisms of all officers. The simplicity, cordiality, and human warmth, combined with personal dignity, displayed on all occasions and with all people of high or low estate by such leaders as Arnold, Doolittle, Vandenberg, and others will serve as a broad pattern to emulate. The day of the austere leader is waning. A "Good morning, Sergeant," with a friendly smile when returning a salute is certainly "military" if the practices of some of our greatest leaders are to establish a pattern.

**Sanctity of Official Statements.** Ordinarily, people accept an officer's official word or statement without question. The knowledge that a false official statement not only is a high crime but also is contrary to the ethics of the military profession has placed personal and official responsibility for an official statement on a high level.

**The Officer-Airman Relationship.** Good officers strive to develop their organizations to their maximum efficiency while providing for their people effective leadership, impartial justice, and wise and fair attitudes in every way. Good officers also strive to avoid those things that militate against this necessary result. Because undue familiarity breeds contempt, officers and airmen have not generally associated together in mutual social activities. No officers could violate this ancient custom with one or two people of their command and convince the others of their unswerving impartiality.

The civilian and the inexperienced cannot possibly understand the officer-airman relationship, nor can they realize that it often develops into something far deeper and more valuable. Only those officers and airmen who have endured together the grueling hardships of bitter campaigns or the ordeals of battle can understand. Those conditions often develop a mutual trust and complete confidence between officer and airman that carries each forward to acts of sacrifice, courage, and leadership to the end that the one shall not be seen as wanting in the eyes of the other. This deep tie may be the force that wins wars.

**Provide for the Needs of Airmen.** The officer must always provide for the needs and requirements of the airman. Officers in command of or responsible for airmen must provide for the airmen's housing, feeding, and comfort before the officers take care of their own personal needs. For example, officers with a military vehicle and a military driver (usually an airman) must provide for the driver's meals and lodging while on extended trips unless suitably timed stops occur at military installations where the airman can obtain military meals and lodging.

Air Force personnel and other authorized passengers on a normal cross-country training flight pay for their own expenses.

**Public Breaches of Discipline and Misconduct of Airmen.** Officers are responsible for making proper corrections and taking the necessary actions whenever and wherever they see airmen conducting themselves in an improper fashion. Officers must not fail to take the necessary preventive or corrective steps because the offenders are not from the same organization or because they are off duty. Officers are never off duty. Generally, it is a matter of protecting the airmen from their own indiscretions to save them from more serious trouble.

Approach the delinquent offenders in a quiet, dignified, unobtrusive manner. Talk in an impersonal officerlike way. Use a tone of voice no louder than necessary to be heard. Avoid threats. Do not scold or argue. Tell the airmen the things they have done that bring discredit upon the uniform they are wearing. Get their passes or travel orders, and record their names and organizations. If necessary, get their names and numbers from their identification cards. Generally, a contact of this sort will be sufficient. If the airmen have been drinking and are unable to care for themselves, take further measures. If the situation worsens, summon security police. Like commissioned officers, noncommissioned officers are never off duty, and you may place recalcitrants in their charge. You may also place sober and better behaved associates in charge of mild offenders with a caution to keep the offenders under control, because airmen do look out for one another. Most officers avoid turning airmen over to civil police except as a last resort, when the offense clearly warrants it, because the military looks out for itself. Whatever action you take, you must follow up, or the deterring effect will likely vanish as soon as you are out of sight. No officers worthy of their positions of trust will fail or avoid their responsibilities, however unpleasant they may seem to be at the time.

Drunkenness in public, foul language and cursing, and other acts that discredit the uniform are the things to curb and control. For the most part, the standards of airmen are high, and they will give their loyal support to the necessary measures. Officers must distinguish clearly between acts that are merely unwise or on the boisterous side and those that are actually offensive. You should ignore the former. A word of caution should suffice for the borderline cases. With force and judgment, you must "handle" the others.

## RANK HAS ITS PRIVILEGES (RHIP)

**General.** The military system is a hierarchy. Leaders placed in charge of units in the military structure exercise control. These leaders are officers and noncommissioned officers. All must display disciplined obedience combined with loyalty, in accordance with law and regulations. From the highest to the lowest, subordinates must extend an unfailing respect to the authority that issues their orders. Personal admiration is a voluntary tribute to another that the military service does not demand. But the service does demand, and without equivocation, manifesting respect for authority by unfailing courtesy to people who exercise it.

The privileges of rank do not include the privilege of abuse of position. The needs of the organization as a whole come first. Officers who use official transportation for personal use are abusing the position. Officers who divert equipment to their own use do likewise. In general, officers who take the stand that they are above the regulations that guide others, especially their own subordinates, are in abuse of their positions, and other people will thus regard and condemn their acts.

The privileges of rank and position are privileges indeed, well worth striving for and attaining. They exist in about the same ratio and for the same reasons as in other walks of life. Position may mean more in the Air Force than in many civil professions because, in most instances, the civilian leader receives far greater pay or other monetary allowances.

**"I Wish" and "I Desire."** When the commander states, "I wish," or "I desire," rather than, "I order you to do so-and-so," this wish or desire has all the force of a direct order.

**The Place of Honor.** The place of honor is on the right. Accordingly, when juniors walk, ride, or sit with seniors, they take the position abreast and to the left of the seniors. The deference young officers should pay to elders pertains to this relationship. The junior should walk in step with a senior, step back and allow the senior to be the first to enter a door, and show similar acts of consideration and courtesy. Usually, in the relations between seniors and juniors, the senior will never think of the difference in rank; the junior should never forget it.

**Addressing a Senior.** In military conversation, junior officers address senior officers and all airmen address officers as either "Sir" or "Ma'am." The "Sir" or "Ma'am" precedes a report and a query; it follows the answer of a question. For example: "Sir, do you wish to see Sergeant Brown?" "Sir, I report as Officer of the Day." "Sergeant Brown, Ma'am." "Thank you, Sir." Address a general officer, however, as "General."

**Departing after the Commander.** Officers should remain at a reception or social gathering until after the commander has departed. The corollary: Thoughtful commanders leave early.

**Reception of a Newly Joined Officer.** Customarily, newly joined officers receive a cordial welcome, and most installations extend many acts of courtesy to the officers and families to make their arrival more pleasant and convenient. People assume that newly joined officers know their professional duties and that they have every intention of performing them ably.

Whenever conditions permit such niceties, the base commander or unit commander sends a letter of welcome to officers under orders to join, informing them of local conditions that may be important or interesting for them to know before arrival. The commander will inquire as to the date and hour of arrival, whether traveling by automobile, airplane, or train, and the number of persons accompanying. If the arrival is by airplane or train, an officer with transportation will meet the new arrivals at the airport or at the station. The commander will detail sponsor officers to assist newly joined officers.

If quarters are available, commanders should make them ready for immediate occupancy; if not available, they should take steps to provide temporary accommodations at the BOQ or elsewhere.

Sponsors usually introduce newly joined officers to the commander and to the other officers of their units. Sponsors should also inform the newcomers as to local regulations and customs they will need to know at once. Copies of base regulations and maps of the base are especially useful to strangers.

**Military Weddings.** Military weddings follow the same procedures as any other except for additional customs that add to their color and tone.

At military weddings, all officers should wear the prescribed uniform for the occasion. Officers may wear their medals or ribbons. Whether the wedding is held in the morning, afternoon, or evening has no bearing on the selection of appropriate uniforms. For the wedding party, the thoughtful servicemember should express a preference as to the uniform.

**Birth of a Child.** When a child is born to the family of an officer, the base commander sends a personal letter of congratulations to the parents on behalf of the command.

The same procedure is appropriate for a child born to the family of an airman except that the organization commander writes the letter of congratulation, and the gift, if any, is from the airman's unit.

**Death of an Officer or a Member of an Officer's Family.** When an officer dies, the commander immediately designates an officer to give every possible assistance to the bereaved family. The base commander writes a letter of condolence on behalf of the base, and sends flowers in the name of the officers and spouses of the base.

**Death of an Airman.** When an airman dies, the immediate commander of the deceased writes a letter of condolence to the airman's nearest relative.

Flowers sent in the name of the members of the deceased's unit accompany the body.

All officers and members of the deceased airman's unit, the commander, the band, and other members who so desire and whose duties permit attend the funeral.

## SUPPORT OF BASE AND ORGANIZATION ACTIVITIES

**General.** Your commander expects you to support the activities of your unit, such as wing, group, or squadron, as well as the activities of the entire base. Your unit is a closely knit group around which official duties and athletic, social, religious, and cultural activities intertwine for the benefit of all. You are a member of an official family. Your assignment must mean more than the place where you perform required and official duties, important as they may be. Your commander expects you to support and assist, at least by your presence, many events that form a part of military life. A proper interest and pride in all activities of your unit and base stimulate morale. An officer should be a good military citizen, sharing with other good citizens responsibility for the unofficial life and activities of the base.

**Officers' Open Mess.** An officers' open mess is a membership association of commissioned officers established to provide food and beverage services, entertainment, and social and recreation programs for its members and their families and bona fide guests. Depending upon space accommodations, some installations extend membership to retired officers of all armed services of the United States, officers of the National Guard and reserve components, and authorized Department of Defense civilian employees working on the installation, as determined by the installation commander. Because all officers are eligible for voluntary membership, they cannot use the officers' open mess unless they become members. In this sense, the officers' open mess resembles a private civilian club because the members themselves generate funds from sales, fees, and dues to support the services and programs of the mess. Traditionally and historically, the officers' open mess is the social center of the Air Force community life for officers and their families. As such, it is customary for every officer to join the officers' open mess on the base of assignment.

The scope of activities and programs offered by the officers' open mess may vary from base to base. Membership in your installation's officers' open mess, however, assures you of reciprocal privileges in all other officers' open messes of the armed forces. Basically, the benefits and services offered include dining and beverage services, private party catering, special events, check cashing, charge privileges, swimming, childcare, charge system, tennis, and live entertainment attractions. The check-cashing service is an important and convenient privilege of membership, especially during the evenings, weekends, and holidays when banks may be closed. The officers' open mess charge system provides you a 30-day credit policy without incurring any finance charge. Membership dues may vary from $12 to $25 monthly. For further information, see AFR 215-11.

**Attendance at Athletic Events.** As a matter of policy, to demonstrate an interest in base affairs, as well as for personal enjoyment, officers should attend athletic events in which their teams participate.

**Attendance at Chapel.** Similarly, officers should show their support of base religious activities by periodic attendance at services at the base chapel, to the extent that individual religious preferences permit.

**Armed Forces Day.** The third Saturday in May is usually designated Armed Forces Day. Undoubtedly, each base will hold a special ceremony or review and invite civilians. This day unifies all the former service days and is symbolic of the unity of action and purpose of all our armed services.

## FAREWELL TO A DEPARTING OFFICER

Before an officer departs from his unit or station on change of assignment or upon retirement, the officers and spouses usually give a reception or other suitable function in honor of the departing officer and family. Customarily, the unit gives a memento to the one departing.

## RETIREMENT CEREMONY

Retirement of an officer or an airman is an occasion that merits special commemoration. It is a just reward for long, faithful, and honorable service. For most individuals, it is a day of serious realization of the value of military friendships accompanied by heart tugs of regret that these fine associations will change. It is a day that all military people will reach, provided they live, serve honorably, and remain on the active list. Therefore, a suitable ceremony should mark the occasion.

**Retirement of an Officer.** The officer's unit or the personnel of the base should arrange for a final ceremony, such as a parade, in the officer's honor with a reception for the officer and family.

A custom followed by many organizations is to present a scroll with suitable heading, signed by appropriate members of the base or unit. Such a remembrance costs little and therefore does not violate laws or regulations regarding gifts. If suitable for framing, it is a highly cherished memento.

Friends and family of the retiring officer will wish to hold farewell parties of various informal types.

## TABOOS

**Do Not Defame the Uniform.** Officers must not defame their uniform or their official or social position. Conduct unbecoming an officer is punishable under the Uniform Code of Military Justice. The confidence of the nation in the integrity and high standards of conduct of officers is an asset that the military may permit no one to lower.

**Do Not Bad-mouth Members of Other Services.** Never belittle members of the Army, the Navy, or the Marines. They are part of our team. For that matter, don't downgrade your own service.

**Interview the Commander Only through the Aide or the Executive.** Customarily, officers ask the commander's aide or the executive for an appointment with the commander. Often, you may do so informally by asking when the commander can see you.

**Proffer No Excuses.** Never volunteer excuses or explain a shortcoming unless someone requires an explanation. Proffering unsought excuses does more damage than good.

**Scorn Servility.** Servility, "bootlicking," and deliberate courting of favor are beneath the standard of conduct expected of officers, and any who practice such things earn the scorn of their associates.

**Say Things like "Old Man" with Care.** Some commanders acquire the accolade "the old man" by virtue of their position and without regard to their age. Although the term usually implies approbation and admiration, using it in the presence of the commander is disrespectful.

**Avoid "Going over an Officer's Head."** Jumping an echelon of command is called "going over an officer's head." For example, a squadron commander may make a request of the group commander concerning a matter that should first have gone through the group operations officer. The act is contrary to military procedure and decidedly disrespectful.

**Avoid Harsh Remarks.** Gossip, slander, harsh criticism, and faultfinding are unofficerlike practices. In casual conversation, follow this guide: "All the brothers and all the sisters are valiant and virtuous." Don't criticize or correct fellow officers in front of airmen.

**Avoid Vulgarity and Profanity.** Although you certainly will hear profanity in the military, you need to know that foul and vulgar language larded with profanity is repulsive to many self-respecting people and that to them its use by officers is reprehensible. Officers should avoid foulness, repulsiveness, and vulgarity if they are to gain respect, and no officer can lead others without their respect.

**Avoid Excessive Indebtedness.** Few offenses injure the standing of an officer more than earning the reputation of being a poor credit risk. Officers are people, and they are subject to the same temptations and the same hazards of life as any other adults. Sometimes you may find that assuming debt is unavoidable and necessary, but you must, of course, repay all debts. When circumstances intervene that prohibit the payment that is due, you should write or visit the creditor and make a mutually satisfactory arrangement. You should make some payment, however small, at the time a payment is due; this practice protects the legal standing of the obligation and shows the intention to pay. The practice of permitting bills to accumulate, with no attempt to pay or to arrange a method of payment, is reprehensible and subject to official military censure.

Officers enjoy an exceptional individual and group credit standing earned and deserved because of the scrupulous care officers have taken through the years to meet obligations when due. An officer who violates this custom brings discredit upon the entire officer corps. For further information, see AFR 35-18.

**Never Lean on a Senior Officer's Desk.** Avoid leaning or lolling against a senior officer's desk. Most officers resent such familiarity, and it is unmilitary. Stand erect unless invited to be seated. Don't lean.

**Never Keep Anyone Waiting.** Report on time when notified to do so. Never keep anyone waiting unnecessarily.

**Avoid Having People Guess Your Name.** Do not assume that someone whom you have neither seen nor heard from for a considerable period will know your name when you renew contact. Say at once who you are, and then renew the acquaintance. If this act of courtesy is unnecessary, the other person will view it only as an act of thoughtfulness; if it happens to be necessary, you will save the other person and perhaps yourself embarrassment. *At official receptions, always announce your name to the aide.*

**Don't Trade on Your Commission.** Officers may not use or permit others to use their military titles in connection with commercial enterprises of any kind. (See chapter 7.)

**Stay out of Politics.** Don't become embroiled in politics. Political activity is contrary to American military tradition. As a citizen, you have a right to your opinions and a *duty* to vote, but keep your opinions to yourself, within your home, or within your own circle of friends. You can do this without being an intellectual eunuch. Also remember that criticism of the president is particularly improper because the president is, after all, the commander in chief of the armed forces.

**Look Smart in Public.** Avoid smoking or chewing gum when on the streets in uniform. Keep your hands out of your pockets, your uniform coat (blouse) buttoned, your tie tight, and your cap squared away properly.

AN AIR FORCE CUSTOM—THE THUNDERBIRDS PERFORM.

**What Not to Discuss.** Avoid talking shop at social occasions, and of course, *never* discuss classified matters, no matter how obliquely. At the mess, use discretion in discussing politics and religion.

## CUSTOMS CONCERNING AIRCRAFT

The base airdrome officer (AO) meets all transient aircraft and determines crew and passenger transportation requirements. If possible, the base commander usually meets general and flag officers.

Pilots of aircraft carrying classified material are responsible for safeguarding it unless they can remove it from the aircraft and store it in an adequately guarded area.

Only the AO can authorize passenger vehicles on the ramp or flight line.

Regardless of rank, aircraft commanders are the final authority on operation of their aircraft. If they decide to alter their flight plan, passengers of whatever rank or service will not question their decision.

Aircraft passengers must be prompt, obey safety regulations, and avoid moving around unnecessarily. Don't be one of those passengers that pilots castigate as "waltzing mice"—moving around requires frequent trimming of the aircraft.

The pilot is the last to leave an abandoned aircraft.

Parades and other ceremonies honoring dignitaries often use aircraft flyovers.

When airplanes participate in the funeral of an aviator, they fly in tactical formation, less one aircraft, over the graveside service, but not so low as to drown out the service with noise.

## SOME ARMY CUSTOMS

Because the Army is the parent of the Air Force, most of our military observances are similar. There are a few differences, however, and the Air Force officer should know them. For instance, the Air Force no longer employs the cannon salute, but Army posts fire it at reveille and retreat and at ceremonies honoring distinguished visitors entitled to gun salutes. On Independence Day, the Army fires a 50-gun salute to the Union, one shot for each state. At this salute, one comes to attention but does not salute.

**Organization Day.** Army regiments and separate battalions celebrate the anniversary of their units' founding as Organization Day. This festive occasion often includes a parade and review with the reading of the unit's history and feats of arms, an athletic field day, a holiday dinner, and a ball.

**Regimental Traditions.** Some of the older Army units are rightly proud of their traditions, and if you are with Army units on joint service, you should ascertain them. Such units include the oldest Regular Army unit, Battery D, 5th Field Artillery Battalion, commanded by Capt. Alexander Hamilton in the Revolutionary War; the 3d Infantry "Old Guard," oldest Regular Army regiment, stationed at Fort Myer, Virginia, for ceremonial duties in the capital; the "Cottonbalers" of the 7th Infantry with 60 battle streamers dating back to the Battle of New Orleans; the 9th Infantry with their Liscum Bowl from Peking; and the "Garry Owens" of the 7th Cavalry, Custer's regiment. Some National Guard regiments are even older: Massachusetts's 182d Infantry, formed in 1636 as the Puritans' "Train Bands"; and Mississippi's 155th Infantry, commanded by Col. Jefferson Davis at Buena Vista in the Mexican War. The other services also uphold unit traditions, such as the Navy ships named *Wasp, Hornet, Essex,* and *Bonhomme Richard;* the "China 4th" Marines; and the 5th and 6th Marines of Belleau-Wood fame.

Despite the organizational changes imposed by modern military technology, we of the Air Force have units with prideful histories, too: Capt. Eddie Rickenbacker's "Hat-in-the-Ring" 94th Fighter Squadron, part of TAC's 1st Fighter Wing at Langley AFB; SAC's 2d Bomb Wing, which flew in Billy Mitchell's great Meuse-Argonne bomber offensive; TAC's 4th Fighter Wing, formed from the RAF Eagle Squadrons; TAC's 23d Fighter Wing, formed from Chennault's Flying Tigers of the AVG (American Volunteer Group); and SAC's 19th Air Refueling Wing, which went on from Clark Field in December 1941 to win nine U.S., one Philippine, and one Korean Presidential Unit Citations.

**"How."** The traditional Old Army toast, "How," in drinking one's health is the equivalent of "Cheers," *"Prosit,"* or *"Skoal."* Several stories attempt to explain its origin, and it apparently results from the old Indian-fighting days. One story is that it began in Florida in 1841 during the Seminole Wars, when Chief Coacoochee tried to imitate the officers' toasts by shouting "Hough!" The officers of the 8th Infantry and the 2d Dragoons picked it up and spread it through the Army.

**Massing the Colors.** Some Army posts, in conjunction with local chapters of the Military Order of the World Wars, have adopted the British ceremony of the massing of the colors and the searchlight tattoo.

**Dancing Old Year Out and New Year In.** Officers and their partners customarily dance the old year out and the new year in. Formerly, a bugler sounded tattoo at 11:50 P.M. and taps at midnight, and immediately afterward, the orchestra played the reveille of the New Year.

## NAVY CUSTOMS AIR FORCE OFFICERS SHOULD KNOW

**Courtesies.** Air Force officers sometimes visit Navy ships. On ships having 180 or more men of the seaman branch, "side boys" attend visiting officers of our armed services, except when in civilian clothes, and officers of the foreign service when the officer comes onboard and departs. This courtesy also extends to commissioned officers of the armed services of foreign nations. Officers of the ranks of lieutenant through major receive two side boys; from lieutenant colonel through colonel, four side boys; from brigadier general through major general, six side boys; and lieutenant general and above, eight side boys. General officers receive full guard and band; colonels, the guard of the day but no music.

During the hours of darkness or low visibility, the hail for an approaching boat is usually "Boat ahoy?" which corresponds to the sentry's challenge, "Who is there?" The answers identify the senior in the boat:

- "Aye aye": Commissioned officer
- "No no": Warrant officer
- "Hello": Enlisted man
- "Enterprise": CO of Enterprise
- "Third Fleet": Admiral commanding Third Fleet

Similarly, if the commander of the 1st Tactical Fighter Wing or of Langley Air Force Base is in the boat, the answer would be "1st Wing" or "Langley Air Force Base."

On arrival, at the order "Tend the side," the side boys fall in fore and aft of the approach to the gangway, facing each other. The bos'n's mate-of-the-watch takes station forward of them and faces aft. When the boat comes alongside, the bos'n's mate pipes and again when the visiting officer's head reaches the level of the deck. At this latter instant, the side boys salute.

On departure, the ceremony repeats in reverse: The bos'n's mate begins to pipe and side boys to salute as soon as the departing officer steps toward the gangway between the side boys. As the boat casts off, the bos'n's mate pipes again (shore boats and automobiles are not piped).

You uncover when entering a space where people are at mess and in sick bay (quarters) if sick personnel are present. You uncover in the wardroom at all times if you are junior. All hands except when under arms uncover in the captain's cabin.

Admirals and captains when in uniform fly colors astern when embarked in boats. When on official visits, they also display their personal flags (pennants for commanding officers) in the bow. The appropriate number of stars on each side of the barge's hull distinguishes flag officers' barges. The name or abbreviation of ships surcharged by an arrow distinguishes captains' gigs.

**Visiting.** Where gangways are on both sides, the starboard gangway is for officers and the port for enlisted. Stress of weather or expedience, in the discretion of the officer of the deck (OOD), may make either gangway available to both officers and enlisted.

Seniors come onboard ship first. When reaching the deck, you face toward the ensign (or aft if no ensign) and salute the ensign (quarterdeck). Immediately thereafter, you salute the OOD and request permission to come onboard. The usual form is, "Request permission to come onboard, Sir." The OOD must return both salutes.

On leaving the ship, observe the inverse order. You salute the OOD and request permission to leave the ship. The OOD will indicate when the boat, if used, is ready. Each person, juniors first, salutes the OOD and then faces toward the ensign (quarterdeck), salutes, and embarks.

The OOD onboard ship represents the captain and as such has unquestioned authority. Only the executive and commanding officers may order the OOD relieved. The authority of the OOD extends to the accommodation ladders or gangways and to the decision of when a boat may approach.

The OOD normally conveys orders to the embarked troops via the troop commander, but in emergencies the OOD may issue orders directly to you or to any other person onboard.

The *bridge* is the command post of the ship when under way, as the quarterdeck is at anchor. The officer of the deck is in charge of the ship as the representative of the captain. Admittance to the bridge when under way should be at the invitation of or with the permission of the captain. You may usually obtain permission through the executive officer.

The *quarterdeck* is the seat of authority and respected as such. The starboard side of the quarterdeck is for the captain (and admiral if a flagship). No person trespasses upon it except when necessary in the course of work or official business. All persons salute the quarterdeck when entering it. When pacing the deck with another officer, the place of honor is outboard, and when reversing direction, each turns toward the other. The port side of the quarterdeck is for commissioned officers, and the crew has all the rest of the weather decks of the ship. Every part of the deck (and the ship) belongs to a particular division, however, so that the crew has ample space, and every division naturally considers it has a prior though unwritten right to its own part of the ship. For gatherings, such as smokers and movies, all divisions have equal privileges at the scene of assemblage. Space and chairs are for officers and for chief petty officers, where available, and mess benches are for enlisted personnel. The seniors have the place of honor. When the captain (and the admiral) arrive, those present come to attention. The captain customarily gives "carry on" at once through the executive officer or master-at-arms who accompanies him to his seat.

**Messes.** If you take passage onboard a naval vessel, the ship will assign you to one of several messes onboard ship, the wardroom, or the junior officers' mess. In off hours, particularly in the evenings, you can gather there for cards, yarns, or reading. Generally, coffee is available.

The executive officer is ex officio the president of the wardroom mess. The wardroom officers are the division officers and the heads of departments. All officers await the arrival of the executive officer before sitting at lunch and dinner. If it is necessary for you to leave early, ask the head of your table for permission. The seating arrangement in the messes is in order of seniority.

Naval officers must pay their mess bills in advance. The mess treasurer, chosen by election every month, takes care of the receipts and expenditures and the management of the mess. When assigned to a mess, you are an honorary member. Consult the mess treasurer as to payment of mess bills. Stewards will serve your meals, clean your room, make up your room, make up your bunk, and shine your shoes. Because these tasks are their regular work, do not tip them.

The cigar mess is the successor of the old wine mess. You may make purchases from this mess, for example, of cigarettes, cigars, pipe tobacco, and candies. The cigar mess treasurer will make out your bill at the end of the month or before your detachment. Before you depart, be sure that the mess treasurer and the cigar mess treasurer have sufficient warning to make out your bills before you leave. Once a ship has sailed, long delays usually occur before remittances can overtake it. The unpaid mess bill onboard is a more serious breach of propriety than the unpaid club bill ashore because of the greater inconvenience and delay in settlement.

**Calls.** Passenger officers should call on the captain of the ship. If there are many of you, you should choose a calling committee and consult with the executive officer, who will make arrangements with the captain as to a convenient time to call.

**Ceremonies.** Gun salutes in the Navy are the same as in the Army except that flag officers below the rank of fleet admiral or general of the Army or Air Force, by Navy regulations, receive a gun salute upon departure only.

**Other Naval Customs.** Address commanders of any ships, regardless of grade, as "Captain," Navy officers below the rank of commander as "Mister," chief petty officers as "Chief," and other ratings usually by their last names. Some people also address Marine lieutenants as "Mister" (this address was also the practice in the Old Army) and Marine NCOs by their rank titles.

The naval services do not salute when uncovered.

If overtaking a senior, draw abreast of him on the left, slow down, salute, and say, "By your leave, Sir." The senior normally will reply, "Granted." A senior overtakes a junior on the right, and the junior initiates the salute when he sees the senior out of the corner of his eye.

In sending verbal messages, the junior uses the formula: "My respects to Captain Hornblower, and." The senior uses the phrase: "My compliments to Mr. Roberts, and." In correspondence, a senior "calls attention" to something; a junior only "invites" it. A junior closes a letter with "Very respectfully"; a senior, with "Respectfully."

## ORIGINS OF SOME MILITARY CUSTOMS

Newly commissioned officers may find some military customs more meaningful if they understand how the customs began. The origins of many are shrouded in antiquity, and some of the stories may be apocryphal, but they should be of interest.

The dress parade was originally supposed to impress visiting emissaries with the strength of the monarch's troops, rather than to honor the visitor.

Inspecting the guard of honor began with the restoration of Charles II to the throne of England. When one of Cromwell's regiments offered its allegiance, the king carefully scrutinized the face of each soldier in ranks looking for signs of treachery. Convinced of their sincerity, he accepted the escort.

The "Sound off," in which the band plays the "Three Cheers" and marches down the front of assembled troops, stems from the Crusades. Those selected as crusaders were at the right of the line of troops, and the band matched past them in dedication while the populace gave three cheers. "The right of the line" was the critical side in ancient battle formations and is the unit place of honor in ceremonies.

The saber salute, still employed on occasion of ceremony in the other services, demonstrated the officer's dedication to Christ in his bringing the hilt (symbolic of the cross) to his lips, while dipping the saber tip signified submission to his liege lord commanding him.

Age determines precedence among units, and for that reason, Air Force units usually follow the sister services in parades.

Raising the right hand in taking the oath stems from ancient days when the taker called upon God as his witness to the truth and pledged with his sword hand. If gloved, people taking the oath remove the right glove, supposedly because criminals were once branded on the right palm, and courts could thus determine whether one was a reputable witness.

Wearing decorations and medals on the left breast also goes back to the crusaders, who wore the badge of honor of their order over their hearts and protected by their shields, which they carried on the left arm.

The origin of the aiguillette and the fourragère is open to debate. One story has it that squires used to carry metal-tipped thongs (aiguillette is French for little spike or lace-tag) in a roll over their shoulders to lace their knights into their armor, and it thus became the badge of an aide-de-camp. Another yarn concerns the fourragère, which states that Marlborough's foragers carried fodder sacks for their mounts attached to their shoulders by a looped-up cord hooked to the jacket.

The white flag of truce may derive from the Truce of God arranged on certain days by Pope Urban V in 1095 between warring medieval barons.

The use of the arch of sabers in military weddings recalls the days when the groomsmen pledged to protect the wedded couple, particularly elopers.

The term "chaplain" supposedly derives from Saint Martin of Tours, who gave half his military cloak, or "cappa," to a beggar. The kings of France made of it a relic and war talisman guarded by special clerical custodians, who celebrated services in the field.

Saluting a ship's quarterdeck apparently derives from ancient times when the ship's stern carried a pagan altar to propitiate the gods. Later, it carried the Christian crucifix, and it is still the seat of authority.

At a military funeral, the national flag is on the coffin to indicate that the dead died in service of the state, which acknowledges its responsibility.

The firing of three volleys over the grave may derive from the Romans, who honored their dead by casting earth thrice on the grave, calling the name of the dead, and saying "Vale" (farewell) three times.

A military funeral plays taps to mark the beginning of the servicemember's last sleep and to express hope in the ultimate reveille.

# 4

# Pay and Personal Allowances

*The nation which forgets its defenders will itself be forgotten.*

—Calvin Coolidge, 1920

An officer's pay and allowances consist of four fundamental elements (Department of Defense Military Pay and Allowances Entitlement Manual—DODPM):

- Basic pay.
- Basic allowance for subsistence (BAS).
- Basic allowance for quarters (BAQ).
- Incentive and special pay.

## FUNDAMENTAL ELEMENTS

**Basic Pay.** Because of inflation, military pay has increased annually since 1964 to reflect the increased cost of living. That trend seems likely to continue, so consider the accompanying pay table as merely a guide, a reflection of 1995 military pay. On the other hand, as federal budget constraints increase, cost of living allowance increases (COLAs) could decrease or end. Therefore, if you want to find out the exact current rate, check with your base accounting and finance office. For detailed information about the pay system, see AFP 177-4.

# Monthly Military Basic Pay
(effective 1 January 1995)

| GRADE | Under 2 | 2 | 3 | 4 | 6 | 8 | 10 | 12 | 14 | 16 | 18 | 20 | 22 | 24 | 26 |
|---|---|---|---|---|---|---|---|---|---|---|---|---|---|---|---|
| | Years of Service | | | | | | | | | | | | | | |
| **Commissioned Officers** | | | | | | | | | | | | | | | |
| 0–10 | 6978.30 | 7223.70 | 7223.70 | 7223.70 | 7223.70 | 7501.20 | 7501.20 | 7916.70 | 7916.70 | 8482.80 | 8482.80 | 9051.00 | 9051.00 | 9051.00 | 9614.70 |
| 0–9 | 6184.50 | 6346.50 | 6481.80 | 6481.80 | 6481.80 | 6646.50 | 6646.50 | 6923.10 | 6923.10 | 7501.20 | 7501.20 | 7916.70 | 7916.70 | 7916.70 | 8482.80 |
| 0–8 | 5601.60 | 5769.60 | 5906.40 | 5906.40 | 5906.40 | 6346.50 | 6346.50 | 6646.50 | 6646.50 | 6923.10 | 7223.70 | 7501.20 | 7686.00 | 7686.00 | 7686.00 |
| 0–7 | 4654.50 | 4971.00 | 4971.00 | 4971.00 | 5193.90 | 5193.90 | 5494.80 | 5494.80 | 5769.60 | 6346.50 | 6783.00 | 6783.00 | 6783.00 | 6783.00 | 6783.00 |
| 0–6 | 3449.70 | 3790.20 | 4038.60 | 4038.60 | 4038.60 | 4038.60 | 4038.60 | 4038.60 | 4176.00 | 4836.30 | 5082.90 | 5193.90 | 5494.80 | 5680.80 | 5959.50 |
| 0–5 | 2759.10 | 3239.70 | 3463.80 | 3463.80 | 3463.80 | 3463.80 | 3568.50 | 3760.80 | 4012.80 | 4313.10 | 4560.00 | 4698.60 | 4862.70 | 4862.70 | 4862.70 |
| 0–4 | 2325.60 | 2832.00 | 3021.00 | 3021.00 | 3077.10 | 3212.70 | 3432.00 | 3624.90 | 3790.20 | 3956.70 | 4065.60 | 4065.60 | 4065.60 | 4065.60 | 4065.60 |
| 0–3 | 2161.20 | 2416.50 | 2583.30 | 2858.10 | 2994.90 | 3102.30 | 3270.30 | 3432.00 | 3516.30 | 3516.30 | 3516.30 | 3516.30 | 3516.30 | 3516.30 | 3516.30 |
| 0–2 | 1884.60 | 2058.00 | 2472.90 | 2556.00 | 2608.80 | 2608.80 | 2608.80 | 2608.80 | 2608.80 | 2608.80 | 2608.80 | 2608.80 | 2608.80 | 2608.80 | 2608.80 |
| 0–1 | 1636.20 | 1703.10 | 2058.00 | 2058.00 | 2058.00 | 2058.00 | 2058.00 | 2058.00 | 2058.00 | 2058.00 | 2058.00 | 2058.00 | 2058.00 | 2058.00 | 2058.00 |
| **Commissioned Officers with More than 4 Years' Active Duty as Enlisted or Warrant Officer** | | | | | | | | | | | | | | | |
| 0–3E | 0.00 | 0.00 | 0.00 | 2858.10 | 2994.90 | 3102.30 | 3270.30 | 3432.00 | 3568.50 | 3568.50 | 3568.50 | 3568.50 | 3568.50 | 3568.50 | 3568.50 |
| 0–2E | 0.00 | 0.00 | 0.00 | 2556.00 | 2608.80 | 2691.60 | 2832.00 | 2940.60 | 3021.00 | 3021.00 | 3021.00 | 3021.00 | 3021.00 | 3021.00 | 3021.00 |
| 0–1E | 0.00 | 0.00 | 0.00 | 2058.00 | 2199.00 | 2280.00 | 2362.50 | 2444.40 | 2556.00 | 2556.00 | 2556.00 | 2556.00 | 2556.00 | 2556.00 | 2556.00 |

**Basic Allowances.** The *basic allowance for subsistence* (BAS) is the same for all officers of all grades, with or without dependents. ($146.16 per month in 1995.)

The amount of pay provided as *basic allowance for quarters* (BAQ) for officers authorized but not occupying government quarters differs between officers having dependents and those without dependents. A detailed definition of what constitutes a dependent appears later in this chapter.

The monthly quarters allowance for officers varies with the pay grade and follows either of two schedules, with dependents and without dependents. The dependents schedule is the same regardless of the number of dependents.

## Basic Allowance for Quarters
(effective 1 January 1995)

| Pay Grade | Without Dependents Full | Without Dependents Partial | With Dependents |
|---|---|---|---|
| O-10 | $749.40 | $50.70 | $922.50 |
| O-9 | 749.40 | 50.70 | 922.50 |
| O-8 | 749.40 | 50.70 | 922.50 |
| O-7 | 749.40 | 50.70 | 922.50 |
| O-6 | 687.60 | 39.60 | 830.70 |
| O-5 | 662.10 | 33.00 | 800.70 |
| O-4 | 613.80 | 26.70 | 705.90 |
| O-3 | 492.00 | 22.20 | 584.10 |
| O-2 | 390.00 | 17.70 | 498.90 |
| O-1 | 328.50 | 13.20 | 445.80 |
| O3E | 531.00 | 22.20 | 627.60 |
| O2E | 451.50 | 17.70 | 566.40 |
| O1E | 388.20 | 13.20 | 523.20 |
| W5 | 623.40 | 25.20 | 681.30 |
| W4 | 553.80 | 25.20 | 624.60 |
| W3 | 465.30 | 20.70 | 572.40 |
| W2 | 413.10 | 15.90 | 526.50 |
| W1 | 345.90 | 13.80 | 455.40 |
| E-9 | 454.80 | 18.60 | 599.40 |
| E-8 | 417.60 | 15.30 | 552.60 |
| E-7 | 356.40 | 12.00 | 513.00 |
| E-6 | 322.80 | 9.90 | 474.30 |
| E-5 | 297.60 | 8.70 | 426.30 |
| E-4 | 258.90 | 8.10 | 370.80 |
| E-3 | 254.10 | 7.80 | 345.00 |
| E-2 | 206.40 | 7.20 | 328.50 |
| E-1 | 183.90 | 6.90 | 328.50 |

**Variable Housing Allowance.** The 1980 Nunn-Warner Bill authorizes additional quarters allowances up to the difference between 115 percent of the basic allowance for quarters and the average cost of off-base housing in each area.

**Incentive and Special Pay.** *Flight pay* for aircrew officers ranges from a minimum of $125 per month to a maximum of $650 after six years on flying status and at 18 years' service decreases to $585, falling gradually to $250 after 25 years' service. Brigadier generals may receive no more than $200 per month; major generals and above, $206. *Hazardous duty incentive pay* for parachutists on jump status and divers is $150 per month for officers. *Hostile fire pay* for military members serving in areas where they are subject to injury as a result of enemy action is $110 per month. *Special medical pay* for medical officers ranges from $250 to $1,000 per month for physicians, depending on grade and length of service, and from $100 to $350 for dentists. Veterinary and optometry officers receive special pay of $100 per month. *Engineering and scientific career continuation pay* to a maximum of $3,000 per year is payable to those officers in selected critical skills.

**Pay and Allowances.** With these facts in mind, you may determine from the tables the four fundamental elements of your pay and allowances as an officer: base pay, BAS, BAQ, and incentive or special pay.

Officers in pay grade 0-4 and above may choose to live off base and receive the BAQ for their grade without dependents even if government quarters are available.

Generals receive these personal money allowances: lieutenant general, $500 a year; general, $2,200 a year; the chief of staff, USAF, $4,000 a year.

**Leave and Earnings Statement (LES).** Each month you receive a copy of Air Force Form 141, *Leave and Earnings Statement,* a personal account of your pay status. (See chapter 8 for information about computation of leave credits.) You should save these statements and keep them in a safe place. They are useful for tax purposes, for making inquiries at the Accounting and Finance Office (AFO), and for helping AFO personnel determine amounts of casual or partial payments. If you are paid twice a month and use the Sure Pay system, the AFO also sends an abbreviated pay notice at the middle of the month, telling how much was deposited to your account at that time.

## INTERMITTENT AND NONRECURRING ELEMENTS OF PAY AND ALLOWANCES

**Family Separation Allowance.** This allowance is payable only to servicemembers with dependents. The family separation allowance is of two types, both of which you may receive if you meet the following qualifications for both, regardless of any other allowance or per diem to which you may be entitled:

• One allowance, equal to the basic monthly allowance for quarters payable to a member in the same pay grade without dependents, is payable to a member with dependents, who is on permanent duty in Alaska or anywhere outside the United States, when:

—Movement of dependents to the permanent station or place nearby is not authorized at government expense and dependents are not residing at or near the station.

—No government quarters are available for assignment to the member.

• The other type of family separation allowance, equal to $75 per month, is payable (except in wartime or national emergency declared by Congress) to a member with dependents who is authorized a basic quarters allowance, when:

—Movement of dependents to the permanent station or place nearby is not authorized at government expense and dependents are not residing at or near the station.

—The member is on duty aboard ship away from the ship's home port continuously for more than 30 days.

—The member is on temporary duty away from his permanent station continuously for more than 30 days and dependents do not reside at or near the temporary duty station.

**Uniform Allowances.** Reserve officers upon initial appointment are entitled to $200 to purchase required uniforms. This amount accrues upon first reporting for active duty for more than 90 days, upon completion as a member of a reserve component of at least 14 days' active duty or active duty for training, or upon completion of 14 periods of not less than two hours each in the Ready Reserve that required wearing the uniform. After 90 days of duty, you may receive an additional allowance of $100. As a regular officer commissioned from AFROTC, you would receive $300.

*The Allowance for Reentry on Active Duty.* A reserve officer who has been on inactive duty for a period of two years and then goes back on active duty for more than 90 days may qualify for $100 as reimbursement for additional uniforms and equipment required on such duty.

**Dislocation and Trailer Allowances.** *Dislocation Allowance.* The allowance is to partially reimburse servicemembers for the expense incurred in closing out households at one location and setting up again at a new place when they are transferred on permanent change of station (PCS). The allowance is an amount equal to two months of basic allowance for quarters. The Air Force pays it only once in connection with any one PCS and only when dependents have completed travel in connection with a PCS that authorizes transportation of dependents or travel allowances. The Air Force does not pay it for the move from home to first duty station or from last duty station to home. Under normal conditions, servicemembers are not entitled to payment of the dislocation allowance more than once in any fiscal year, and the following conditions apply:

• For the purpose of determining the fiscal year in which entitlement to a dislocation allowance occurs, the date of departure (detachment) from the old permanent duty station in compliance with PCS orders shall govern.

• Computation excludes prior PCSs in the same fiscal year for which a dislocation allowance was not authorized.

• Computation excludes PCS to, from, or between courses of instruction conducted at an installation of the uniformed services.

*Trailer Allowance.* The trailer allowance is in lieu of transportation of baggage and household effects when a member transports a house trailer or mobile dwelling within the United States for use as a residence, provided the member would otherwise be entitled to transportation of baggage and household effects. A member receiving a trailer allowance would not be authorized to receive a dislocation allowance for the same move.

The allowance is payable in advance of the movement of the trailer.

**Travel Allowance.** An allowance of $50 per diem and 15 cents a mile for the official distance is authorized for officers moving under PCS orders by private vehicle (with 2 cents per mile for each dependent, up to a total of 20 cents per mile).

**Station Allowances, Overseas.** Uniformed personnel stationed in a number of foreign countries may receive station allowances to equalize the cost of living and housing in the foreign station with those in the United States if the cost is greater in the oversea station.

**Advance Pay.** An officer may draw PCS advance pay of not more than three months' net basic pay.

**Temporary Lodging Allowance.** Servicemembers on PCS orders with families can draw $110 per day for ten days.

**Imminent Danger Pay** of $150 per month currently is authorized at two dozen locations around the world (foreign duty pay is authorized only for enlisted members). Also, there is a tax break in a combat zone: An officer may exclude $500 per month of his pay from federal income tax while serving in a war zone. There is also a savings plan when serving in a major conflict. During the Gulf War, military members could bank as much as $10,000 annually of unallotted pay and allowances at 10 percent interest.

## DEPENDENTS

**Definition.** The term "dependents" includes the lawful spouse and unmarried children, under 21 years of age, of any member of the uniformed services, and the father or mother of such member, provided he or she is in fact dependent on such member for more than half of his or her support. It also includes unmarried children, over 21 years of age, of such member who are incapable of self-support because of being mentally or physically incapacitated and who are in fact dependent on such member for more than half of their support. The term "children" includes stepchildren and adopted children dependent upon such member. The term "father" or "mother" shall include a stepparent or parent by adoption and any other person, including a former stepparent, who has stood in loco parentis to the person concerned at any time for a continuous period of not less than five years during the minority of such member. No member claiming a dependent may receive increased allowances on account of such dependent for any period during which such dependent is entitled to receive basic pay for active or training duty.

**Credit for Dependent Parents.** An officer will receive credit for basic allowance for quarters because of a dependent parent only when the dependent parent actually is residing in the household of the officer claiming the increased allowance.

## DEDUCTIONS

**Social Security Tax.** The law requires the Air Force to deduct Social Security taxes from individual pay. The percentage deducted and the amount on which it is computed has edged upward gradually. For details, check your finance office.

**Federal Income Tax.** Members of the armed services are subject to the federal law providing for payroll deductions for income tax. Taxable income includes all pay but does not include subsistence and quarters allowances.

**State Income Tax.** Members of the armed services are subject to the laws of their state of official residence providing for payroll deductions for state income taxes.

## INCOME TAX EXEMPTION

**Taxation of Pay for Retired Service Personnel.** Members of the armed services who are retired for length of service or age pay the same federal income taxes as other citizens. The accounting and finance officer makes the same tax withholdings as for active-duty officers.

Members retired for physical disability receive an important exemption in the computation of federal income tax. The amount of their exemption depends upon the degree of disability and applies to their active-duty base pay at the time of retirement. Assume, for example, that an officer with active-duty base pay of $1,085 retired with 30 percent disability. By tax rulings, apply the 30 percent to the active-duty base pay, which is $325.50, the amount exempt from income tax. The retired pay is $813.75. Deduct the nontaxable $325.50, and the remainder of $488.25 is taxable. Moreover, this officer could deduct $5,200 as sick pay ($100 weekly) until reaching statutory retirement age under an Internal Revenue Service ruling. The officer would therefore pay no tax at all if retired pay was his sole income.

## ALLOTMENTS AND STOPPAGES

**Allotments.** Air Force regulations permit you to make allotments from your pay for various purposes.

The word "allotment" means a definite portion of your pay that you authorize the Air Force to pay to another person or institution.

The "allotter" is the person who makes the allotment, in this case you.

The "allottee" is the person or institution to whom you make the allotment.

Generally, you can make an allotment for an indefinite time beginning on the first of the month for which you want to make the deduction but not before your date of commission or appointment.

Allotments can make life simpler for you, especially because you may have to go anywhere in the world at any time for temporary duty (TDY) or permanent change of station (PCS). With allotments, although you still have control of your money, you don't have to physically write out the checks and stamp the envelopes every month. You may want to consider making allotments for the following purposes:

- Buy government bonds.
- Donate to charity (Combined Federal Campaign).
- Support dependents.
- Repay home loans.
- Pay commercial life insurance premiums.
- Pay Servicemen's Group Life Insurance premiums.
- Add to savings accounts.

**While Prisoner of War or Reported Missing.** Any officer who is interned, taken prisoner of war, or reported missing and who has made an allotment of pay for the support of dependents or for the payment of insurance premiums is entitled to have such allotments or insurance deductions continued for a period of 12 months from the date of commencement of absence. Allotments of officers under any of the above conditions may not continue beyond 12 months following the officially reported date of commencement of absence, except that when that 12 months is about to expire and the Air Force has received no official report of death or of being a prisoner of war or of being interned, the Air Force can fully review the case. Following such review and when the 12 months' absence has expired or following any subsequent review of the case, the Air Force may direct the continuance of the officer's missing status, if the Air Force can reasonably presume the officer is still alive. Such missing officers continue to be entitled to have pay and allowances credited and payment of allotments as authorized to be continued, increased, or initiated.

In the absence of an allotment or when the allotment is not sufficient for reasonable support of a dependent and for the payment of insurance premiums, the Air Force may direct payment of an appropriate allotment, not to exceed the total basic pay of the person concerned.

**Authorized Stoppages.** The Air Force may withhold the pay of officers on account of an indebtedness to the United States admitted or shown by the judgment of a court, but not otherwise unless specifically ordered by the Secretary of the Air Force.

## CREDITABLE SERVICE FOR BASIC PAY

DODPM establishes the rules for counting the various conditions of active duty in computing cumulative years of service for credit toward basic pay. This manual is so long and detailed that if you have an unusual background of service you should peruse it carefully, but you may find the following general statements helpful.

**Active Duty.** You will receive full time credit for all periods of active duty served in any regular or reserve component of any uniformed service in any military status, commissioned or enlisted.

**Retired Status.** You will receive additional credit for any period of time you are on any retired list. This provision does *not* increase retired pay, but if you return to active duty from a retired list, you benefit from inclusion of your time on the retired list in computing basic pay.

**Academies.** Service as a cadet or midshipman in the service academies or ROTC is *not* creditable.

**Fraudulent Enlistment.** You may receive credit for service in a fraudulent enlistment not voided by the government.

**Beginning Dates of Service.** Service as an officer begins from the date of acceptance of appointment; as an enlisted member, from the date of enlistment.

## REIMBURSEMENT FOR TDY TRAVEL EXPENSES

**Travel at Personal Expense.** When you perform authorized travel at personal expense, the Air Force will reimburse you a monetary allowance in lieu of transportation at the rate of 25 cents per mile for the official distance in addition to authorized per diem. Daily mileage allowance is 350 miles.

**Travel by Privately Owned Vehicle.** For travel actually performed by privately owned vehicle under orders authorizing such mode of transportation as more advantageous to the government, you will receive a monetary allowance in lieu of transportation at the rate of 24 cents per mile for the official distance in addition to authorized per diem.

**Per Diem.** The per diem allowance within the United States ranges from $66 to $151, depending upon the city. This allowance covers the cost of quarters, subsistence, and other necessary expenses.

In instances requiring certificates of availability of government quarters and messing facilities, you must adhere to the provisions of paragraph M4451 of the Joint Travel Regulations (JTR) if you wish to receive proper per diem reimbursement.

**Interrupted Leave.** When you are called back to your permanent station within 24 hours after your departure on a leave of five or more days, your travel will be at government expense. The government will also pay the cost of returning you to your point of leave if resumption of leave is feasible.

**Reimbursable Travel Expenses.** When traveling under orders, keep a detailed record of all expenses, however minor. Many are reimbursable. Note the following list of reimbursable items:

*Taxi Fares.* You may receive reimbursement for taxi fares between home or business and stations, wharves, airports, other carrier terminals or local terminus of the mode of transportation used, between carrier terminals, while en route when free transfer is not included in the price of the ticket or when necessitated by change in mode of travel, and from carrier terminals to lodgings and return in connection with unavoidable delays en route incident to the mode of travel. Itemization is required.

*Allowed Tips.* You may receive reimbursement for tips incident to transportation expenses as follows: tips of 15 percent to taxi drivers and tips to baggage porters, red caps, and so on, not to exceed customary local rates, but not including tips for baggage handling at hotels. Itemization is required, including the number of pieces of baggage handled.

*Checking and Transfer of Baggage.* Expenses incident to checking and transfer of baggage are reimbursable. The number of pieces of baggage checked must appear on the claim. Itemization is required.

*Excess Baggage.* When excess baggage is authorized, actual costs for such excess baggage in addition to that carried free by the carrier are reimbursable.

*Government Aircraft.* Cost of gasoline, oil, repairs, nonpersonal services, guards, and storage are reimbursable when such expenses are necessary because you land at other than a government field. Receipts are required.

*Government Auto.* Cost of storage of government automobiles when necessary is reimbursable if government storage facilities are not available. Receipt is required.

*Telephone, Telegraph, Cable, and So On.* Cost of official telephone, telegraph, cable, and similar communication services is reimbursable when incident to the official duty or in connection with items of transportation. Such services when solely in connection with reserving a hotel room and so on are not, however, considered official. Copies of messages sent are required for all mechanical transmissions unless the message is classified, in which case a full explanation and a receipt will suffice. Local calls are allowable when itemized. Long distance calls require full explanations.

*Local Public Carrier Fares.* Expenses incident to travel on streetcar, bus, or other usual means of transportation may be reimbursable in lieu of taxi fares under certain conditions and limitations. Itemization is required.

*Toll Fares.* Ferry fares and road, bridge, and tunnel tolls are reimbursable when travel is by special conveyance or government highway transportation. Itemization is required.

*Local Transportation.* Reimbursement is authorized for transportation obtained at personal expense in the conduct of official business within and around either the permanent or temporary duty station. See JTR.

**Nonreimbursable Travel Expenses.** The government cannot reimburse you for the following travel expenses:

• Expenses incurred during travel that are incidental to other duties (such as traveling aboard a vessel in performance of temporary duty on such vessel).
• Travel under permissive orders to travel, in contrast to orders directing travel.
• Travel under orders but not on public business, such as travel as a participant in an athletic contest. Unit or command welfare funds, which come from such sources as operation of exchanges and motion picture theaters, may reimburse you for such travel, but appropriated funds cannot.
• Return from leave to duty abroad. Unless government transportation is available, such as space on a transport, you must pay your own return expenses from leave in the United States.
• Attendance at public ceremonies or demonstrations paid for by the sponsoring agency.

**Travel outside the United States.** The government will pay you in advance or reimburse you for travel expenses for travel outside the United States essentially the same as for temporary duty travel performed in the United States. You are entitled to the costs of transportation, per diem allowance, and cost of incidental necessary expenses.

**Certificates of Nonavailability.** When government quarters are available, the government will deduct 54 percent of the travel per diem allowance. You must certify that government quarters were available even though, in connection with the occupancy of such quarters, you had to pay incidental room or service charges. You must get certificates from the commander or designated representative of an installation at which you perform temporary duty as follows if you want reimbursement for nongovernment lodging and meals:

"I certify that government quarters as defined in paras. 1150-5, JTR, were not available to . . . on the following dates: . . . and that a government mess, as defined in paras. 1150-4, JTR, was not available on the following dates for the number of meals indicated: (such as Feb. 22 (1); 23 (3); 24-26 (9); 27 (0)). . . ."

You must also certify that you did not use quarters and mess for the same periods.

**Amount of Oversea Travel Allowances.** The allowances for TDY travel costs overseas vary. You may expect allowances for necessary expenses provided you use reasonable care.

Before undertaking travel outside the United States, you should consult local transportation or accounting and finance officers to determine the exact amount of the expected allowances, which appear in appendix A, *Joint Travel Regulations*.

**Preparation of Vouchers for Payment.** Consult the local accounting and finance officer. Learn to save every receipt from your trip, keep them together with your draft voucher paperwork, and take everything to finance when you file your voucher. Go to finance *before* your TDY trip, get a copy of the voucher and actual expenses sheet you may have to fill out, and ask the people at finance what they will need from you. They usually prefer to help travelers before the trip. Often, installations have handy checklists or how-to-take-a-TDY-trip booklets for you.

**Advance Payment of Travel and Transportation Allowances.** You may receive travel and transportation allowances in advance, except in connection with retirement or movement of household goods.

## WEIGHT ALLOWANCES FOR CHANGE OF STATION

Although Congress has proposed increasing weight allowances, the accompanying table shows weight allowances authorized for shipment of household goods at government expense on change of station.

TABLE OF WEIGHT ALLOWANCES (Pounds)

| Grade* | Temporary Change of Station | Permanent Change of Station With Dependents | Without Dependents |
|---|---|---|---|
| General of the Air Force and General | **2,000 | 18,000 | 18,000 |
| Lieutenant General | 1,500 | 18,000 | 18,000 |
| Major General | 1,000 | 18,000 | 18,000 |
| Brigadier General | 1,000 | 18,000 | 18,000 |
| Colonel | 800 | 18,000 | 18,000 |
| Lieutenant Colonel | 800 | 17,500 | 16,000 |
| Major | 800 | 17,000 | 14,000 |
| Captain | 600 | 14,500 | 13,000 |
| 1st Lieutenant | 600 | 13,500 | 12,500 |
| 2d Lieutenant | 600 | 12,000 | 10,000 |

*Members of reserve components and officers holding temporary commissions in the Air Force of the United States are entitled to weight allowances for corresponding relative grades listed. The weight allowance of an individual depends upon grade or rating at the time of detachment from the last duty station.

**The respective secretaries or the chiefs of staff, U.S. Air Force and Army, and chief of naval operations may authorize exceptions to this limitation in such additional amounts, not exceeding 2,000 pounds, as they may consider appropriate.

# 5

# Uniforms and Insignia

*A soldier must learn to love his profession, must look to it to satisfy all his tastes and his sense of honor. That is why handsome uniforms are useful.*

—Napoleon

The Air Force is a uniformed service and, as such, requires all members to maintain a high standard of dress and personal appearance. Pride in each member's daily personal appearance and uniform wear greatly strengthens the esprit de corps essential to an effective military force. Officers who violate the specific prohibitions of AFR 35-10 are subject to appropriate administrative action and prosecution under the Uniform Code of Military Justice.

Officers must provide, at their own expense, many uniforms and uniform items. For information concerning uniform allowances for newly commissioned officers, see chapter 4.

## WEARING THE UNIFORM

**When to Wear the Uniform.** Air Force personnel must wear the prescribed service uniform at all places of duty during duty hours, except as specifically authorized by AFR 35-10. The installation commander designates the appropriate uniform combinations in accordance with local climatic and mission requirements. Special occasions require wearing the dress uniform.

**Standards of Dress and Appearance.** Although all Air Force personnel must maintain a high standard of dress and appearance, officers in particular, whose manner of dress and personal appearance provide a visual example for enlisted personnel, must wear the uniform in a manner that emphasizes pride and must keep their personal appearance above reproach.

The elements of the Air Force standard are neatness, cleanliness, safety, and military image. The first three are absolute, objective criteria required for the efficiency and well-being of the Air Force. The fourth standard, military image, is subjective in that the American public and its elected representatives draw certain conclusions based on the image presented by Air Force members. The military image, therefore, must instill public confidence and leave no doubt that Air Force members live by a common standard and respond to military order and discipline.

Appearance in uniform is an important part of the military image. Because judgment as to what constitutes the proper image differs in and out of the military, the Air Force must spell out what is and what is not acceptable. The image of a disciplined and reliable servicemember excludes the extreme, the unusual, or the fad.

**Uniform Standards.** Keep your uniforms clean, neat, correct in design and specification, properly fitted, pressed and in good condition—not frayed, worn out, torn, faded, patched, or stained. Keep uniform items, including pockets, buttoned, snapped, or zippered as appropriate. Keep your shoes shined and in good repair. Keep your badges, insignia, belt buckles, and other metallic devices clean and free from scratches or corrosion. Keep your ribbons clean, and replace them when they begin to look frayed.

You may wear wristwatches and identification bracelets, but they should be of conservative design. An identification bracelet must be no wider than one inch and must not subject you to potential injury. You may also wear rings but only a total of three rings on both hands at any one time.

Women members with pierced ears may wear, on a daily basis, small, conservative, spherical earrings in gold, silver, or white pearl. When worn, earrings must fit flat against the ear and must not extend below the earlobe. Do not wear earrings when safety considerations dictate.

Keep the gig line—shirt placket, belt buckle, and trouser fly—in alignment.

**Personal Appearance and Grooming Standards.** One of the most important elements of your personal appearance as an officer is your hair. Keep your hair clean, well groomed, and neat. Avoid extreme or fad hairstyles, such as mohawks, ducktails, or cornrows. If you dye your hair, it must look natural. When groomed, your hair must not touch your eyebrows or protrude in front below the band of properly worn headgear. Women members, however, must have their hair visible when wearing the beret.

For men, hair must not touch the ears, and only the closely shaved hair on the back of the neck may touch the collar. The bulk of a man's hair may not exceed 1¼″. Sideburns can be no longer than the lowest part of the exterior ear opening. Women may not wear their hair longer than the back bottom edge of their shirt collar. Hair bulk may not exceed 3″.

Hair ornamentation is not permitted. To keep their hair in place, however, women may wear plain pins, combs, or barrettes similar in color to their own hair.

Men who choose to wear mustaches must ensure that they do not extend downward beyond the lip line of the upper lip or sideways beyond a vertical line drawn upward from the corner of the mouth. The Air Force does not allow its members to wear handlebar mustaches or beards. On the advice of a medical officer, however, the commander may authorize otherwise.

## CLASSIFICATION OF UNIFORMS

Uniforms worn by USAF personnel fall into three categories: service uniforms, fatigue uniforms, and dress uniforms.

**Service Uniforms.** Wear the service uniform during regular duty hours while performing assigned work. You may wear all service uniform combinations year-round, but installation commanders may prescribe when members will wear certain combinations. If the commander does not prescribe specific combinations, use good judgment, based on weather conditions and duties, when selecting the particular service uniform combination to wear.

Personnel assigned to a non-Air Force military installation will wear the service uniform that most closely matches the host service order of dress.

The blue maternity uniform is mandatory for all pregnant members.

**Fatigue Uniforms.** Wear the fatigue uniform whenever mission requirements make the service uniform inappropriate. Do not wear the fatigue uniform to off-base businesses if you anticipate or intend extended shopping, dining, or socializing. When wearing the fatigue uniform, especially if you will be making an off-base stop, you must present the proper standards of cleanliness, neatness, and military image.

**Dress Uniforms.** The formal dress, the mess dress, and the winter and summer ceremonial dress uniforms are for year-round wear at the discretion of the installation commander.

## THE NEW AIR FORCE UNIFORM

In 1991 USAF Chief of Staff Gen. Merrill A. McPeak ordered the most sweeping changes in USAF service uniforms since 1948, when the present uniform replaced the Army Air Force's "pinks and greens." The new uniform will be issued beginning 1 October 1995, but the present uniform may be worn until 1 October 1999. As of press time, the new AFR 35-10, *USAF Uniforms and Insignia,* had not been published, but enough information has been released to provide a preview. Information on the present uniform has been retained in this edition of the *Guide* for the transition period 1995–99.

**Men's New Service Dress Uniform.** Air Force shade 1620, 55/45 percent polyester/wool blend serge weave. Equivalent civilian attire is the business suit. The coat is semidrape and single breasted with three buttons, one welt pocket on the left breast for alignment of ribbons, and two lower pocket flaps. Metal buttons bear the old Army Air Corps "wing and star" design. Officers will wear aluminum-color grade insignia on sleeve cuffs (see illustration). Trousers are of matching color and material.

*Belt.* Same as current one, except that general officers may wear a buckle bearing the wing and star design.

*Shirt.* Any of the present long- or short-sleeved light blue shirts with epaulets and tie may be worn.

*Tie.* Polyester herringbone twill, Air Force shade 1621.

*Footwear.* Three types are authorized: low-quarter shoes, dress boots, or combat boots. They may be of smooth or scotch-grained leather or man-made material, either of high gloss or patent finish.

*Socks.* Plain black (or white with boots).

*Outergarments.* The present all-weather coat, raincoat, or overcoat.

*Gloves.* Gray wool knit, gray or black leather, or black mittens.

MEN'S NEW SERVICE DRESS UNIFORM.

*Scarf.* Worn only with outergarments, not more than 10 inches wide, white or gray, wool or cotton, with or without napped surface (Air Force shade 1155 or 1164), worn tucked in.

*Headgear.* Either the optional service cap or flight cap; shade and material need not match that of the coat and trousers.

*Earmuffs.* Commercial design of any material, plain in solid blue, black, or gray.

*Cuff links.* Any of three kinds: wing and star design, oval bearing Air Force coat of arms, or plain satin silver finish. Wear is optional.

**Women's New Service Dress Uniform.**

*Coat.* Same as men's. Coat and skirt or slacks must match.

*Blouse.* Any of the present ones. Tab must be worn (polyester herringbone, Air Force shade 121).

WOMEN'S NEW SERVICE DRESS UNIFORM.

*Skirt.* Straight with belt loops, kick pleat in back, pleated front with two pockets.

*Belt.* Same as present one.

*Footwear.* Four types are authorized: dress shoes, dress boots, oxfords, or combat boots, material same as men's.

*Hose.* Plain commercial sheer nylon in neutral, dark brown, black, off-black, or dark blue will be worn with the skirt. Socks may be worn with slacks.

*Headgear.* Beret, flight cap, or service cap.

*Outergarments.* The present all-weather coat, raincoat, or overcoat.

*Scarf.* Similar to men's.

*Gloves.* Plain white cotton knit or nylon tricot, black leather, knitted wool, or cotton simplex, suede or combination, or black mittens.

*Earmuffs.* Similar to men's.

*Handbag.* Air Force-approved vinyl handbag, optional leather handbag, or clutch-style purse.

## SERVICE UNIFORMS

**Men's Service Dress.** Dark blue service coat and trousers of matching shade and fabric; dark blue belt with silvered buckle and tip; light blue long-sleeved shirt with epaulets; undergarments; black socks and shoes; dark blue necktie; service cap or flight cap; name tag; insignia, badges, and ribbons.

**Women's Service Dress.** Dark blue semibox coat and skirt of matching shade and fabric; light blue overblouse, standard length with epaulets and dark blue tie tab; undergarments; nylon hose of a neutral or dark shade; black pumps, oxfords, or dress boots; service cap or beret; name tag; insignia, badges, and ribbons. (The dark blue blazer may substitute for the semibox coat.)

**Men's Light Blue Shirt with Long Sleeves.** Same as service dress, except that the service coat is not worn and ribbons are not required.

**Women's Light Blue Blouse with Long Sleeves.** Same as service dress, except that the semibox coat is not worn and ribbons are not required.

**Men's Light Blue Shirt with Short Sleeves, Epaulets, and Necktie.**

**Men's Light Blue Shirt with Short Sleeves, Epaulets, No Necktie.**

**Men's Light Blue Shirt with Short Sleeves, No Epaulets, No Necktie.**

**Women's Light Blue Blouse with Short Sleeves.**

**Men's and Women's Pullover Sweaters with Shoulder Mark Insignia.**

**Maternity Blouse or Tunic.**

**Women's Combinations.** Eight other combinations of women's uniforms substitute slacks for skirts and/or overblouses for blouses in these combinations.

## FATIGUE UNIFORMS

**Camouflage Fatigue Uniform (Battle Dress Uniforms—BDUs).** Wear either subdued color metal or cloth grade insignia with these uniforms.

**Leather Flying Jacket.** The brown Army Air Force's World War II leather flying jacket has been revived for aircrew wardrobes only. It is worn without grade insignia but with an embossed leather name tag showing the grade.

## DRESS UNIFORMS

(*Note:* This section describes the newer dress uniforms, for which no illustrations were available at press time.)

**Men's Mess Dress.** *Required items:* Blue mess jacket with officers' silver sleeve braid, blue shoulder boards, miniature badges and decorations; blue trousers with striping; plain white pleat-fronted shirt; blue bowtie; blue cummerbund, silver studs, links, and chain buttons; suspenders; plain black socks and low-quarter shoes; blue dress cap with silver chin strap. *Optional items:* blue overcoat or raincoat, gray or white gloves, and scarf.

WOMEN'S AND MEN'S SERVICE DRESS.

WOMEN'S AND MEN'S LIGHT BLUE BLOUSE OR SHIRT WITH LONG SLEEVES.

WOMEN'S AND MEN'S LIGHT BLUE BLOUSE OR SHIRT WITH SHORT SLEEVES, EPAULETS, AND NECKTIE.

WOMEN'S AND MEN'S LIGHT BLUE BLOUSE OR SHIRT WITH SHORT SLEEVES, EPAULETS, NO NECKTIE.

WOMEN'S AND MEN'S PULLOVER SWEATERS WITH SHOULDER MARK INSIGNIA.

MATERNITY SMOCK WITH SKIRT.
Note: Skirt and shirt may also be worn with or without smock.

CAMOUFLAGE FATIGUE UNIFORM (BATTLE DRESS UNIFORM—BDU).

MEN'S AND WOMEN'S MESS DRESS UNIFORMS.

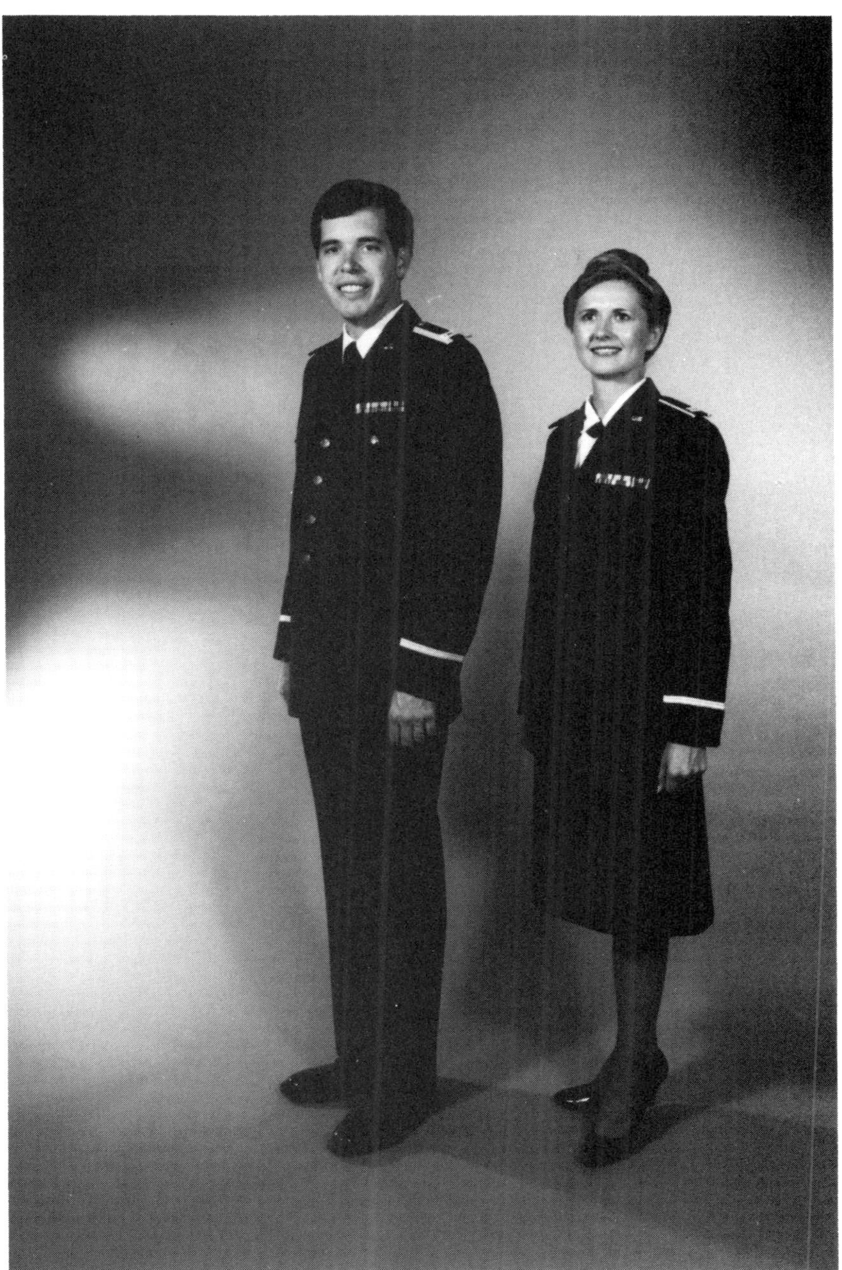

MEN'S AND WOMEN'S BLUE CEREMONIAL DRESS UNIFORMS.
Note: Sleeve braid should be blue for company-grade officers and silver for field graders.

MEN'S AND WOMEN'S WHITE CEREMONIAL DRESS UNIFORMS.

**Women's Mess Dress.** *Required items:* Blue mess jacket with officers' silver sleeve braid, blue shoulder boards, miniature badges and decorations; blue ankle-length skirt; white mess shirt with blue tie tab, blue cummerbund. *Optional items:* blue overcoat or raincoat, white gloves, and black vinyl, leather, or suede clutch handbag.

**Men's Formal Dress.** Same as the mess dress, except that a white wing-collar full dress shirt, white bow tie, white single-breasted vest, and pearl studs and links replace the white pleated-front shirt, blue bow tie, cummerbund, and silver studs and links.

**Women's Formal Dress.** Same as the mess dress, except that a silver tie tab and silver cummerbund replace the blue ones.

**Men's Ceremonial Dress Uniform (Blue or White).** Blue or white coat with silver sleeve braid, blue shoulder boards, insignia, badges, and ribbons; blue or white trousers; plain white shirt; blue necktie; blue or white silver-tip belt with silver buckle; black or white socks; plain black or white shoes; blue or white cover service cap with silver chin strap.

**Women's Ceremonial Dress Uniform (Blue or White).** Blue or white blazer-style coat with silver sleeve braid, blue shoulder boards, insignia, badges, and ribbons; blue or white street-length skirt and matching coat; white overblouse (optional); stockings in appropriate shade; black or white pumps; blue beret or blue or white service cap.

*Note:* The blue and white ceremonial dress uniforms are optional for company-grade officers (lieutenants and captains), but mandatory for field grade officers (majors through colonels) and general officers. Officers will wear them at daytime and evening social occasions and at authorized official functions and ceremonies.

## OPTIONAL UNIFORM ITEMS

Certain other optional uniform items are also available.

**Outergarments.** There are five kinds of outerwear, besides sweaters, for men and women: cotton/polyester poplin lightweight blue jacket, polyester/wool gabardine lightweight blue jacket, all-weather coat, raincoat, and overcoat.

**Sweater.** You may wear the pullover sweater with epaulet grade insignia indoors and outdoors.

**Umbrella.** You may carry a black umbrella, but you need to know that old-guard officers frown on male officers carrying umbrellas when in uniform because they consider umbrellas "wimpy."

**Attaché Cases and Gym Bags.** Carry them with the left hand so that you can salute.

**Gloves.** You may wear black or gray leather gloves with all outergarments or with the service dress uniform.

**Light Blue Long-Sleeved Shirt.** Women may wear the light blue long-sleeved shirt (must be tucked in) as follows: with skirt with waistband and blazer jacket combination only; with skirt with waistband only; without restrictions with the other uniform combinations.

**Religious Headgear.** You may wear yarmulkes or Sikh turbans.

MEN'S AND WOMEN'S ALL-WEATHER COAT.

## OTHER UNIFORM REGULATIONS

**Reserve Officers.** Except as otherwise prescribed, a reserve officer on active duty will wear the uniform, including insignia, prescribed for officers of the Regular Air Force.

Reserve officers not on active duty, when within the limits of the United States or its possessions, may wear the uniform when participating in inactive duty training, on occasions of military ceremony, at social functions and informal gatherings of a military character, when engaged in military instruction, or when responsible for the military discipline at an educational institution.

Reserve officers will wear the uniform when participating in an inactive duty training period, when performing equivalent or appropriate duties, or when engaged in equivalent training or instruction, when such duty, training, or instruction is within the confines of a military installation.

Reserve officers will wear the appropriate uniform when engaged in military flying activities.

Reserve officers not on active duty and outside the United States or its possessions, except when granted authority by the Secretary of the Air Force, will *not* wear the uniform. These officers on occasions of military ceremony or other military functions, upon reporting to the nearest military attaché and having their status accredited, may receive authority to appear in uniform. In a country without a military attaché, these officers should obtain authority to wear the uniform for a specific occasion from the proper civil or military authorities of the country concerned.

**Retired Officers.** Retired officers on active duty wear the uniform prescribed for officers on the active list.

The uniform of retired officers not on active duty will be, at their option, either that for officers of corresponding grade at date of retirement or that for officers on the active list, but not a mixture of the two uniforms.

Retired officers not on active-duty status when attending ceremonies and social functions of an official character or when calling at or visiting the White House may wear the appropriate civilian dress for the occasion, except that, when attending New Year's Day receptions in formation with officers on the active list, they will wear the uniform.

Retired officers not on active duty are prohibited from wearing the uniform in connection with nonmilitary, civilian, or personal enterprises or business activities.

Medal of Honor winners may wear the uniform any time AFR 35-10 does not prohibit its wear.

Retirees and honorably discharged veterans may on ceremonious occasions wear either full-size or miniature decorations and service medals on appropriate civilian clothing, such as "black tie" or "white tie" evening wear or equivalents.

**Responsibilities.** Individuals are responsible for ensuring that their uniforms are neat, correct, and in good condition and that their appearance reflects credit upon themselves and the Air Force.

Commanders are responsible for ensuring that their people both singly and collectively present an excellent appearance, reflecting credit on the Air Force. This responsibility does not, however, permit commanders to prescribe the purchase of optional items.

**Special Occasions.** The proper uniform for special occasions, such as ceremonies, weddings, funerals, and White House social functions and similar duties, depends on the circumstances in each case. Such occasions may also require white silk, cotton, or nylon gloves or gray suede or double-weave cotton gloves.

**In Foreign Countries.** Air Force personnel departing for foreign countries in an official capacity will be responsible for getting proper information regarding uniform matters before they leave the United States. The U.S. Air Attaché or the Defense Attaché can answer questions regarding uniforms that arise in a foreign country.

Members of the Air Force, active or retired, visiting or residing in a foreign country in an unofficial capacity will *not* wear the uniform except when attending, by formal invitation, ceremonies or social functions that, by the terms of the invitation or by the regulation or customs of the service, require wearing the uniform.

AFR 35-10 prescribes wearing civilian clothes when you travel through foreign countries.

**Uniforms for Civilians.** The Secretary of the Air Force may authorize civilians to wear uniforms when their duties require identification of this type.

**Former Members of the Armed Forces.** All persons honorably separated from the armed services of the United States may wear on ceremonious occasions the uniform of the highest grade held during that service (Sec. 125 of the National Defense Act, as amended). The uniform may be either that authorized at time of separation or that authorized by current regulations. Ceremonious occasions means those with military significance. Persons honorably discharged from the service may wear their uniform from the place of discharge to their homes, provided such wear is within three months of the date of discharge.

**Illegal Wearing.** Any person within the jurisdiction of the United States who wears a uniform or a distinctive part of a uniform of the armed services without authority is subject to the penalties prescribed by the U.S. Code, Crimes and Criminal Procedure, as amended (AFR 35-10 and AFR 900-48).

**Illegal Manufacture, Sale, and Possession.** The protection of law extends to wearing, manufacture, sale, possession, and reproduction in regular size of any U.S. decoration, medal, badge, and insignia that require the approval of the Secretary of the Air Force (AFR 35-10 and AFR 900-48).

## CARE AND PRESERVATION OF UNIFORMS

Good uniforms and the accessories worn with them deserve the treatment that will assure maximum durability and appearance to the owner. Rumpled and soiled uniforms and frayed service ribbons present an unsightly appearance, regardless of the quality of the articles.

The care you should give to uniforms and equipment is considerable but need not be burdensome. Regulations require the uniform to be neat, clean, and well pressed. Obviously, an old uniform of good quality that fits well and is clean, neat, and unfaded will look far better than a new and costly one that is slightly soiled or out of press.

So, to save money and to look good, take care of your uniform. Put your coat on a good hanger whenever you remove it. If any moisture is in the garment, hang it where it can dry. The hanger should be wide enough at the shoulders to hold the garment in shape; wire hangers won't do. Put trousers on hangers so that they may hang full length. Because dust harms clothing, put uniforms worn infrequently in containers that provide protection, that close tightly to exclude dust, and that contain moth balls. Use a clothing brush with stiff bristles each time you wear a garment to remove loose dust and freshen the nap.

**Dry Cleaning Precautions.** Trust only a competent cleaner with removal of spots or stains, especially those from unusual causes. Report the nature of unusual stains to the cleaner so that he may select the correct solvent without experimentation. Underarm sweating is especially injurious to the color and wearing qualities of fabrics, so consider attaching an impervious lining at the armpit.

## ITEMS OF INSIGNIA

Air Force insignia identifies the wearer as a member of the U.S. Air Force. Air Force uniforms have five different types of insignia: lapel insignia, grade insignia, cap and hat insignia, specialty insignia, and aides' insignia.

**Lapel Insignia.** Lapel insignia is different for officers and enlisted personnel, but both identify the wearer as a member of the U.S. Air Force. Officers wear the letters

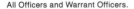

All Officers and Warrant Officers.

All Enlisted Personnel.

LAPEL INSIGNIA.

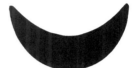

General Officers.

Colonel and
Lieutenant Colonel.

Other Officers and
Airmen.

SERVICE CAP VISORS.

Service Cap (Colonel and Lieutenant Colonel).

CAP INSIGNIA (women).
Large U.S. Coat of Arms is on all service hats except women's beret.

"U.S." in oxidized silver-color or shiny chrome metal, 7/16″ high. Enlisted personnel wear the same "U.S." letters, but they are within a 1″ circle.

**Grade Insignia.** Officer grade insignia is available in two different styles. Use metal grade insignia on all outergarments, on some service uniforms, and on the maternity uniform. Use embroidered epaulets on all other uniform combinations.

**Cap and Beret Insignia.** The insignia on the men's service cap, the women's service cap, and the women's beret is the U.S. coat of arms. The women's beret has the miniature coat of arms, and the service cap has the full-size device. The flight cap has metal grade insignia in either regular or miniature size, except that general officers' caps have a 5/8″ star or connecting bar. The utility cap has subdued cloth grade insignia sewn onto the front of the cap. Service caps for lieutenant colonels and above have a design of lightning, clouds, and darts on the visor.

ENLISTED
ARMY
MARINES
NAVY
AIR FORCE
COAST GUARD
Sergeant Major of the Army (SMA)
Sergeant Major of the Marine Corps (SgtMajMC)
Master Chief Petty Officer of the Navy (MCPON)
Chief Master Sergeant of the Air Force (CMSAF)
Master Chief Petty Officer of the Coast Guard (MCPOCG)
Command Sergeant Major (CSM)
Sergeant Major (SGM)
Sergeant Major (SgtMaj)
Master Gunnery Sergeant (MGySgt)
Fleet/Command Master Chief Petty Officer
Master Chief Petty Officer (MCPO)
Chief Master Sergeant, E-9 (CMSgt)
First Sergeant (E-9)
Master Chief Petty Officer (MCPO)
First Sergeant (1SG)
Master Sergeant (MSG)
First Sergeant (1stSgt)
Master Sergeant (MSgt)
Senior Chief Petty Officer (SCPO)
Senior Master Sergeant, E-8 (SMSgt)
First Sergeant (E-8)
Senior Chief Petty Officer (SCPO)
Platoon Sergeant (PSG) or Sergeant First Class (SFC)
Gunnery Sergeant (GySgt)
Chief Petty Officer (CPO)
Master Sergeant, E-7 (MSgt)
First Sergeant (E-7)
Chief Petty Officer (CPO)
Staff Sergeant (SSG)
Staff Sergeant (SSgt)
Petty Officer First Class (PO1)
Technical Sergeant, E-6 (TSgt)
Petty Officer First Class (PO1)
Sergeant (SGT)
Sergeant (Sgt)
Petty Officer Second Class (PO2)
Staff Sergeant, E-5 (SSgt)
Petty Officer Second Class (PO2)
Corporal (CPL)
Specialist 4 (SP4)
Corporal (Cpl)
Petty Officer Third Class (PO3)
Petty Officer Third Class (PO3)
Private First Class (PFC)
Lance Corporal (LCpl)
Seaman (Seaman)
Airman First Class, E-3 (AIC)
Seaman (Seaman)
Private E-2 (PV2)
Private First Class (PFC)
Seaman Apprentice (SA)
Airman, E-2 (Amn)
Seaman Apprentice (SA)
Private E-1 (PV1) (no insignia)
Private (Pvt) (no insignia)
Seaman Recruit (SR)
Airman Basic, E-1 (AB) (no insignia)
Seaman Recruit (SR)

ENLISTED INSIGNIA OF GRADE.

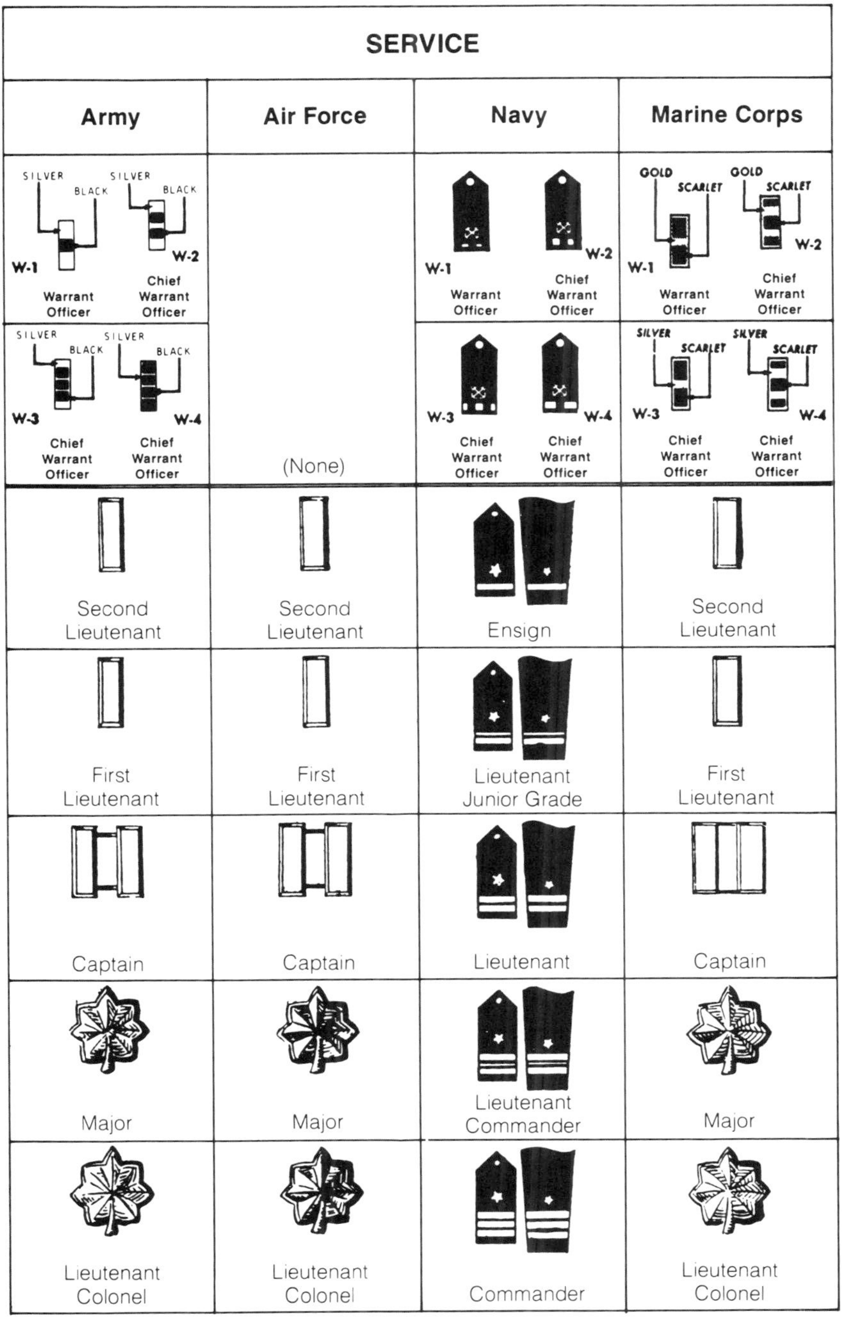

| SERVICE | | | |
|---|---|---|---|
| **Army** | **Air Force** | **Navy** | **Marine Corps** |
| SILVER, BLACK — W-1 Warrant Officer; SILVER, BLACK — W-2 Chief Warrant Officer | | W-1 Warrant Officer; W-2 Chief Warrant Officer | GOLD, SCARLET — W-1 Warrant Officer; GOLD, SCARLET — W-2 Chief Warrant Officer |
| SILVER, BLACK — W-3 Chief Warrant Officer; SILVER, BLACK — W-4 Chief Warrant Officer | (None) | W-3 Chief Warrant Officer; W-4 Chief Warrant Officer | SILVER, SCARLET — W-3 Chief Warrant Officer; SILVER, SCARLET — W-4 Chief Warrant Officer |
| Second Lieutenant | Second Lieutenant | Ensign | Second Lieutenant |
| First Lieutenant | First Lieutenant | Lieutenant Junior Grade | First Lieutenant |
| Captain | Captain | Lieutenant | Captain |
| Major | Major | Lieutenant Commander | Major |
| Lieutenant Colonel | Lieutenant Colonel | Commander | Lieutenant Colonel |

OFFICERS' INSIGNIA OF GRADE.

Note: Grade insignia of 2d Lieutenant and Major are gold; of other officer grades in Army, Air Force, and Marine Corps, silver. Naval insignia are gold color. The Navy pin-on (collar) insignia are the same as for the other services except that the devices are smaller, and the enamel bands on the warrant officers' bars are Navy blue.

| SERVICE | | | |
|---|---|---|---|
| **Army** | **Air Force** | **Navy** | **Marine Corps** |
|  Colonel |  Colonel |  Captain |  Colonel |
|  Brigadier General |  Brigadier General |  Rear Admiral (Lower Half) |  Brigadier General |
|  Major General |  Major General |  Rear Admiral (Upper Half) |  Major General |
|  Lieutenant General |  Lieutenant General |  Vice Admiral |  Lieutenant General |
|  General |  General |  Admiral |  General |
|  General of the Army |  General of the Air Force |  Fleet Admiral | (None) |

OFFICERS' INSIGNIA OF GRADE *(continued)*.

Note: All insignia above are silver color except Navy, which is gold.

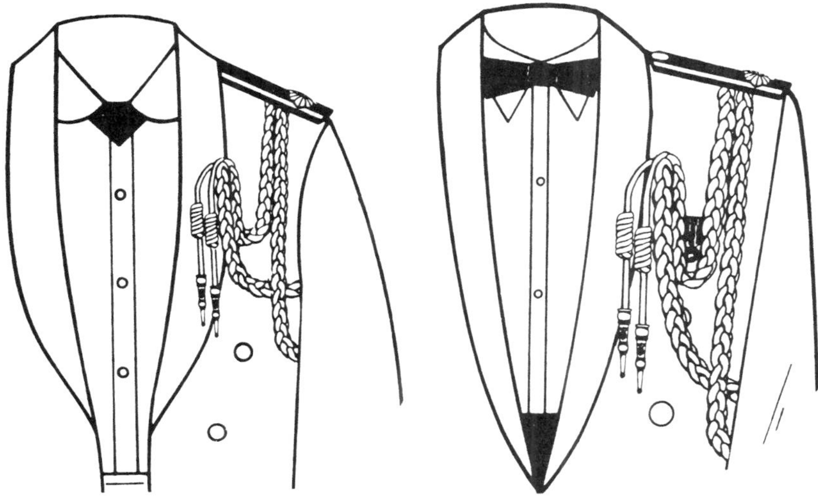

DRESS AIGUILLETTES.

Loop-type ends should go over the shoulder board strap approximately midway. The button on the lapel should be sewn to the body of the jacket under the lapel. Although the button is hidden, it should be the same color as the jacket, and of the smallest size that will adequately accommodate the loop on the aiguillette. Women may shorten aiguillettes. Description: Silver color rayon or metallic cord.

Note: Aides to the president, White House social aides, and aides to foreign heads of state will wear aiguillettes on the right side.

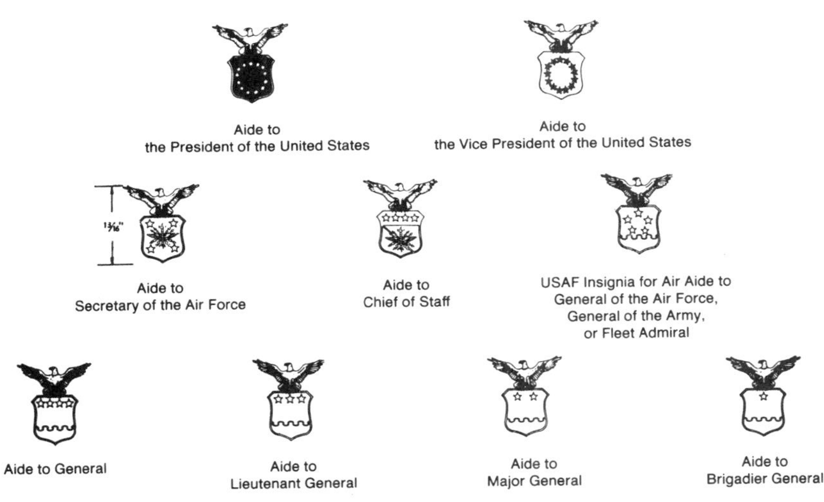


AIDES' INSIGNIA.

**Specialty Insignia.** Chaplains and medical personnel have distinctive specialty insignia worn on all uniform combinations.

**Aides' Insignia.** Aides and attachés are distinguished by aiguillettes of silver-color rayon or metallic cord worn with the service and dress uniforms. Presidential aides wear their aiguillettes on the right shoulder, while all others use the left. Aides are distinguished by metal insignia designating the office or the commander to which they are assigned.

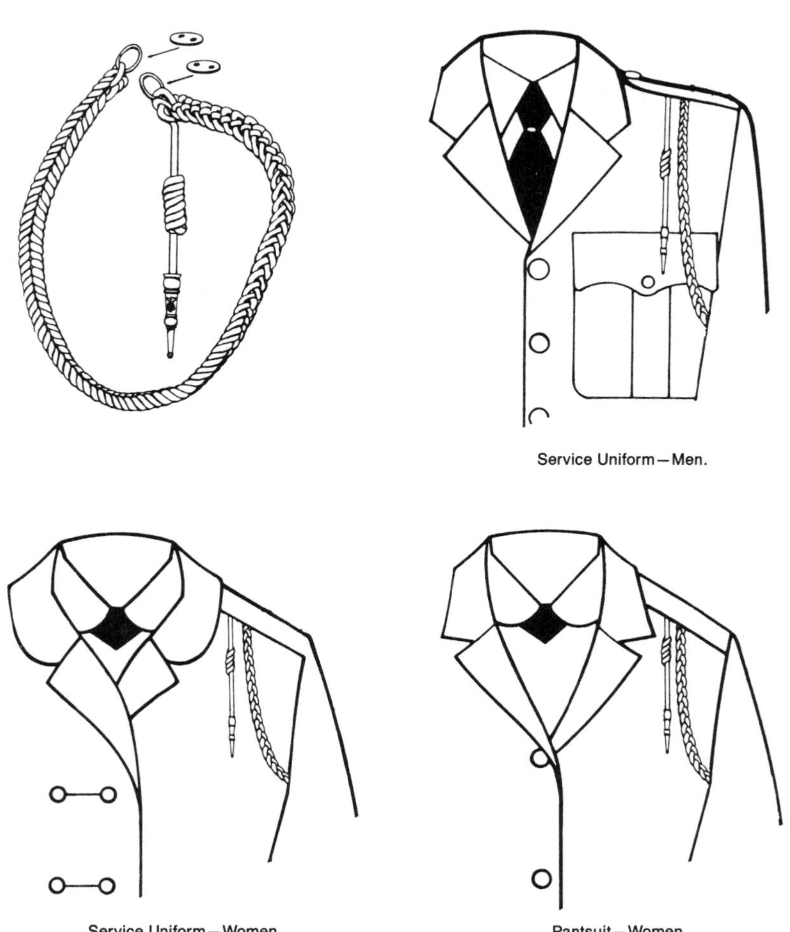

Service Uniform—Men.

Service Uniform—Women.

Pantsuit—Women.

SERVICE AIGUILLETTES (Men and Women).

Secure loop-type ends by sewing button or hook fastener to the underside of the epaulet about midway between the epaulet button and the shoulder seam to avoid interfering with the clutch fasteners on the officer grade insignia.

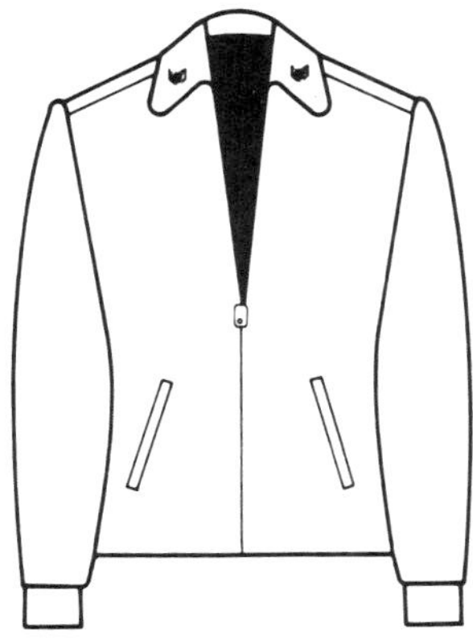

LIGHTWEIGHT BLUE JACKET
(Cotton/Polyester Poplin)

LIGHTWEIGHT BLUE JACKET
(Polyester/Wool Gabardine)

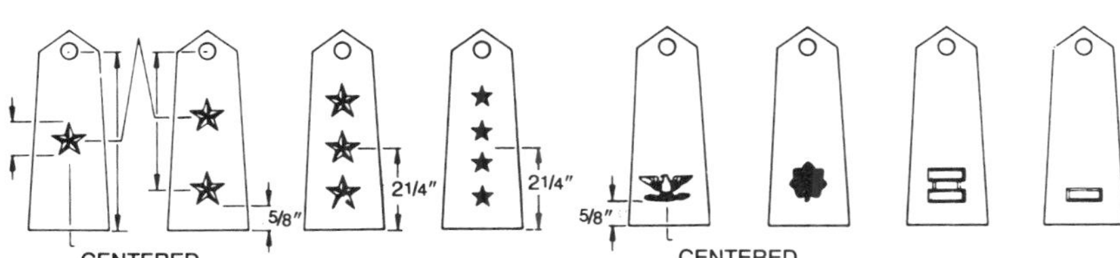


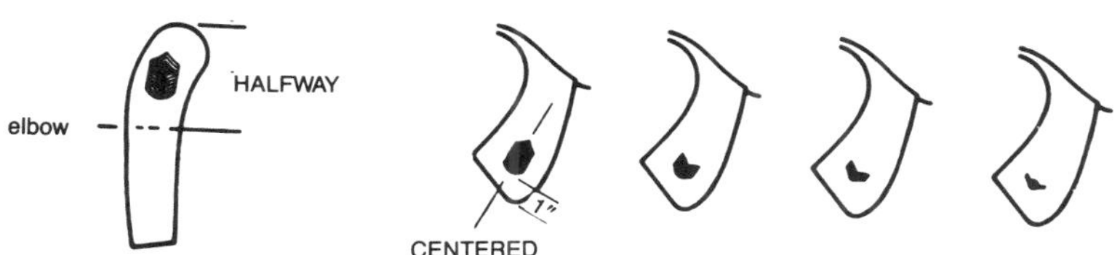


MEN'S LIGHTWEIGHT BLUE JACKETS.

Notes:

1. Officers wear regular size metal grade insignia on epaulets. Enlisted personnel wear standard 4″ sleeve chevrons on sleeve or metal collar insignia. Examples show proper placement of each type grade insignia authorized.

2. Generals wear ¾″ or ⅝″ stars. Lieutenant, major, and brigadier generals wear 1″ stars.

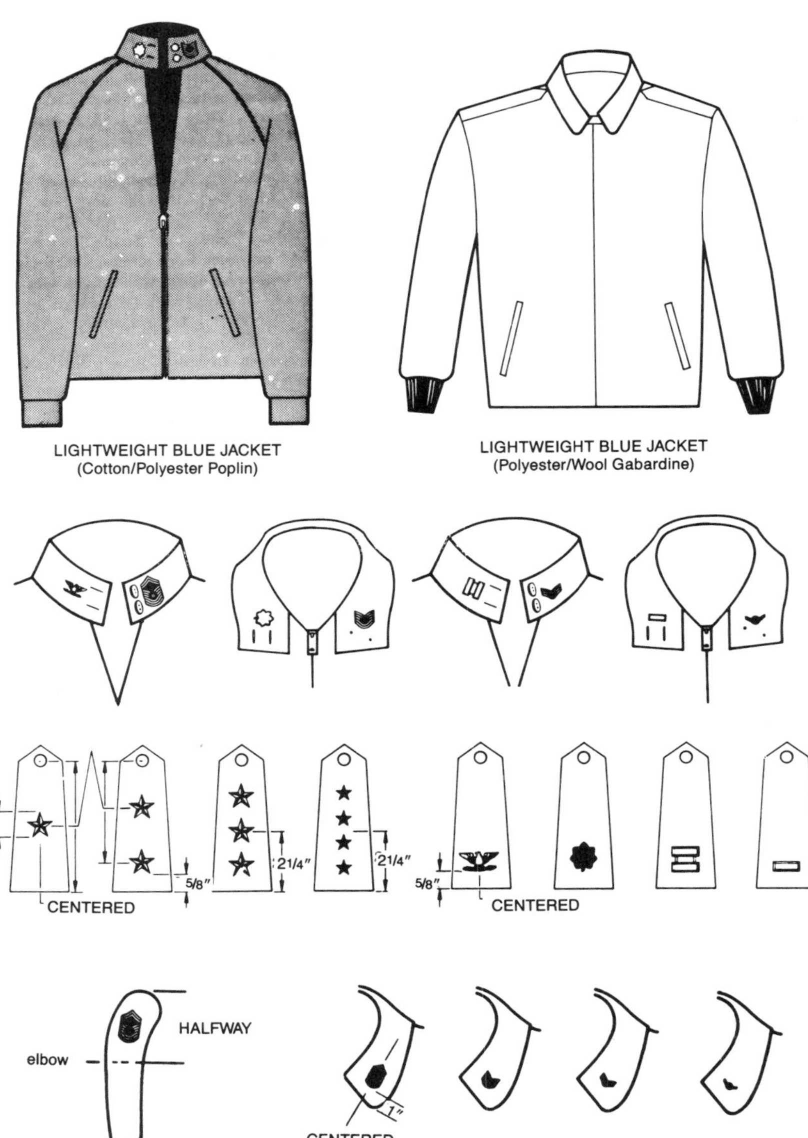


WOMEN'S LIGHTWEIGHT BLUE JACKETS.

Note: Officers wear miniature metal grade insignia on epaulets. Enlisted personnel wear standard 3″ sleeve chevrons on sleeve or metal collar insignia. Examples show proper placement of each type grade insignia authorized.

**Buttons.** U.S. Air Force buttons are oxidized silver-color metal of suitable composition and weight, circular and slightly convex with raised rim, with the Great Seal of the Department of the Air Force in clear relief against a horizontally lined background.

**Brassards.** Armbands may be of blue, shade 1083, felt background and gray, shade 1155, letters, except for noncombatant personnel who come under the provisions of the Geneva Convention of 12 August 1949, who may wear white brassards with a red cross superimposed thereon.

## WEARING OF INSIGNIA, DEVICES, BADGES, AND DECORATIONS

**Appurtenances.** Appurtenances identify and distinguish grades, services, and specialties of people wearing the uniform.

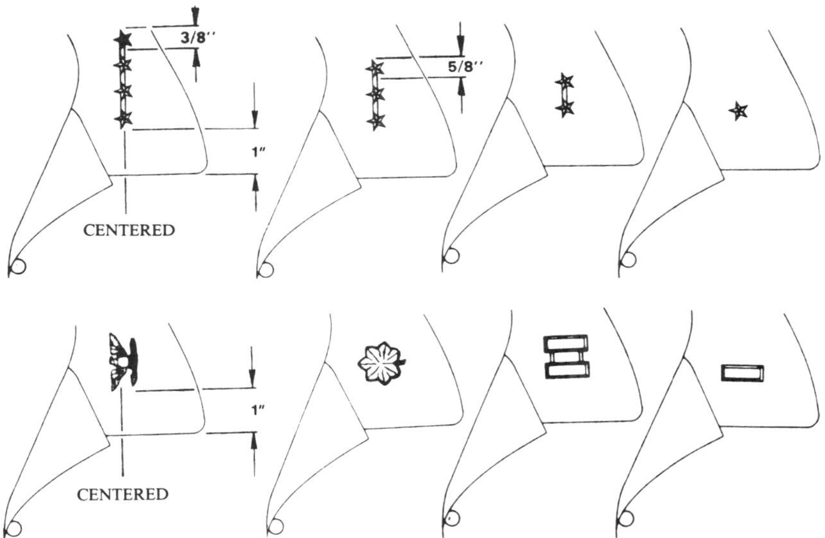


WEAR OF MINIATURE GRADE INSIGNIA ON COLLAR OF MEN'S LIGHT BLUE SHORT-SLEEVED SHIRT.

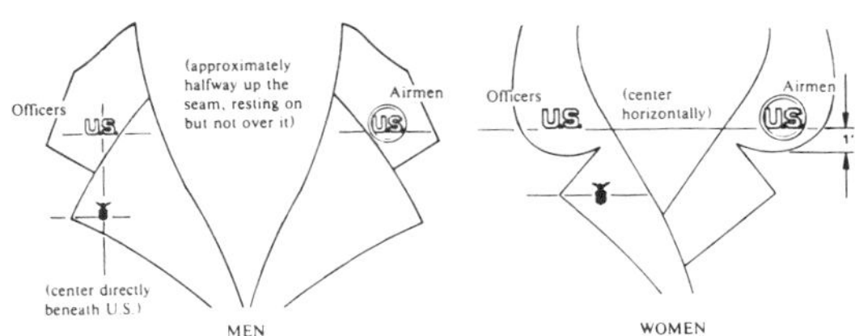


WEAR OF U.S. AND AIDE INSIGNIA ON SERVICE UNIFORMS.

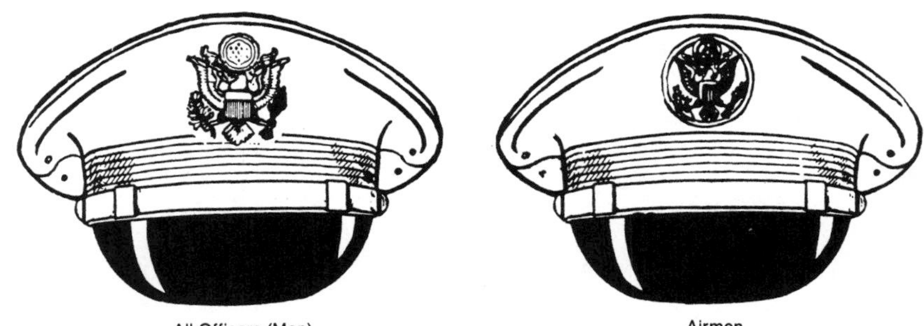

SERVICE CAP INSIGNIA (Men).

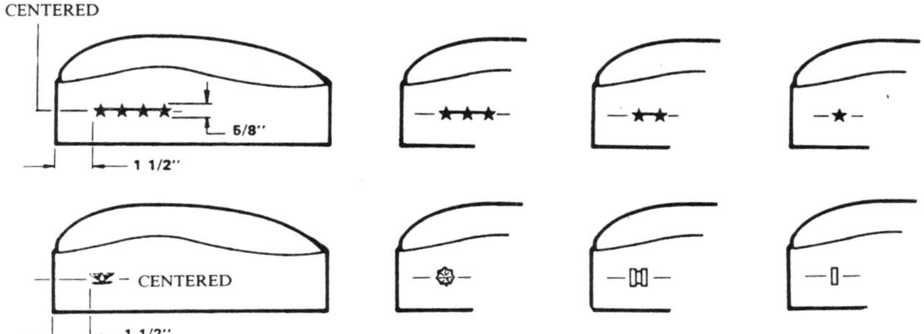

WEAR OF METAL GRADE INSIGNIA ON THE FLIGHT CAP, EITHER REGULAR OR MINIATURE.

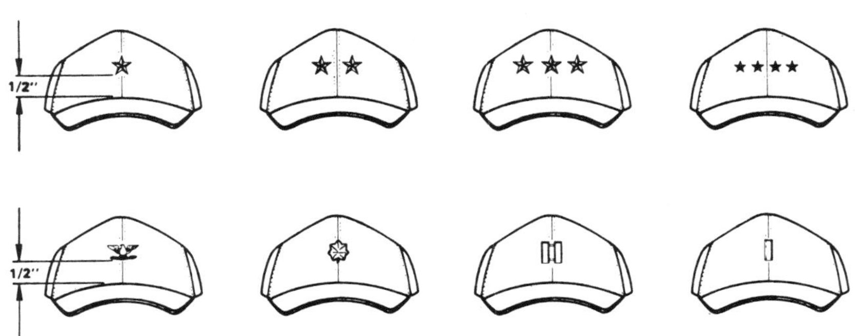

ON THE FATIGUE CAP, SUBDUED CLOTH GRADE INSIGNIA IS SEWN ONTO THE CENTER FRONT OF THE CAP.

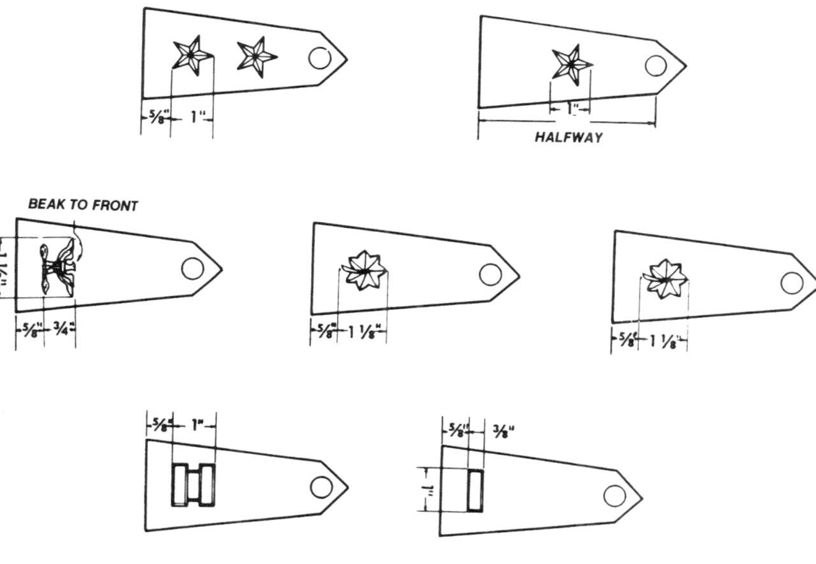


WEARING SHOULDER LOOP INSIGNIA.

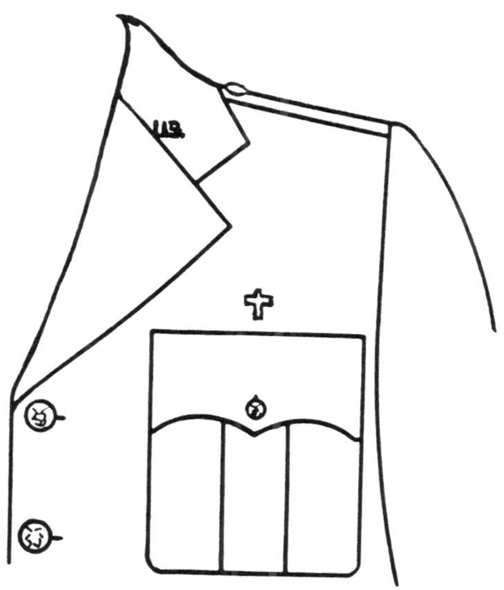


CHAPLAIN'S INSIGNIA.

**Collar Insignia.** Wear insignia on the collar when you wear the shirt as an outergarment. Officers wear grade insignia, and airmen wear the regular-size "U.S." insignia. Miniature-size grade insignia is optional. Nurses and women medical specialists wear miniature grade insignia on both sides of the collar of the hospital-duty uniform.

**Lapel Insignia (All Personnel).** The lower edges of "U.S." insignia are centered on each upper part of lapel (collar) measured on a horizontal line from upper lapel peak. Aides' insignia are centered on each lower part of lapel on a horizontal line from lower lapel peak.

**Cap Insignia.** *Service Cap and Sun Helmet.* Insignia for the service cap is centered on the front rise of the cap, and insignia for the sun helmet is worn in the guide hole.

*Flight Cap.* Insignia of grade (officers only) is worn on the curtain as illustrated.

**Shoulder Loop Insignia.** All officers and warrant officers wear insignia of grade on the shoulder loops of overcoat, topcoat, and coat.

**Identification Tags.** All military personnel of the Air Force will wear identification tags (dog tags) when engaged in field training or when outside the continental limits of the United States.

**Name Plates.** You must wear a name plate just above the right pocket of your coat or your shirt. The plate is blue plastic, 3³⁄₁₆″ long by ⅝″ wide, and your last name only appears in block white letters.

**Distinctive Badges and Specialty Insignia.** See chapters 8 and 9, AFR 35-10, for a list of distinctive badges and specialty insignia authorized for wear on the uniform, such as chaplain and medical insignia, and see table 8-1, AFR 35-10, for their correct placement.

# 6

# Decorations, Achievement Awards, Service Medals, and Badges

*Let him who has won the palm bear it (Palmam qui meruit ferat).*

—Latin proverb

Decorations awarded to members of the armed services are a symbol of acknowledgment by the government of our nation for a job well done. They consist of awards for heroism, the highest of which is the Medal of Honor, and awards for achievement and service, the highest of which is the Distinguished Service Medal. Just as the degree of heroism or achievement above and beyond the call of duty varies, so too does the importance or rank of the several awards given for these two purposes.

## HISTORY

The granting of awards by governments stems at least as far back in history as the Roman era. During that period, Roman rulers took the laurel wreath unto themselves. The Greeks crowned citizens who were outstanding in war, athletics, literature, and oratory with the laurel wreath, so naturally, it forms a part of our nation's highest award for valor. During the age of feudalism, a system of rewards in the form of titles and prerogatives developed. Monarchs would honor barons and knights who performed valiant feats of arms, not only by giving them titles, lands, and pensions, but also by encouraging them in the growing habit of decorating their shields and other armor with insignia that were, in effect, a pictorial history of their deeds. As additional deeds increased the number and complexity of insignia, the whole field of heraldry and heraldic art developed, along with the production of coats of arms for the families that were granted them.

Before the Napoleonic period, such rewards were for the aristocracy, for the few. The rewards given the drafted peasantry, the yeomen, and the lowly fighting men were infrequent indeed.

Napoleon started the modern concept. He originated a decoration that could be worn by anyone, regardless of rank or social background: the *Légion d'Honneur* (Legion of Honor). It was the spearhead of the system he so shrewdly used to instill loyalty in the nation he led—because anybody could win it. Thereafter arose the Russian Order of Saint George, the German Iron Cross, and the British Victoria Cross. They were products of the era of nationalism, created to reward citizens for their loyalty to their state and their courage.

The Purple Heart was the first military decoration established in the United States. It was authorized by General George Washington in 1782 as a decoration for "singularly meritorious action." Three men received it in 1783, but the records show no others. In the early years, the republic awarded six other medals. A resolution of the Continental Congress approved on 25 March 1776 gave the first to General Washington. General Horatio Gates received the second on 25 November 1777 for the defeat of the British at Saratoga. The third went to Henry Lee, father of Robert E. Lee, who won the nickname "Light Horse Harry," on 24 September 1779 in recognition of his successful attack on the British at Paulus Hook, New Jersey, in July of that year, during which he captured 160 of the enemy without loss to his own forces. Enlisted men received the fourth, fifth, and sixth, known as the "André" medals. These were given to the three American militiamen who captured the British intelligence major John André while he was en route to New York from West Point, wearing civilian clothes, after having plotted with Benedict Arnold for the betrayal of the American cause. In 1932, the United States reestablished the Purple Heart.

In the first winter of the Civil War, a feeling developed that a way must be found to recognize and honor the heroism and gallantry of American soldiers who had distinguished themselves in the fighting. There was great argument and discussion at the time that the awarding of decorations was unbecoming a republic. However, the award of a naval medal was approved by Mr. Lincoln on 21 December 1861, and on 12 July 1862 a Medal of Honor was provided for award to enlisted men of the Army "who shall most distinguish themselves by their gallantry in action, and other soldierlike qualities." It was amended by an act approved 3 March 1863, which extended its provisions to include officers as well as enlisted men. This legislation stood as the basis upon which the Army Medal of Honor could be awarded until 9 July 1918 when it was superseded by a completely revised statute.

All other present decorations have been authorized in 1918 or later years.

## PRINCIPLES GOVERNING THE AWARD OF DECORATIONS

The award of decorations is a powerful stimulus to pride of service and to the encouragement of heroism or achievement. But if the greatest benefit is to be obtained, the process of making awards must be most carefully administered.

Awards must be made only to those who have truly earned them. The making of unmerited awards is cheapening and destructive of the purpose for which authorized. But to fail to recognize true valor or merit promptly and make the awards also defeats the purpose. Both a proper evaluation of facts plus promptness in making awards are required.

This requirement presents a serious problem of decision to all commanders of combat organizations. Evidence is often sketchy. The witnesses may be dead as a consequence of combat. The weighing of facts as to which of the several awards is most appropriate is also a delicate choice. To justify any award, the act must be above and beyond the call of duty. Final consideration of the facts before decision by a senior commander will rest with a board of officers who can establish a reasonable yardstick against which to measure and compare these events. Individual commanders, especially junior commanders, must recognize or identify those acts that are truly above and beyond the call of duty, they must make prompt recommendation for the awards they consider most appropriate, and they must document those awards with the statements of witnesses, all to the end that the reviewers may arrive at an independent and accurate decision. Unless a careful process is followed by all, there will be many serious errors, anomalies, and variations among organizations, the sum of which may be to reduce greatly or even to nullify the powerful stimulus to pride of individual service that may be attained through awards.

AFR 900-48 describes the policy on award of decorations.

**Decorations, Service Medals, and Achievement Awards.** *Decorations* are awarded in recognition of and as a reward for extraordinary, unusual, or outstanding acts or services. They are the visible evidence of such acts or services. Properly used, they are potent incentives to greater effort and instrumental in building and maintaining morale. Decorations are of two categories: those awarded for heroism and those awarded for achievement. While most decorations are awarded for one or the other distinct purpose, the Distinguished Flying Cross and the Bronze Star Medal may be awarded for either reason.

*Service medals* are awarded to members of the active military service of the United States for performance of specified duty, usually during periods of war or national emergency.

*Achievement Awards* are presented to recognize specific types of achievements for individuals serving on active duty in the Air Force or as members of the Air Reserve Forces.

**Oak Leaf Clusters.** The oak leaf cluster is awarded in lieu of a second award of the same decoration. It consists of a bronze twig of four oak leaves with three acorns on the stem. It is 13/32″ long and is affixed to the ribbon. One silver oak leaf cluster is worn in lieu of five bronze ones.

**Award by Foreign Governments.** No person holding any office of profit or trust under the United States shall, without the consent of Congress, accept any present, emolument, office, or title, of any kind whatever, from any king, prince, or foreign state.

In this connection special authority was granted by the Congress with respect to foreign decorations awarded during World War II, the Berlin Airlift, the Korean War, the Vietnam War, and the Gulf War. Officers to whom such awards may be tendered are advised to obtain the advice of their headquarters personnel division or judge advocate.

**Penalty for Unauthorized Wearing of Decorations, Service Medals, or Badges.** A federal statute provides for a fine of not more than $250 or imprisonment for not more than six months for individuals convicted of unauthorized wearing of any decoration, service medal, ribbon or rosette, or badge.

The same penalty applies to any person who wears the uniform or decorations of a foreign nation for the purpose of deception.

## USAF DECORATIONS FOR HEROISM

The accompanying chart lists decorations for heroism in their order of precedence.

SUMMARY OF UNITED STATES AIR FORCE DECORATIONS

| Decoration | Awarded for | Rank of awards for valor | Rank of awards for achievement | May be awarded to civilians | May be awarded in peacetime |
|---|---|---|---|---|---|
| Medal of Honor | Gallantry and intrepidity at the risk of life above and beyond the call of duty. | 1 | — | No | No |
| Air Force Cross | Extraordinary heroism in military operations against an armed enemy. | 2 | — | Yes | No |
| Distinguished Service Medal | Exceptionally meritorious service in a duty of great responsibility. | — | 1 | Yes | Yes |
| Silver Star | Gallantry in action. | 3 | — | Yes | No |
| Legion of Merit | Exceptionally meritorious conduct in the performance of outstanding services. | — | 2 | No | Yes |
| Distinguished Flying Cross | Heroism, extraordinary achievement while participating in aerial flight. | 4 | 3 | No | Yes |
| Airman's Medal | Heroism not involving actual conflict with an enemy. | 5 | — | No | Yes |
| Bronze Star Medal | Heroic or meritorious achievement or service against an enemy not involving aerial flight. | 6 | 4 | Yes | No |
| Purple Heart | Wounds received in action against an enemy of the United States. | 7 | — | Yes | No |
| Meritorious Service Medal | Outstanding noncombat meritorious achievement or service. | — | 5 | No | Yes |
| Air Medal | Meritorious achievement while participating in aerial flight. | — | 6 | Yes | Yes |
| Aerial Achievement Medal | Meritorious achievement while participating in aerial flight. | — | 7 | Yes | Yes |
| Air Force Commendation Medal | Meritorious achievement not in operations against enemy. | — | 8 | No | Yes |
| Air Force Achievement Medal | Awarded for meritorious achievement. | — | 9 | No | Yes |

**Medal of Honor (MH).** The Medal of Honor is awarded for conspicuous gallantry and intrepidity at the risk of life above and beyond the call of duty while a member of the Air Force was engaged in armed conflict against an enemy of the United States. Each recommendation for the Medal of Honor must incontestably prove that the self-sacrifice or personal bravery involved conspicuous risk of life, the omission of which could not justly cause censure.

The Medal of Honor is a gold star with the head of the Statue of Liberty centered upon it and surrounded with green enamel laurel leaves suspended by rings from a trophy consisting of a bar inscribed with the word VALOR above an adaptation of the thunderbolt from the U.S. Air Force Coat of Arms. The bar is suspended from a light blue moire silk neckband behind a square pad in the center with corners turned in and charged with 13 white stars in the form of a triple chevron.

**Air Force Cross (AFC).** On 6 July 1960, Congress established the Air Force Cross to parallel the U.S. Army Distinguished Service Cross and the U.S. Navy Cross. Earlier, the Air Force had awarded the Distinguished Service Cross.

The Air Force Cross is our nation's second highest military decoration and is awarded to U.S. Air Force airmen for extraordinary heroism in military operations against an enemy of the United States. The Air Force Cross may be awarded to members of foreign military forces and to American and foreign civilians serving with the armed forces of the United States.

The Air Force Cross is a bronze cross with an oxidized satin finish. Centered on the cross is a gold-plated American bald eagle with wings spread against a cloud formation. The eagle is encircled by a laurel wreath finished in green enamel. The cross is suspended from a ribbon of brittany blue, edged with Old Glory red, and bears a narrow white vertical stripe inside the red edges.

**Silver Star (SS).** The Silver Star was instituted by Congress in 1918. It is granted to persons serving in any capacity with the Air Force cited for gallantry in action that does not warrant the award of a Medal of Honor or the Air Force Cross.

It is a small silver star within a wreath centered on a larger star of gold-colored metal. The ribbon has a center band of red, flanked by equal bands of white; the white bands are flanked by equal blue bands having borders of white lines with blue edgings.

**Distinguished Flying Cross (DFC).** *As an Award for Heroism.* The Distinguished Flying Cross has been awarded to airmen since 1917 for heroism while participating in an aerial flight. The heroism must be evidenced by voluntary action in the face of great danger and beyond the line of duty.

The Distinguished Flying Cross is a bronze cross with rays on which is displayed a propeller. The ribbon is predominantly blue, with a narrow band of red bordered by white lines in the center. The edges of the ribbon are outlined with equal bands of white inside blue.

**Airman's Medal (AmnM).** The Airman's Medal is awarded for heroism involving voluntary risk of life under conditions other than conflict with an armed enemy of the United States.

The Airman's Medal is a bronze metal disk with an oxidized satin finish. The pendant bears a representation of Hermes, son of Zeus, releasing an American bald eagle. The ribbon is brittany blue displaying alternately in the center 13 vertical stripes of the Air Force colors, golden yellow and ultramarine blue.

**Bronze Star Medal (BSM).** *Awarded for Valor.* The Bronze Star Medal is awarded for heroism while engaged in military action against an enemy of the United States.

The medal consists of a bronze star bearing in the center a small star of the same color. The ribbon, on which there is a small bronze letter "V," is predominantly red with a white-edged narrow blue band in the center and white lines at each edge.

**Purple Heart (PH).** The Purple Heart is our nation's oldest medal. It was first established by General George Washington on 7 August 1782. The Purple Heart is awarded for wounds received or death after being wounded in action against an enemy of the United States or as a direct result of an act of such enemy.

The Purple Heart is a heart-shaped pendant of purple enamel bearing a gold replica of the head of General George Washington in relief and the Washington arms. The shield is in colors. The ribbon is dark purple with white edges.

## USAF DECORATIONS FOR ACHIEVEMENT

The accompanying chart also lists the decorations for achievement in their order of precedence.

**Distinguished Service Medal (DSM).** The Distinguished Service Medal is awarded to members of the armed forces who, while serving in any capacity with the Air Force, distinguish themselves by exceptionally meritorious service to the government in a duty of great responsibility. (It is awarded to a foreign national only rarely.)

The term "duty of great responsibility" means duty of such a character that exceptionally meritorious service therein has contributed in high degree to the success of a major command, installation, or project. The performance of the duty must be such as to merit recognition of the service as clearly exceptional. A superior performance of the normal duties of the position will not alone justify the award. The accomplishment of the duty for which the award is recommended should have been completed, or it should have progressed to an exceptional degree if the person rendering the service has been transferred to other duties before its full accomplishment.

The Air Force Distinguished Service Medal features a blue stone representing the firmament at the center of a sunburst of 13 gold rays separated by 13 white enamel stars. The center motif represents the vault of the heavens; the stars symbolize the 13 original colonies. The stylized wings on the ribbon bar are symbolic of the USAF.

**Legion of Merit (LM).** *As to United States Armed Forces.* The Legion of Merit, without reference to degree, is awarded to members of the armed forces of the United States who, while serving in any capacity, distinguish themselves by exceptionally meritorious conduct in the performance of outstanding services. In peacetime, awards by the Air Force are generally limited to recognizing services of marked national or international significance, services that aided the United States in furthering national policy or national security.

This decoration, like the Purple Heart, stems from the Badge for Military Merit, America's oldest decoration, established by George Washington in 1782. As was the case with the Badge for Military Merit, it will be awarded for "extraordinary fidelity and essential service." It will constitute a reward for service in a position of responsibility, honorably and well performed.

The design of the Legion of Merit has been developed from the Great Seal of the United States, also approved by Congress in 1782.

The obverse, or front, of the badge of the Legion of Merit is a five-pointed American star of heraldic form, bordered in purplish red enamel, centered with a constellation of the 13 original stars on a blue enameled field breaking through a circle of clouds. The star is backed by a laurel wreath, the symbolic award for achievement, which is interlaced with crossed war arrows in gold pointing outward, representing the protection afforded by the armed forces to the nation.

On the reverse are the words "United States of America" inscribed on a circling ribbon. In the center is space left for inscription of the name and grade of the individual to whom the award is made. Surrounding this is a band that carries the words (taken from the reverse of the Great Seal) "Annuit Coeptis" (He [God] has favored our undertakings), and the date MDCCLXXXII, the year of the founding of the decoration. The ribbon is a purple-red color edged with white.

*Legion of Merit to Armed Forces of Foreign Nations.* The Legion of Merit, in four degrees, is awarded to *personnel of the armed forces* of friendly foreign nations who distinguish themselves by exceptionally meritorious conduct in the performance of

# DECORATIONS, AWARDS, AND SERVICE MEDALS

## USAF AND DEPARTMENT OF DEFENSE MILITARY DECORATIONS

Medal of Honor (Air Force)

Air Force Cross

Defense Distinguished Service Medal

Distinguished Service Medal (Air Force)

Silver Star

Defense Superior Service Medal

Legion of Merit

Distinguished Flying Cross

Airman's Medal

Bronze Star Medal

Purple Heart

Defense Meritorious Service Medal

Meritorious Service Medal

Air Medal

Joint Service Commendation Medal

Air Force Commendation Medal

Joint Service Achievement Medal

Air Force Achievement Medal

## USAF AND DEPARTMENT OF DEFENSE UNIT AWARDS

Presidential Unit Citation (Air Force)

Joint Meritorious Unit Award

AF Outstanding Unit Award

AF Organizational Excellence Award

## USAF ACHIEVEMENT AWARDS

Prisoner of War Medal

Combat Readiness Medal

Good Conduct Medal (Air Force)

Good Conduct Medal (Army)

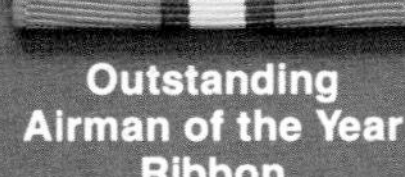
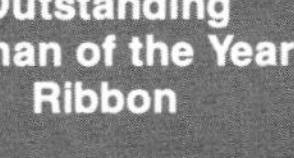

Outstanding Airman of the Year Ribbon

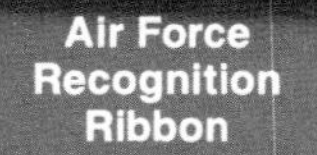

Air Force Recognition Ribbon

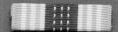

Air Force Overseas Ribbon (short tour)

Air Force Overseas Ribbon (long tour)

Air Force Longevity Service Award Ribbon

Air Reserve Forces Meritorious Service Medal

NCO Professional Military Education Graduate Ribbon

USAF Basic Military Training Honor Graduate Ribbon

Small Arms Expert Marksmanship Ribbon

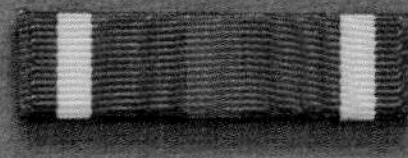

Air Force Training Ribbon

# U.S. MILITARY SERVICE MEDALS

**Army of Occupation Medal**

**Antarctica Service Medal**

**National Defense Service Medal**

**Armed Forces Expeditionary Medal**

**Vietnam Service Medal**

Humanitarian
Service Medal

Armed Forces
Reserve Medal

## NON-U.S. SERVICE MEDALS

United Nations
Medal

Republic of Vietnam
Campaign Medal

Multinational Force
and Observers Medal

outstanding service. The degrees are Chief Commander, Commander, Officer, and Legionnaire.

The criteria for award of the various degrees are these:

- Chief Commander: Chief of state or head of government.
- Commander: Equivalent of U.S. military chief of staff.
- Officer: Other general or flag rank, equivalent assignments, and foreign attachés.
- Legionnaire: All other eligibles.

**Distinguished Flying Cross (DFC).** *As an Award for Achievement.* The Distinguished Flying Cross is awarded to members of the armed forces who, while serving in any capacity with the Air Force, distinguish themselves by heroism or extraordinary achievement while participating in aerial flight.

To warrant an award of the Distinguished Flying Cross for extraordinary achievement while participating in aerial flight, the results accomplished must be so exceptional and outstanding as clearly to set the individual apart from comrades who have not been so recognized.

**Bronze Star Medal (BSM).** *For Achievement.* The Bronze Star Medal is awarded to members of the armed forces who, while serving in any capacity, distinguished themselves by meritorious achievement or meritorious service not involving participation in aerial flight in connection with military operations against an enemy of the United States.

The required meritorious achievement or meritorious service for award of the Bronze Star Medal is less than that required for award of the Legion of Merit, but must nevertheless be accomplished with distinction. The Bronze Star Medal may be awarded to recognize meritorious service or single acts of merit.

**Meritorious Service Medal (MSM).** The Meritorious Service Medal is awarded for outstanding noncombat meritorious achievement or service to the United States, although the required achievement or service is less than that required for the award of the Legion of Merit. It must, nevertheless, be accomplished with distinction and be above and beyond that for the award of the Air Force Commendation Medal. The Meritorious Service Medal ranks with, but after, the Bronze Star.

The Meritorious Service Medal is bronze, with six rays issuing from the upper three points of a five-pointed star, beveled edges, and two small stars defined by an incised outline. In front of the lower part of the star appears an eagle with wings upraised, standing upon two upward curving branches of laurel tied with a ribbon beneath the feet of the eagle. The ribbon is predominantly ruby with white vertical stripes and ruby lines at each edge.

**Air Medal (AM).** Authorized by executive order of the president in 1942, the Air Medal is awarded to people who, while serving in any capacity with the Army or Air Force of the United States subsequent to 8 September 1939, distinguish themselves by meritorious achievement while participating in an aerial flight. This decoration is awarded in those cases where the act of meritorious service does not warrant the award of the Distinguished Flying Cross.

The pendant from a ribbon striped with the Air Force colors of blue and gold is a fleur-de-lis that surmounts a compass rose. In relief on the rose is a swooping eagle with lightning bolts clutched in its talons.

**Aerial Achievement Medal (AAM).** The Aerial Achievement Medal may be awarded for sustained meritorious achievement while participating in aerial flight. The achievement must be accomplished with distinction above and beyond that normally expected of professional airmen.

**Air Force Commendation Medal (AFCM).** The Air Force Commendation Medal may be awarded for outstanding achievement or meritorious service rendered specifically on behalf of the Air Force, for acts of courage that do not meet the requirements for award of the Airman's Medal or the Bronze Star Medal, or for sustained meritorious performance by crew members. The medal is a bronze hexagon medallion bearing eagle, shield, and arrows from the Air Force seal, and the ribbon is predominantly yellow with blue edges and three bands of blue in the center.

**Air Force Achievement Medal (AFAM).** Awarded for outstanding achievement, meritorious service, or acts of courage not meriting award of the AFCM, this award is intended primarily for outstanding junior officers and airmen. The pendant is a silver-colored nebular disc bearing the winged thunderbolt from the USAF seal. The ribbon is predominantly silver-gray with 12 vertical ultramarine stripes.

## DOD DECORATIONS FOR ACHIEVEMENT

Besides the USAF decorations listed above, the Department of Defense awards five military decorations that take precedence with their service counterparts but are worn before them.

**Defense Distinguished Service Medal (DDSM).** Worn before the service DSM, this medal may be awarded to any U.S. armed forces officer assigned to a joint staff or other DOD joint activity for exceptionally meritorious service in a position of unique and great responsibility. The pendant is basically a blue enamel pentagon superimposed by a gold eagle bearing the U.S. Shield and grasping three crossed arrows. The ribbon has blue, yellow, and red stripes.

**Defense Superior Service Medal (DSSM).** Worn before the LM, this medal may be awarded to U.S. military personnel who display superior meritorious service in a position of significant responsibility on a joint staff or in a joint activity. The pendant design is that of the DDSM, except that the eagle and so on are in silver. The ribbon has yellow, blue, white, and red stripes.

**Defense Meritorious Service Medal (DMSM).** Worn before the MSM, this medal may be awarded to U.S. military personnel who give incontestably exceptional meritorious service on a joint staff or in a joint activity. The pendant consists of a bronze laurel wreath and overlapping pentagon surmounted by an eagle. The ribbon is light blue broken by a gold band that is broken by a smaller red band.

**Joint Service Commendation Medal (JSCM).** The Joint Service Commendation Medal is awarded to personnel on duty in the Office of the Secretary of Defense, the Joint Staff, the Defense Supply Agency, the National Security Agency, other joint agencies reporting to the Joint Chiefs of Staff, joint task forces, or NATO organizations. The award is for meritorious achievement. Its ribbon is blue, white, and green stripes. It takes precedence with the AFCM, but is worn before it. A bronze "V" is authorized for a combat award after 25 June 1963.

**Joint Service Achievement Medal (JSAM).** Worn before the AFAM, this medal may be awarded to any members of the U.S. armed forces below the rank of colonel who distinguish themselves by meritorious achievement or service while serving in specified joint activities after 3 August 1983.

## UNIT AWARDS

The following types of unit awards are authorized as recognition of certain types of service and as a means of promoting esprit de corps:

- Unit decorations.
- War service streamers.
- Campaign and expeditionary streamers.

**U.S. Unit Decorations.** The following U.S. unit decorations have been established to recognize outstanding heroism or exceptionally meritorious conduct in the performance of outstanding services:

- Presidential Unit Citation.
- Joint Meritorious Unit Award
- Air Force Outstanding Unit Award.
- Air Force Organizational Excellence Award.

*Presidential Unit Citation (PUC).* The Presidential Unit Citation (formerly Distinguished Unit Citation [DUC]) is awarded to units of the armed forces of the United States and co-belligerent nations for extraordinary heroism in action against the armed enemy. The unit must display such gallantry, determination, and esprit de corps in accomplishing its mission under extremely difficult and hazardous conditions as to set it apart and above other units participating in the same campaign. The degree of heroism required is the same as that which would warrant award of an Air Force Cross to an individual. Extended periods of combat duty or participation in a large number of operational missions, either ground or air, is not sufficient. Only on rare occasions will a unit larger than a battalion or air group qualify for award of this decoration. It is a blue ribbon set in a gold-colored metal frame of laurel leaves; it is worn above the pocket of the left breast, after decorations and preceding service ribbons.

*Joint Meritorious Unit Award (JMUA).* This ribbon is awarded in the name of the Secretary of Defense to Joint Activities of the Department of Defense for meritorious achievement or service, superior to that normally expected, during combat with an armed enemy of the United States, during a declared national emergency, or under extraordinary circumstances that involved the national interest.

*Air Force Outstanding Unit Award (AFOUA).* Established in 1954, this award consists of a predominantly blue streamer with a narrow red band center bordered by white lines and red bands. Theater or area of operations is embroidered in white on the streamer. The individual emblem is a ribbon of the streamer color. It is awarded to units not larger than a wing for meritorious achievement or service in support of military operations or of great significance in accomplishment not involving combat operations. The ribbon bar is worn on the left breast pocket.

*Air Force Organizational Excellence Award (AFOEA).* Established in August 1969, this ribbon is predominantly red with a narrow blue band center bordered by white lines and blue bands at each edge separated by white lines. It is awarded to Air Force internal organizations that are organizational entities within larger organizations. The organizations are unique, unnumbered organizations or activities that perform staff functions and functions normally performed by numbered wings, groups, squadrons, and so on. The ribbon is worn on the left breast pocket.

**War Service Streamers and Campaign and Expeditionary Streamers.** War service streamers are awarded to organizations for service in a theater or area of operations. They represent the unit's service in the same manner that service medals represent the individual's service in a theater or area of combat operations. Campaign and expeditionary streamers represent the unit's participation in a campaign in the same manner that battle stars and arrowheads on the service medal represent the individual's participation in a campaign or in an airborne landing or amphibious assault. The streamers are carried on the organizational flag or guidon on ceremonial occasions.

## ACHIEVEMENT AWARDS

Air Force achievement awards recognize specific types of achievement by members serving on active duty in the Air Force or in the Air Reserve Forces.

**Prisoner of War Medal (POWM).** This award is authorized for all U.S. military personnel who were taken prisoner of war after 6 April 1917 during an armed conflict and who served honorably during the period of captivity.

**Combat Readiness Medal (CRM).** The Combat Readiness Medal is authorized for members of combat crews of manned weapons delivery systems for sustained meritorious performance. The medal is a circle marked with arrowheads and the points of overlapping triangles to indicate the hours of round-the-clock duty and performance. The ribbon is predominantly Old Glory red and banded in blue with a narrow dark blue stripe separated by two wider stripes of light blue.

**Air Force Good Conduct Medal (AFGCM).** This medal is awarded only to enlisted persons in recognition of exemplary behavior, efficiency, and fidelity under prescribed conditions as to time and ratings. A distinctive clasp is awarded for each successive period of three years' service that meets the requirements. The ribbon is light blue with red, white, and blue vertical stripes to the right and the left of the center.

**Air Reserve Forces Meritorious Service Medal (ARFMSM).** This medal was approved in April 1964 to be effective 1 April 1965 as an award equivalent to the Air Force Good Conduct Medal for issuance to Air Reserve personnel who meet the following qualifications: exemplary behavior, efficiency, and fidelity for four continuous years; attendance at 90 percent of all scheduled training periods each of four continuous years; completion of active-duty requirements in the four-year period. The ribbon is predominantly light blue with white, ultramarine, and yellow stripes at the edges.

**Outstanding Airman of the Year Ribbon (OAYR).** This ribbon is awarded to airmen nominated by major air commands and separate operating agencies for competition in the 12 Outstanding Airmen of the Year Program sponsored by the Air Force Association. The ribbon is oriental blue with a white center bordered by equal strips of ultramarine blue and flaming red.

**Air Force Recognition Ribbon (AFRR).** This ribbon is awarded to named individual Air Force recipients of special trophies and awards listed in AFR 900-29, except 12 Outstanding Airmen of the Year nominees. The ribbon is predominantly turquoise blue centered with a wide red stripe and with red and white stripes at either end.

**Air Force Overseas Ribbon (AFOSR).** This ribbon is awarded for completion of an overseas tour of duty after 1 September 1980, provided the tour is not recognized by another service award. Ribbon is predominantly brittany blue with three vertical narrow white stripes on either side.

**Air Force Longevity Service Award (AFLSA).** All members of the Air Force on active duty and all reservists not on active duty are eligible for the Longevity Service

Award. Requirements for the basic award are four years of honorable active federal military service with any branch of the U.S. armed forces. A bronze oak leaf cluster is worn on the ribbon for each additional four years of service. A silver oak leaf cluster is worn in lieu of five bronze clusters.

The Air Force Longevity Service Award is an ultramarine blue service ribbon divided by four equal stripes of turquoise. No medal is authorized.

**NCO Professional Military Education Graduate Ribbon (NCOPMEGR).** This ribbon is awarded to graduates of certified Noncommissioned Officer Professional Military Education Schools, Phases III, IV, and V. The ribbon is red with a narrow white stripe near each edge and two blue stripes near the center.

**USAF Basic Military Training Honor Graduate Ribbon (BMTHGR).** This ribbon is awarded to honor graduates of BMT who have demonstrated excellence in all phases of academic and military training and is limited to the top 10 percent of the training flight. The ribbon has an ultramarine blue center with yellow, brittany blue, and white bands on either side.

**Small Arms Expert Marksmanship Ribbon (SAEMR).** Awarded after 1 January 1963 to persons qualifying as "expert" on weapons specified in AFR 50-36, the ribbon has a green center with a wide blue stripe at each edge and two narrow yellow stripes separating the green and the blue.

**Air Force Training Ribbon (AFTR).** Awarded to Air Force members on completion of initial military accession training (BMT, OTS, ROTC, academy, medical services, judge advocate, chaplain orientation, and so on), the ribbon is predominantly Air Force blue centered with a red stripe with one gold stripe near each end.

## SERVICE MEDALS

Service medals are awarded to members of the armed forces of the United States to denote the honorable performance of duty. Most service medals pertain to federal duty in a time of war or national emergency. A person's entire service during the period for which the award is made must be honorable.

**Service Medals Authorized before Vietnam War.** Service medals, appurtenances, and devices that pertain only to wars or campaigns before the war in Vietnam are not included since there are few, if any, officers still on active duty who might wear such items. See AFR 900-48 for details on these awards.

**Army of Occupation Medal (AOM).** This medal requires 30 days' consecutive service with any of the following armies of occupation:

Germany (exclusive of Berlin), 9 May 1945-5 May 1955.
Austria, 9 May 1945-27 July 1955.
Italy, 9 May 1945-15 September 1947.
Japan, 3 September 1945-27 April 1952.
Korea, 3 September 1945-29 June 1949.

An appropriately inscribed clasp is issued with each award to denote the area in which occupation duty was performed. The Berlin Airlift Device, awarded for 90 days' consecutive service in the Berlin Airlift between 26 June 1948 and 30 September 1949, is worn on the service ribbon or the suspension ribbon of the Army of Occupation Medal. The ribbon consists of a white stripe, black band, red band, white stripe.

**Antarctica Service Medal (ASM).** This medal is awarded to members of any of the armed forces who as members of a U.S. expedition participated in scientific, direct support, or exploratory operations on the Antarctic Continent or in a foreign expedition cooperating with U.S. expeditions, or who participated in flights to and from Antarctica in support of such operations, or who have served in a U.S. ship operating south of the 60th parallel in support of such U.S. operations. The medal includes a "Wintered Over" clasp for those who stayed in Antarctica during the winter months. There is a corresponding circular device for wear on the ribbon bar, depicting the map of the Antarctic Continent.

**National Defense Service Medal (NDSM).** This medal has been authorized for honorable active service for any period between 27 June 1950 and 27 July 1954. Persons on active duty for purposes other than extended active duty are not eligible for this award. The medal is of bronze. The ribbon is red with a yellow center bordered with white, blue, white, and red. The NDSM has also been authorized for cold war service from 1 January 1961 to 14 August 1974 and again for service during Operations Desert Shield and Desert Storm from 2 August 1990 to a cut-off date not yet announced as of press time. A bronze service star is authorized for persons who have served during more than one such period.

**Armed Forces Expeditionary Medal (AFEM).** This medal is awarded to members of the U.S. armed forces who have served during the cold war in places where there was fighting or the threat of it, such as Berlin, Quemoy, Matsu, Lebanon in 1958, the Dominican Republic, Laos, Vietnam, or Korea after 1 October 1966. (Those who served in Vietnam between 1 July 1958 and 3 July 1965 may wear either the AFEM or VNSM for such service, but not both.)

**Vietnam Service Medal (VNSM).** The Vietnam Service Medal has been authorized by the president to be awarded to personnel who served in Vietnam, Cambodia, Thailand, Laos, or contiguous waters or airspace, from 4 July 1965 through 28 March 1973. The ribbon is yellow, edged in green, with three red stripes in the center.

**Southwest Asia Service Medal (SWASM).** The Southwest Asia Service Medal has been authorized to those servicemembers who served in the Persian Gulf area in Operations Desert Shield and Desert Storm from 2 August 1990 to a cut-off date not yet announced as of press time. The medal is suspended from a sand-colored ribbon with red, white, blue, green, and black stripes incorporating the colors of the United States and of the Gulf area. The obverse of the medal depicts the desert and the sea with tank, armored personnel carrier, helicopter, ship, and aircraft in recognition of joint service participation. The reverse depicts an upraised sword entwined with a palm frond symbolizing military might and preparedness in defense of peace.

**Humanitarian Service Medal (HSM).** This medal is awarded to those who after 1 April 1975 distinguished themselves by meritorious direct participation in approved military acts of a humanitarian nature. Bronze pendant displays an opened right hand on obverse and a sprig of oak on reverse. Ribbon has vertical stripes of purple, white, and light and dark blue.

**Armed Forces Reserve Medal (AFRM).** Required is honorable and satisfactory service in one or more of the reserve components of the armed forces for a period of 10 years, not necessarily consecutive, provided such service was performed within a period of 12 consecutive years. Periods of service as a member of a regular component are excluded from consideration.

The ribbon consists of stripes of blue, buff, blue, buff, blue, buff band, continuing with stripes of blue, buff, blue, buff, blue.

*10-Year Device.* One 10-year device is authorized to be worn on the suspension and service ribbon to denote service for each 10-year period in addition to and under the same conditions as prescribed for the award of the medal. It is a bronze hourglass with a 5/16″ Roman numeral "X" superimposed.

## NON-U.S. SERVICE MEDALS

**United Nations Medal (UNM).** The United Nations Medal is awarded by the United States to specific individuals for service with United Nations Forces, specifically with the UN Observer Group in Lebanon or the UN Truce Supervisory Organization in Palestine. The medal is a round disc with the United Nations emblem and the letters "UN" on the obverse, and on the reverse is the inscription "In the Service of Peace." The ribbon is of United Nations blue with two single narrow white stripes 1/4″ from each edge.

**Republic of Vietnam Campaign Medal (RVNCM).** This silk moire ribbon of vertical green and yellow stripes has a metal device reading "1960- ." Republic of Vietnam Armed Forces Order No. 48, dated 24 March 1966, authorized award of this RVN service medal to U.S. military personnel serving six months or wounded in the Vietnam War. U.S. military personnel outside Vietnam who contributed direct combat support to the RVNAF for six months were also eligible.

**Multinational Force and Observers Medal.** This medal may be awarded to those who served with the international peacekeeping force, the MFO, in the Sinai Peninsula for at least 90 days after 3 August 1981 or for six months after 15 March 1985. Subsequent awards are designated by numeral appurtenances.

**Kuwait Liberation Medal, Kingdom of Saudi Arabia (KLM).** Awarded to U.S. military personnel who served in the theater of operations of the Gulf War between 17 January and 21 February 1991.

## BADGES

Badges are appurtenances of the uniform. In the eyes of their wearers, several badges have a significance equal to or greater than all but the highest decorations. Although there is no established precedence among badges, aerospace badges are worn above any others, with the exception of the chaplain insignia.

New specialty badges for all USAF personnel were authorized in 1994, but only one may be worn at a time. Detailed descriptions were unavailable as of press time, but should appear soon in a revision of AFM 35-10.

Six categories of badges and specialty insignia are currently approved for wear: aerospace badges, noncombatant designation badges and insignia, special service badges, duty identification badges, Air Force specialty qualification badges, and other badges.

**Aerospace Badges.** These include the astronaut, pilot, navigator or observer, flight surgeon, flight nurse, officer aircrew member, enlisted aircrew member, and parachutist badges.

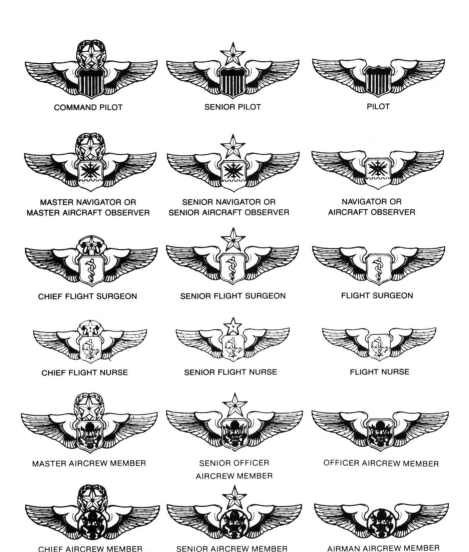

COMMAND PILOT

SENIOR PILOT

PILOT

MASTER NAVIGATOR OR
MASTER AIRCRAFT OBSERVER

SENIOR NAVIGATOR OR
SENIOR AIRCRAFT OBSERVER

NAVIGATOR OR
AIRCRAFT OBSERVER

CHIEF FLIGHT SURGEON

SENIOR FLIGHT SURGEON

FLIGHT SURGEON

CHIEF FLIGHT NURSE

SENIOR FLIGHT NURSE

FLIGHT NURSE

MASTER AIRCREW MEMBER

SENIOR OFFICER
AIRCREW MEMBER

OFFICER AIRCREW MEMBER

CHIEF AIRCREW MEMBER

SENIOR AIRCREW MEMBER

AIRMAN AIRCREW MEMBER

ASTRONAUT DESIGNATOR
(This design is embossed on top of badge member is awarded.)

AIR FORCE ASTRONAUT AND AVIATION BADGES.

MASTER SPACE OPERATIONS

SENIOR SPACE OPERATIONS

SPACE OPERATIONS

SPACE BADGES.

**Noncombatant Designation Badges and Insignia.** These include the physician, dentist, nurse, biomedical scientist, medical service corps, judge advocate, chaplain, and Air Force Academy permanent professor badges.

**Special Service Badges.** These include the presidential service, vice-presidential service, office of the secretary of defense, and joint chiefs of staff badges.

**Duty Identification Badges.** These include the combat crewmember, security police, ATC instructor, Air Force recruiting service, fire protection, Junior AFROTC instructor, Air Force Reserve recruiting service, and Defense Language Institute instructor badges.

**Air Force Specialty Qualification Badges.** These include air traffic controller, aircraft maintenance/munitions, explosive ordnance disposal, missile, security police qualification, space, weapons controller, administration, communications-electronics maintenance, medical technician, meteorologist, and supply-fuels badges.

**Other Badges.** These include distinguished international shooter, USAF distinguished rifleman, USAF bronze excellence-in-competition rifleman, USAF distinguished pistol shot, USAF distinguished-in-competition pistol shot, and USAF bronze excellence-in-competition pistol shot badges.

**Eligibility to Wear Badges.** See AFR 35-10 for eligibility requirements for wearing aerospace badges. Those granted aeronautical ratings no longer current are authorized to wear the aerospace badge that was in effect when the rating was granted.

## DEVICES

**Service Ribbons.** The service ribbon is a strip of ribbon identical to that from which the service medal is suspended. (Not all ribbons reflect the award of a medal, such as service longevity ribbons.) Service ribbons will not be impregnated with unnatural preservatives nor worn with artificial protective coverings.

**Clasps.** Clasps are authorized for the Good Conduct Medal and the Antarctica Service Medal.

**Service Stars.** The service star is a bronze or silver five-pointed star 3/16″ in diameter. A silver service star is worn in lieu of five bronze service stars.

*Wearing on Suspension Ribbons.* Service stars are authorized to be worn with one point of each star up in a vertical position and all stars arranged in a horizontal row on the suspension ribbon of the Vietnam Service Medal (and some pre-Vietnam medals) to represent combat service.

*Wearing on Service Ribbons.* Service stars are authorized to be worn on the service ribbons of some pre-Vietnam medals and the following medals only:

CHIEF PHYSICIAN
SENIOR PHYSICIAN
PHYSICIAN
CHIEF DENTIST
SENIOR DENTIST
DENTIST
CHIEF NURSE
SENIOR NURSE
NURSE
CHIEF BIOMEDICAL SCIENTIST
SENIOR BIOMEDICAL SCIENTIST
BIOMEDICAL SCIENTIST
CHIEF MEDICAL SERVICE CORPS
SENIOR MEDICAL SERVICE CORPS
MEDICAL SERVICE CORPS

MEDICAL BADGES.

PRESIDENTIAL SERVICE BADGE

VICE-PRESIDENTIAL SERVICE BADGE

OFFICE OF THE SECRETARY OF DEFENSE BADGE

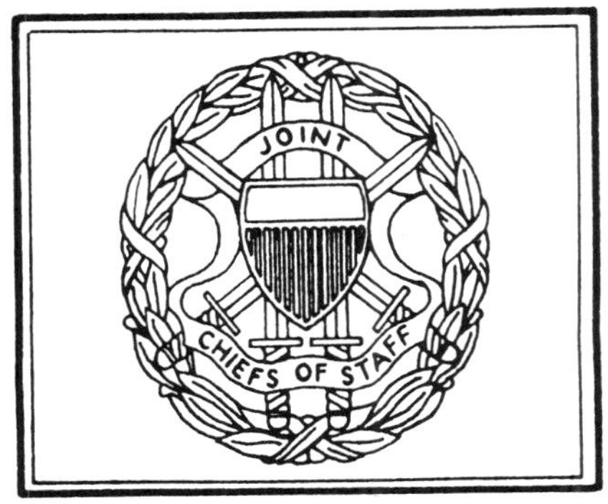


JOINT CHIEFS OF STAFF BADGE

PERMANENT PROFESSOR USAF ACADEMY BADGE

IDENTIFICATION BADGES.

MASTER PARACHUTIST

SENIOR PARACHUTIST

PARACHUTIST

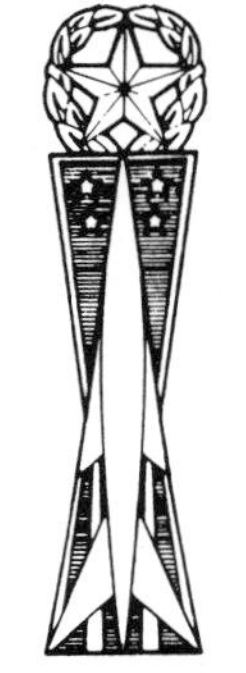

MASTER MISSILE

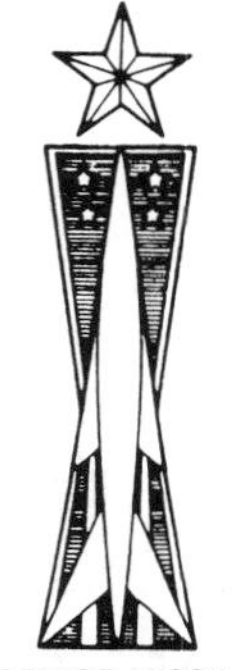

SENIOR MISSILE

MISSILE

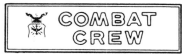

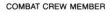

COMBAT CREW MEMBER

RECRUITING SERVICE

ATC INSTRUCTOR INSIGNIA

SECURITY POLICE BADGE

PARACHUTIST, MISSILE, COMBAT CREW, RECRUITING SERVICE, ATC INSTRUCTOR, AND SECURITY POLICE BADGES.

USAF
DISTINGUISHED
RIFLEMAN

USAF
EXCELLENCE-IN-COMPETITION
RIFLEMAN

USAF BRONZE
EXCELLENCE-IN-COMPETITION
RIFLEMAN

USAF
DISTINGUISHED
PISTOL SHOT

USAF
EXCELLENCE-IN-COMPETITION
PISTOL SHOT

USAF BRONZE
EXCELLENCE-IN-COMPETITION
PISTOL SHOT

USAF DISTINGUISHED AND EXCELLENCE-IN-COMPETITION RIFLEMAN AND PISTOL SHOT MARKSMANSHIP BADGES.

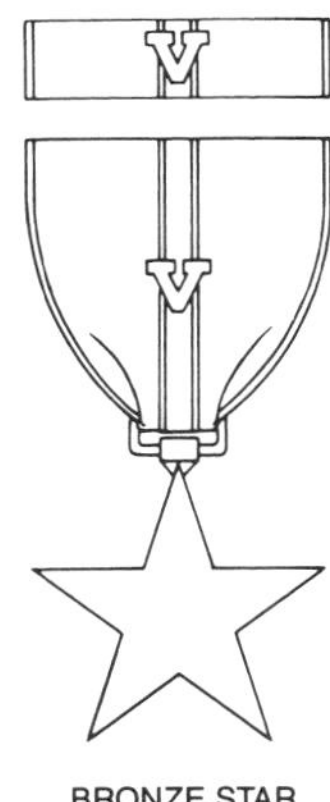


BRONZE STAR
WITH V DEVICE.

SERVICE RIBBON
WITH V DEVICE
AND OAK LEAF
CLUSTER.

- Vietnam Service Medal to represent possession of service stars on the suspension ribbons.
- National Defense Service Medal to represent a second award.
- Small Arms Expert Marksmanship Ribbon to represent qualification with M-16 rifle and with handgun.

Silver service stars are worn to the wearer's right of bronze service stars, but to the left of the arrowhead.

**Letter "V" Device.** The bronze letter "V" device indicates an award for valor in combat.

**Arrowheads.** The arrowhead is a bronze replica of an Indian arrowhead 1/4" high and 1/8" wide. It is authorized for wear on the appropriate service medal ribbon to signify that the wearer participated in a combat parachute jump, a combat glider landing, or an amphibious assault landing.

**Miniature Decorations, Service Medals, and Appurtenances.** Miniature decorations, service medals, and appurtenances are replicas of the corresponding decorations and service medals on the scale of one half. The Medal of Honor is not worn in miniature, but its rosette is authorized for civilian wear.

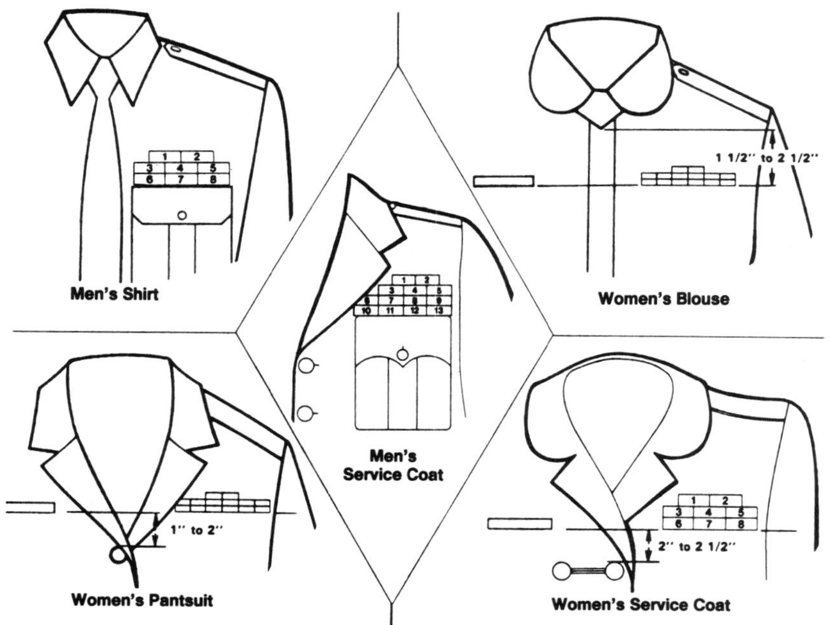


PLACEMENT OF AIR FORCE RIBBONS.

Note: Numbers indicate arrangement of ribbons with smaller numbers representing ribbons with highest precedence. Women are authorized option of four or six miniature ribbons per row. If option of six miniature ribbons is elected, multiples of six will continue with the top row centered. If four miniature ribbons are elected, the same rule applies.

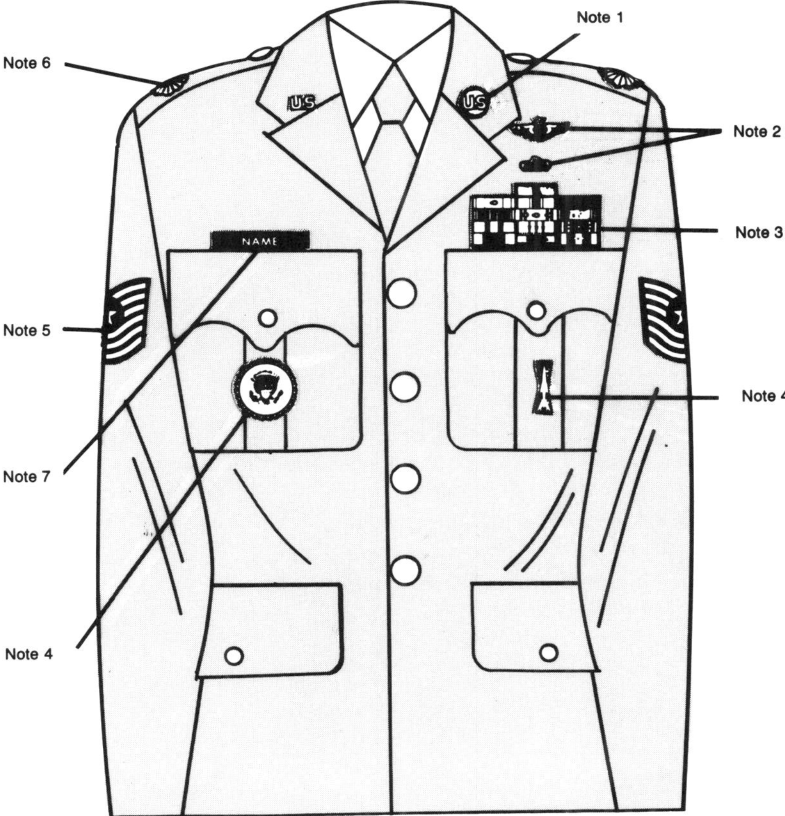


PLACEMENT OF ACCOUTERMENTS ON MEN'S SERVICE DRESS UNIFORM.

Notes:

1. (Mandatory) Place the insignia approximately halfway up the seam resting on but not over it. Bottom of the U.S. is horizontal with the ground. The finish may be satin or highly polished; however, the finish of all badges and U.S. insignia must match.

2. (Aerospace and chaplain badges are mandatory.) Center badge ½″ above the top row of ribbons. Center additional badge ½″ above first badge. The finish may be satin or highly polished; however, the finish of all U.S. insignia and badges must match.

3. (Mandatory) Ribbons must be resting on but not over the top edge of the pocket and centered between the left and right edges. May be worn four in a row and the left edge of ribbons aligned with left edge of pocket to keep the lapel from covering the ribbons.

4. (Optional) Center badge on the lower portion of pocket between left and right edges and bottom of flap and pocket.

5. (Mandatory) Center 4″ sleeve chevron halfway between the shoulder seam and elbow when elbow is bent at a 90° angle.

6. (Mandatory) Commissioned officers center regular-size grade insignia ⅝″ from the end of the epaulet.

7. (Mandatory) The name tag rests on but not over the top edge of the pocket, centered between the left and right edges.

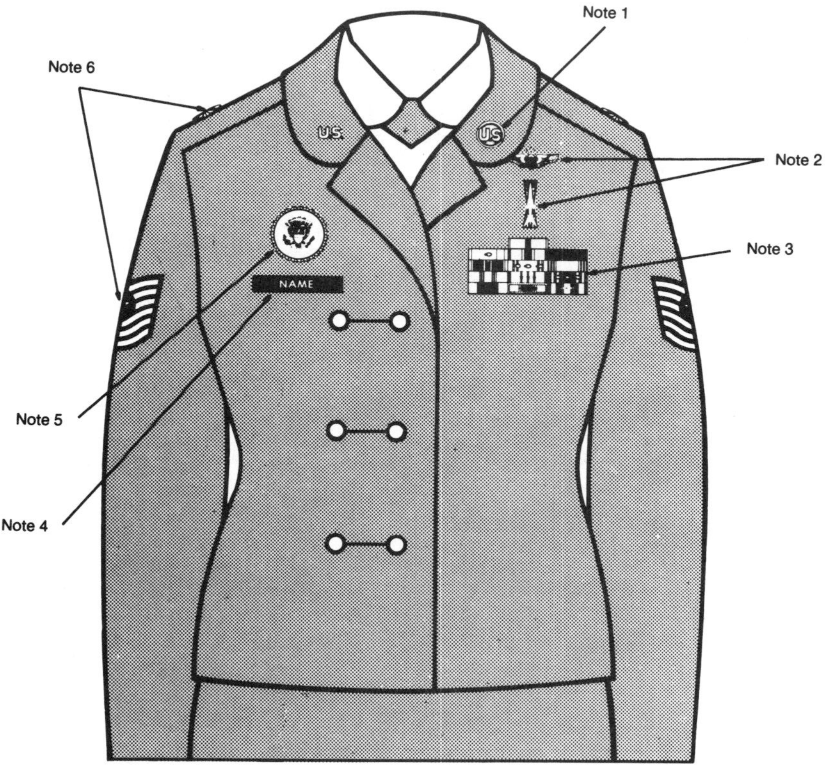


PLACEMENT OF ACCOUTERMENTS ON WOMEN'S SERVICE DRESS UNIFORM.

Notes:

1. Centered with bottom of U.S. horizontal with the ground.
2. Center badge ½″ above the ribbons. When no ribbons are authorized, center ½″ above imaginary row of ribbons. Center additional badge or insignia ½″ above other worn.
3. Centered on left side between lapel and arm seam, 2″ to 2½″ higher than top buttons, horizontal with ground. Bottom of the ribbons will be even with the bottom of the name tag.
4. Centered on right side between lapel and arm seam, 2″ to 2½″ above the buttons, horizontal with ground.
5. Center badge ½″ above name tag.
6. General officers: See illustration above. Other officers: Center regular size grade insignia ⅝″ from end of epaulet (imaginary seam line). Airmen: Center 3″ sleeve chevron halfway between imaginary shoulder seam and elbow when elbow is bent at 90° angle.

**Miniature Service Ribbons.** Miniature service ribbons are replicas of corresponding service ribbons on a scale of about one half.

**Lapel Buttons.** *For All Decorations and Service Medals.* The lapel button is 21/32″ long and 1/8″ wide, in colored enamel, being a reproduction of the service ribbon. Miniature appurtenances may be placed on lapel buttons.

**Air Force Lapel Button.** This is a small metal replica of the Air Force star and wings. It is authorized for wear by all active-duty and reserve (including AFROTC cadets) personnel.

**Air Force Retired Lapel Button.** This button is presented to each retiree.

**Supply of Appurtenances.** Only the following appurtenances will be supplied by the Department of the Air Force:

- Service ribbons.
- Clasps
- Service stars.
- Letter "V" device.
- Arrowheads.
- Lapel buttons for U.S. military decorations (except Medal of Honor).
- Air Force lapel button.
- Air Force retired lapel button.

An initial issue of the above appurtenances will be made with the corresponding service medals. Replacements for military personnel on active duty will be supplied to commanders on requisition in the usual manner. Replacements for others will be made at cost upon request to USAFMPC/DPMSAA, Randolph AFB, TX 78148.

The following appurtenances for service medals will *not* be sold by the Department of the Air Force:

- Miniature service medals and ribbons.
- Lapel buttons, except the Air Force lapel button.

**Manufacture, Sale, and Illegal Possession.** AFR 900-48 prescribes:

- Restrictions on manufacture and sale of service medals and appurtenances by civilians.
- Penalties for illegal possession and wearing of service medals and appurtenances.

## GUIDE FOR WEARING AWARDS

Individuals entitled to wear decorations, service medals, ribbons, and badges should be certain that they place them on the uniform in the prescribed location and in the prescribed order.

**U.S. Military Service Medals.** U.S. military and naval service medals fall into the following categories:

- Service medals awarded by the Department of the Air Force and the Department of Defense, as listed in this chapter, and by the Department of the Army and Navy.
- The Republic of Vietnam Campaign Medal, awarded by that government for service in Vietnam between 1 March 1961 and 18 March 1973.

*Occasions for Wearing.* Commanders may prescribe the wearing of decorations and service medals on the following occasions:

- Parades, reviews, inspections, and funerals.
- Ceremonies and formal occasions.

The servicemember has the option of wearing decorations and service medals on the following occasions:

- Holidays when not on duty with troops.
- Social occasions of a private nature ("black tie" or "white tie").

*Prohibited Wearing.* Decorations and service medals will not be worn on the following occasions:

- When equipped for combat or simulated combat.
- By officers while suspended from either rank or command.
- By airmen while serving a sentence of confinement.

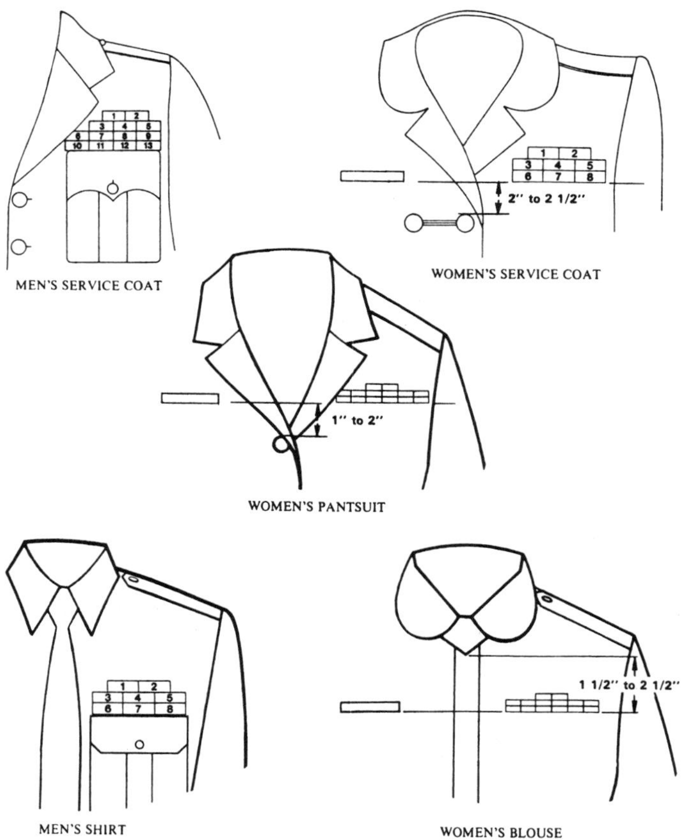


WEAR OF RIBBONS ON SERVICE UNIFORM COMBINATIONS (men's and women's).

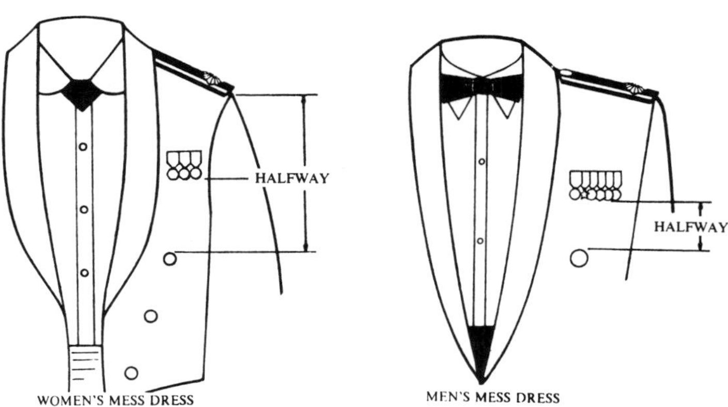


WEAR OF MINIATURE MEDALS ON THE MESS DRESS UNIFORM (men's and women's).

**U.S. Nonmilitary Decorations.** The following nonmilitary decorations may be worn only if military decorations or service medals are worn: the Medal for Merit, the National Security Medal, the Presidential Medal for Freedom, and decorations awarded by NASA, the Treasury Department, Public Health, and Maritime Services. Nonmilitary service awards may not be worn on the Air Force uniform.

State decorations and service awards may be worn only by Air National Guardsmen in nonactive duty status.

**Foreign Service Medals.** The acceptance or wearing of foreign decorations and service medals for service performed while a member of the armed forces of the United States is prohibited except as provided in AFR 900-48.

Decorations and service medals awarded by the national government of a friendly country may also be worn provided such service medals were earned during service as a bona fide member of the armed forces of that friendly foreign nation. At least one U.S. decoration or service medal must be worn at the same time that a foreign service medal is worn.

The wearing of foreign service medals (except those indicated above), including civilian service medals awarded by a foreign national government and all service medals awarded by an inferior foreign jurisdiction, is prohibited.

**Wear of Decorations and Service Medals.** Decorations and service medals are worn on the service coat. The Medal of Honor is worn pendant from the cravat (ribbon placed around the neck) outside the shirt collar and inside the coat collar, the medal proper hanging over the necktie near the collar. Other decorations and service medals are worn in order of precedence from right to left of the wearer immediately above the pocket on the left breast in one or more lines, which are overlapped. The top line consists of those decorations and service medals highest in the order of precedence, which is as follows: decorations (in order listed at the end of this chapter); U.S. unit citations; achievement awards; service medals, in order earned; foreign decorations; UN service awards; and foreign service awards.

A *bronze oak-leaf cluster* is authorized for wear for each additional Presidential Unit Citation received by a unit. A *silver oak-leaf cluster* is authorized for wear in lieu of five bronze oak-leaf clusters.

*Wear of Decorations and Service Medals on Civilian Clothing.* The wearing of decorations, service medals, or miniatures on civilian clothes should be limited to ceremonial occasions—and then only when strictly appropriate to the occasion.

When permitted by the employing agency, employees of federal, state, and city government who served honorably in active service and whose duties require that they wear special uniforms to denote their authority may wear U.S. service ribbons.

**Wear of Unit Awards.** An individual assigned to, or permanently attached to, and present for duty with a unit in the action for which a unit award was given may wear the award as a permanent part of the uniform.

The framed awards (the Presidential Unit Citation and the Joint Meritorious Unit Award) are worn with the laurel leaves pointing up. The unit award emblems may be worn with service ribbons or full-size medals but are not worn with miniature medals. Foreign unit awards from the Vietnam era, authorized only for permanent wear, are the Vietnam Presidential Unit Citation, the Republic of Vietnam Gallantry Cross Unit Citation, and the Republic of Vietnam Civil Actions Unit Citation.

**Wear of Badges.** Only one U.S. aerospace badge may be worn at a time. Medical Corps and Nurse Corps officers may wear both the aviation medical badge and authorized medical insignia.

For placement of badges, see the accompanying illustrations of placement of accouterments. For further information, see AFR 35-10.

## BRASSARDS

A brassard is a cloth band worn around the upper arm to designate its wearer as a member of a special group or service and usually bearing an identifying mark, such as the Red Cross. Special duty brassards are worn centered on the left sleeve of the outer garment—overcoat, raincoat, topcoat, coat, jacket, or shirt when worn as an outer garment—halfway between elbow and sleeve shoulder seam.

## ORDER OF PRECEDENCE OF DECORATIONS AND AWARDS

There is a definite ranking among decorations and awards. Consult this listing before you assemble authorized decorations and awards on your uniform to be sure you have them in the proper sequence. U.S. military decorations of the Air Force, Army, Navy, and Coast Guard are worn by Air Force personnel in the following order:

Medal of Honor (Air Force, Army, Navy)
Air Force Cross
Distinguished Service Cross
Navy Cross
Defense Distinguished Service Medal
Distinguished Service Medal (Air Force, Army, Navy, Coast Guard)
Silver Star
Defense Superior Service Medal
Legion of Merit
Distinguished Flying Cross
Airman's Medal
Soldier's Medal
Navy-Marine Corps Medal
Coast Guard Medal
Bronze Star Medal
Purple Heart
Defense Meritorious Service Medal
Meritorious Service Medal
Air Medal
Aerial Achievement Medal
Joint Service Commendation Medal
Air Force Commendation Medal
Army Commendation Medal
Navy Commendation Medal
Coast Guard Commendation Medal
Joint Service Achievement Medal
Air Force Achievement Medal
Army Achievement Medal
Navy Achievement Medal
Coast Guard Achievement Medal
Combat Action Ribbon
Presidential Unit Citation (Air Force-Army)
Presidential Unit Citation (Navy)
Joint Meritorious Unit Award

Air Force Outstanding Unit Award
Air Force Organizational Excellence Award
Valorous Unit Award
Navy Unit Commendation
Coast Guard Unit Commendation
Meritorious Unit Commendation (Army/Navy/Coast Guard—worn in order earned)
Navy "E" Ribbon
U.S. nonmilitary decorations (see AFR 35-10)
POW Medal
Combat Readiness Medal
Air Force Good Conduct Medal
Army Good Conduct Medal
Navy Good Conduct Medal
Marine Corps Good Conduct Medal
Coast Guard Good Conduct Medal
Air Reserve Forces Meritorious Service Medal
Outstanding Airman of the Year Ribbon
Air Force Recognition Ribbon
Army of Occupation Medal
Antarctica Service Medal
National Defense Service Medal
Armed Forces Expeditionary Medal
Vietnam Service Medal
Southwest Asia Service Medal
Humanitarian Service Medal
Air Force Overseas Ribbon
Army Overseas Ribbon
Coast Guard Restricted Duty Ribbon
Sea Service Deployment Ribbon (Navy/Marine)
Coast Guard Sea Service Ribbon
Air Force Longevity Service Ribbon
Reserve Medals (Armed Forces/Navy/Marine Corps—worn in order earned)
Army Reserve Component Achievement Medal
Naval Reserve Meritorious Service Medal
Coast Guard Meritorious Service Medal
Organized Marine Corps Reserve Medal
NCO PME Graduate Ribbon (USAF)
Army NCO Professional Development Ribbon
USAF BMT Honor Graduate Ribbon
Coast Guard Reserve Honor Graduate Ribbon
Small Arms Expert Marksmanship Ribbon
Navy Pistol Shot Medal
Air Force Training Ribbon
Army Service Ribbon
Foreign decorations (see AFR 35-10)
Foreign unit citations (see AFR 35-10)
United Nations Medal
Republic of Vietnam Campaign Medal
Multinational Force and Observers Medal
Foreign service medals (see AFR 35-10)

# 7

# Your Rights, Privileges, and Restrictions

*I believe that every right implies a responsibility; every opportunity, an obligation; every possession, a duty.*

—John D. Rockefeller, Jr.

When citizens enter military service, they undergo a change in legal status. Some civilian rights are restricted or modified. They take on additional hazards and obligations that are balanced by additional benefits not enjoyed by civilians. To a lesser degree, officers in inactive status and retired officers enjoy benefits and are also subject to restrictions. Some former members of the armed forces whose separation was honorable enjoy very important benefits administered by the Department of Veterans Affairs.

## JUSTIFICATION FOR BENEFITS

Strong reasons justify granting military rights and privileges called benefits. Those citizens who are members of the Army, the Navy, the Marines, or the Air Force have the primary mission of protecting and preserving the Constitution, including our free institutions and way of life, the prosecution of wars with the incidental hazard, and the service of the federal government wherever duty is directed. They give up many freedoms of choice civilians take for granted.

The hard core of the armed forces consists of the officers and members of the regular components who are volunteers. They are backed up by the several categories of reserves, also volunteers. Volunteers will not be obtained in the number required or the quality necessary unless the conditions of their life and lot are acceptable. Beset as we are by international strains and recurrent wars, our country needs as its first essential the armed forces necessary to protect itself, and this armed force must be strong enough, brave enough, and proud enough to do its job. Let no thoughtful person attack the principle of rights and privileges for the military.

A phase of this subject invariably overlooked by the critic of things military is that the bulk of officers of the regular and reserve components are beyond the age of being subject to military service. Even in wartime, the officer is a volunteer. As long as the nation has need of the best military leadership of all grades and ages, it will be wise to recognize this condition by granting appropriate benefits, first to attract good people to service and then to hold them.

There is an inescapable difference between the individual in civilian employment and the member of the service. The civilian may quit or refuse a task with no greater penalty than loss of employment, being thereafter free to choose another job. But the wearer of the uniform can do so only at the peril of punishment by action of court-martial, which, if refusal to obey or cowardice before any enemy is involved, may result in a death penalty.

**Justification for Restrictions.** There is a sufficient case also for imposing restrictions upon military people, especially commissioned officers, that civilians do not bear.

The government must have a clearly defined power to deploy its forces and require individuals to perform specific missions, however unpleasant or hazardous such locations or duties may become.

The government must insist upon full service of its officers and thus is justified in defining and prohibiting improper outside activities of individuals.

Since procurement officers and others in the business end of government have many prerogatives incident to the letting of contracts, the government must require high standards of ethics as well as clearly codified methods of conducting these affairs.

In order to assure fair treatment for all and to prevent abuses in the exercise of federal power, limitations must be placed on authority, especially in the field of punishments, sentences of courts-martial, and the like.

## RIGHTS

Let us be sure of our meaning in this matter of rights. To do so, if followed by consideration of some examples, will identify many benefits in their true perspective. While there are many obligations of service, there are not many actual rights.

**Definition.** A right in the sense of this discussion is a benefit established for military people by federal law. Unless a benefit is established by law, in contrast to a departmental regulation that is subject to administrative change or withdrawal, it is something less than a right.

**Acquisition of Military Rights.** A citizen who has subscribed to his oath of office as an officer, or oath of enlistment if an airman, becomes entitled at once to certain rights of military service, such as the right to wear the uniform. Other rights accrue only by completing specified requirements, such as the right to retire after completing a stipulated period of service.

**The Right to Wear the Uniform.** Members of the military service have the right to wear the uniform of their service. That the department may require the wearing of the uniform off duty as well as on duty is beside the point. First of all, it is a right.

Members of the reserve components on inactive status, retired personnel, and former members of the service who have been honorably separated have the right to wear the uniform only at stipulated times or circumstances, and unless these conditions exist, the right is denied. Chapter 5 describes these conditions fully.

**The Right of Officers to Command.** In the commission granted an officer by the president are these words: "And I do strictly charge and require those officers and other personnel of lesser rank to render such obedience as is due. . . ." The commission itself may be regarded as the basic document that gives military officers the right to exercise command and to exact obedience to proper orders.

AFR 35-54 establishes this right in further detail, along with definite restrictions on this right.

**COMPARISON OF CITIZENS' DUTIES**

| *As a Civilian* | *As a Servicemember* |
|---|---|
| 1. To take part in civic affairs; to accept public office. | 1. Modified—Duty and right to vote remains; may express private opinion informally and become candidate for public office, but must not campaign actively. |
| 2. To serve on a jury. | 2. Modified—May be exempted from jury service; subject to appointment on court-martial. |
| 3. To respect and obey laws; to assist public officials in preventing crime and courts by giving evidence. | 3. Unchanged—Sometimes officially assigned to assist public officials. |
| 4. To pay taxes. | 4. Modified—May be exempted by statute from taxes of state where stationed, if not legal resident thereof. |

**COMPARISON OF CITIZENS' RIGHTS**

| *As a Civilian* | *As a Servicemember* |
|---|---|
| 1. Freedom of worship. | 1. Unchanged. |
| 2. Freedom of speech and press. | 2. Altered slightly by duty to maintain respect toward the president, vice president, Congress, and other officials. |
| 3. Right to assemble peaceably and to petition government. | 3. Subject to maintenance of good order and military discipline; must not go beyond "petition" stage. |
| 4. Right to keep and bear arms. | 4. Unchanged. |
| 5. Protection against unreasonable search and seizure of person and property. | 5. Similar safeguards applied by executive order. |
| 6. Right to vote secretly in national and local elections. | 6. Unchanged—Military authorities required to facilitate absentee voting. |
| 7. Freedom to make contracts, start and manage businesses, etc. | 7. Some limitations—Must not do business with government, reflect discredit on the uniform, interfere with duties, or use military titles (other than in authorship). |

**The Right to Draw Pay and Allowances.** Pay scales for grade and length of service are established by law. See chapter 4, "Pay and Personal Allowances."

The rights as to pay and allowances may be suspended, in part, by action of a court-martial or forfeited in part by absence without leave.

**The Right to Receive Medical Attention.** Members of the military service and in general their dependents are entitled to receive appropriate medical or dental care for the treatment of their wounds, injuries, or disease. In fact, refusal to accept treatment ruled to be necessary may be punishable by court-martial. For rights of dependents to receive medical care, see chapter 20.

**The Right to Individual Protection under the Uniform Code of Military Justice (UCMJ).** All members of the military service are under the jurisdiction established by the Articles of the Uniform Code of Military Justice. Many persons regard the *Manual for Courts-Martial,* which contains this code, merely as the authorization of courts-martial and the implementation of their procedures as a means of maintaining discipline or awarding punishment for crime. This view is shallow. Except for the punitive articles, the Uniform Code of Military Justice pertains in considerable measure to the protection of individual rights, such as these:

- No people may be compelled to incriminate themselves before a military court.
- No people shall without their consent be tried a second time for the same offense.
- Cruel and unusual punishments of every kind are prohibited.
- While the punishment for a crime or offense is left to the discretion of the court, it shall not exceed such limits as the president may from time to time prescribe.

**The Soldiers' and Sailors' Relief Act.** The Soldiers' and Sailors' Relief Act, passed in 1940 and still in effect, has for its purpose the relief of draftees, enlistees, and reservists on active duty of some of the pressure of heavy financial obligations they may have assumed in civil life. See chapter 20, "Personal Affairs and Aid for Your Dependents."

**Redress of Wrong.** Each of the armed services provides a procedure by which any members of the military service may seek redress of wrong. All officers should become fully acquainted with this matter. Officers may have occasion to register official objections or complaints with respect to their own treatment, although such occasions should be rare because most officers complete their entire service without finding it necessary to use this privilege. But officers should certainly know that their juniors also enjoy this right and that if they take action that is grossly injurious to an individual or action that is so considered, they may be obliged to endure the process as the injuring party rather than the injured.

There may come a time in the service of all people when they feel that they have been wronged by a superior, such as under such conditions as these: an unfavorable ruling regarding pay or allowances, unsatisfactory living conditions, undeserved stigma, or treatment by a superior that is directly contrary to military laws or regulations.

Any person contemplating registering an official complaint should first get the facts straight and be quite certain of sustaining them. It is contrary to regulations to punish anyone for filing a complaint. But a person can be punished for knowingly making statements that are unfounded, untruthful, or unjustly harmful to another person's good name. No person need fear the aftereffects of filing an honest complaint or stating a genuine grievance. But the basis of the grievances must be factual and subject to proof.

After getting the facts straight, the person should normally state the entire situation to the commander and seek advice. In most instances, this step will end the matter because, if the grievances are real, the commander may take action that will correct the situation.

In the event the conference with the commander is insufficient or for some sufficient reason is not held, a person may bring the problem to the attention of the inspector general who serves the organization, in person or in writing. More than likely, the inspector general will require a written statement in any event. This officer will advise the complainant of the final action taken on the complaint or grievance. Nor need this be all. The officer or airman may write directly to the inspector general of the major command or to the inspector general of the Air Force.

**Right to Request Correction of Military Records.** Military records serve as the basis for recording the fact, nature or character, and duration of military service. Accordingly, the military records that pertain to each individual are of inestimable value. When, therefore, any individual military record contains an error of commission or omission, means have been made available to petition for correction.

Each service secretary, acting through boards of civilian officers or employees of their respective services, is authorized to correct any military record where such action is necessary to correct an error or remove an injustice. In the Air Force, this board is known as the Air Force Board for Correction of Military Records.

Application for correction should be submitted by the person requesting corrective action on DD Form 149, *Application for Correction of Military Record.* Application may be made by other persons as authorized by the board when the person concerned is unable to submit application. In general, a statute of limitations of three years applies to applications. There must be a showing of exhaustion of normal administrative remedies. Hearing on an application may be denied if a sufficient basis for review has not been established or if effective relief cannot be granted. When an application has been found to be within the jurisdiction of the board and sufficient evidence has been presented indicating probable error or injustice, the applicant will be entitled to a hearing before the board either in person or by counsel or in person with counsel. Detailed instructions concerning the entitlement to hearing, notice, counsel, witnesses, and access to records are set forth in AFR 31-3 and AFR 31-11.

**The Right to Vote.** Legislation enacted by the Congress establishes the right of voting by members of the armed forces, and commanders are required to establish facilities for absentee voting for members of their commands. See AFR 211-19. Exercise of the right to vote is, of course, subject to state laws with which the servicemember must comply.

**The Right to Retire.** After satisfying specific requirements of honorable service or having endured physical disability beyond a fixed degree, commissioned officers of the armed forces have the right to retire. See chapter 17, "Retirement."

**The "GI Bill of Rights."** Former members of the armed forces and retired personnel may obtain benefits under the "GI Bill of Rights." VA benefits for eligible veterans, their dependents, and beneficiaries include these:

- Servicemen's Group Life Insurance.
- Educational aid.
- Guarantee of loans for the purchase or construction of homes, farms, or business property.
- Readjustment allowances for veterans who are unemployed.
- Disability compensation.
- Vocational rehabilitation.
- Physical examinations, hospital care, and outpatient medical and dental treatment.
- Domiciliary care and guardianship service.
- Pensions.
- Death benefits to survivors.

These are discussed in chapter 20, "Personal Affairs and Aid for Your Dependents."

**Social Security Benefits of Retired Personnel.** Retired officers, including those who are employed or self-employed, qualify for Social Security benefits in the same manner as other citizens. See chapter 17, "Retirement."

**The Right to Be Buried in a National Cemetery.** The rights of a deceased servicemember to be buried in a National Military Cemetery are discussed in chapter 20.

## PRIVILEGES

**The Privileges of Rank and Position.** That "rank has its privileges" is a saying as old as the armed forces. It is the deference in all walks of life to one's elders or seniors. It is no more or less pronounced, although it may be more codified, than among faculty members, in a business establishment, in a legislative body, or among doctors, lawyers, ministers. Throughout chapter 2, "Military Courtesy," and chapter 3, "Customs of the Service," are numerous examples.

**Leave.** Under current laws and regulations, military people become entitled to accumulate leave and to take it when their duties permit (see chapter 8, "Leave"). But people in uniform must apply for permission to take leave from station and duties, regardless of how much leave they have accumulated. Their applications may be denied. The training or tactical situation will govern the decision. If they absent themselves without permission, they are subject to forfeiture of pay and to disciplinary action. Hence, it is a privilege, rather than a right.

**Election to Public Office.** Members of the Air Force other than the Regular Air Force, while on active duty, may become candidates for election to public office without the tender of resignation and may file such evidence of their candidacy as required by local laws. Their candidacy must not interfere with duty. If elected, the officers must not, while in active-duty status, act in their official capacity as the holders of the offices or perform any of the duties. Members of the Regular Air Force on the active list do not enjoy this privilege.

Because this particular privilege has been altered several times in recent years, servicemembers considering becoming a candidate for office should consult local military authority, for otherwise they may vacate their commissions.

**Membership in Officers' Clubs and Messes.** All officers assigned at a station have the privilege of club membership, if clubs are provided. They must follow the rules of the club or mess as to payment of dues, bills, and other matters, and unless they do so, this privilege may be curtailed or denied.

**The Privilege of Writing for Publication.** Traditionally, active-duty officers have been permitted to add to their income by writing for publication, as long as it was done on their own time and was not part of their official duties. One need only remember William J. Hardee, West Point commandant of cadets before the Civil War, whose *Rifle and Light Infantry Tactics* became the officer's manual for both Union and Confederate armies; Gen. John J. Pershing's World War I and Dwight D. Eisenhower's World War II memoirs (neither went off the active rolls); Hap Arnold's "Billy Bruce" children's books; and Marine Col. John W. Thomason's stories written between the world wars, which his friend Ernest Hemingway held in highest esteem. Maj. Gen. A. J. Kinney, the first author of this *Guide,* wrote it for more than 20 years on active duty.

However, in 1992 in an effort to clean its own house, the U.S. Congress passed a law (5 U.S.C., App. 501(b)) prohibiting federal officials and employees from accepting honoraria for public appearances, speeches, or articles. Enforced throughout the U.S. government, this proved unworkable and was challenged as a violation of the First Amendment, and the U.S. Court of Appeals did find the law unconstitutional.

The status quo ante apparently applies now, as it did traditionally within certain regulatory provisions. See Hq USAF/JA letter "Honoraria" of 9 February 1994, with two attachments for guidance and stay current with your SJA.

*Publishing Articles on Military Subjects Is Authorized.* Subject to restrictions stated below, any member of the military service may publish articles on military subjects that contain nothing prejudicial to military discipline.

If publication is not objectionable, such permission will be granted, but no reference to approval by the Department of the Air Force will appear in the publication.

If the author offers the work to the Department of the Air Force and it is accepted and published by the Department of the Air Force in original form, proper recognition will be given to the individual.

The inclusion of classified military information (top secret, secret, or confidential) in any article published by a member of the Air Force is prohibited.

*Manner of Obtaining Clearance on Proposed Addresses and Military Publications.* The Office of Public Affairs, Department of Defense, is responsible for reviewing for security and coordination with existing policies of the Department of Defense and its components information disseminated to the public on a national scale by individuals or agencies of the Departments of the Army, the Navy, and the Air Force.

The agency is charged with reviewing manuscripts, speeches, advertising material, radio scripts, and still and motion pictures submitted for clearance by individuals and agencies of the Department of Defense and its components.

*Active-Duty Personnel.* All material containing information about the Air Force prepared by officers or airmen on active federal service will be submitted to appropriate public affairs authority for review before publication. Material not relating directly to the Air Force is governed only by the dictates of propriety and of good taste. Review of such material is not required.

*Retired Personnel.* Retired military personnel are responsible for the security and propriety of material prepared by them.

*Inactive Personnel.* Inactive Air Force Reserve and National Guard personnel assume civilian status upon completion of terminal leave and are not required to submit material prepared by them for review.

Attention is called to a long-standing policy prohibiting military and civilian personnel assigned to public affairs divisions from accepting direct remuneration from civilian agencies for any type of public affairs activity without topside approval. Exceptions may be granted in cases where the subject matter is in no way related to the official duties of the personnel.

**Inventions and Rights to Profit Therefrom.** Another way in which active-duty personnel may seek to add to their incomes is through an invention. The armed forces have many people with inventive minds and good ideas. It is likely that many good ideas are unexploited because of lack of information on how to proceed.

An officer who makes an invention has the same right as any other citizen to profit therefrom provided it does not refer to and is not evolved in the line of duty.

A free pamphlet on the subject is issued by the Commissioner of Patents, Washington, D.C. Novice inventors should obtain it before disclosing anything about their projects.

**Defense Department Exchange Privileges.** The following persons, identified as prescribed by AFR 147-7 when purchases are made, and organizations are entitled to all exchange privileges:

- All uniformed personnel on active duty more than 72 hours and their dependents.
- Officers and airmen of foreign nations when on duty with U.S. armed services under competent orders issued by one of the armed services.
- Widows and widowers of servicemembers of the following categories who have not remarried: members of the uniformed services who at the time of death were on active military duty for a period exceeding 72 hours; members of the reserve components of the armed forces who died in line of duty while on active duty; and retired personnel.

Retired personnel entitled to the privilege include these people:

- All personnel carried on the official retired lists of the armed services.
- Contract surgeons during the period of their contract.
- Uniformed personnel of the Red Cross assigned to duty within an activity of the armed services.

*Patrons Entitled to Limited Privileges.* The following people are entitled to make limited purchases at exchanges (see departmental exchange regulations for details):

- Honorably discharged veterans who are receiving medical treatment at a facility where exchanges are operated.
- Exchange employees.
- Fountain, snack bar, and restaurant privileges may be extended when civilian facilities are not conveniently available to the following: civilian employees; Red Cross nonuniformed personnel working in offices within an activity of the armed forces; visitors; reserve components members on duty for periods less than 72 hours.
- Members of reserve components not on active duty are entitled at all times to purchase such necessary articles of uniform clothing, accouterments, and equipment as would be required immediately when called to active duty.
- Unlimited exchange privileges are authorized for reserve component personnel who participate in regularly scheduled inactive duty training on the basis of one day of exchange use privileges for each day of inactive duty training performed. This training must be appropriately documented by the individual's commander.

*Identification.* All patrons must identify themselves as a person entitled to full or restricted privileges at the time purchase is made. Dependents and nonuniformed people are required to obtain an official DD Form 1173, *Identification and Privilege Card.* Widows and widowers and retired personnel will be obliged to establish their right to purchase by the same card. Uniformed people should be prepared to display their official identification card or official orders as may be required by the exchange officer before a sale is made.

**Private Practice by Medical and Dental Officers.** Private practice by medical and dental officers is strictly regulated by the Air Force. Established application procedures must be followed. Approval is not ordinarily granted unless there is demonstrated community need, including a letter in support of such need from the local medical or dental society. In no case may such practice be in conflict with military requirements, and the establishment of an office for the purpose of engaging in civilian practice is prohibited. Medical officers engaging in private practice must be licensed in that state and must provide their own professional liability insurance.

The same provisions govern private practice for dental officers.

**Concessions and Scholarships at Civilian Educational Institutions.** Several civilian educational institutions offer concessions to service children and grant scholarships to discharged airmen whose records and educational qualifications warrant the action. Any person in the military service who desires information relating to scholarships should apply directly to the sponsoring activity, or at base level, go through the personal affairs office in the military personnel flight (MPF) or the education office, which is under the director of personnel.

**Privileges Extended by Civilian Organizations.** In many localities, it is quite common for civilian professional, civic, golf, or social clubs to extend the privilege of membership to officers stationed at a nearby military establishment. This custom (which is by no means universal) is of great importance to officers. It enables some among them to obtain a desired membership without the costly entrance fees charged in some instances.

**Abuse of Privilege.** The evil that has been practiced by the few and that has discredited many of the officer corps is *abuse of privilege.* It consists of taking advantage of position or rank to secure pleasures or facilities to which one is not entitled by law, regulation, or custom. It is "getting away with something." This chapter is an attempt to clarify what is meant by proper benefits so that the proper officer may observe and evaluate alleged rights and privileges before practicing them. The selfish and grasping may not be deterred. But the officer who might offend innocently may be helped on a correct course.

Here is a simple way to determine whether an alleged benefit or privilege is genuine or spurious. Find the answers to these two questions:

- Can you establish authorization in any current departmental or major command document?
- Observe the five or ten best officers of experience known to you whom you observe frequently. They must have high standing as good officers among their colleagues. Is the questioned privilege used or practiced by half or more of them?

## THE TREATMENT OF PRISONERS OF WAR

Applying this analysis of rights and privileges to the status and situation of a prisoner of war is especially important to all who wear their country's uniform.

**Prisoner of War Code of Conduct.** The following executive order established rights and restrictions that apply to servicemembers under the code of conduct for members of the U.S. armed forces, which also appears here:

### EXECUTIVE ORDER 10631

*Code of Conduct for Members of the Armed Forces of the United States.* By virtue of the authority vested in me as President of the United States and as Commander in Chief of the armed forces of the United States, I hereby prescribe the Code of Conduct for Members of the Armed Forces of the United States which is attached to this order and hereby made a part thereof.

Every member of the armed forces of the United States is expected to measure up to the standards embodied in this Code of Conduct while he is in combat or in captivity. To ensure achievement of these standards, each member of the armed forces liable to capture shall be provided with specific training and instruction designed to better equip him to counter and withstand all enemy efforts against him, and shall be fully instructed as to the behavior and obligations expected of him during combat or captivity.

The Secretary of Defense (and the Secretary of the Treasury with respect to the Coast Guard except when it is serving as part of the Navy) shall take such action as is deemed necessary to implement this order and to disseminate and make the said Code known to all members of the armed forces of the United States.

Dwight D. Eisenhower

The White House
August 17, 1955

---

**CODE OF CONDUCT FOR MEMBERS OF THE U.S. ARMED FORCES***

**I**

**I am an American, fighting in the forces which guard my country and our way of life. I am prepared to give my life in their defense.**

**II**

**I will never surrender of my own free will. If in command I will never surrender the members of my command while they still have the means to resist.**

**III**

**If I am captured I will continue to resist by all means available. I will make every effort to escape and aid others to escape. I will accept neither parole nor special favors from the enemy.**

**IV**

**If I become a prisoner of war, I will keep faith with my fellow prisoners. I will give no information or take part in any action which might be harmful to my comrades. If I am senior, I will take command. If not, I will obey the lawful orders of those appointed over me and will back them up in every way.**

**V**

**When questioned, should I become a prisoner of war, I am required to give my name, rank, service number, and date of birth. I will evade answering further questions to the utmost of my ability. I will make no oral or written statements disloyal to my country and its allies or harmful to their cause.**

**VI**

**I will never forget that I am an American, fighting for freedom, responsible for my actions, and dedicated to the principles which made my country free. I will trust in my God and in the United States of America.**

---

*As amended, May 1988.

The Secretary of Defense has directed training under the code in three main phases:

• A general citizenship type of orientation.

• A formal course for combat crews likely to fall into enemy hands, which could include training in avoiding capture, survival while evading or during captivity, resistance to giving information and making false "confessions," and escape attempts.

• A specialized course for selected students, which could include prisoner interrogation, and treatment courses of definite duration designed to toughen individual students and to let them test their resistance ability and determine their physical and mental weaknesses.

## RESTRICTIONS

There are many *Thou shalt nots* in the military life. They consist for the most part of restrictions or standards of conduct inapplicable to the civilian. Some are in federal laws. Others are in departmental regulations. A few are in observed customs. They need not be regarded as onerous. They have come about through experience and necessity. In any event, they are well balanced by military benefits. Because their violation would be regarded as a serious matter, at the worst resulting in trial by a court-martial, officers should know of them.

**Effect of Conduct Unbecoming an Officer.** Article 133 of the Uniform Code of Military Justice reads as follows: *"Any officer, cadet, or midshipman who is convicted of conduct unbecoming an officer and a gentleman shall be punished as a court-martial may direct."* (Manual for Courts-Martial, United States, 1951.)

There are certain moral attributes common to the ideal officer, a lack of which is indicated by acts of dishonesty or unfair dealing, of indecency or indecorum, or of lawlessness, injustice, or cruelty. Not everyone is or can be expected to meet ideal standards or to possess the attributes in the exact degree demanded by the standards of the time; but there is a limit of tolerance below which the individual standards of officers or cadets cannot fall without their being morally unfit to be officers or cadets. This UCMJ article contemplates such conduct by officers or cadets that, taking all the circumstances into consideration, satisfactorily shows much moral unfitness.

This article includes acts made punishable by any other article of the code, provided such acts amount to conduct unbecoming an officer; thus, an officer who embezzles military property violates both this and the article dealing with embezzlement.

Instances of violation of this article include such as these: knowingly making a false official statement; dishonorable neglect to pay debts; opening and reading another's letters without authority; giving a check on a bank where one knows or reasonably should know there are no funds to meet it and without intending that there should be; using insulting or defamatory language to other officers in their presence or about them to other military persons; being grossly drunk and conspicuously disorderly in a public place; public association with notorious prostitutes; cruel treatment of airmen; committing or attempting to commit a crime involving moral turpitude; failing without good cause to support one's family.

**Sexual Harassment.** The problem of sexual harassment (a form of gender discrimination) in the workplace has received much attention in recent years, and military officials have been challenged to define sexual harassment and develop investigation procedures that protect the rights of accusers and accused. Sexual harassment often is hard to identify and even harder to prove. The number of sexual harassment complaints within the military has risen recently, and about 25 percent come from men.

It should go without saying that officers should behave in a professional manner at all times, offering all associates the respect due fellow members of the Air Force. Anyone, regardless of sex, who experiences sexual harassment should try to rectify the situation through the chain of command. Harassers may receive administrative punishment or be court-martialed, depending on the nature and severity of the offense.

**Fraternization.** To fraternize, according to Webster's, is "to associate in a brotherly manner; be on friendly terms." What the Air Force means by the word is any improper relationship between persons of different ranks. A relationship is improper if it meets one of the following criteria: It causes actual or perceived partiality or favoritism; it involves the improper use of rank or position for personal gain; or it would have a clearly predictable, adverse impact on discipline, authority, or morale.

Usually, fraternization is thought of as occurring between officers of different ranks or between officers and enlisted personnel. Under Article 134 of the Uniform Code of Military Justice, if an officer's fraternizing meets any of the elements of proof listed there, criminal charges may be brought to bear. An officer who has direct command or supervisory authority over others or who has the capability to influence personnel or disciplinary actions, assignments, or other benefits or privileges, must exercise the utmost restraint in social, commercial, or duty relationships with lower-ranking personnel.

**Removal from the Active List for Cause.** AFR 36-2 provides procedures by which the Secretary of the Air Force may remove from the active list any officer who is derelict in respect to meeting standards of moral conduct or of professional performance or otherwise in the interests of the national security.

**Liability Regarding Classified Documents.** By the very nature of their duties, officers are required to have possession of and to use classified documents. Officers must be mindful of the restrictions placed upon such documents and the punitive action that may be taken against them for improper handling or use.

AFR 205-1, *Information Security Program,* is the principal source of instructions for dealing with classified information. The inclusion of classified military information in any article, speech, or discussion by a member of the Air Force of the United States is prohibited unless specifically authorized:

> Whoever, being entrusted with or having lawful possession or control of any document, writing, code book, signal book, sketch, photograph, photographic negative, blueprint, plan, map, model, note, or information, relating to the national defense, through gross negligence permits the same to be removed from its proper place of custody or delivered to anyone in violation of his trust, or to be lost, stolen, abstracted, or destroyed, shall be punished by imprisonment for not more than ten years and may, in the discretion of the court, be fined not more than $10,000. (June 5, 1917, c. 30, Title I, Sec. 1; 40 Stat. 217. Act of March 28, 1940; Public Law No. 443, 76th Congress, 3d Session.)

**Officer in Arrest.** An officer in arrest cannot exercise command of any kind. (Para. 20a, *Manual for Courts-Martial*, U.S., 1951.)

**Officers Suspended from Rank or Command.** Officers suspended from either rank or command and airmen serving sentence of confinement are prohibited from wearing decorations, medals, or substitutes therefor.

**Effect of Disrespectful Language Concerning Certain Government Officials.** The 88th Article of the Uniform Code of Military Justice reads as follows:

*Any officer who uses contemptuous words against the President, Vice President, Congress, Secretary of Defense, or a Secretary of a Department, a Governor or a legislature of any State, Territory, or other possession of the United States in which he is on duty or present shall be punished as a court-martial may direct.*

**Restrictions on Outside Activities.** Officers will not engage in or permit their names to be connected with any activity, participation in which is incompatible with the status of an officer.

There are limitations on officers and other personnel subject to military law relating to the activities outside of their military duties in which they may properly engage and upon the outside interests they may have without impropriety. Some outside activities and interests are specifically prohibited by statute or regulation or both; but there are many others from which certain military personnel are barred by the high standards of conduct required of persons in the military service. The general principle underlying the limitations mentioned above is that every member of the military establishment, when subject to military law, is bound to refrain from all business and professional activities and interests not directly connected with military duties, participation in which activities or interests would tend to interfere with or hamper in any degree full and proper discharge of such duties or would normally give rise to a suspicion that such participation would have that effect. Any substantial departure from this underlying principle would constitute conduct punishable under the articles of the Uniform Code of Military Justice.

It is impossible to enumerate all the various outside activities to which the above restriction applies. The following examples may be regarded as typical: (1) Acceptance by an officer or, with the approval of the officer, by a member of the officer's immediate family of a substantial loan or gift or any emolument from a person or firm with whom it is the officer's duty as an agent of the government to carry on negotiations. (2) Acquisition or possession by an officer of a financial interest in any concern whose business includes the manufacture and sale of articles of a kind of which it is the duty of the officer to make purchases for the government.

An officer who is engaged or who contemplates engaging in outside professional or business activities should learn pertinent laws, regulations, and standards of the service, in order to determine conscientiously and impartially whether or not such activities or interests might be considered as being in any way incompatible with the proper performance of official duties or in any sense adverse to the interests of the government. If after such investigation there is any doubt, the individual concerned should report all pertinent facts to the Department of the Air Force and request instructions. An officer who has certain outside interests that have no bearing upon the performance of military duties at the time of acquiring such interests, and who is later assigned to duties in the performance of which the possession of such interests might normally be suspected of having an influence adverse to the interests of the government, will immediately dispose of such outside interests and report the facts to superior military authority or without disposing of such interests will report all pertinent facts and circumstances to superior authority with a view to change assignments or such other action as may be deemed appropriate.

*Acting as Attorney or Agent.* No member of the military establishment on the active list or on active duty or a civilian employee whose official duties are concerned with patent activities shall act as agent or attorney in connection with the inventions or patent rights of others, except when such action is a part of the official duties of the person so acting.

*Acting as Consultant for Private Enterprise Prohibited.* No member of the military establishment on the active list or on active duty, or a civilian employee of the Air Force or of the Department of the Air Force shall act as a consultant for a private enterprise with regard to any matter in which the government is interested (AFR 30-30).

**Assistance to Persons Preparing for Civil Service Examinations Prohibited.** No officer or employee of the government will, directly or indirectly, instruct or be concerned in any manner in the instruction of any person or classes of persons, with a view to their special preparation for the examination of the U.S. Civil Service Commission or of the boards of examiners for the diplomatic and consular services. *The fact that any officer or employee is found so engaged will be considered sufficient cause for removal from the service.*

**Solicitation for Contributions for Gifts Prohibited.** No officer, clerk, or employee in the U.S. government employ shall at any time solicit contributions from officers, clerks, or employees in the government service for a gift or present to those in a superior official position. *Every person who violates this section shall be summarily discharged from the government employ* (R.S. 1784).

**Acceptance of Gifts from Subordinates Prohibited.** No official or clerical superior shall receive any gift or present offered or presented as a contribution from persons in government employ receiving a lesser salary. *Every person who violates this section shall be summarily discharged from government employ* (R.S. 1784).

**Receiving Gifts from Civilian Sources in Recognition of Services Prohibited.** The practice of receiving presents from persons not in the military establishment or in the employ of the government in recognition of services or from firms or their representatives with whom the officer has negotiated as an agent of the government is prohibited. Officers will exercise their influence over members of their immediate families to ensure that contributions or gifts are not received or accepted from such persons or firms (AFR 30-30).

**Effect of Refusal of Medical Treatment.** An officer or airman may be brought to trial by court-martial for refusing to submit to a surgical or dental operation or to medical or dental treatment at the hands of the military authorities if it is designed to restore or increase fitness for service and is without risk of life.

**Communication with Members of Congress.** Communication with members of Congress by personnel of the Air Force on matters of personal interest is restricted only by the provisions of AFR 11-7, as amended, and the provisions of 10 USC 1034, which states, "No person may restrict any member of an armed force in communicating with a member of Congress, unless the communication is unlawful or violates a regulation necessary to the security of the United States." All members of the Air Force, however, are advised that all legislative matters affecting the Department of the Air Force program shall be conducted through the office of the Secretary of the Air Force or as authorized by that office.

**Action on Attempts to Secure Personal Favor.** Except when properly made by the officers themselves, requests for personal favor or consideration for any officers will be referred to the officers in question for statement whether they directly or indirectly procured the request to be made and whether they avow or disavow the request as one on their behalf.

**Writing Checks with Insufficient Funds and Payment of Debts.** When considered necessary, commanders concerned will take action under Article 133 or 134, Uniform

Code of Military Justice, in cases in which members of their command issue checks against accounts with insufficient funds therein or fail to clear their personal accounts before departure from their station. When information of indebtedness is received after the departure of an individual, the commander of the station at which personal accounts remain unsettled will correspond with the person's new commander to obtain prompt settlement.

**Restrictions on Using Franked Envelopes and Letterheads.** All Department of the Air Force letterheads, envelopes, and other stationery are for OFFICIAL use only and will not be used as personal stationery.

# 8

# Leave

*A certain amount of leave, although not in any contract of service, is a recognized part of a soldier's life.*

—Winston Churchill, 1943

The privilege of taking leave is a valuable attribute of military service, and the Air Force encourages its members to take leave. Arrange duties so that both you and your subordinates can take all leave due. Particularly encourage any members who are exhibiting signs of impending physical or mental breakdown to take leave to help lessen the effects of job stress leading to burnout, which too often can lead to the loss of very fine, dedicated, competent, conscientious Air Force officers and enlisted members.

Commanders should bear in mind that the persistence of conditions within their commands in time of peace that preclude granting leave to their officers is a most direct indication of poor organization, poor administration, or poor leadership. No military organization should rest on seemingly indispensable people. Moreover, commanders who grumble that they are so short of officers that they "can't afford" to permit their officers to take leave are admitting that they have no workable plan to meet the occurrence of sickness, accident, or death among their officers. Ultimately, such commanders will receive a cold letter from the inspector general pointing out their failure to comply with Air Force policy.

Conversely, if you are reluctant to take leave because you're afraid your unit can't get along without you for two weeks or a month, consider these thoughts: Your unit survived before you arrived; your unit will survive after you leave; if you died today of a heart attack at your duty station, your unit would survive and find time to do the paperwork for your death, attend your funeral, mourn your loss, request a replacement, and do your work in the meantime. It's your responsibility to organize your work so that both your seniors and your subordinates can function well in your absence; sometimes, it's good to let them miss you for a while.

## AIR FORCE POLICIES

Commanders will ensure that members of their commands have an opportunity and the encouragement to take leave. AFR 35-9 requires using leave as you earn it and discourages hoarding leave to build up large cash payments for unused leave upon discharge or retirement. Periods of cessation from routine work for the purpose of travel, healthful recreation, and diversion are essential to the efficiency of people in the military service. Commanders at all levels should encourage people in their commands to avail themselves frequently of accrued leave, and subject only to military necessity, all commanders will approve such requests of leave.

**Holidays.** The following days in each year are public holidays established by law, and the Air Force observes them except when military reasons prevent:

New Year's Day—1 January
Martin Luther King's Birthday—Third Monday in January
Washington's Birthday—Third Monday in February
Memorial Day—Last Monday in May
Independence Day—4 July
Labor Day—First Monday in September
Columbus Day—Second Monday in October
Veterans Day—11 November
Thanksgiving Day—Fourth Thursday in November
Christmas Day—25 December

When a holiday falls on a Sunday, the following day is a holiday. When a holiday falls on Saturday, the preceding day is a holiday.

## TYPES OF LEAVE

**Ordinary Leave.** Leave the Air Force grants you upon your request at any time during a fiscal year to the extent of the leave that you may earn during that fiscal year, plus your leave credit from previous years.

**Sick or Convalescent Leave.** Leave the Air Force grants you for absence because of illness or convalescence upon recommendation of the surgeon. It is not chargeable as leave.

**Advance Leave.** The Air Force may grant you advance leave in anticipation of the future accrual of leave. In the case of officers, such leave would apply in case of emergency leave and pre-embarkation leave.

**Emergency Leave.** Leave the Air Force may grant you upon assurance that an emergency exists and that granting of such leave will contribute to the alleviation of the emergency. The total leave advanced, including emergency leave, may not exceed 45 days. Emergency leave does not affect granting future leave, but the Air Force does charge it against present or future accrued leave.

**Excess Leave.** Leave the Air Force grants you that is in excess of the amount you have accrued, that is, except for such advance or ordinary leave as specifically authorized, without pay and allowances, and that you may take only under exceptional circumstances upon authority of commanders up to 30 days and of the Department of the Air Force for more than 30 days, such as to go to law school.

**Graduation Leave.** The Air Force grants graduates of the service academies leave (30 days not charged against accrued leave credits) from date of graduation if they are commissioned in the Air Force.

**Prenatal and Postpartum Leave.** Normally, a woman who becomes pregnant while on active duty goes into "sick in quarters" status about four weeks before delivery, as determined by the attending physician. Time spent in the hospital for delivery is duty time. Following completion of inpatient care, the member receives convalescent leave until her medical condition permits her to return to duty, normally not more than six weeks after her release from the hospital.

**Delays en Route in Executing Travel.** The Air Force counts and charges as leave authorized delays stated in travel orders.

## COMPUTATION OF LEAVE CREDITS

The Air Force credits leave on a fiscal year basis. In any case in which the Air Force considers only a part of the fiscal year, it will prorate earned leave at the rate of 2½ days for each month of active (honorable) service.

In all computations, the Air Force credits leave for portions of a month as follows:

1 to 6 days duty inclusive—½ day leave.
7 to 12 days inclusive—1 day leave.
13 to 18 days inclusive—1½ days leave.
19 to 24 days inclusive—2 days leave.
25 to 31 days inclusive—2½ days leave.

Leave may not accumulate in excess of 60 days (except that personnel in a combat zone may accumulate 90 days). Members of USAF Reserve Forces ordered to active duty for periods of 30 days or more will receive leave in accordance with these computations. Those ordered to active duty for periods of less than 30 days will not receive leave.

## COMPENSATION WHILE ON LEAVE

Personnel in the following circumstances shall receive the same pay and allowances while on leave that they would receive if on a duty status: when absent on sick or convalescent leave; absent with leave not exceeding the aggregate number of days' leave standing to their credit or authorized to be advanced to their credit; absent awaiting orders on disability retirement proceedings in excess of the number of days' leave accrued or authorized; and absent awaiting orders for initial duty station assignment for newly appointed officers of the Regular Air Force.

Personnel granted excess leave shall receive no pay or allowances while so absent from duty. The Air Force may, however, grant advance leave with pay and allowances, but if the member is separated before accruing sufficient leave to cover the advance leave, the Air Force will consider the unaccrued portion excess leave without pay and allowances.

## APPLICATION FOR LEAVE

Use AF Form 988 to apply for leave. State the amount of leave desired and the amount of accumulated leave due. Generally, you must also give an address where the

Air Force can reach you while you are on leave. For form and channels, consult your personnel officer.

**Day of Departure; Day of Return on Duty Days.** The Air Force will charge you both the day of departure and the day of return as leave unless you were present for duty all or nearly all of the normal working day on either the day of commencement or termination of the leave period.

**Day of Departure; Day of Return on Nonduty Days.** When you sign out on a nonduty day, the Air Force will charge that day as leave. When you sign in on a nonduty day, the Air Force will not charge that day as leave.

**Leave to Visit outside the United States.** Air Force officers may visit foreign countries on leave, either from the United States or from their oversea station, in accordance with procedures set forth in AFR 35-9. Such leaves are chargeable as ordinary leave.

To visit communist or communist-oriented countries, officers must comply with the provisions of Ch. 4, Para. 1, AFR 35-9.

**Warnings.** As an officer, you are responsible to report to your *duty* station, not just any Air Force station, at the expiration of your leave. You may use military air transport on a space-available basis during leave, but a delay in securing a flight is no excuse for failing to return from leave on time.

Above all, use your leave as a time for mental and physical rejuvenation. Toward this end, avoid killing yourself on the highway, drinking all the liquor available, or spending next year's income. Have fun, but take it easy.

# 9

# Leadership

*Leadership is the most important consideration, if any one thing is more important than another.*

—General of the Army George C. Marshall

Leadership is essential to a successful officer. If you glanced at the other chapter titles of this book, you would note topics of importance to officers, such as the art of training, the preparation of performance reports, and the proper way to wear the uniform. Increased proficiency in these matters will make a good officer a better officer. But such proficiency is not essential to an officer. *Leadership is essential.* When we consider other attributes of successful officers, we can recall specific exceptions to all save leadership. General Ulysses S. Grant almost never wore his uniform properly and used liquor to excess, yet he knew how to win a war. General Forrest, he of the "git thar fustest with the mostest" philosophy, was nearly illiterate. Yet, he was a genius in battle. Robert E. Lee, the model, combined every desirable attribute of an officer within himself. But of all his galaxy of military attributes, that which shone brightest in Lee was leadership. Renowned Air Force officers such as Arnold, Vandenberg, and LeMay were men of many talents, but their outstanding talent was leadership.

A young officer should look forward with pleasure and keen anticipation to the opportunity to lead. It is the most exciting and interesting experience the service can offer you. The Air Force does not expect that you will equal an Arnold, a Vandenberg, or a LeMay, but who can tell? Some writers have described the leaders wanted so badly and in such large numbers as "the good, common, garden variety of leaders; officers who can inculcate those under them with knowledge of their tasks and imbue them with the spirit to do them well." That goal is not impossible. With application, a person who meets the standards for commissioned officers can be that sort of good leader.

A *leader* is one fitted by force of ideas, character, or genius or by strength of will or administrative ability to arouse, incite, and direct individuals in conduct and achievement.

*Leadership* means the art of imposing one's will upon others in such a manner as to command their respect, their confidence, and their wholehearted cooperation. The core of the definition is that you must impose your will on others; they must do what you direct them to do.

The martinet accomplishes this goal by simple reliance upon his position of authority and his power of punishment. The leader accomplishes it through that quality of leadership the Air Force seeks. In the case of the martinet, the people commanded do what the martinet directs them to do, but often in a sullen and grudging manner. In the case of the leader, the people carry out directions with zip and enthusiasm, contributing their own native American ingenuity and drive to the task at hand.

The remainder of this chapter is largely taken from AFP 35-49, *Air Force Leadership,* prepared by the Military Personnel Center in the office of Maj. F. L. Johnson and written and edited by Ms. Barbara Carver. The material provides a basic guide for Air Force leaders.

## THE AIR FORCE LEADERSHIP CONCEPT

Leadership is the art of influencing and directing people to accomplish a mission. As an effective leader, the basic concept you must keep in mind encompasses two fundamental elements: the mission and the people. This is the Air Force concept of leadership, and all facets of Air Force leadership should support these two basic elements. They are embedded in the definition of leadership.

**The Mission.** The primary task of a military organization is to perform its mission. This is paramount, and everything else must be subordinate to this objective. As a leader, your primary responsibility is to lead people to carry out the unit's mission successfully. Former Air Force Chief of Staff General Curtis E. LeMay emphasized, "No matter how well you apply the art of leadership, no matter how strong your unit or how high the morale of your men, if your leadership is not directed completely toward the mission, your leadership has failed." Yet you must never forget the importance of the unit's personnel.

**The People.** People perform the mission. They are the heart of the organization and without their support a unit will fail. Your responsibilities include the care and support of your unit's personnel. To be a successful leader, you must continually ensure that the needs of the people in your unit are met promptly and properly.

Clearly, the two "simple" parts of the leadership concept—mission and people—are actually two very complicated elements. Successful leaders who effectively deal with this complex concept have certain characteristics or traits.

## LEADERSHIP TRAITS

Effective leaders have certain distinguishing characteristics that are the foundation for their approach to the leadership situation. The list of a leader's desirable qualities is virtually endless. While many characteristics (such as truthfulness) are expected of all members of the military profession, six traits are vital to Air Force leaders.

**Integrity.** Integrity is a total commitment to the highest personal and professional standards. As a leader, you must be honest and fair. Integrity means establishing a set of values and adhering to those values. Air Force Chief of Staff General Charles A. Gabriel said, "Integrity is the fundamental premise of military service in a free society. Without integrity, the moral pillars of our military strength—public trust and self-respect—are lost."

**Loyalty.** Loyalty, a three-dimensional trait, includes faithfulness to superiors, peers, and subordinates. You must first display an unquestionable sense of loyalty before you can expect members of your unit to be loyal. General George S. Patton, Jr., highlighted the importance of loyalty when he said, "There is a great deal of talk about loyalty from the bottom to the top. Loyalty from the top down is even more necessary and much less prevalent."

**Commitment.** Commitment means complete devotion to duty. As a leader, you must demonstrate total dedication to the United States, the Air Force, and your unit. Plato said, "Man was not born for himself alone, but for his country." Dedicated service is the hallmark of the military leader.

**Energy.** Energy is an enthusiasm and drive to take the initiative. Throughout history, successful leaders have demonstrated the importance of mental and physical energy. You must approach assigned tasks aggressively. Your preparation should include physical and mental conditioning that will enable you to look and act the part. Once a course of action is determined, you must have the perseverance and stamina to stay on course until the job is completed.

**Decisiveness.** Decisiveness is a willingness to act. As a leader you must have the self-confidence to make timely decisions. You must then effectively communicate the decisions to your unit. British Admiral Sir Roger Keyes emphasized that "in all operations a moment arrives when brave decisions have to be made if an enterprise is to be carried through." Of course, decisiveness includes the willingness to accept responsibility. You are always accountable—when things go right and when things go wrong.

**Selflessness.** Selflessness requires sacrificing personal requirements for a greater cause. You must think of performing the mission and caring for the welfare of the men and women in your organization. As an Air Force leader, you cannot place your own comfort or convenience before the mission or the people. Willingness to sacrifice is intrinsic to military service. Selflessness also includes the courage to face and overcome difficulties. While courage is often thought of as an unselfish willingness to confront physical dangers, equally important—and more likely to be tested on a daily basis—is the moral courage you need to make difficult decisions. General Douglas MacArthur said, "No nation can safely trust its martial honor to leaders who do not maintain the universal code which distinguishes those things that are right and those things that are wrong." It requires courage and strength of character to confront a tough situation head-on rather than avoiding it by passing the buck to someone else.

These traits are essential to effective leadership. Developing these characteristics will improve your ability to employ the principles of leadership.

## LEADERSHIP PRINCIPLES

Leadership principles are rules or guides that have been tested and proven over the years by successful leaders. The most important of these principles are discussed below.

**Know Your Job.** People will follow you if you are a competent person who has the knowledge needed to complete the mission successfully. You should have a broad view of your unit's mission, and you must make sure all members of your unit understand how their jobs relate to mission accomplishment.

Between World War I and World War II, the United States Army Air Corps was fortunate to have men like General Henry Arnold and General Carl Spaatz. These men learned their jobs and knew how they could enhance the Air Corps mission. Their preparation and vision paid substantial dividends when they were charged with building a force to fight and win the air battles of World War II.

Just as important as your own competence is ensuring that assigned people know their responsibilities. Former Chairman of the Joint Chiefs of Staff General Maxwell D. Taylor stated, "One expects a military leader to demonstrate in his daily performance a thorough knowledge of his own job and further an ability to train his subordinates in their duties and thereafter to supervise and evaluate their work."

**Know Yourself.** Knowing your own strengths and weaknesses is important to successful leadership. You, the leader, must recognize your personal capabilities and limitations. Former Chief Master Sergeant of the Air Force Robert D. Gaylor put it this way: "Sure, everyone wants to be an effective leader, whether it be in the Air Force or in the community. You can and will be if you identify your strengths, capitalize on them, and consciously strive to reduce and minimize the times you apply your style inappropriately."

**Set the Example.** You must set the standard for your unit. People will emulate your standards of personal conduct and appearance. They will observe your negative characteristics as well as your positive ones. If you are arrogant or domineering, you will deserve no respect, only resentment. If you violate basic standards of morality, you will invariably end up in a compromising situation. If you drink excessively or abuse controlled drugs, you send a dangerous message: I cannot control myself; how can I control you? Lack of self-discipline in a leader destroys the unit's cohesion and, ultimately, impairs its ability to perform the mission.

Self-discipline also pertains to physical fitness. When you are in good physical condition, you are better prepared for any assigned mission. Setting the right example includes supporting a unit physical fitness program and enforcing Air Force weight standards. As a military leader, you must be a positive example of professional conduct, appearance, and physical conditioning. As General George S. Patton, Jr., once remarked, "You are always on parade."

**Care for People.** General of the Army George C. Marshall believed, "A decent regard for the rights and feelings of others is essential to leadership." Take care of the people. Find out what their requirements are and be sensitive to human needs. Are the people housed adequately; are they well fed; are they paid promptly; are there personal problems with which they need help? When people are worried about these conditions, they cannot focus their full attention on their job, and the mission will suffer. If people believe they are cared for as well as circumstances will permit, you, as leader, are in a position to earn their confidence, respect, and loyalty.

**Communicate.** Information should flow continuously throughout the organization. Former Air Force Chief of Staff General Thomas D. White believed, "Information is the essential link between wise leadership and purposeful action." Communication is a two-way process. Only as an informed leader will you be able to evaluate realistically your unit's progress toward mission accomplishment. You must listen to what your people have to say and always look for the good ideas that can flow up the chain. It is also key to emphasize the importance of feedback. The worker who is well informed concerning the quality of the work and its importance within the job will be more effective and highly motivated. It is your job to keep all channels open. The more senior you become, the more listening skills will be required.

**Educate.** People should be properly trained to do their jobs. Professional military education, professional development education, technical training schools, and on-the-job training are formal means by which Air Force personnel are trained. Informal training, practice, and personal experience at the unit level are crucial reinforcements to formal training. General of the Army Douglas MacArthur observed, "In no other profession are the penalties for employing untrained personnel so appalling or so irrevocable as in the military."

**Equip.** It is also your responsibility to ensure the unit is equipped properly. Just as an aircrew should never be expected to engage in combat without a well-armed aircraft, personnel should not be sent ill-equipped to the office, shop, or flightline. Your leadership responsibilities include identifying needs, securing funds, and then obtaining the necessary weapons, tools, and equipment.

**Motivate.** Your greatest challenge is motivating subordinates to achieve the high standards set for them. Motivation is the moving force behind successful leadership. In fact, the ability to generate enthusiasm about the mission may be the single most important factor in leadership. Recognition of the efforts people put forth is one positive way in which motivation toward mission accomplishment pays dividends. When you publicly applaud the efforts of unit personnel, you build a cohesive organization that will accomplish the mission.

To motivate people, you must understand their needs and work to align these needs with unit requirements. Most people will work for an organization that they know cares about them, and one in whose mission they believe. Remember, the most powerful form of lasting motivation is self-motivation. One of your goals as a leader should be to provide an environment that fosters and rewards self-motivation.

**Accept Your Responsibility.** General LeMay was once asked to provide a one-word definition of leadership. After some thought, he replied, "If I had to come up with one word to define leadership, I would say responsibility." As a leader, you are responsible for performing the unit's mission. If you fail, you are accountable for the consequences. Any unwillingness to accept responsibility for failure destroys your credibility as a leader and breaks the bond of respect and loyalty. Accountability also includes the requirement for discipline within a unit. A leader should reward a job well done and punish those who fail to meet their responsibilities or established standards. The former is easy and enjoyable; the latter is much more difficult, but equally necessary. George Washington observed, "Discipline is the soul of an Army. It makes small numbers formidable; procures success to the weak, and esteem to all."

**Develop Teamwork.** As a leader, you must mold a collection of individual performers into a cohesive team that works together to accomplish the mission. The unit's mission will suffer if each person in your organization is "doing his own thing" in isolation. As the leader, you should know how the various functions within the unit fit together and how they must work in harmony. You should create and maintain an atmosphere of teamwork and cooperation to meet mission demands. Teamwork comes when people are willing to put the unit's mission before all else.

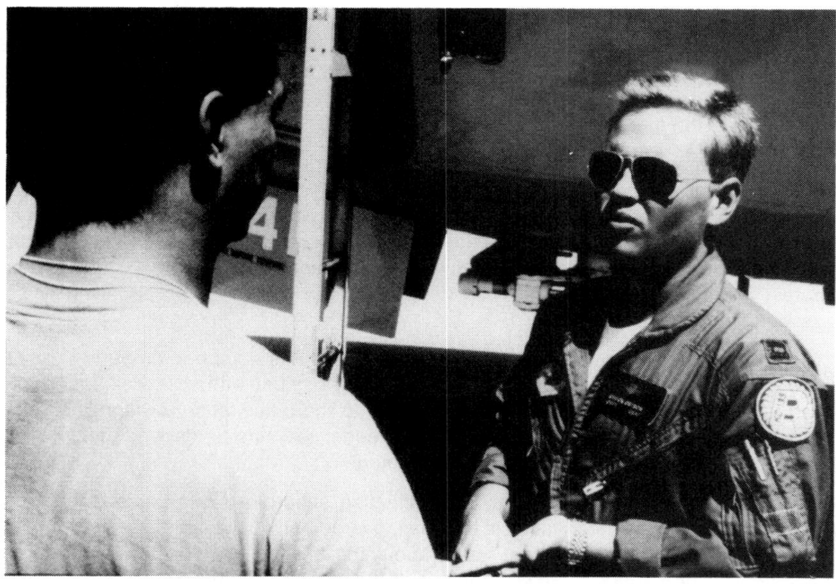

OFFICER-AIRMAN TEAMWORK IN THE PERSIAN GULF.

## THE LEADERSHIP SITUATION

Leadership has been defined as the art of influencing and directing people to accomplish the mission. Management is the manner in which resources are used to achieve objectives. As a military leader, you should also be aware of your responsibility as an Air Force manager. British Field Marshal Lord Slim made a clear distinction:

> There is a difference between leadership and management. The leader and the men who follow him represent one of the oldest, most natural, and most effective of all human relationships. The manager and those he manages are a later product with neither so romantic, nor so inspiring a history. Leadership is of the spirit, compounded of personality and vision—its practice is an art. Management is of the mind, more a matter of accurate calculation, statistics, methods, timetables, and routine—its practice is a science. Managers are necessary; leaders are essential.

In essence, you lead people and you manage things. The Air Force needs people who can do both. The requirement is for the proper division of attention between the two, with the proportion dependent on the situation. You should approach each leadership situation by paying careful attention to the four primary factors: the mission, the people, the leader, and the environment.

**The Mission.** Most missions involve many tasks that must be completed if your unit is to fulfill its responsibilities. As the leader, you must define the mission and set priorities for its various components. In many instances the mission has been defined by higher headquarters, but you should translate the higher direction into goals with which people will relate. When possible, you should involve unit personnel in setting these goals to ensure their support. Individual involvement is very important when total effort is needed from everyone. The goals must be challenging but attainable. Goals that are unrealistic frustrate even the most dedicated people.

Set reasonable and acceptable standards of job performance to make sure that goals are met. These standards must be consistent with the mission and defined clearly for every individual. Recognize those who meet or exceed standards, prescribe additional training for those who cannot, and take corrective action for those who will not. When standards are not met, you must determine the reason and move quickly to correct the situation through training or, if appropriate, administrative or disciplinary action. Get the facts, then act.

**The People.** Be sensitive to people. People perform the mission. Understanding people helps determine the appropriate leadership action to take in a given situation. You cannot be totally successful at getting the most out of people without first knowing the capabilities of those you are leading. Capability has two principal elements: training and experience.

*Training.* You should assess the level of your unit's training. If the people are not trained, do what it takes to get them the necessary training. People joined the Air Force to be part of a team with an important mission. They cannot do it without proper training. Medal of Honor recipient Sgt. John L. Levitow credited his heroic action under fire to the training he had received from the Air Force.

*Experience.* Levels of experience vary widely. You should learn each individual's experience and ability to perform in various situations. Do not base your evaluation of an individual's experience solely on rank. While rank may be a good overall experience indicator, the person may have never done a particular job or been in a particular environment before—and there are those who learn faster than others. Knowing the experience or knowledge level of the unit's personnel is an important aspect of your leadership style.

**The Leader.** Successful military leaders adapt their leadership style to meet the mission demands, and use an approach that capitalizes on their strengths. For example, if you are able to communicate effectively with people on an individual basis but are uncomfortable when speaking to large groups, then use personal conferences as much as possible. If you write well, take advantage of this skill by writing letters of appreciation or using other forms of correspondence. If you are a good athlete, organize and participate in unit sports activities.

In addition to capitalizing on your strengths and minimizing your weaknesses, your style of leadership must correspond to the people's job knowledge. When they lack sufficient knowledge to do the job at hand, you must spend much of your time directing their efforts to accomplish the mission.

On the other hand, if people have some training or experience, you are not required to direct their every action and should not do so. Still, you must motivate them to complete the task. Work with them, but keep your eye on the objective.

Occasionally, you may discover that people are only moderately motivated to do a job they are capable of completing. In such circumstances, let them participate in planning the task. Motivate them by maintaining a job-related working relationship. Their capabilities will do the rest.

When the people have extensive experience and are enthusiastic about the task, you should provide them greater freedom to complete it the way they choose. You, as the leader, are still ultimately responsible for the mission, so stay informed of the group's progress.

There is no one perfect leadership style. Rather, the most effective style is the one that the leader tailors to the mission, the people, and the environment, which is discussed next.

**The Environment.** You should carefully consider the environment in which you work. Leadership methods that worked in one situation with one group may not work with the same group in a different environment. Consider the squadron that is permanently based in the United States but deploys overseas for an extended period of temporary duty. Billeting or food service difficulties, equipment or parts shortages, family separation problems, inclement weather, and so forth may occur. Any of these problems creates an entirely new environment with which you must cope. As a unit leader, you must alter your leadership behavior, as necessary, to accommodate changes in the environment of the given mission. Be sensitive to your surroundings.

## LEADERSHIP PREPARATION

Now that we have explained some of the basics of Air Force leadership, here is how you can best prepare yourself to lead:

**Think about Leadership.** What would you do in a given situation, and why? If you were placed in charge of your work unit tomorrow, how would you act? Remember the traits and principles of Air Force leadership.

**Observe Leaders in Action.** How does your boss handle a given situation? Why did a particular action succeed or fail? How does your wing commander, squadron commander, first sergeant, or supervisor lead?

**Study Leadership and the Profession of Arms.** The military has a long tradition of leadership. Read about the successful leaders in our history and how they led. Alfred Thayer Mahan wrote, "The study of history lies at the foundation of all sound military conclusions and practice." You must have detailed professional knowledge to develop perspective and to meet the challenges of the future.

**Practice Leadership.** Look for opportunities to exercise leadership. It can be as simple as taking the initiative and leading one person to complete a task. Learn from your efforts, seek feedback, and evaluate your efforts. Always lead by positive example.

The United States was fortunate that between the world wars, several members of its military services prepared themselves to be leaders. Their preparation resulted in strong leadership during some of the most crucial years in our history. The Air Force has inherited a legacy of strong, dynamic leadership from the early air pioneers. As one of today's leaders, you must continue this tradition of excellence.

Don't confuse leadership with management, as some of your predecessors did. Leadership is about people; management is about things. First learn to lead and only then to manage.

## CONCLUSION

The Air Force depends on positive, effective leaders at all levels to perform the mission. Leadership is not the private domain or responsibility of senior officers or of noncommissioned officers. It is a responsibility for which every member of the Air Force must prepare.

General LeMay's words continue to serve us well: "I'm firmly convinced that leaders are not born; they're educated, trained, and made, as in every other profession." To ensure a strong, ready Air Force we must always remain dedicated to this process.

# 10

# Responsibilities of Command

*If officers desire to have control over their commands, they must remain habitually with them, industriously attend to their comforts, and in battle lead them well.*

—Stonewall Jackson

To the more junior officers of the Air Force nothing seems more remote from current or prospective duties than command of an Air Force unit. Command is indeed a rare assignment for Air Force officers of any grade. The officer strength of the Air Force is more than 100 times the number of Air Force units available to command: hence the rarity of command jobs. Yet consider another aspect of command. Command is not a function exercised solely by one officer, such as the squadron commander. The squadron commander cannot exercise command other than through the officer and noncommissioned officer members of the squadron. Each officer of the squadron not only is subject to command but also helps exercise command. Thus, every officer participates in the function of command. For this reason, all officers, whatever their grades or assignments, should understand the basic elements and objectives of the command function. They are part of the command operation, and it is one of the most important responsibilities. The command function has to do with the mission of the squadron or unit, with training, with discipline, with supply, and with morale. How could an officer not be involved in these factors? All officers should appreciate the responsibilities of their squadron or unit commander to better comprehend the reasons for the decisions of the commander, for one of the hallmarks of a professional is to appreciate the responsibilities of other members of the team and to assist in the discharge of those responsibilities.

## IMPORTANCE OF THE MILITARY MISSION

In the exercise of command, the very first necessity is to perform the mission. Orders may assign the mission. If so, just go ahead and do it. Often the assignment is general with an overall objective. You may then need to select and adopt successive missions, the sum of which will accomplish the requirement. Successful commanders are the ones who accomplish their missions on time with minimum expenditures of personnel and means and in a professional manner.

## TAKING CARE OF THE TROOPS

Next to the mission, the welfare of his or her people is a leader's most important responsibility because of its effect on their morale and their consequent ability to perform the mission. All leaders must interest themselves in all matters affecting the welfare of their people, including food, career guidance, adequate clothing and equipment, health and sanitation, recreation and entertainment, and personal problems. This responsibility involves planning, procurement and distribution of necessary supplies, training, frequent inspections, and corrective measures, which may include disciplinary action.

**Food.** Food must be well prepared, special efforts being made to ensure the best possible meals even under the most adverse conditions. The storing of food, the health and cleanliness of kitchen workers, the control of insects, the disposal of wastes, and the cleaning of utensils and other equipment are matters of strict daily supervision.

**Clothing.** Clothing must fit properly, must be properly worn and cared for, and be promptly salvaged and replaced when no longer usable. The uniform must be worn with pride. Care of clothing must be stressed as a necessary means of conserving national resources and government property and as a habit that will ensure dependable functioning under battle conditions when failure may prove costly.

**Health.** The sick rate is an indication of a unit's efficiency. Sanitary conditions in kitchens, mess halls, sleeping quarters, washrooms, latrines, and other sources of infection must be watched carefully. Instructions in health habits, provisions of the means for protecting health, and insistence on development of proper habits are equally important, especially under oversea conditions. Constant vigilance and frequent inspections are necessary.

**Recreation.** Wholesome recreation and entertainment must be provided, especially that which encourages active participation, physical development, and team spirit.

Leaves and passes must be granted impartially and as freely as the situation permits.

Consideration and, when possible, help must be given in dealing with personal problems. Young people away from home for the first time may need unsolicited advice.

The spirit behind the leader's interest must be one of genuine helpfulness and thoughtfulness. In matters involving the proper care of government property, protection of health, and fitness of the airman to perform assigned duties, stern measures are taken, if necessary.

## MILITARY SECURITY

Always there is the problem of security. Personnel must be ready to detect attack from the air or the ground. The repeated sudden attacks on Air Force bases during the Vietnam War are sufficient examples of the necessity for vigilance. Teach your people thoroughly the difficult art of security (see AFR 205 Series, AFR 206-2, and AFR 208-1).

## IMPORTANCE OF UNIT ADMINISTRATION

Administration begins in the squadron. That is where the airmen live and work and where changes in their status take place. That is where they are fed, housed, disciplined—and trained to become efficient, high-spirited fighting teams. The entire process of administering their affairs depends in large measure upon the initial action of the commander. If that first action by the commander and his lieutenants is speedy and accurate, the administrative process may then become a smooth-running operation of which the tactical commander is scarcely conscious.

Command of a unit includes a diversified responsibility over several different but interdependent phases of operation. The breakdown of one will have an injurious effect upon the others. Balance is required. These phases are organization, morale, discipline, training to develop battle efficiency, administration, food management, and supply.

**Classification and Assignment.** The Air Force has an excellent classification system that identifies special skills possessed by our airmen. After classification, people are assigned to units or other assignments in accordance with these skills. This knowledge is of inestimable value, because the use of skills reduces the training burden. Record is made of the classification, and it follows the airmen wherever they go.

There is no system of classification and assignment that cannot be nullified or destroyed by thoughtless commanders. Unfortunately, this happens too often. If a unit needs 10 truck drivers and gets them and 10 cooks and then assigns the truck drivers to the kitchen and the cooks to the trucks, the entire system becomes useless. This may sound silly or improbable, but search your own unit carefully, and see the extent to which you may be guilty!

Look at a unit manning document. Note the numbers along the edge; they are the Air Force specialty classification numbers, which refer to a particular classified skill or Air Force Specialty (AFS). Take the service records of your people; ascertain the classification numbers of their skills. Determine the exact job each person performs. Decide whether the skill of each individual is being fully used. As you proceed, study the training of each person to see whether that person is assigned to give the maximum value to the government. Check to see whether you have people of special skills that you do not require in your organization. You may be able to uncover some of the "rare birds" so badly needed by other units. If you find such individuals, report them, and perhaps by a little judicious trading, you can obtain people of skills you need in exchange for people who have skills you do not need.

The Air Force is vitally interested in placing all members where they can use their best talents. In so doing, we use the training of our industry, our schools, and our colleges. Don't be guilty of hiding a radio operator or an airplane mechanic, for example, when the Air Force is running great schools to develop such individuals without experience.

## THE SQUADRON COMMANDER

The commander is responsible for the execution of all activities pertaining to the unit, including the successful accomplishment of all missions assigned either in training or war. Commanders are responsible in every way for all that their organizations do or fail to do.

To a greater degree than other commanders, squadron commanders must be in intimate touch with their people and know their individual characteristics and capacities, their degree of training, their morale, and their discipline. They must provide for the welfare of their people in all ways and under all conditions. In training, they must prepare their own people to undergo the most rigorous hardships. In war or even on maneuvers, they must save them from all unnecessary trials to preserve their stamina. The conditions airmen experience in their own squadron determine their opinion of the Air Force as a whole.

There are several duties commanders cannot decentralize, such as responsibility for organization property, responsibility for the unit fund, nonjudicial punishment under Article 15 of the Uniform Code of Military Justice, and the authentication of many official records.

**Use of Subordinate Leaders.** The commander who attains high success will be adept at obtaining maximum efficiency from subordinate leaders. Their responsibilities should be clearly defined so that each may proceed with confidence.

Events that depart from routine must be disclosed to subordinate leaders in time to permit them to make their plans and prepare to do their several parts. A meeting may be held at which the requirement is discussed. Thought should be given to the manner of presenting the project before the group assembles. At the assembly, the commander should state the mission with its time and place of execution. Opportunity to ask questions should be provided. At the end of the meeting, the commander will have announced the decision and plan for the joint execution of a mission for which the commander alone is responsible.

Meetings of the key officers of a squadron should be held frequently. This is an opportunity for the commander to announce new work to be undertaken, specific small tasks to be completed in anticipation of a later action, and inspections and other matters that affect the squadron as a whole. Opportunity to make suggestions for improvement in conditions should be extended. A healthy reaction is obtained by asking opinions as to matters of general concern and interest. These meetings should be informal and brief. They provide an opportunity for the commander to obtain the cooperation of all subordinate leaders because they will know exactly what is wanted.

**Understudies and Replacements.** The services of key persons are often lost to an organization with disconcerting suddenness. The Air Force must maintain itself so that any officer, noncommissioned officer, or specialist may be immediately replaced without affecting the efficiency of any unit or activity. The training of understudies must be continuous.

The best people must convince themselves that they will receive consideration for appointment to higher responsibility or position if they prepare themselves for the task. Some regular procedure must be followed for the training of ambitious airmen who wish to demonstrate their capacity for advancement. As opportunity offers, airmen should be given a chance to exercise command or control of others to provide a means of further development. When this is done, the selection of the best people for advancement or for replacements is made more likely.

**Preparations to Be Relieved of Command.** The conditions of military service often result in a limited tenure of command by individual officers. While one should approach each current duty as if it would continue for a lifetime, officers know well that one day they must turn their outfits over to their reliefs.

Someone has said that the efficiency of a commander can be better judged after his or her relief from command. When command is relinquished it should be "clean" with no hidden skeletons, no loose ends to confound a successor unfamiliar with the problems. Property should be in good condition with no shortages not adjusted by the responsible officers, all required entries should be made in official records, and the unit fund should be built up and its exact status made entirely clear. The principle of *noblesse oblige* should be observed to the utmost.

It would seem to be a questionable practice for an officer about to be relieved to embark upon a program of expenditure of the unit fund. The successor may have ideas on these matters and be prevented from carrying them into execution.

The new commander should not be embarrassed by requests that are just within permissible practices. It is an imposition to ask a new commander to receipt for "overages" or "shortages," and if such request is made it should be refused. The successor should not be asked to complete transactions that should be finished by the officer being relieved.

It is reprehensible in the extreme to criticize the predecessor in command. Even in those few instances when it may be well deserved, it should be strictly avoided. But the officer being relieved can eliminate much of the chance of such criticism by being very certain to complete every required transaction, to inform the successor of every helpful bit of information (not forgetting the special desires and requirements of the immediate commander), and finally to transmit to the new commander an organization to be proud of.

## FOOD SERVICE MANAGEMENT (AFR 146 SERIES)

Food service management is the supervision and control exercised over every phase of the operation of a mess. The term *mess* is applied to those military groups who for convenience, sociability, or economy eat together. As used herein the term applies to squadron messes. Mess supervision is a function of command and is exercised, in some degree, by all commanders over the messes within their respective organizations. Direct control is exercised by the food service officer, who is assisted by the steward, cooks, and other food service personnel. Within the squadron, the food service officer may be either the commander or a designated officer. The phases of operation involved are the preparation of menus; the procurement and storage of food; the preparation, cooking, and serving of food; the proper use of the mess equipment; the economical and efficient use of rations; sanitation; and mess accounting.

**Object of Good Management.** The object of good food service management is to build and maintain an efficient, economical, and attractive mess. Nothing contributes more to the morale of an organization than the fulfillment of this mission. A good mess is the sum of good food ingredients, good cooks, good tools with which to work, and painstaking supervision. It is not necessary for a food service officer to be an expert in cooking and nutrition to accomplish this task; only to apply fundamental principles and check the operation daily to see that a variety of good food, balanced and properly cooked, is served under sanitary conditions, without waste, in an attractive manner.

## SUPPLY (AFM 67–1)

The United States has been lavish with money and effort to make our armed forces the best equipped of any. Most individuals understand this point clearly when they consider outstanding single items. The total number of separate items is infinite, and the cost, prodigious. The job of commanders is to obtain the items allowed for their units, see that they are issued to their people, and thereafter see that they are maintained in top-notch condition.

Tables of organization and tables of allowances show the articles authorized. The unit supply officer can provide all the necessary information. The unit commander must supply the energy, care, and attention to detail that are necessary to attain the required results. This is what unit commanders must do: find out the equipment authorized for their units; obtain it; distribute it; maintain the required records with accuracy; inspect the equipment; and maintain it always ready for use.

**Supply Personnel.** Responsibility for property is a function of command. The squadron administrative unit is the place of final distribution of supplies to airmen. Supplies are of small use unless they reach this ultimate point of distribution at the right time, in the right amounts, and in good condition. Tables of organization provide personnel for this function. Zealous, efficient, capable supply personnel are worth their weight in gold and will be much appreciated. Select the best individuals available for this assignment.

**Supply in the United States.** Unit commanders constantly face supply problems. The supply procedures require considerable bookkeeping and responsibility. It cannot be otherwise. The whole problem resolves itself into accomplishing two primary objectives: first, to equip the unit with the items needed; and second, to keep every last item of equipment in thoroughly serviceable condition.

The procedures for supply in the United States are adequately covered in instructions distributed to all organizations. Unit commanders should be certain they have in their possession the necessary current regulations and consult their unit supply officer to make certain they are fully informed as to the regulations pertaining to their own units. Thereafter, it is only a matter of execution.

**Supply in the Field.** As soon as a unit enters field conditions, as in the Persian Gulf, it faces a different sort of supply problem. But if any officers conclude that their "responsibility" has been left behind, they are in for a rude awakening. An officer is responsible for seeing that the enlisted personnel are provided with the items of equipment they require, in combat especially, and the penalty for carelessness or inefficiency may be to do without, which in combat may be the difference between victory and defeat.

Let us assume that a unit reaches an oversea area fully equipped. At once, things will happen that must be handled promptly. People are careless and they lose things. Property is lost by pilferage. It has been stated authoritatively that during the early years of World War II, losses from pilferage exceeded losses from enemy submarine action. There is also the temptation for sympathetic and liberal American airmen to give articles of clothing, food, and other necessities of life to poverty-stricken natives. The airmen may feel that they can obtain replenishment or have more equipment than they will need, anyway. There is even the temptation to sell articles to natives for disposal on thriving black markets. In any event, the commander of a small unit is responsible for having personnel of the unit fully equipped, and these are some of the matters that must be solved lest precious equipment vanish into thin air. The saying that lost articles will be found "on the payroll" may be exploited to curb carelessness. It will not solve the problem. Training to impress personnel with the importance to themselves of guarding their equipment jealously will help. Frequent and thorough property checks will also reduce losses and inform the commander of the unit's situation.

Wear and tear is a most difficult problem, especially in combat zones. Clothing especially wears out quickly. Lack of normal laundry facilities is an important factor. Higher commanders will provide for reserve stockage in bases and depots, but the unit commander must reduce wastage and present the needs in time for the supply or repair machinery to operate.

Commanders of units must gain a complete understanding of the system of supply. The supply of rations will be automatic, and quantity will depend upon the number of people they must feed. They must, however, know the time and place of deliveries and take the steps necessary to obtain them. The supply of fuel and ammunition will be automatic in the sense that it will be available at distribution points. But they must know where these points are and the things that must be done to replenish stockage.

The problems of supply of food, ammunition, fuel, and clothing are with unit commanders day and night. They must provide for them and plan for them.

In combat, supply lines are life lines. Every item is in short supply. Squadrons unaccustomed to frugality with supplies pay for this failing in inconvenience, inefficiency, and sometimes in lives.

**Importance of Maintenance.** Americans have become so accustomed to the garage around the corner that they have often not taken the trouble to learn how to repair and maintain mechanical devices. In combat any failure to maintain equipment in perfect condition may be disastrous. A gun that fails to fire may be the difference between life and death. Rockets or bombs that fail to explode can waste the effort and increase the risk involved in a mission. Continual training and inspection are necessary. A landing gear that is improperly lubricated will be subject to unnecessary breakage and wear. It may fail in a crucial moment. Adequate maintenance will reduce the necessity for returning vast quantities of supplies to the United States for extensive overhaul. Unit commanders are in direct charge of the equipment and the people who use it, must understand the whole problem, must see the need for maintenance, and must acquaint themselves with the condition of their equipment by unremitting inspections and corrective action. Maintenance may be the difference between success and failure.

## MORALE PROBLEMS

**Personal Problems of Airmen.** All airmen have left interests, roots, or problems behind them that may require their attention or action while in the military service. At home, they would turn for advice to parents, friends, lawyers, ministers or priests, or other people in whom they have trust and confidence. In the service, they will usually turn to their commander.

These occasions provide a fine opportunity for commanders to show deep interest in the welfare of their men and women. They should adopt an impersonal and kindly attitude in hearing these problems. If the matter is confidential, it must never be divulged improperly. When it is proper to do so, they should give the counsel they feel is correct, obtain the necessary information, or direct the airmen to an authority who can supply the information.

Good leaders must have a genuine understanding of human relations. Their tools are people, and therefore they must be able to deal with people. The necessary warmth of military leadership may be demonstrated when individuals carry their baffling personal problems to their commander for advice or solution.

**The Complaint Problem.** The commander must be accessible to members of the unit who wish to state a complaint. Some of the complaints will be petty. Others may be deliberate attempts to injure the reputation of another with a charge that is without foundation. There are other occasions, however, even in the best organizations, where genuine cause for dissatisfaction may occur. This is information the commander must obtain lest the morale of the unit be seriously impaired. Personnel must know that they may state a cause for complaint to their commander with the knowledge that the commander will give them a hearing and correct the grievance if convinced of its truth. They must believe that the commander will wish to remove causes for dissatisfaction.

Poor airmen find many causes for grievance. Their petty or unfounded accusations must be heard, but they may receive the treatment or disposition they merit. Good airmen will seek to avoid making a complaint. When ideas, suggestions, or reports are stated to the commander that affect the welfare, the efficiency, or the morale of the unit, or any individual therein, they must be heard sympathetically. If the condition reported can be corrected or deserves correction, the action should be taken at once.

**Absence without Leave.** Commanders must face and solve the problem of unauthorized absences from duty. Particularly, commanders must analyze the causes and find solutions to the AWOL situation in their own units. It is not a new problem, and it exists during times of peace as well as in times of war. It is "the status of a person subject to military law who has failed to repair at the fixed time to the properly appointed place of duty, or has gone from the same without proper leave, or has absented himself from his command, guard, quarters, station, or camp without proper leave." In time of war the punishments authorized in Article 86 of the Uniform Code of Military Justice depend upon the circumstances of the absence; but in a crucial situation in contact with the enemy, this is a most heinous offense.

But the punitive approach is inadequate and will not provide the cure. Commanders who rely on punishment will fail to eliminate the cause of unauthorized absence; while guardhouse population may increase, they will not maintain the on-duty strength of their organizations, which is the vital thing. Officers must get acquainted with unit personnel. It is important for reasons of administration and leadership, but is especially necessary in connection with understanding the AWOL problem. They may facilitate this process by get-acquainted interviews preceded by an analysis of the airmen's service records and related forms so that they will know in advance of the interviews the individual's age, education, aptitudes, length of service, training status, dependency situation, and conduct as shown by the disciplinary record. With that information in mind, commanders should proceed with an informal interview to get acquainted with the airmen and let the airmen get acquainted with them. Seek to find the views of the airmen as to family responsibilities and any worries they may have with respect to their families. By so doing commanders may be able to correct oversights in dependents' benefits provided by the government and thus remove at once the cause for people absenting themselves without leave. Inquire of the airmen as to their progress, and determine whether they are satisfied that they are contributing a maximum of talents. Find out about civilian training and background to determine whether the airmen should be assigned to duty for which they are better fitted. Encourage them to talk freely and take the time to explain to the airmen those misunderstood things that may confuse or disappoint young people. Knowledge of pass and leave regulations should be tested, for it is true that some personnel absent themselves without leave when by asking they might have received an authorized absence. In this interview, the airmen should be invited to bring problems to the commander when in need of help or advice so that they will feel they have someone to lean on when confused by personal problems.

The Department of the Air Force authorizes commanders to grant leaves so that people receive an average of 30 days leave per year. Like leaves for officers, they are a privilege and not a right. The requirements of training, work, or operations come first. These requirements must take precedence. Commanders should be informed thoroughly on the regulations governing leaves prescribed by the department and local senior commanders. Commanders should study the program of the organization and determine periods most suitable for granting leaves and those periods when they should not be granted except for important emergency reasons. They must *plan* their leave procedures. Personnel who are designated for shipment overseas are required to be granted leaves before departure unless they have had a recent absence or military necessity prohibits a delay in departure. To the extent practicable, persons in units likewise should receive leaves before departure overseas. Military necessity must govern, and it will not always be possible to grant these absences. The personnel must be informed. It is most unwise for commanders to announce leave policies in a manner that can be interpreted as a promise. Broken promises are themselves a cause for some absence without leave. Commanders can inform unit personnel of the regulations, can tell them of their plans and their intentions, can inform them that circumstances at the time the leave is desired must determine their action, can seek opportunities to send personnel on leave, and can see to it that opportunities are equitably distributed to all personnel. These measures will replace ignorance with understanding and serve to reduce the causes for unauthorized absence.

The regulations for passes over weekends and in evenings are likewise important. Local policies will govern in this matter, and people must be thoroughly instructed. Just as in the case of leaves, the granting of passes must not interfere with requirements of training or work. Liberality in granting short passes within the scope of prescribed policy is a wise practice. Where this is combined with sincere efforts to provide recreational activities on the base for people who do not wish to visit neighboring communities, many of the small but human dissatisfactions can be prevented.

The whole subject of eliminating unauthorized absences is of primary importance in building an effective Air Force. It is likewise of importance in developing pride in an organization. Success will identify the commanders who study causes of AWOL and remove them. Few people will absent themselves without leave from a well-commanded organization.

**Delivery of Mail.** In priority, next to food, airmen might place the prompt delivery of mail. Indeed, for the airmen with spouses, children, sweethearts, or beloved parents, mail may be of far greater lasting importance than food. Commanders of units must pay particular attention to mail delivery. They must see to it that the airmen's mail reaches them quickly and safely. They must make very certain that none is lost and that chance of malicious opening and violation of privacy is reduced to the vanishing point. Letters from home are of the highest importance to airmen because they unite them for a moment with those they love. For the most part, letters will quiet their apprehensions and dispel the worries that beset those who are far removed from their homes. Knowledge that all is well at home secures a peace of mind so strong that it justifies every effort a good mail system requires.

Commanders are urged to check the methods of receiving, guarding, and distributing the mail as it reaches their organizations. Are the individuals charged with handling it completely trustworthy? Are there unsolved complaints of rifled or stolen letters? Is the mail guarded scrupulously from the time of receipt until it is handed to the airmen? Is it allowed to lie about, subject to scrutiny and mishandling? Is it tossed promiscuously into a milling throng with small regard to its actual delivery? Is it handed to the individual to whom addressed? Is it held for long hours after receipt to be distributed at the whim of some individual? Is the mail delivered as promptly as circumstances permit after receipt? Are registered and special delivery pieces handled with due regard to postal regulations? Are your receipts for these classes of mail maintained exactly as prescribed? Airmen treasure packages from home. Are packages zealously guarded so that petty pilfering is surely prevented? These are all matters that are very important in the daily life of the airmen.

**Importance of Letters to Parents.** In a number of organizations, commanders make it a practice to write letters to parents of their people when important personal events have occurred in which they may take pride. The people of the United States are tremendously and vitally concerned about the progress of the Air Force to which they have given the services of their sons and daughters. Their impressions are formed by the reports they receive from their children and their neighbors and friends. No amount of big-name announcements as to morale and conditions will offset the local effect of an unfavorable report from a personal acquaintance. The interests and satisfaction that can be developed by contact, even by letters, with the folks at home are worth the effort required.

Many leaders write these letters. "Dear Mrs. Brown," they may write, "I am pleased to tell you that I have recommended your son for promotion to the grade of Airman 1st Class. He has worked hard here and his record is splendid. He is quite a good airman." Or this: "As you know, your daughter has been confined in the base hospital. I have visited her several times and have had frequent reports about her condition from her medical officer, the chaplain, and others. I can tell you now that she is well on the road to recovery, and her return to her organization will occur very soon." American airmen are young people. In many instances, they are away from home for the first time. Parents are eager for them to perform creditably.

Have you been present when a letter is received from a young airman? Do you know how it is discussed and passed around or read aloud to others? Can you not imagine the effect of a letter from an airman's commander? Form the habit of writing personal letters to the parents of your airmen on proper occasions. It places a human touch on a relationship that is otherwise impersonal and detached.

**Personal Appearance and Morale.** The uniform is supposed to improve the appearance and standing of the wearer. It will do so only to the extent that it is well designed, clean, neatly pressed, and well fitted. There is nothing glamorous about a soiled, rumpled, ill-fitting uniform. Airmen cannot feel the pride in their service we strive to develop unless they look the part of good airmen (see AFR 35–10).

**Health as an Aid to Morale.** It is an accepted principle that commanders are responsible for the health and physical well-being of the members of their units. In this responsibility, they are assisted by the medical officers. Medical officers serve as staff officers and advisers of the commander in all matters that pertain to the care of the sick and the evacuation of the wounded, as well as in matters of sanitation or hygiene, all in addition to their professional duties within the fixed or mobile hospitals serving the needs of the armed forces. There is nothing so destructive of the morale of service personnel as the knowledge or even the suspicion that the sick or wounded are being inadequately attended. In the execution of normal command functions, officers of the Air Force have, in the medical officers, a material source of assistance upon which they may draw.

**Religion and Morale.** Freedom of religion and of religious belief is one of the most important doctrines in our governmental philosophy. This principle must be extended to the airman and proper respect extended to religious convictions.

The religious and spiritual welfare of the members of a command is an important factor in the development of individual pride, morale, and self-respect, all essentials in a military organization. While Kipling may have overemphasized the sordid side of the life led by military personnel in saying that people in barracks do not grow into plaster saints, it is a fact that the environment in some instances leaves a little to be desired. We are a religious people, and our airmen are subject to a wholesome, religious influence. There is a relation between morals and morale just as there is a relation between fair and just treatment and morale, or cleanliness and morale. The organization commanders who are mindful of the religious and spiritual environment of their people will be able to make a strong appeal to the better instincts of all.

**The Chaplain (AFR 265–1).** The chaplains of a command are charged with the religious responsibility and a host of others. While they conduct the routine religious services and attend as a matter of course to baptisms, marriages, and funerals, their most important work may lie in the close and personal human contacts they enjoy throughout a command. Unless they receive the cooperation of the commander, their work cannot possibly achieve the utmost. The task of chaplains is always a difficult one. A word of suggestion to the chaplain as to a needed service for an individual will often result in the solution of a baffling problem. A word of encouragement to the chaplains to let them know their service is recognized and valued will stimulate further effort. Commanders who cooperate with the chaplains and seek thereby to improve the spiritual, religious, and moral standard of their units will receive important dividends for their efforts (see AFR 265–1).

**Morale, Welfare, and Recreation (MWR) (AFR 215–1).** The morale, welfare, and recreation officer leads the recreational services, including voluntary athletics. The closest coordination and support should be developed between commanders and the MWR officer.

The overall mission of MWR is to provide an attractive off-duty environment for personnel. Such a program should have a direct effect upon reenlistment rates, which are a matter of direct continual concern to commanders.

Athletic programs that encourage maximum participation by individuals constitute the heart of all MWR activities. The airmen's club should be the hub around which many activities of high interest to airmen will revolve. The library service is taken for granted at most stations and its popularity accepted, but in prewar days it was not generally of high order. Organization commanders should inform their people of its location and facilities and encourage its use. Hobby shops with manual arts programs should be encouraged. Music programs and shows in which airmen take part constitute a part of these activities.

The goal is to increase the degree of satisfaction experienced by all military personnel. The effect should be that the airmen find interesting things to do at their stations near their units, rather than seek every opportunity to visit nearby civilian communities.

Commanders of small units are their own MWR officers. They should be thoroughly familiar with facilities available for their use and make it possible for their people to make use of them to the fullest degree.

**The Public Affairs Officer (AFR 190–1).** Commanders who learn the objectives, opportunities, and value of the public affairs program have added an important tool to their own professional capacities. The public affairs officer is trained to control the program. The time has come when the Air Force must recruit an even higher type of individual than it has in the past. It must provide a social and mental environment with full opportunity for intellectual development and professional advancement.

The Armed Forces Information and Education Division operates three major activities: the Troop Information Program; the Armed Forces Radio and Television Service; and service newspapers. The Armed Forces Institute is the core of the educational program. It offers correspondence courses, self-teaching courses, group study materials, and testing services. Young officers are well advised to investigate these matters in their own behalf, as well as in the interests of the airmen.

**The American Red Cross and Morale (AFR 211-11).** The American Red Cross acts as the medium of communication between the military and the civilian community. This organization has chapters or representatives in all parts of the United States and its foreign possessions. At many stations, there is a Red Cross field director to serve the needs of the base. While this nationwide organization stands ready always to perform a wide variety of worthy missions, its services are often useful in cases where airmen are troubled about conditions at home. In such instances, it is common practice to call upon the representative of the Red Cross, explain the problem fully, and ask for an investigation of the actual conditions. The situation can often be adjusted. In any event, the officers will obtain reliable information that will enable many baffling human problems concerning the airmen of their organizations to be handled in a judicious manner based upon facts as they exist.

**Air Force Aid Society (AFR 211-1).** The work of the Air Force Aid Society is another valuable adjunct to the efforts of commanders to provide for the welfare and morale of their airmen. For a fuller discussion of the society, see chapter 20.

**Use of Allocation of the Organization Fund (AFR 176-1).** Through nonappropriated fund channels, base commanders receive allotments of funds applicable to units on their bases for the purpose of improving morale. Squadron commanders can apply for an allocation from this fund for specific morale-building activities of the squadron. A typical use of such a fund allocation would be to hold a squadron picnic or beer party. Any worthwhile, enjoyable entertainment for squadron personnel can be financed in this manner. The squadron commander must make application for the allocation of funds, indicating the intended use.

Members of a unit are entitled to know the status of the fund at all times because, after all, it is *their* fund. They should be informed of the intent to make future purchases. The commander who announces, however, that a purchase will be made and fails to make it soon nullifies any beneficial effect such announcements can provide.

**Athletics and Morale (AFR 215 series).** Provisions for athletics for all is an important factor in the physical development of the individual airman and in the problems of maintaining high morale. Officers must sponsor and develop athletic facilities. For the most part, airmen are young, strong, and energetic people. They need an outlet for these energies. A variety of athletic facilities should be available to meet the varying preferences of members of the unit. The use of the facilities should be encouraged by all proper means. Ask your MWR officer for help. For more information on athletics programs and their effect on morale, see the following regulations: AFR 215-20, *Air Force Outdoor Recreation Program*; AFR 215-22, *Air Force Sports Program*; AFR 215-24, *Air Force Competitive Recreation and Sports Activities*; and AFP 215-38, *Air Force Sports Program Guide*.

**Housing (AFR 90 series).** One of the most frequently overlooked factors affecting morale is housing. When officers or airmen report to your base, the first consideration in their minds is where they are to live. If bachelors, their concern is less acute than if married. Nevertheless, married or unmarried, there must be housing for them. Unit commanders should consider housing their first and most important duty relative to newly arrived people. Do not wait until the incoming airmen or officers have arrived. Contact them by mail as soon as you know about the orders to your unit. (Check with the base Family Services Center; perhaps they have already done this.) Determine the housing needs through your communication. Establish whether there will be quarters provided on the base. If so, check them for adequacy and readiness. If they must live off-base, seek out several suitable rentals for them to consider. While awaiting their arrival, arrange temporary quarters for them, on base if possible. Meet them at the base Family Services Center. Give your assistance in getting settled temporarily, including arranging for items needed until their furniture arrives. (Playpen? Bottle warmer?) Later, see to any help needed in occupying the permanent housing. You cannot expect to have effective officers or airmen until they and their families are adequately housed.

**Family Support Centers (FSCs) (AFP 30-44).** Family Support Centers have been expanded considerably at base level over the past few years. They are a result of the Air Force's recognition that family issues have a direct effect on the morale and productivity of Air Force members and on decisions for making the Air Force a career. They serve as a focal point for responding to family issues that affect the Air Force mission.

Their services include the following:

1. Information/referral center, where airmen or officers can get information or specialized assistance.
2. Relocation assistance, for help when moving to another base.
3. Support during family separations.
4. Financial management programs.
5. Spouse employment programs, which offer information about job opportunities and programs on how to develop job-hunting skills.
6. Special-needs programs, such as single parents' groups.
7. Family skills, which offer programs on communication and enhancing a family's quality of life.
8. Private and professional assistance for personal crisis issues, marital, child-related, and so forth.

## DISCIPLINE

**Discipline Defined.** Military discipline is intelligent, willing, and cheerful obedience to the will of the leader. Its basis rests upon the voluntary subordination of the individual to the welfare of the group. It is the cohesive force that binds the members of a unit, and its strict enforcement is a benefit for all. Its constraint must be felt not so much in the fear of punishment it evokes as in the moral obligation it imposes on the individual to heed the common interest of the group. Discipline establishes a state of mind that produces proper action and prompt cooperation under all circumstances, regardless of obstacles. It creates in the individual a desire and determination to undertake and accomplish any mission assigned by the leader.

Discipline is a controlling factor in the combat value of airmen. The combat value of a unit is determined by the military qualities of the leader and members and its "will to fight." A point too often overlooked is the fact that poorly trained and poorly disciplined units reap the defeats and greatest losses. The greater the combat value of the organization, the more powerful will be the blow struck by the commander.

People are and always will be the vital element in war. In spite of the advances in technique, the worth of the individuals is still decisive. They must be disciplined and must have good morale.

In war, discipline is a matter of the gravest importance, affecting both the questions of life and death of individuals and also the question of localized or global war. Those who disobey sanitation regulations risk poisoning. Pilots may be briefed to avoid violating the borders of unfriendly nations. An incident leading to open world conflict may result from infringements of this order, whether intentional or unintentional. Discipline is the cement in the structure of the Air Force: Without it, an Air Force would be merely a mob. We *must* have a disciplined Air Force; otherwise, ultimately, we shall have none.

**Relationship of Superiors toward Subordinates.** Superiors are forbidden to injure those under their authority by tyrannical or capricious conduct or by abusive language. While maintaining discipline and the thorough and prompt performance of military duty, all officers, in dealing with airmen, will bear in mind the absolute necessity of preserving their self-respect. A grave duty rests on all officers and particularly upon organization commanders in this respect. Officers will impress upon the young airmen lessons of patriotism and loyalty and above all will impress upon them the necessity of obedience in the service. These lessons will be repeated again and again. The difference in the status of airmen compared with that of civilians will be carefully explained to make them understand that in becoming airmen they are subject to a new control and have assumed obligations that did not rest upon them as civilians. Officers will keep in as close touch as possible with the personnel under their command, will take an interest in their organization life, will hear their complaints, will endeavor on all occasions to remove the existence of those causes that make for dissatisfaction, and will strive to build such confidence and sympathy that their people will come to them for counsel and assistance, not only in military and organizational matters but also in personal or family distress or perplexity. This relationship may be gained and maintained without relaxing the bonds of discipline.

**Punishment.** The maintenance of control requires the promulgation of regulations for the guidance of members of the organization. These regulations must include positive matters, things to do, and negative matters, things to avoid doing. Good management requires that these regulations be few, entirely justified by conditions, easily understood, necessary for the accomplishment of unit objectives, and at least reasonably in harmony with those in use by neighboring organizations. There is small occasion for the adoption of extra-official restrictive orders that serve only to gratify the aversions of the commander. The application of restrictive regulations on an entire organization because of the transgressions of one or of a small number is a lazy and ineffective form of control. The process of "beating down the bush to kill the snake" is poor leadership. An error of leadership method is the use of threats or naming a penalty in issuing an order. Such a practice causes antagonism. The *Manual for Courts-Martial,* regulations of the Air Force, and the orders of higher authority prescribe the methods of control, and they should be well and carefully studied. An understanding of the requirements that must be enforced is an important part of the maintenance of control.

In any organization, there will be violations of standing orders and offenses committed that are punishable under the Uniform Code of Military Justice. The proper exercise of command requires that personnel be fully informed of the regulations they are to observe. The commander must be alert to prevent offenses, for very often a kindly word of caution may prevent an offense. Offenses may be committed in ignorance, through carelessness, or with deliberate intent. The skilled commander can eliminate many of those that might be done through ignorance or carelessness.

An immediate recognition and reward of the deserving do much to prevent the commission of offenses. The officer need not be voluble. A softly spoken "good work" may be more stimulating to pride than a flowery and lengthy oration. The award of extra privileges, promotion, or mere recognition of merit has much to do with the development of both a sound discipline and a high morale.

The commander of a unit should prefer to take disciplinary action under Article 15, Uniform Code of Military Justice, rather than submit charges that will result in a trial by court-martial. For first offenders or for petty offenses, this will usually suffice. Careful investigation must be made before any decision as to punishment is made. This investigation must be impersonal, fair, and just, and it must include an opportunity for the accused airman to refute the charge.

The method of maintaining discipline must be such that it will stand the test of battle. Reliance upon trial by court-martial as the sole means of securing obedience to law and regulations will certainly fail. A trip to the guardhouse may be considered, by some, far preferable to participation in a combat mission.

**Military Courts-Martial.** There are three kinds of courts-martial: the summary court, the special court, and the general court. The summary court consists of one commissioned officer, the special court of three or more members, and the general court of five or more members. Officers may serve as members of any court-martial. Airmen may serve on a general or a special court-martial for the trial of airmen when, before the convening of the court, the accused requests in writing the airmen be so detailed. When so requested, the membership of the court must include at least one-third airmen. Punishing power of the two inferior courts, summary and special, is limited by statute, the summary not being empowered to adjudge confinement in excess of one month and forfeiture of more than two-thirds of one month's pay. The special court may not adjudge confinement in excess of six months and forfeiture of more than two-thirds pay per month for six months. The punishing power of the general court is usually, by the wording of the Uniform Code of Military Justice denouncing a particular offense, left to the discretion of the court. That apparently unlimited power does not, however, exist. In a few instances, the Article itself prescribes the punishment for a particular offense. In all other cases, the president, under authority given him by an article of the Uniform Code of Military Justice, has prescribed a table of maximum punishments. The punishment of nearly all offenses that are denounced by the common law and by nonmilitary codes has been similarly limited by the president. In the rare event that an offense is committed that is not covered by the president's limit of punishment order, the punishment may not exceed that fixed as a maximum for the offense by the U.S. Penal Code or the Criminal Code for the District of Columbia. The sentence of a court-martial has no validity until it has been approved by the officer appointing the court. The sentences of all general courts-martial are subject to a series of reviews and approvals or disapprovals in which the record of trial is examined not only to determine its legal sufficiency but also to ensure that no sentence of unnecessary harshness is finally executed.

## DISCIPLINARY PROCEDURES

Officers repeatedly find it necessary to determine what procedure to adopt in disciplinary and quasi-disciplinary matters. This recurrent problem most often takes one of these forms:

- Courts-martial.
- Nonjudicial punishment.
- Administrative discharges.

**Commander's Disciplinary Measures.** The Uniform Code of Military Justice provides two procedures by which commanders may enforce discipline: the courts-martial procedure, and the application of Article 15 of the Uniform Code, which authorizes punishment without resort to courts-martial.

**Courts-Martial.** *Restraint.* Any person in the military service may sign and swear to charges that are an offense under military law. Usually, however, the person having knowledge of the alleged offense makes the information known to the immediate commander of the accused airman or officer. Ordinarily, this commander would be the squadron commander. The commander must then make an immediate decision as to whether the accused person should be put under any degree of restraint, such as confinement to barracks. If restraint seems indicated, the commander should issue the necessary orders at once.

*Informal Inquiry.* The commander (or a representative) must promptly make a preliminary inquiry of the accusations. This inquiry may be no more than a consideration of the charges and such evidence as is offered by the accuser. It may include a search of barracks, quarters, or other pertinent areas. Collection of documentary evidence may be desirable, depending on the nature of the charge. Individuals may be questioned informally. It is most important to remember, however, that before questioning an accused person, that person must be informed of the accusations made and warned that any statement he utters may be used against him if a trial results. (Article 31, UCMJ.)

The commander must reach decisions as matters proceed. If it appears that court-martial action is probable, the commander should obtain written, signed testimony from all persons involved. If the preliminary inquiry leads to a conclusion that court-martial action is not indicated, the commander may wish to adopt lesser punitive procedures or none at all. In many cases, accusations will be found to lack substance and may simply be dismissed.

*Charges for Courts-Martial.* If commanders believe that court-martial procedure is proper, they should have formal charges (DD Form 458) executed at once and so inform the accused. In carrying out this action, commanders are well advised to consult with the office of the staff judge advocate (see AFR 111-1, *Military Justice Guide*).

**Punishment under Article 15.** Article 15 of the UCMJ provides authority to squadron or unit commanders to impose punishment of a degree less than that for which court-martial action is required. This authority, however, is qualified by the fact that any airman may demand trial by court-martial rather than accept punishment under Article 15. Nonetheless, when commanders have conducted a preliminary inquiry or are otherwise satisfied that court-martial action is not desirable, they should inform the offender in writing of the intent to impose punishment under Article 15. The offender must state, in writing, a willingness to accept Article 15 punishment or a demand for court-martial. If the offender demands court-martial, the matter is then handled by preferring formal charges. If the offender certifies willingness to accept Article 15 punishment, the commander proceeds to impose the punishment. In this correspondence, the commander does not indicate what punishment is intended until after the offender has accepted punishment under Article 15.

Under Article 15, commanders may impose a wide variety of punishments. Commanders in the grade of major or above may adjudge punishment to airmen of their command as follows: not more than 30 days correctional custody, forfeiture of half of their pay for two months, extra duty of 45 days, restriction for two months, or reduction in grade (an E-4 or higher may not be reduced more than two grades).

Commanders below the grade of major may under Article 15 punish airmen of their command by imposing not more than one week of correctional custody, forfeiture of one week's pay, extra duty for two weeks, restriction to limits for two weeks, detention of two weeks' pay, or reduction of one grade (provided the commander has the authority to promote to the grade from which the airman is to be demoted).

Commanders have authority to admonish or reprimand officers under their command.

Commanders in general officer grade may under Article 15 punish officers under their command by imposing not more than suspension from duty for two months, arrest in quarters for one month, or forfeiture of half their pay for two months.

The commander should consult with the staff judge advocate if the punishment intended approaches the levels for which court-martial action is required. In general, the use of Article 15 is preferred by commanders, as against court-martial, when it is an appropriate procedure. The court-martial procedure is costly to the government and consumes the time of valuable people. Article 15 should be employed when the offender accepts it, when the punishments available under Article 15 are considered adequate, and when court-martial is not mandatory.

**Administrative Discharges.** Under AFR 39-10, commanders are given authority to eliminate the unfit and the undesirable from the Air Force. AFR 39-10 authorizes commanders to remove airmen who are mentally or psychologically unable to perform acceptably as airmen. Such people may well want to perform properly, but cannot. They should be discharged.

AFR 39-10 provides for the separation of those who can be useful airmen but will not do so. These are the alcoholics, the drug users, the rebels, the repeating offenders, the undisciplined. They should be removed from the Air Force as quickly as possible.

AFR 39-10 authorizes the separation of airmen who are sentenced by civil authorities to confinement for more than one year.

In preparing action to eliminate airmen, commanders must formulate a record of offenses, instances, or other evidence of unsuitability. Usually, it will be necessary to show that efforts have been made to correct the situation, through counseling or other methods. This record is attached to a letter to the group commander, asking that a board of officers be formed to review the case and determine disposition.

Officers dealing with cases of unsuitability should be guided entirely by the needs of the Air Force. An unfit airman stands in a space that might be filled by a productive airman. There is no room for the unfit or the undesirable. Each person in the total strength of the Air Force must be first class.

**Crime and Punishment.** In dealing with offenders against military law, officers should be guided wholly by a desire to serve the best interests of the Air Force. Vengeance has no place in such a consideration. The object is not to punish for the sake of "an eye for an eye." The object is to deter airmen from offenses, to exact recompense when property of the government has been lost, to rehabilitate offenders when possible. It is usually wise to be lenient with first offenders, particularly when the subsequent attitude of the offender is commendable. It is equally wise to be rough on second offenders; usually, it is best to evict them from the Air Force. Seek no reputation for mercy, nor one for ruthlessness. Seek, instead, to advance the good reputation of the Air Force for level-headed action in the interests of the national security.

## TRAINING (AFR 50 SERIES)

**Purpose of Military Training.** The ultimate purpose of all military training is the assurance of victory in war. We want a fighting Air Force composed of officers and enlisted people who can do their complex jobs better than the enemy. If we train well, the task of winning the victory will require far less time than that which will be necessary if we train poorly.

One of the outstanding lessons derived from experiences in World War II, Korea, Vietnam, and the Gulf War is that the state of training of units is the governing factor determining the combat capability of an Air Force unit. Air Force equipment in general is excellent in quality and adequate in quantity. Air Force morale is high. Supply and maintenance standards are superior. Discipline, while not perfect, is very commendable. Leadership, from the top down to the lowest unit, is superb. In the field of training, however, lapses may be noted. Every commander should heed this lesson: *Training is never good enough; improvement is always possible.* Training is a round-the-clock function for the squadron. A great deal of it may seem dull and tiresome. Nonetheless, it must be accomplished thoroughly, for it pays off in lives saved and in battles won.

War also points up the tremendous importance of the less dramatic aspects of Air Force training. The officers in control of support activities, such as the supply of munitions and aviation fuel, actually hold the throttle of the Air Force. It is of critical importance that those officers in command of support organizations realize the controlling nature of their units' performance and bring those units to the highest possible state of training. Aircrews cannot soar off into the wild blue without fuel, ammunition, spare parts, operating weapons, well-maintained air bases, and in-commission aircraft. The Air Force is a chain involving many links, only one of which is the operating combat force. The air depots, the engineers, the researchers, the administrators, the hospitals, the maintenance crews, the tactical control parties, the intelligence agencies—all of these and many more are absolutely indispensable links in the chain of air power. Everyone has a crucial job to do; everyone must be highly trained to do it.

**Joint Training.** All squadron commanders will sooner or later find their units engaged in some form of joint training with the Army or the Navy or both. In the past, there has been too much of a "to hell with that" attitude about joint training. Some of this attitude stemmed from a false belief that the Air Force could win wars alone, that joint training was superfluous. Some stemmed from the feeling that there was already too much to be accomplished in the training program without adding joint training. If any single fact stood out in Korea, Vietnam, and again in the Gulf War, it is the need for more and better joint training. The Air Force, the Army, the Marines, and the Navy fight in close coordination. Each depends upon the others.

For the unit commander, the point is this: Wars are won by teamwork among the services; your unit must not only want to take part in this teamwork but it must also be well trained in joint operations. Mere willingness to cooperate in an emergency will never take the place of a practiced know-how. It would be a sickening thing to think that Americans were dying because of a low state of joint training of *your* unit; nor would you find it any solace to reflect that such Americans were in the Army, the Navy, or the Marines rather than in the Air Force.

**Analysis of the Training Process.** Training doctrines, principles, methods, and management are covered in various training publications. A point that stands out is that the training of individuals is essentially identical. The qualities to be developed in the individual or the unit are the same for all. Differences in training are confined to subjects relating to tactical and technical proficiency. All must be good airmen. And all must have the same high standard of discipline, of health, strength, and endurance, and of morale, initiative, and adaptability; and all must have the same fine leadership in order to produce the final goal of teamwork.

**Estimate of the Training Situation.** Higher headquarters prescribe the training objectives, allot the use of facilities to units in turn, and designate periods for maneuvers and tactical exercises. Commanders of subordinate units must make a careful analysis of the objectives to be met and the steps required to attain each objective, survey their own problems with reference to the existing state of training of their units, determine the facilities that will be required, and make detailed plans for the best use of the time available to them to execute all of their missions. Foresight combined with careful planning is required from unit commanders who succeed in executing with smoothness and efficiency the training missions prescribed.

Commanders must make an estimate of the training situation just as they would make an estimate of the tactical situation. A logical process of thought assists commanders in arriving at sound conclusions in view of all of the facts. This estimate includes consideration of the following subjects:

- Mission (training objective).
- Essential subjects (relative importance of each): basic, technical, tactical, logistical.
- Time available.
- Equipment and facilities available.
- Personnel available as instructors.
- Local conditions.
- Existing state of training.
- Organization for training.
- Obstacles: administrative, physical, human.

After commanders have made the estimate and arrived at a plan, they are ready to state the plan in orders or in a schedule, which may well include delegation to subordinate leaders the task of conducting phases of the training process. The next and final step is that of carrying out the plan. Commanders must supervise the instructions given by others to make very certain that they are given correctly and that they will be completed satisfactorily within the available time.

## THE CONDUCT OF INSTRUCTION (AFM 50-2)

Every officer has responsibilities for the conduct of instruction. Some officers are engaged in formal instructional activities, such as in the schools of the Air Education and Training Command. Others are confronted with the regular influx of new airmen into their units or offices. These latter airmen will have received instruction in their specialties, through the formal training processes of the Air Force. But instruction never ceases. All airmen should be brought to a higher state of competence as rapidly as possible, particularly in respect to the specific tasks they must perform in the unit of assignment. Officers must engage themselves in this process, either through direct participation or through supervision of the noncommissioned instructors who perform the training tasks.

**Instruction Should Be Planned.** Officers should examine the plans of instruction to ensure that they exist and are properly geared to the objective. Further considerations include these:

- Timing and duration of instruction periods.
- Availability of competent instructors.
- Availability and use of adequate instructional tools.
- Procedures applied in carrying out instruction.

No single method of instruction works best in all circumstances. But all instruction reduces to four basic moves:

- Explanation.
- Demonstration.
- Practice.
- Correction.

Whatever and wherever may be the instructional objective sought—in the United States, in the Pacific, in Europe—instruction must accomplish these four phases. It is the responsibility of all officers to ensure that within their areas of responsibility, instruction is carried on constantly and well. They cannot safely assume that this will be automatically accomplished by noncommissioned officers or that the formal training of airmen is sufficient. In the Air Force, change is constant, and almost every change requires new instruction of airmen. This is a prime responsibility of command.

## THE SOUND OF COMBAT

Only a very few words will be devoted to the subject of combat duty. Officers of the Air Force who have seen the sights and heard the sounds of battle express no undue concern over the reactions of untried Air Force officers. Most experienced officers state that inexperienced officers show more aplomb, more bravery, more unconcern for enemy fire than do those who have sweated through more deadly circumstances on a number of earlier occasions.

Combat is too often described as being only the event of deadly encounters between two adversaries, each possessing and directing an attacking vehicle, such as an airplane. Not so. Combat is much more often the tiresome struggle to supply aviation materiel, such as fuel, at the proper time and place in the theater of war. Combat is frequently the effort to produce sanitary water and food in an area where is it impossible to do so; to build revetments around fighter aircraft; to operate a decent mess in indecent surroundings; to predict weather from totally inadequate soundings; to furnish needed parts for inoperational aircraft when the parts are 10,000 miles away. Combat is doing the best you can under the circumstances; but the "best" means *best*. It is a sharp realization that your life or death or someone else's, someone else whom you value, hangs in the balance between your performance and that of your enemy counterpart.

No officers of the U.S. Air Force need be unduly afraid of combat, provided they have done their best to prepare themselves for the test.

For testimony to that, read this statement by Lt. Gen. Joseph Moore, then Commander, 7th Air Force, Vietnam:

> The story of the battle of Plei Me would have had a different ending without the men and aircraft of the 2d Air Division [now 7th Air Force] reacting instantaneously to the tactical situation. Fighter bombers, flying low-level missions around the clock under intense ground fire, were able to disperse and rout heavy concentrations of the enemy whenever called upon. Our airlift forces, under the most adverse conditions day and night, flew weapons, food, and equipment without which the Special Forces outpost could not have survived. Airpower, working in close coordination with the U.S. and Vietnamese Army ground forces, saved the day at Plei Me.

# 11

# The Code of the U.S. Air Force

*It is not the critic who counts, nor the man who points out how the strong man stumbled, or where the doer of deeds could have done them better. The credit belongs to the man who is actually in the arena; whose face is marred by dust and sweat and blood; who strives valiantly; who errs and comes short again and again; who knows the great enthusiasms, the great devotions, and spends himself in a worthy cause; who, at the best, knows in the end the triumph of high achievement; and who, at the worst, if he fails, at least fails while daring greatly, so that his place shall never be with those cold and timid souls who know neither victory nor defeat.*

—Theodore Roosevelt

The code of the Air Force is a standard of life. It is a set of principles at which all officers aim, both in their official duties and in their personal concerns, in actions seen and known by the world, and in the deepest privacies of the mind. These things, these ideals, do not appear in regulations. The Air Force has no checklist, no approved solution for each individual's every situation. Rather, the code of the Air Force is an attitude of the spirit, rarely arrived at consciously but strongly governing the reactions of Air Force officers to all the many sides of Air Force life. Insofar as this spirit of the Air Force runs strong in the veins of its officers, the nation will have a military air arm of indomitable quality, and freedom will have a champion more able than any it has ever before known.

## PRINCIPLES OF THE AIR FORCE CODE

The printed word cannot capture the code of the Air Force in its entirety, for this code is a living reality that you as an officer must experience to fully understand. Yet, we can identify some of the deep foundations upon which our code rests. These are criteria by which we have lived and fought and some of us have died; these are values we have sought to uphold, the true hallmarks of the U.S. Air Force.

**Patriotism.** Patriotism as practiced in the Air Force is an intelligent devotion to the interests of the United States *above every other consideration.* It rests upon the conviction that preservation of the American system of life, with its noble traditions, free institutions, and infinite promise is at once the highest practical morality and the most enlightened self-interest. Patriotism springs from deep knowledge that this land and this people are in truth the hope of the earth. Such patriotism is not jingoism, blindly unaware of faults of our American system, stupidly touting it as perfect. Rather, such patriotism works to remove faults that do exist, while remaining confident that here in America the fallible hands and limited minds of humans have done their best work, that ours is the most promising road yet found toward a goal of maximum human welfare, toward freedom, dignity, and justice for each individual, and peace for the world. We know we have not yet reached this goal, but we believe the United States is the human race's longest stride in that direction, and we mean to see to it that the ground thus far gained is not lost, nor the path onward blocked.

Not only in the high drama of war does patriotism invoke a readiness to make personal sacrifices, but also in the humdrum of routine duties, during off-duty hours, in the thousands of small choices with which daily life confronts us. Patriotism invests the duties assigned to an Air Force officer with an importance far beyond their apparent measure. Thus, patriotism in the Air Force is intelligent devotion to the interests of the United States day by day, at work or at leisure, in war or peace, in life or, if need be, in death.

**Honor.** Honor is the highest form of self-respect. You must live with yourself alone for a very substantial part of your life. It is imperative to peace of mind and peace of soul that you respect your own character. Thus, honor is that code of conduct that springs not only from a "do unto others as you would have done unto you" philosophy but also from a determination to do only those things about which your inner thoughts are serene. A person of honor does not lie, steal, cheat, or take undue advantage of another. The question here is not whether you would be seriously hurt if someone did such things to you. The question is whether you yourself could be proud of such practices on your own part. To be known as a man or a woman of honor has many practical advantages, but these are incidental. The greatest reward of honorable people is that they respect themselves. Somehow such self-respect shows, and others recognize it as the sign of an honorable human being. We of the Air Force seek to be counted as such.

**Courage.** Courage is ascendancy over fear. Note that where there is courage there must be fear. In this sense, a lion is not courageous, for it does not know fear. The Air Force wants no officers who are unafraid. The perils that threaten the United States in this nuclear era, in this time of limited wars that could escalate to Armageddon, are such that a person who is without fear is either foolish or ignorant. The Air Force *does* want officers who can conquer their fears, suppress them in the interests of the nation, and courageously carry on despite fear. Such officers are dangerous to the enemies of the United States, whereas a rash fool is not. Nor is the Air Force satisfied with officers whose courage is a thing of a moment, a flash of strength invoked for a brief instant only. Instead, we need officers whose courage is as steady and long-enduring as the threat to the nation, who can steel themselves for the long pull over the years.

**Loyalty.** Loyalty is the quality of sincere confidence in and support for the purposes, methods, and capabilities of one's associates, whether superiors or subordinates. Loyalty is a quality that precludes sneering comment on the faults of your squadron commander or bleating complaints about the errors of your new crew chief. It is basically an attitude of warm friendship toward your comrades. Perhaps an illustration would make this point more plain. Two little boys were discussing their dogs. The one pointed out that his dog was a thoroughbred of impressive lineage, including champions. The other lad, gazing at his mongrel pup, said: "Spotty is the best little black and brown dog with one ear half gone that there is in the whole world." That is loyalty, and it was probably richly deserved. If you look carefully, you will find that many more of your associates than you may imagine well deserve your loyalty.

**Discipline.** Discipline is the cement that binds together any military force. Without it, the Air Force would be a mob. Obedience of orders in letter—and, more important, in spirit—is the heart of discipline. Air Force officers who grudgingly, complainingly, or unenthusiastically obey orders are poorly disciplined officers who encourage poor discipline in the airmen they are supposed to lead. Such are not the officers who build and maintain an effective fighting force. Almost everyone agrees that discipline is a fine thing—for everyone else. Too many of us are tempted to believe that orders and regulations were meant for the masses, but not for the Great Me. Yet, we all should be aware that unless we practice discipline in our routine conduct, the stress of combat, of emergency, and of violent uncertainties can easily force us from the iron path of obedience to orders, with results disastrous to our cause and to ourselves. One thing seems certain: We shall have disciplined officers of our Air Force, or we will one day have no Air Force, no nation, and no freedom.

**Readiness.** One of the most striking qualities of Air Force officers is their relative readiness to meet whatever tasks arise. The Far East Air Forces transformed themselves overnight from a slow-paced occupation force to the combat sword of the United Nations over Korea. Yet, two days before the entry of U.S. air forces into combat in Korea, not an officer of the Far East Air Forces had an inkling such a task would arise. Eight days later, they had totally destroyed the North Korean air force of more than 300 aircraft. Once again, the nation called upon the Air Force for quick reaction to the combat situation in Vietnam. Thousands of Air Force members deployed into battle in Southeast Asia to fight a bitter, difficult war. Our officers can be ready, as they were in Grenada and Panama. They can be well-trained, well-informed, clear-headed, and physically fit masters of their duties. We must maintain such readiness, for some day a bigger gong than Korea or Vietnam may suddenly ring out a dread alarm, as it did in the Persian Gulf, calling Air Force officers to the trial of the ages. For this possibility, each of us must stand prepared.

**Frugality.** We of the Air Force represent the largest single item in the U.S. budget. We are an expensive force, using extremely costly equipment and supplies. In fairness to all American taxpayers (including ourselves), we ought to hold this expense to the minimum consistent with national safety. This quality of frugality involves more than just these measures, however. Air Force units in Vietnam sometimes found to their sorrow that the cost of wastefulness was ineffectiveness and that the price of ineffectiveness was a longer war with more lives lost. One of the dark hopes of the communist world is that the United States will bankrupt itself through its far-flung national security programs. Let's not contribute to that enemy scheme.

**Caution.** Caution has a proper place in the code of the Air Force. The great strength we hold poised is the chief defense of the United States. The most massive power for evil ever assembled threatens this defense. The situation is dangerous and explosive. A mistake can lead to total war. Has any condition of affairs ever more strongly recommended caution? Moreover, Air Force officers operate equipment noted for its great speed and awesome effects. Recklessness often costs lives; it certainly costs millions of dollars annually. In these circumstances, no Air Force officer is justified in abandoning caution. A famous Air Force combat ace once said: "When I get in an airplane, I slow down." When you get into an Air Force uniform, consider doing the same.

**Sense of Responsibility.** The quality known as responsibility is one of the most valued in an officer. Its most frequent evidence is the execution of work that should be done whether or not one is directly charged with that work. How many times can you hear the phrase from the substandard officer: "Oh, well, it's not my headache." But it *is* your headache, if it hurts the Air Force. The sense of responsibility found in the best of Air Force officers will not be satisfied with a job merely well done. The question is: Has the job been done to the best of my ability? If not, it isn't finished. On an air base in the Far East, a very high ranking Air Force general walked across a runway. As he hurried toward the operations building, the general looked back over his shoulder, hesitated, and finally said: "Damn it, I've got to go back. I saw a bolt on that runway. Should have picked it up. They ruin tires, you know." Here was a busy officer not too busy to ignore that deep-rooted sense of responsibility.

**Teamwork.** Teamwork is the method by which officers of the Air Force do the impossible more rapidly. Teamwork makes football champions of eleven people who, if they all insisted on being ball carriers, would gain nothing. Teamwork makes every officer's task easier, and yet the overall result is greater success. It is the nearest thing in life to getting something for nothing. If you insist on playing a lone hand, always want to carry the ball, and feel that associates should do their own work without bothering you, you will find that the path is rough and leads not very far. Cooperation with others is a first essential. The Air Force is a team organization, and teamwork is the oil of the machine.

**Ambition.** To be ambitious is the mark of a superior officer. Every officer has a right to be ambitious and will be a better officer for it. People will tend to assess you according to the evaluation you place upon yourself. If you exert yourself to become qualified for higher positions and greater responsibilities, you will eventually become convinced that you are ready for advancement. Thus, ambition based on qualification will give you confidence and aggressiveness, qualities indispensable to superior officers. Stonewall Jackson said: "You can be what you determine to be." When Jackson used the word *determine,* he meant willingness to do the work, gain the qualifications, and seek the opportunity necessary for advancement to your goal. Ambition can be a driving force for self-improvement and should be. Only one caution is relevant: Set the sights of your ambition no higher than the level of your willingness to work, for the two are linked as with iron.

**Adaptability.** One of the qualities Air Force officers must employ the most is adaptability, meaning the ability to make the best of any situation. Life in the Air Force is a rough-and-tumble of wildly varying conditions. Officers serve in all parts of the world, in an almost infinite number of differing conditions. Aircraft change endlessly, new maintenance problems arise constantly, and all things are subject to frequent change. As an officer, you must be prepared to adapt to the conditions you may find in any assignment. Living accommodations, offices, operational facilities, the quality of superiors and subordinates, all may differ radically from your previous assignment. Yet, you must work with these new factors. You, not they, must adapt. Adaptability and flexibility are essential to meet such diametrically different situations as are the routine experiences of Air Force officers.

**Ascendancy of the Civil Power.** It's important that you know where your loyalty lies. Under our system of government, you have a dual allegiance to the U.S. Constitution, which you swore to uphold, and to the president as commander in chief.

In this system of divided civilian supremacy—between the president and the Congress—over our armed forces, you must not allow yourself to become involved in the tug of war between an administration and Congress. You should keep informed about politics, and it is your duty to vote, but on active service you should not speak out about your personal views on political policy. If you can't support established policy, you should take the honorable course and resign.

**Relations with Civilians.** One of the most important accomplishments expected of you as an Air Force officer is the maintenance of favorable relations with civilians. This fact becomes doubly important when you realize that about 90 percent of the American public's attitude toward the Air Force is a direct reflection of the impression individual Air Force officers make. The continued strength of the Air Force demands that American citizens hold a favorable view of the Air Force. The future of the service, in a very large measure, turns on the relations of Air Force personnel with their civilian neighbors.

All Air Force officers are public affairs officers, sources of information about the Air Force to civilians with whom they come in contact. Not only words convey such information. If you, an Air Force officer, are irresponsible toward your just debts, conduct yourself in an obnoxious manner in your civilian neighborhood, display yourself in a drunken condition, or ignore the laws and the customs of the community—how much confidence would you expect the civilian observer of these malpractices to place in the Air Force you are a part of? On the contrary, if you conduct yourself as a sober, responsible citizen of the civilian community, your civilian acquaintances will tend to feel that the Air Force is an organization in which they can safely repose confidence. Thus, by your *pattern of conduct,* you form important impressions regarding the Air Force.

Your civilian friends are interested in their Air Force. They have a right to be. It is their best hope for averting total war and their most effective instrument with which to win victory in limited war. The Air Force is close to their vital interests, for it is the force that stands between their homes and the bombs of the enemy. Incidentally, the Air Force is one of their greatest single reasons for taxes, so they have a lively and legitimate interest in the Air Force, and they most frequently turn to the individual Air Force officer for information. The manner in which you meet that interest will have a decided effect on the future of the Air Force. Accordingly, each officer should *welcome* the opportunity to provide factual, proportioned information about the Air Force to civilian friends, taking care always, of course, to avoid classified matters. If your civilian friends point with alarm to a report that a C5A aircraft has blown up, explain how such things happen and how infrequently they happen. If civilians ask whether your quarters allowance is tax exempt, tell them yes. Also, explain to them the *overall* financial status of Air Force personnel. In other words, so far as security considerations permit, give your civilian friends the *whole* truth. Throughout, remember that the U.S. Air Force is the property of American citizens. They have built it, manned it, and paid for it. They have an awful lot of blue chips riding on its wings.

Air Force officers should seek to take a full part in the life of the civilian community. Be sociable with your neighbors. Become a member of their clubs, societies, and churches. Take your share in community enterprises. In short, be a good neighbor, a respected and desired neighbor. While doing so, you will not only perform well a duty expected of you as an Air Force officer but also add greatly to your own enjoyment of life.

## ON HEALTH AND HAPPINESS

Many lists of attributes considered essential to a successful Air Force officer omit two critically important items: health and happiness. The traditional picture of an officer of our armed services is that of a man or a woman so dedicated to duty, so disciplined, that they carry on despite illness of the body, sickness of the soul, or agonized turmoil of the mind. Baloney! An officer in such condition may indeed carry on, but is a menace to all. Such an officer is incapable of doing an adequate job in assigned tasks and is almost as dangerous as someone who is drunk or insane. The Air Force has issued an order *requiring* all Air Force officers to take action to guard their own physical health and mental freshness. Thus, the Air Force recognizes a fact: Officers cannot do their best work unless they are healthy and happy. Let's consider the matter.

Mental health—we'll call it happiness—is a natural state. We must concern ourselves, therefore, with those things that disturb happiness, those troubles that beset us with such intensity or persistence as to destroy our natural serenity.

**Physical Troubles.** The most common and perhaps the most serious disturber of our inner peace is bad health. Officers who are suffering from ulcers or heart trouble are worried officers, anxious about the future and that of their families. They may well be uncomfortable officers, suffering often or constantly from the illness. They may be afraid the next physical examination may end their careers in the Air Force, leaving the serious problem of finding a new way to earn a living of sufficiently high standard for their dependents. Such officers are in trouble. How did it happen?

Young, vigorous officers have some difficulty imagining themselves other than healthy when they *are* healthy. Still, though you are healthy now, you may do well to look ahead a bit. The Air Force is a tense organization, bearing the most grave and urgent responsibilities ever assigned to a military force. Officers of the Air Force lead lives characterized by steady pressure, sudden change, and taut occasions. Unless Air Force officers are more than usually careful of their health, the long years of tension may finally make their mark, perhaps grievously.

*Fast Lunches.* Being specific, consider the matter of eating. In 20 years of service, you could just "grab a bite to eat" for lunch from the junk food vending machine more than 5,000 times! What does this procedure of eating rapidly and without regard to a balanced diet do to health? Any doctor can give answers ranging over a wide variety of physical troubles. Which one would finally hit *you* depends on your particular makeup. One of them certainly would.

*Liquor.* One of the most certain though expensive methods of breaking down good health is excessive use of liquor. All right, what's excessive? Unfortunately, there's no pat answer. Life would be far simpler for most people if there *were* a pat answer—if it could be said that two drinks of an evening are *not* dangerous, but that three drinks *are* dangerous. Not so. It all depends on you. One thing is certain, however: If you drink to the point of being "high" each evening or even a few evenings a week, something is going to give. Perhaps it will be your stomach, perhaps your heart, or perhaps your liver. Sooner or later.

If you prefer, you need not drink at all. No one will think the less of you. And if they do, it's their choice, not yours.

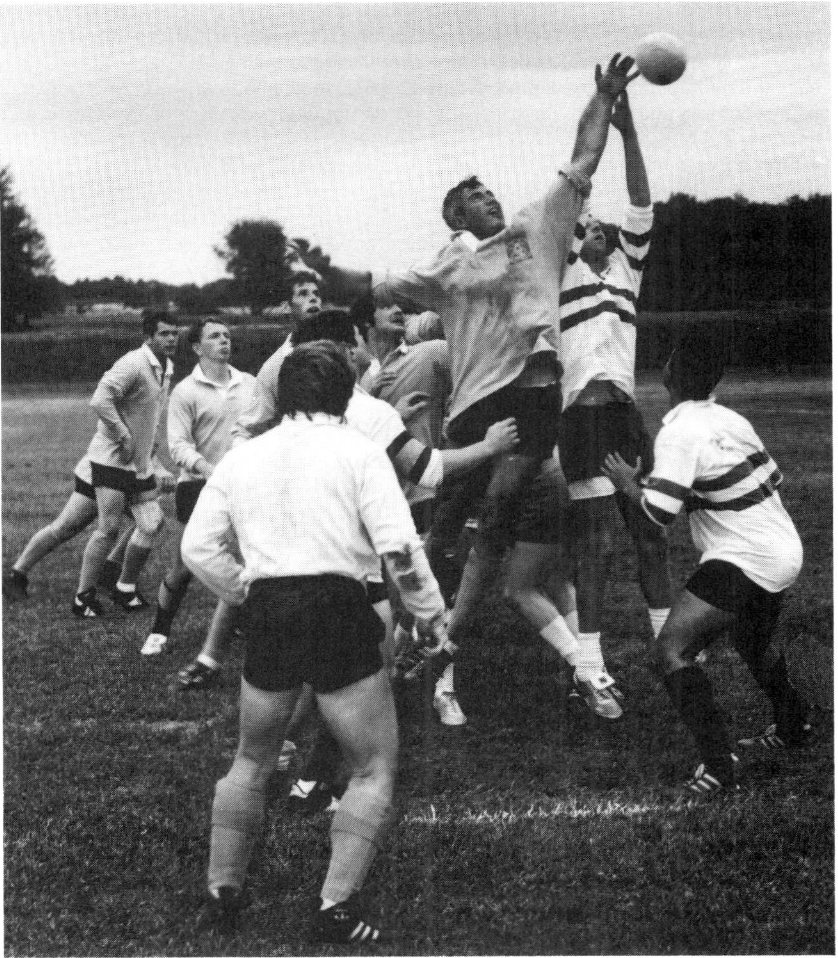

THE AIR FORCE TAKES UP RUGBY.

*Drugs.* Just say no. If you don't care about your health yet, at least consider your career. Mandatory urinalysis is as deadly for some careers as drugs are for some people.

*Smoking.* The Department of Defense is making a concerted effort to discourage smoking among members of the armed forces. This is in response to the evidence that smoking puts the smoker's health at risk. Today in the military, nonsmoking offices and workplaces are often the rule. During off-duty hours, it is your choice to smoke or not, but if you smoke, you are responsible for being considerate of those who do not.

*Exercise.* Smart exercise is good health insurance, and the Air Force's weight control program and physical fitness program underline the responsibility of the officer to keep trim and fit so as to be able to carry out often arduous duties (AFR 35-11). If nothing else, the perhaps 20 years of physical training (PT) tests ahead of you should convince you to get into shape and stay in shape, no matter what your age or exercise preferences are.

Find some different kinds of activities you enjoy and take part in them, such as running, cycling, racquetball, squash, handball, soccer, basketball, golf, football, baseball, tennis, weightlifting, aerobics, walking, or swimming. Play them with your spouse, your friends, and your colleagues. As you process in at every new base you're assigned to, sign up for a locker at the gym and sign up for a soccer team or a racquetball court or the next local 10K and soon you'll find like-minded souls who may become friends for a lifetime. If you think such play is frivolous and beneath the dignity of an Air Force officer, consider this question: If you had to parachute into enemy territory tomorrow, could you run five miles to safety or to complete your mission?

*Weight.* Watch the weight. Almost all people tend to pick up weight as they grow older. The trouble with this tendency is that the more weight one carries, the more work the heart must do. Thus, the normal strain on the heart due to age doubles because of the greater amount of tissue it must support. Keeping the weight down will *not* prevent a heart attack or cure heart trouble. Excessive weight *will* bring on such troubles earlier, aggravate them, and cause them to be more persistent.

*Worry.* Most doctors look on worry as the chief debilitating agent of modern times. Anxiety is their high-priced word for it. Worrying is probably the most expensive of all pastimes, because it not only prevents effective action to remove the cause of worry but also degrades the physical and mental strength of worriers, thus making them less capable of taking any action. Worrying, however, is more a symptom than a disease. This thought brings us to the area of mental health—happiness.

**Happiness.** Mental health—serenity, happiness—this state of mind is usually firm and stable when there is no cause for concern about health, family, career, or finances. It is true that an entire spectrum of special situations does not fall within these four categories. But it is also true that about 99 percent of all unhappiness stems from these fatal four. Officers must take care not only of their own health but also the health of others whose lives touch their own.

*Dependents' Health.* As an officer, you should never allow your official duties of the moment to prevent your taking proper steps to assure the health of your loved ones. This duty may necessitate absenting yourself from your place of work for a few hours to take your child to the doctor for a needed checkup. Do so. Your commander will approve, especially if you ask beforehand. The point is this: If you fail to see that your spouse or child gets proper medical attention at the time it can do the most good, sooner or later your spouse or child may become seriously ill. Then you become deeply disturbed, and the Air Force loses your most effective services, not for a few hours but for weeks or months.

*Family Problems.* Turning more generally to the matter of the officer's family, no person enjoys the best mental health when family relationships are abnormal. The foremost consideration in this area is the relationship between husband and wife. Air Force officers ought to realize that they cannot live a daily home life full of strain and turmoil and at the same time do a top-notch job at work. If trouble persists between husband and wife, they should not allow it to fester. Rather, the two should agree to discuss their problem with the chaplain or the doctor, as they choose. They should thresh it out, bring it up into the light of day. False pride is poor justification for suppressing a situation that can wreck lives, careers, and the health of all involved. Officers *must* realize that marital problems are the proper concern of the Air Force because these strains can and very often do result in poor health, poor efficiency, or both. Officers suffering from appendicitis do not hesitate to lay this problem before a doctor. They should as quickly seek competent advice on family problems because these can be, in the long run, more damaging than most bodily ailments.

*Career Dissatisfaction.* Concern about your career can become a source of worry, of bitterness, of frustration amounting to a major menace to mental health. Perhaps you feel you have been forced into a career channel to which you are unsuited. Perhaps you believe you have been mistreated in the matter of promotion. These thoughts can lead to a state of mind incompatible with serenity and will markedly degrade your performance in your assignment. Should such a problem develop, you should talk it over with your commander in complete frankness. The commander may not agree with you, but will at least know your state of mind. By sharing your problem with someone, you lighten it somewhat. Better still, the commander may be able to do something about it. If you don't feel comfortable talking to your commander, go see a chaplain or a lawyer or a community mental health professional. But do something—don't just keep it inside you until you make yourself ill.

*Finances.* Finances are perhaps the greatest single source of worry among officers. Finances are also the greatest single source of career and marital troubles. All officers should spend ample time *thinking*—not worrying—about their finances. Trite as it may sound, there is no good substitute for a budget. A budget is simply a financial plan, a program for matching obligations and income. All officers can draw up a budget for themselves. The trick is to stick to it.

*Easy Credit.* Foremost among the financial traps awaiting officers is the easy credit of these times. Officers are considered excellent credit risks because the services require them to meet their just debts. They can buy on credit almost anything they are willing to sign for. There is a great temptation, therefore, to go for the high-priced car, the deluxe television set, and the best quality furniture. The best help in resisting these temptations is the cold logic of a personal budget. A budget will show you exactly what you can afford to buy with your income.

If, however, you slip into a welter of debts, the best action is to consult with a reputable bank. Seek to consolidate a number of debts into one large one, to be paid off in a manner consistent with your income. When you pay off your credit cards, however, make sure you don't simply run them up again, or you'll face the original pile of bills plus the new one from the consolidation loan from the bank. An oversea assignment in a low-cost-of-living area may help to solve a temporary financial problem, but don't bank on it.

Other than by such notably stupid practices as spending too much money on liquor or gambling, the chief methods of encountering financial troubles are in connection with renting or buying a house, buying a car, and purchasing furniture or appliances (AFR 35-18).

*Renting an Apartment or a House.* Renting is an experience that often befalls Air Force officers, so consider these points: First of all, a lease is binding on you as an Air Force officer unless you get PCS orders. Make sure your lease has a military clause.

Second, be very clear as to what the rent covers. How about utilities? Water? Heat? Who pays for these? Third, if the landlord requires an extra month's rent as a deposit in advance, exactly what are the conditions under which you would be able to get your deposit back? Is fair wear and tear chargeable? Before renting, ask to see a few utility bills for the *winter* and *summer* months. These are, in effect, additional rent. Determine such matters firmly before you sign the lease.

*Buying a House.* Buying a house is probably the most serious financial move you as an officer will ever make. Thorough investigation of all angles is imperative, especially in these days of conventional, variable rate, and creative financing in addition to your eligibility for VA and FHA guaranteed loans. Current four-year tours often make buying a house seem like a very good investment. But before you buy, research the housing market in your area to assess your chances of being able to resell or rent your house if you wish when you PCS.

*Buying Cars.* The primary mistake of most officers in buying an automobile is to sign up for a Cadillac on a Chevrolet budget. Any fully equipped automobile is a very expensive item, especially if it's also equipped with finance charges. Further, the higher the initial price, the higher the upkeep cost. When it comes to spare parts, another factor sets in with a vengeance. Compare the cost of a new muffler for a Porsche with the same item for a Toyota. Generators, starters, water pumps, tires—you must replace these, too, when they wear out. In this area you find a significant differential. Finally, compare the percentage of turn-in allowance to original cost. Whatever your final decision, at least take these matters into account.

*Buying Furniture.* An officer can easily go overboard in purchasing furniture and appliances. You will be overseas about one-third of your service. Repeated moves or storage will reduce furniture to shambles. Buy only the items of furniture you really must have. Stay away from very expensive, delicate items. Don't try to match the Joneses. Maybe the Joneses do not live a third of their lives in faraway places.

*Bad Checks.* Monitor zealously your checkbook balance and, indeed, your entire credit rating. Impress upon your spouse the need for responsibility, and if you share a checking account, be sure that each party knows the extent to which he or she may use it. Keep an amount in your account as a cushion above your monthly expenditures. If possible, either arrange with your bank to notify you if there is a slip-up before "bouncing" a check, or authorize it to cover the amount by drawing against your savings account (AFR 35-18).

**Summary.** In this section, we have touched only lightly on some of the more common sources of trouble. Whatever may be your specific situation, if you have a problem that menaces your health of mind, of body, or of soul, seek competent advice, and seek it early. Remember that your health is a matter of proper and sincere concern to your superiors in the Air Force, to your doctor, and to your chaplain. Don't ignore the help they can give you and will gladly give if you ask. You are far more important to the Air Force than any piece of machinery, any weapon, any gadget. You, the Air Force officer, are the kingpin of a weapons system that guards the survival of civilization. Take care of yourself.

Moderation—a sense of proportion—in the areas discussed will keep most officers out of trouble. If, nonetheless, troubles arise, don't just worry. Do something!

---

*Note:* See Jonathan P. Tomes, *Servicemember's Legal Guide,* 2nd ed., Stackpole Books, 1992, for more specific guidance.

# Part Two • Your Career and Advancement

# 12

# Promotion

*It is our goal to provide opportunity for everyone to rise to as high a level of responsibility as his talent and diligence will take him.*

—General John D. Ryan, former Chief of Staff, USAF

The subject of promotion comes up for lively discussion whenever and wherever groups of officers gather. Such discussions are only natural because promotion is the avenue to increased responsibility and rank, including the pay and other emoluments that go with increased responsibility. Like the weather, promotion causes heated discussions, but often without full consideration of just what the promotion system is supposed to accomplish, the methods available, or the problems involved in the operation of a career promotion system. Understanding the promotion system—what it is, how it works, and some of the obstacles involved—requires a review of the laws and regulations governing promotion.

## DEFENSE OFFICER PERSONNEL MANAGEMENT ACT (DOPMA)

To an extent unparalleled by any other profession, the law establishes the parameters of the careers of commissioned officers. These laws reflect the concern of the Congress and the nation in maintaining the high quality of our officer force and the recognition that this quality is essential to national security. A landmark in the legislation governing officer personnel management was the enactment of the Defense Officer Personnel Management Act (DOPMA), which became effective on 15 September 1981.

DOPMA updated outmoded aspects of earlier law, introduced important new officer personnel management concepts, and completed the task begun with the Officer Personnel Act of 1947 of unifying and standardizing the law as it applies to officers of the four armed services. While DOPMA deals in comprehensive fashion with all aspects of officer personnel management, the bulk of the legislation concerns the dimensions and characteristics of the career system for officers and the specific rules governing promotion procedures. The changes from earlier systems and procedures were evolutionary, building on experience under previous laws to improve the overall quality of the officer corps.

Two changes DOPMA made are particularly significant to the Air Force: (1) permanent grade relief for the Air Force from the restrictive field grade authorizations contained in the Officer Grade Limitation Act of 1954 and (2) the creation of a single system of permanent promotions for all officers on the active-duty list. In 1954, the Air Force, because its officer corps was young in terms of both age and length of service, was authorized relatively fewer officers in the grades of lieutenant colonel and colonel than were the other services. Beginning in 1959, as the Air Force officer corps matured, these lower limits increased on a temporary basis during development of a more comprehensive proposal for officer career management. The Air Force needed temporary grade relief on nine subsequent occasions before DOPMA provided the Air Force what it had long needed: adequate permanent authorizations in law to meet mission requirements and provide attractive career patterns.

The single system of permanent promotions for all officers on the active-duty list introduced by DOPMA replaced a complex and sometimes confusing system of temporary and permanent promotions. Before DOPMA, officers on active duty typically changed insignia as a result of temporary promotion. Regular officers were also considered for permanent promotions that determined their tenure. A similar permanent promotion system for reserve officers considered reserve officers on active duty in competition with all other reserve officers. With DOPMA, all active-duty-list officers are considered under the same rules governing promotion eligibility and consideration.

With DOPMA in force, the officer corps will continue to have a mix of regular and reserve officers on extended active duty (EAD), although all officers selected for promotion to the grade of major or above will receive regular appointments. Most officers will continue to enter active service as reservists. They will first be considered for a regular appointment when they compete for selection to captain. Subsequent consideration points will be after five and seven years of service.

## PROMOTION SYSTEM OBJECTIVES

Air Force promotion plans for the future have these objectives:

• To fill Air Force positions. The primary purpose of the active-duty promotion system is to select the best qualified officers available to fill Air Force positions; therefore, the system must be responsive to the needs of the Air Force. Promotion is not a reward for past service; it is based on demonstrated potential to serve in positions of greater responsibility.

• To provide reasonably stable, consistent, and visible career progression opportunities. The active-duty promotion system must also provide incentive to the officer. It must make visible reasonable opportunity for promotion, including accelerated promotion from below the promotion zone for officers possessing exceptional potential, to attract the officer toward an Air Force career. The active-duty promotion system should be relatively stable, so as to provide each year group of officers opportunity comparable with that of other year groups.

• To maintain force vitality. To carry out its role in support of national objectives, the military service has a unique requirement to maintain a young and dynamic officer force that is capable of developing and managing a large combat ready force and of assuming wartime leadership. The Air Force promotion system is designed to produce officers in sufficient quality and quantity while maintaining a well-balanced force in terms of age and experience.

Over the past several years, we have seen senior officers retiring who were with us in the post-Korea cold war era. This turnover means that leadership is transferring to the next generation of officers. The Air Force must continue to cultivate a promotion system that will select only those who best meet the challenges for future leadership.

## PROMOTION BOARDS

We have discussed the new officer promotion system that DOPMA provides and the Air Force's promotion philosophy and procedures, but not how one officer gets promoted and another does not. No discussion of the subject is realistic that does not touch upon how one gets oneself promoted. Although cynics may tell you that the prerequisites are to be a general officer's offspring, in-law, or aide, you may reasonably doubt the truth of that idea because there is too much evidence to the contrary. Others more sanguine may subscribe to the fatalistic philosophy that if they do a good job the system will take care of them, but this theory, too, is an insufficient explanation.

Discussing how a typical promotion board operates may help you understand better how the selection process—often shrouded in mystery and distorted by rumor—really works. First, to scotch some rumors, it does not help to have a friend on the board; job descriptions and word pictures *are* important as well as the blocks checked; and the process does not favor select groups.

A selection board uses the following officer records as instruments: all officer performance reports (OPRs) and training reports, an official photograph, citations or orders for approved U.S. decorations, the officer selection brief, letters pertaining to nonattendance at or ineligibility for professional military education (PME), letters to the board from officers eligible in or above the promotion zone, and specified unfavorable information, such as court-martial orders and Air Force forms reflecting the imposition of nonjudicial punishment.

All selection boards use the best-qualified method of selection. Because the board can recommend only a set maximum number, it must arrange those eligible in an order-of-merit listing (best- to least-qualified), apply the quota to this listing, and promote those officers above the line where the quota runs out. Boards evaluate officers using the whole-person concept. Board members review carefully each officer's selection folder, especially in the areas of job performance and responsibility, leadership, breadth of experience, professional competence, and academic and professional military education.

Boards take care to put the different earlier OER and newer OPR systems into their proper historical context. The board knows that records contain evaluations under several different assignments. The ratee's job, unit of assignment, level of responsibility, and OPR endorsements all play a part in evaluation. The selection folder reflects each officer's level of academic and professional military education, but the board judges to what extent these achievements improve performance and potential to assume greater responsibility. The board does not give mere completion of such courses disproportionate credit, nor does the board penalize officers for not having obtained advanced degrees or PME diplomas. Some officers, such as those assigned to engineering or scientific areas or to some particular rated specialty, may not receive an opportunity for career broadening, so boards do not penalize them for that reason. The Air Force needs both specialists and generalists.

Boards must promote the best officers they review for consideration, and the board members—highly qualified officers who have the experience and mature judgment to make accurate assessments of potential—must take an oath to perform their duties without prejudice or partiality, having in view the fitness of the officers considered and the efficiency of the USAF. The Air Force takes pains to ensure that board panels make selections on a uniform basis. Of course, in the last analysis, one's view of the promotion selection process may depend upon whether one is selected, but the Air Force makes strenuous and conscientious efforts to ensure that the selection basis is the best one possible.

## HOW TO GET PROMOTED

This question has no perfect and unequivocal answer, but some observations based on experience may help. First, hit the ground running when you go on active duty. Whether you go first to flight or technical training or get on-the-job training (OJT), master your *job* quickly and thoroughly and give it 110 percent effort. Although your seniors, peers, and subordinates should give you aid and comfort, don't assume that anyone is going to help you learn the ropes. After this step, learn your *profession,* the profession of arms. Even in this age of specialization, just being a specialist—a pilot, a navigator, or an intelligence officer—is not enough. The military profession is one of the oldest and most honorable professions. Learn it, understand it, and respect it.

Along the way, you may want to become an expert in some aspect of the military arts and sciences that few or no others know. If you are *the* expert, your expertise may lead you to some interesting experiences.

Strive for assignments at increasingly higher command and staff levels, including joint staff duties. When you can obtain advanced education and PME, go for it. Try to master at least one foreign language, and it need not be an esoteric one. Thanks to a rather basic knowledge of French, one officer found himself posted to a sensitive joint staff position in Saigon at a crucial period of the Vietnam War and later was picked to help initiate closer relations between the Air University and France's Ecole Superieure de Guerre Aerienne.

Because your fellow officer is at the same time your comrade, your peer, and your competitor for promotion, you must maintain a proper perspective about this business of promotion. Above all, keep a good sense of humor. Always be your own man or woman, never forgetting Polonius's advice to Laertes in *Hamlet:* "This above all, to thine own self be true. Thou canst not then be false to any man." After your career has ended and if you have soldiered as a professional, not only will you cherish the worth of it all, having followed the path of duty, honor, and country, but also you will cherish the camaraderie that was such an essential part of it.

# 13
# Officer Evaluation System

*War must be carried on systematically, and to do it, you must have good officers.*
—General George Washington

The measurement of an officer's performance, with potentials, strengths, and weaknesses, is a matter of the gravest importance to the Air Force, as well as to you, the individual officer. Performance reports constitute the most important single source of information for selection and assignment of people to do the work of the Air Force. They are the means by which all members may be placed where their work will be of greatest value. Here also will be recorded the information that will determine selection for promotion, for favored assignment, for the higher schools, or for actions leading possibly to elimination or termination of service.

Junior officers are not so much concerned with why performance reports are necessary, or even with the responsibility imposed upon the rating officers, as they are with how to obtain a favorable performance report. This chapter will therefore discuss the Officer Evaluation System (OES), how the rating system's forms work, and how you can approach trying to get higher evaluations.

Officers who study this information and apply it will find themselves in the position of writing performance reports on other officers sooner than they may now think.

## THE OES AND OFFICER PROFESSIONAL DEVELOPMENT

Because any appraisal system is an integral part of officer professional development, it is important to understand the Air Force concept of professional development. It has three basic objectives.

First, professional development must increase the officer's qualification and ability to perform duties, now and in the near term. Formal training and discussions with supervisors provide a foundation for building this competence. However, the most important contributor is likely to be the officer's experiences in day-to-day duties.

Second, professional development involves preparing officers for future leadership challenges. Professional Military Education (PME) and most other education assists this effort, but, again, the key to growth in leadership and professionalism is experience in appropriate leadership positions.

The third objective of professional development is to ensure the people who are best qualified are advanced in grade and responsibility. This is where the Officer Evaluation System fits in.

What makes an officer "best qualified" for promotion? The right kind of experience, training, and education at the right time.

Lieutenants and captains become best qualified for promotion by concentrating on depth of experience in their career areas. Staff assignments and other career-broadening experiences are not needed for promotion to major. Some captains will serve in staff jobs because their expertise is needed, but the OES will strongly emphasize performance in the assigned job for company grade officers with neither credit nor penalty for staff jobs.

There is increased opportunity for field grade officers to fill command and staff jobs, with more diverse job opportunities and accompanying broadened career opportunities. Field grade officers who choose to forgo broader opportunities and remain in primary line duties should still have a reasonable prospect for promotion to lieutenant colonel, given a level of performance warranting promotion. The lieutenant colonel seeking promotion to colonel will generally need emphasis on broader considerations as well as job performance.

The point is that lieutenants and captains need not make a long-term career decision between a narrow focus on line jobs and broadening. Whatever their long-term goals, the right focus at the lieutenant and captain level is in their career area. The primary concern of all officers should be doing the very best possible job in their primary duties, day in and day out.

## WHY AN OES?

The Air Force has a high-quality officer force, making competition for promotion inevitable. An evaluation system should not attempt to eliminate or even reduce the intensity of this competition. Rather, the OES must ensure that officers compete on the right basis by measuring the proper accomplishments and qualities.

The number of officers to be selected for promotion by any given board is limited because there is a ceiling imposed by law on the number of officers who can be serving in the field grades. The accompanying table illustrates the select rates for promotion to captain through colonel averaged over five promotion boards and the corresponding promotion opportunity.

**SELECT RATES BY PROMOTION ZONE**
***(Line Only)***

| *To* | *IPZ* | *BPZ* | *APZ* | *Promotion Opportunity* |
|---|---|---|---|---|
| Captain | 96% | N/A | 40% | 97.5% |
| Major | 79% | 1.2% | 14% | 90% |
| Lt. Colonel | 62% | 2.6% | 6% | 75% |
| Colonel | 43% | 3.0% | 3% | 55% |

As an example, the chart shows that, on average, 79 percent of captains are promoted to major when first eligible in the promotion zone (IPZ). Another 1.2 percent have been selected for promotion below the promotion zone (BPZ) and 14 percent of those considered above the promotion zone (APZ) have been promoted. Overall, the opportunity to be selected for major below, in, or above the promotion zone is 90 percent. (Note: The individual selection rate percentages do not add up to 90 percent because group sizes are not the same.) Promotion opportunity and select rates to all grades remain relatively constant regardless of the evaluation system used. The purpose of an evaluation system is to ensure promotion boards have the information to select, within these percentages, officers who are the best qualified.

## PERFORMANCE FEEDBACK

Performance feedback is an important element of the OES. It will be provided during a private, formal meeting between an officer and the officer's supervisor and is designed to provide a realistic assessment of the officer's performance. An initial session requires the supervisor to let an officer know what is expected. This is the basis for later feedback on how well the officer is meeting these expectations. The second feedback meeting will occur midway through the officer's reporting cycle to allow for corrections in deficient areas.

The supervisor will prepare a handwritten form that provides an assessment of the subordinate's performance, and the two will discuss the form. At the conclusion of the session, the rater will give the form to the officer being provided the feedback. The feedback form will not become part of an officer's record, nor can the rater show the form to anyone other than the officer on whom the form has been prepared.

Supervisors will provide feedback on duty performance, job knowledge, leadership skills, organizational skills, judgment and decisions, professional qualities, and communication skills using a scale that ranges from "Needs Significant Improvement" to "Needs Little Improvement." The rater may also add written comments to expand on these ratings.

Performance feedback will be required twice annually for company grade officers. An officer of any grade may request performance feedback at any time, and a supervisor may call for a feedback session whenever the supervisor feels it will be useful.

## OFFICER PERFORMANCE REPORT

The Officer Performance Report (OPR) is designed to build a continuing record of performance. The rater is an officer's immediate supervisor, the same person who provides performance feedback, so the person being rated shouldn't be surprised with the content of the report. The additional rater is the supervisor's boss. For officers below the grade of colonel, the additional rater must be at least one grade senior to the officer being rated.

A senior officer, called the reviewer, will perform quality control on the report. The reviewer will not normally provide a rating and does not make comments about the officer unless there is disagreement with the rating of the rater or additional rater. For lieutenants through majors, the reviewer is the wing commander or equivalent staff officer. For lieutenant colonels and colonels, the reviewer is the first general officer in the rating chain. The reviewer will be in a position to have personal knowledge, or access to such knowledge, of the officer's job performance.

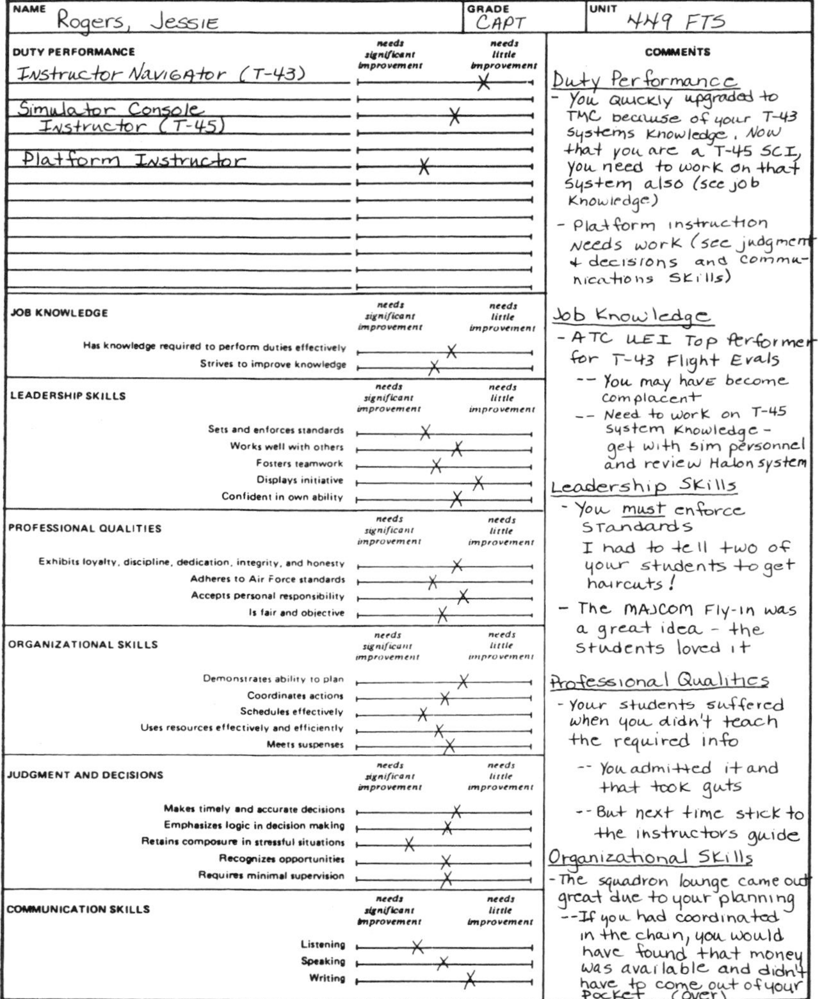

NAME Rogers, Jessie | GRADE Capt | UNIT 449 FTS

**DUTY PERFORMANCE** (needs significant improvement — needs little improvement)

Instructor Navigator (T-43) X

Simulator Console Instructor (T-45) X

Platform Instructor X

**JOB KNOWLEDGE**

Has knowledge required to perform duties effectively X

Strives to improve knowledge X

**LEADERSHIP SKILLS**

Sets and enforces standards X

Works well with others X

Fosters teamwork X

Displays initiative X

Confident in own ability X

**PROFESSIONAL QUALITIES**

Exhibits loyalty, discipline, dedication, integrity, and honesty X

Adheres to Air Force standards X

Accepts personal responsibility X

Is fair and objective X

**ORGANIZATIONAL SKILLS**

Demonstrates ability to plan X

Coordinates actions X

Schedules effectively X

Uses resources effectively and efficiently X

Meets suspenses X

**JUDGMENT AND DECISIONS**

Makes timely and accurate decisions X

Emphasizes logic in decision making X

Retains composure in stressful situations X

Recognizes opportunities X

Requires minimal supervision X

**COMMUNICATION SKILLS**

Listening X

Speaking X

Writing X

**COMMENTS**

Duty Performance
- You quickly upgraded to TMC because of your T-43 systems knowledge. Now that you are a T-45 SCI, you need to work on that system also (see job knowledge)
- Platform instruction needs work (see judgment + decisions and communications skills)

Job Knowledge
- ATC UEI Top Performer for T-43 Flight Evals
-- You may have become complacent
-- Need to work on T-45 system knowledge - get with sim personnel and review Halon system

Leadership Skills
- You must enforce standards. I had to tell two of your students to get haircuts!
- The MAJCOM Fly-in was a great idea - the students loved it

Professional Qualities
- Your students suffered when you didn't teach the required info
-- You admitted it and that took guts
-- But next time stick to the instructors guide

Organizational Skills
- The squadron lounge came out great due to your planning
-- If you had coordinated in the chain, you would have found that money was available and didn't have to come out of your pocket (over)

PERFORMANCE FEEDBACK WORKSHEET *(front)*.

The emphasis of the performance report is on how well officers accomplish their primary duties. The raters will not consider or evaluate the probable impact of professional military education, advanced degrees, or broadening assignments. This information is available elsewhere in an officer's record. The raters' task is to focus on performance and potential based on that performance.

The OPR will provide a brief description of the unit mission, the officer's job description, and a short narrative to document the officer's most significant achievements and

STRENGTHS, SUGGESTED GOALS, AND ADDITIONAL COMMENTS:

ORGANIZATIONAL SKILLS (Cont)

- Your student evals are usually turned in the day they are due. Plan ahead and get them in early so we have more options in the area of student management.

Judgment and Decisions

- As training mission commander, you make good decisions, Continuing that integrated navigation sortie when 1 complexes TACAN failed was just one example. There are more.
- You need to relax when students interupt your planned presentation. Make sure their questions are answered satisfactorily before you go on.

Communication Skills

- Listen to student questions to see where the real problem lies
  -- Does student understand the theory but not know how to use the equipment?
- Don't be so mechanical during academic presentations. Your students have scored below average on several tests Your students are giving you signs that they're not catching everything you're throwing out (quizzical looks, questions, etc). You're missing the signs. If you want, we can set up a video taping of one of your classes.

Additional Comments

- Not many surprises here. We've talked about most of these areas informally and I've already seen some improvement in T-45 Knowledge (still a ways to go, though)
- You need to remember that 50% of our instruction is in the classroom. You work well with students in the airplane and sim (low in: student ratio) but you must become equally comfortable in the classroom
- Last point: It's fine to talk up fighters in the bar, but don't put the other tracks down too hard Some of our Grads will go to TTB + EWT. They don't always have a choice!

| RATER SIGNATURE | DATE |
|---|---|
| Larry Osbourne | 17 Mar 89 |

*AF Form 724, AUG 88 (Reverse)*

PERFORMANCE FEEDBACK WORKSHEET *(reverse)*.

the impact of these accomplishments on the unit mission. In addition, several performance factors will be rated on a two-block scale: "Meets Standards" or "Does Not Meet Standards." The evaluation of these factors will not include narrative remarks. Finally, the form will contain space for brief comments by the evaluators.

Performance reports make up the cumulative record of an officer's performance. They will weigh heavily both in the promotion board's deliberations and in the senior rater's recommendation for promotion, which will be made on a separate form.

**I. RATEE IDENTIFICATION DATA** *(Read AFR 36-10 carefully before filling in any item)*

| 1. NAME *(Last, First, Middle Initial)* | 2. SSN | 3. GRADE | 4. DAFSC |
|---|---|---|---|
| MERRIWEATHER, PAUL E. | XXX-XX-XXXX | Captain | 4024 |

| 5. PERIOD OF REPORT | | 6. NO. DAYS SUPERVISION | 7. REASON FOR REPORT |
|---|---|---|---|
| From: 24 Apr 88 | Thru: 28 Feb 89 | 310 | CRO |

| 8. ORGANIZATION, COMMAND, LOCATION | 9. PAS CODE |
|---|---|
| 432d Aircraft Generation Squadron (PACAF), Misawa Air Base, Japan | MOORFWJT |

**II. UNIT MISSION DESCRIPTION**

Responsible for all on-equipment maintenance for 2 combat-ready 24 primary assigned aircraft (PAA) F-16 squadrons. The AGS supports in-place and deployed contingency operations in the Pacific theater. Peacetime activities include supporting daily flying training at home station and various deployed, joint and combined exercises throughout PACOM.

**III. JOB DESCRIPTION** 1. DUTY TITLE: Officer-in-Charge, 14th Aircraft Maintenance Unit (AMU)

2. KEY DUTIES, TASKS, AND RESPONSIBILITIES: Provides on-equipment maintenance for 24 F-16C/D aircraft in the air-to-air and air-to-ground missions. Responsible for 200 personnel in 14 AFSCs, performing maintenance, launch, recovery, and weapons loading functions. Acts as senior maintenance officer during deployments. Also responsible for training and training records for all unit personnel and $2.5M worth of unit-owned support equipment as well as aerospace ground equipment, vehicles, and AMU facilities. SIGNIFICANT ADDITIONAL DUTIES: Squadron Mobility Officer.

**IV. IMPACT ON MISSION ACCOMPLISHMENT**

- Led AMU in COPE THUNDER 88-3
  -- 200 successful training sorties without maintenance air abort while operating from deployed location
- Developed new flightline mobility procedures
  -- 24 combat-ready aircraft/28 increments of error-free cargo
- Achieved 85 percent systems effectiveness by integrating all electronic combat subsystems into a comprehensive electronic combat program
  -- 75 percent is MAJCOM standard
- Developed computerized maintenance system procedures 2 weeks early

| V. PERFORMANCE FACTORS | DOES NOT MEET STANDARDS | MEETS STANDARDS |
|---|---|---|
| 1. **Job Knowledge** Has knowledge required to perform duties effectively. Strives to improve that knowledge. | ☐ | ☒ |
| 2. **Leadership Skills** Sets and enforces standards. Works well with others. Fosters teamwork. Displays initiative. Self-confident. | ☐ | ☒ |
| 3. **Professional Qualities** Exhibits loyalty, discipline, dedication, integrity, and honesty. Adheres to Air Force standards. Accepts personal responsibility. Is fair and objective. | ☐ | ☒ |
| 4. **Organizational Skills** Plans, coordinates, schedules, and uses resources effectively. Meets suspenses. | ☐ | ☒ |
| 5. **Judgment and Decisions** Makes timely and accurate decisions. Emphasizes logic in decision making. Retains composure in stressful situations. Recognizes opportunities. Requires minimal supervision. | ☐ | ☒ |
| 6. **Communication Skills** Listens, speaks, and writes effectively. | ☐ | ☒ |

**AF Form 707B, AUG 88**

COMPANY GRADE OFFICER PERFORMANCE REPORT *(front)*.

## PROMOTION RECOMMENDATION

To assist promotion boards in selecting those officers best qualified for promotion, there is the Promotion Recommendation Form (PRF), which focuses strongly on duty performance. It is completed 60 days prior to a promotion board on all officers eligible for promotion in or above the promotion zone and on a specific percentage of those officers eligible below the promotion zone. The individual completing the form is the

**VI. RATER OVERALL ASSESSMENT**

Capt Merriweather's leadership had a positive impact on the entire squadron. He took this low-performing AMU and brought most maintenance indicators up to or above command standards. His diligence allowed completion of four urgent action TCTOs while preparing aircraft for COPE THUNDER 88-3. His AMU supported a 21 UTE rate in spite of major aircraft structural restrictions. He demonstrated potential for increased responsibility in his daily integration of the management, technical, and administrative facets required of a successful AMU. Capt Merriweather is an outstanding performer. Send him to intermediate service school in residence.

Performance feedback was accomplished consistent with the direction in AFR 36-10. *(If not accomplished, state the reason.)*

| NAME, GRADE, BR OF SVC, ORGN, COMD, LOCATION | DUTY TITLE | | DATE |
|---|---|---|---|
| MALCOME B. ERVIN, Lt Col, USAF<br>432d Aircraft Generation Sq (PACAF)<br>Misawa AB, Japan | Commander, 432d Aircraft Generation Sq | | 28 Feb 89 |
| | SSN<br>XXX-XX-XXXX | SIGNATURE<br>Malcome B. Ervin | |

**VII. ADDITIONAL RATER OVERALL ASSESSMENT** CONCUR ☒ NONCONCUR ☐

A dedicated maintenance officer with excellent potential. Capt Merriweather provides strong leadership to his AMU. His abilities resulted in his AMU being selected as the 432d Tactical Fighter Wing Aircraft Maintenance Unit of the Quarter for the first time this year. This is indicative of the depth of his experience and knowledge. He is an outstanding maintenance officer and a valued member of the wing.

| NAME, GRADE, BR OF SVC, ORGN, COMD, LOCATION | DUTY TITLE | | DATE |
|---|---|---|---|
| STEVEN A. BURTLESON, Col, USAF<br>432d Tactical Fighter Wing (PACAF)<br>Misawa AB, Japan | Deputy Commander for Maintenance | | 3 Mar 89 |
| | SSN<br>XXX-XX-XXXX | SIGNATURE<br>Steven A Burtleson | |

**VIII. REVIEWER** CONCUR ☒ NONCONCUR ☐

| NAME, GRADE, BR OF SVC, ORGN, COMD, LOCATION | DUTY TITLE | | DATE |
|---|---|---|---|
| ANDREW D. JONES, Col, USAF<br>432d Tactical Fighter Wing, (PACAF)<br>Misawa AB, Japan | Wing Commander | | 7 Mar 89 |
| | SSN<br>XXX-XX-XXXX | SIGNATURE<br>Andrew D Jones | |

Instructions

**All:** Recommendations must be based on performance and the potential based on that performance. Promotion recommendations are prohibited. Do not consider or comment on completion of or enrollment in PME, advanced education, previous or anticipated promotion recommendations on AF Form 709, OER indorsement levels, family activities, marital status, race, sex, ethnic origin, age, or religion.

**Rater:** Focus your evaluation in Section IV on what the officer did, how well he or she did it and how the officer contributed to mission accomplishment. Write in concise "bullet" format. Your comments in Section VI may include recommendations for augmentation or assignment.

**Additional Rater:** Carefully review the rater's evaluation to ensure it is accurate, unbiased and uninflated. If you disagree, you may ask the rater to review his or her evaluation. You may not direct a change in the evaluation. If you still disagree with the rater, mark "NONCONCUR" and explain. You may include recommendations for augmentation or assignment.

**Reviewer:** Carefully review the rater's and additional rater's ratings and comments. If their evaluations are accurate, unbiased and uninflated, mark the form "CONCUR" and sign the form. If you disagree with previous evaluators, you may ask them to review their evaluations. You may not direct them to change their appraisals. If you still disagree with the additional rater, mark "NONCONCUR" and explain in Section VIII. Do not use "NONCONCUR" simply to provide comments on the report.

*AF Form 707B, AUG 88 (Reverse)*

COMPANY GRADE OFFICER PERFORMANCE REPORT *(reverse).*

officer's senior rater. For lieutenants, captains, and majors, this will be the wing commander or equivalent staff officer. For lieutenant colonels, it will be the first general officer in the rating chain. The senior rater is the same individual who acts as reviewer for the OPR. A different term has been chosen to reflect the different function on the PRF. The senior rater completes the PRF based on knowledge of the officer and on a review of the officer's overall record of performance.

| I. RATEE IDENTIFICATION DATA *(Read AFR 36-10 carefully before filling in any item)* | | | |
|---|---|---|---|
| 1. NAME *(Last, First, Middle Initial)* HARRIS, JOHN T. | 2. SSN XXX-XX-XXXX | 3. GRADE Captain | 4. DAFSC 2635 |
| 5. ORGANIZATION, COMMAND, AND LOCATION Department of Physics, Dean of Faculty (USAFA), Colorado Springs, Colorado | | | 6. PAS CODE USOBFBCC |

**II. UNIT MISSION DESCRIPTION**
The Physics Department is one of 19 academic departments. Department teaches 3 introductory physics courses to 2000 cadets annually and 25 advanced physics courses to 93 physics majors. Conducts basic space physics, laser and astronomy research for several operational commands. Provides officer role models and career counseling to cadets.

**III. JOB DESCRIPTION** 1. DUTY TITLE: Course Director and Instructor of Physics
2. KEY DUTIES, TASKS, RESPONSIBILITIES: Supervises 10 instructors who annually teach 25 sections of introductory calculus-based physics to 1200 cadets. Develops curricula, establishes educational standards, and determines grades. Instructor for 42 cadets in subject areas of classical mechanics, thermodynamics, and fluid mechanics. Conducts classes, motivates, and counsels cadets. Conducts basic optics research funded by the Air Force Weapons Laboratory.

**IV. PROMOTION RECOMMENDATION**
Capt Harris is one of our top company grade instructors meeting this board. His superior record of performance--youngest Minuteman crew commander at Minot AFB, ground-breaking research at the Air Force Weapons Laboratory--bring a real-life relevance to his courses. As a result of his research proposals, he acquired $130K worth of laser equipment and organized a research team of 5 officers. He is now the principle investigator for this project which has significant SDI application. His unique blend of operational experience, technical expertise, and supervisory talent mark him for a bright future. Promote to major this board and select for intermediate service school.

| V. PROMOTION ZONE | VI. GROUP SIZE | VII. BOARD | VIII. SENIOR RATER ID |
|---|---|---|---|
| BPZ [ ] I/APZ [ ] | NA | XXXXX | XXXXX |

**IX. OVERALL RECOMMENDATION**

DEFINITELY PROMOTE [X]
PROMOTE [ ]
DO NOT PROMOTE THIS BOARD [ ]

**X. SENIOR RATER**
NAME, GRADE, BR OF SVC, ORGN, COMD, LOCATION
MARTIN W. DALEY, Col, USAF
US Air Force Academy (USAFA)
Colorado Springs, Colorado

DUTY TITLE
Permanent Professor and Head, Department of Physics

SSN XXX-XX-XXXX

SIGNATURE Martin W. Daley

**Instructions**

Review previous OERs, OPRs, Education/Training Reports, and Supplemental Evaluation Sheets. Discuss, if needed, the officer's performance with officials in the supervisory chain. Evaluate the officer's performance and assess his or her potential based on performance. Do not consider or comment on enrollment in or completion of professional military education or advanced academic education.

Provide an accurate, unbiased assessment free from consideration of race, sex, ethnic origin, age, religion, or marital status.

Provide the officer a copy of this report approximately 30 days prior to the board for which this report is prepared.

AF Form 709, AUG 88

PROMOTION RECOMMENDATION FORM.

The Promotion Recommendation Form consists of a brief description of the unit's mission, the officer's job description, narrative comments about the officer's promotion potential, and one of three possible recommendations: *Definitely Promote, Promote*, or *Do Not Promote This Board.* A Definitely Promote recommendation tells the central promotion board that an officer's performance warrants promotion with minimal regard for broader considerations such as variety of job experience, PME, and academic education. A Promote recommendation means that the officer is well qualified for promotion and should compete on the basis of both performance and broader considerations.

The number of Definitely Promote recommendations for in- and above-the-promotion-zone officers will be limited to a number smaller than the total number of officers that a board can select for advancement. These percentages will vary by grade (see accompanying table). Past experience suggests that when promotion boards are given a vehicle to assist them in differentiating among officers on the basis of performance, they will use it. Therefore, officers in and above the promotion zone who receive a Definitely Promote assessment will probably be promoted at a high rate. Even if all officers with a Definitely Promote are selected, a specified number of people who receive a Promote recommendation will also be promoted. The latter is a mathematical reality based on the fact that more officers will be promoted than will meet the board with a Definitely Promote recommendation.

Senior raters will also give a percentage of their below-the-promotion-zone candidates Definitely Promote recommendations. This amounts to a nomination for early promotion and means only that the officer's record will be reviewed by the selection board. Below-the-promotion-zone Definitely Promote recommendations will be limited to 10 percent of eligible officers for promotion to major and lieutenant colonel and 15 percent for promotion to colonel; this percentage will be applied only to those officers eligible for BPZ consideration. PRFs on officers who are BPZ skip the evaluation board process discussed below and go directly to the central promotion board.

After the senior rater makes promotion recommendations on above- and in-the-promotion-zone candidates, the forms are sent to an evaluation board. This group, made up of senior raters, meets at a numbered air force, major command, or equivalent level. The board performs a quality control function and may, in certain circumstances, allocate a limited number of Definitely Promote recommendations. It cannot downgrade a recommendation given by a senior rater.

Allocation of additional Definitely Promote recommendations by an evaluation board occurs in two cases. The first is when a subordinate unit is too small to earn an allocation of at least one Definitely Promote. A minimum group size of three lieutenants, three captains, three majors, or four lieutenant colonels is required to earn an allocation. Units with fewer eligible officers are aggregated in order to produce a group size large enough for valid quality comparisons. This occurs at the evaluation board.

The second case in which evaluation boards allocate Definitely Promote recommendations is when additional Definitely Promote recommendations are available as a result of rounding down. When senior raters determine how many Definitely Promotes they can award, they must round down any fractions to the nearest whole number. For example, a senior rater who computes that 4.5 officers may receive Definitely Promote recommendations can give this rating to four people. Fractional remains accrue into whole number recommendations that are allocated by the evaluation boards based on job performance of officers whose records they have reviewed.

After the evaluation board completes its tasks, it sends all the APZ and IPZ promotion recommendations to the selection board. By law, the central selection board is charged with selecting officers for promotion. While a Definitely Promote recommendation will be a strong signal, it remains up to the selection board to determine which officers are selected for promotion.

Promotion recommendations for APZ and IPZ candidates will be removed after the central promotion board has finished, whether or not the officer is selected for promotion.

**"Definitely Promote" Allocations by Grade**
***(Line Officers)***

| *Grade to* | *A/IPZ* | *BPZ* |
|---|---|---|
| Captain | 90% | N/A |
| Major | 65% | 10% |
| Lt. Colonel | 45% | 10% |
| Colonel | 25% | 15% |

## IT'S YOUR SYSTEM

The OES is not a personnel program; it is an Air Force program. It is a tool that officers can use in their own professional development and in the development of those officers they supervise. It strongly recognizes the importance of performance, both in the current job and over the course of each officer's career. It is up to each officer, especially those entrusted with supervisory responsibilities, to use this tool wisely and properly.

## QUESTIONS AND ANSWERS ABOUT THE REVISED OFFICER EVALUATION SYSTEM

**Why is feedback mandatory for company grade officers, while optional for others?**

In general, company grade officers can benefit the most from more guidance and direction. Further, these officers may be more hesitant to ask for feedback. Making feedback mandatory for company grade officers ensures they receive the necessary guidance, direction, and feedback to help develop those skills and traits essential in field grade officers.

**What will be contained in the "Impact on Mission Accomplishment" section of the Officer Performance Report?**

This section will contain specific information on what the officer has done that impacts the unit's capability to carry out the mission. The unit here refers to the unit of assignment—the communications squadron, the security police, the field maintenance squadron, or the like. Impact on the unit mission is written to this level and not to the overall mission of the wing or equivalent unit. An officer's contribution to the unit mission, by definition, also positively impacts the wing, command, and Air Force missions.

**Why will raters use bullet form in this section?**

Writing in bullet form tends to force the writer to focus on specific accomplishments. This should help eliminate generalities and glowing comments. In addition, selection boards indicate that reports written in bullet form tend to be much easier to assimilate.

**Why does the performance factor section use a two-block scale?**

Performance factor ratings tend to automatically become a two-block system in any case. The two-block approach eliminates inflationary pressures and the resulting inflationary mind-set. It provides the needed information without unnecessary complexity.

**Won't most officers be marked in the "Meets Standards" block?**

Yes. We have a high-quality officer force and most officers will meet the standards listed on the performance report. Officers will know from feedback sessions what sort of abilities are considered important, and they'll be able to work on improving their skills in these areas.

**What happens if an officer is marked in the "Does Not Meet Standards" block?**

If a "Does Not Meet Standards" block is checked, the report will be a referral and the procedures currently used with referral reports will apply. The officer will be given an opportunity to comment and the rater will be obligated to explain how the officer is failing to meet the standard. The two-block rating scale of the new performance report assures an officer whose record is negatively impacted by a performance rating an opportunity to have his or her side of the story heard.

**What are the functions of the "Overall Assessment" sections?**

These sections contain space for a narrative assessment of the officer's performance during the rating period and an overall assessment of potential based on that performance. This could include a continuation of comments from the "Impact on Mission Accomplishment" section, comments on additional duties and other accomplishments that are significant enough to document, and recommendations for promotion, regular augmentation, and so forth. Space is intentionally limited, so comments must be concise. This space is not used to comment on ongoing or recently completed PME or academic education, but it may be used to recommend in-residence PME attendance.

**Will some officers receive elevated endorsements under the revised system?**

No. The regulation is specific as to who the rater, additional rater, and reviewer/senior rater will be. Moreover, the regulation states that all officers within a specific rating group will have the same reviewer/senior rater.

**Can the additional rater or reviewer change a performance factor rating on the OPR?**

The additional rater or reviewer can indicate disagreement with a performance factor rating by initialing a higher or lower block on the OPR. If the rater or reviewer downgrades a block, the report becomes referral. Of course, if the report comes to the reviewer with a factor rated "Does Not Meet Standards," referral procedures will have already occurred. In any case, it is the additional rater's or reviewer's prerogative to disagree with a performance factor rating.

**What types of comments are allowed in the "Promotion Recommendation" section of the PRF?**

The comments in this section are quite different from those in the narrative of the current OER. The senior rater is expected to make a decision on promotion potential based on the officer's performance. The rater first evaluates the cumulative record of job performance reflected in the file of performance reports and applies knowledge of the officer's most recent performance. The narrative section should explain why the senior rater feels the officer should be promoted. The narrative would most likely include a brief synopsis of the officer's cumulative record of performance, a statement linking that performance to advancement qualification, and an appropriate recommendation for promotion. The narrative would not address factors not related to performance, but rather would focus on performance. The rater may highlight any particular aspects of performance that set the officer apart from others and make him or her best qualified for promotion.

**How were senior rater positions and grades chosen?**

These officers must be senior enough in grade to have the scope and breadth of experience to assess long-term performance based on the officer's record as reported on performance reports. At the same time, senior raters need to be close enough to the officers being rated to have reliable knowledge of their most recent performance or access to reliable knowledge and need to understand the significance of that performance as it relates to potential and promotion. The OPR reviewer and PRF senior rater are the same person. The terms are different to depict their different roles in the OES.

**What is the significance of the three levels of recommendation the senior rater can make?**

*Definitely Promote.* This recommendation indicates that the strength of the officer's performance warrants promotion with minimum regard for broader considerations.

*Promote.* This recommendation indicates the officer is well qualified and should compete at the promotion board on the basis of both performance and broader considerations. A Promote recommendation means exactly that—promote. The senior rater believes the officer should be promoted.

*Do Not Promote This Board.* This recommendation means that, based on the cumulative record of the performance and on personal knowledge of the most recent performance, the senior rater believes that the officer should not be promoted on the board for which the promotion recommendation is being prepared. As with all promotion recommendations prepared on IPZ and APZ officers, the Do Not Promote This Board recommendation is removed after the central promotion board reviews the record and makes final consideration. Thus, a Do Not Promote This Board does not become a permanent part of an officer's selection folder.

**If an APZ or IPZ officer receives a Definitely Promote recommendation, does this mean promotion is virtually guaranteed?**

*Definitely Promote* recommendations will have a very powerful effect, and APZ and IPZ officers receiving such recommendations have a strong probability of promotion. However, by law, the promotion decision may be made only by the central promotion board. It is possible that an officer receiving a Definitely Promote will not be promoted. However, there will, in all likelihood, be some indicator in the officer's selection folder, other than performance, of why this has occurred.

**Why will all Promotion Recommendation Forms be pulled from the record once an officer is promoted?**

The promotion recommendation is intended to be a direct communication between a senior rater and a specific central selection board. This recommendation evaluates the officer's potential for advancement to a specific rank at a specific point in time based on a cumulative record of performance. Removing recommendations eliminates any potential stigma from having been selected for promotion with a Promote versus a Definitely Promote recommendation.

**Why are there limits for Definitely Promote recommendations?**

Limits are the result of two facts of life. First, the services cannot promote everyone. Public law limiting the number of officers who may serve in the field grades forces tough choices. Second, without such limits, past experience has shown that inflation is inevitable. Inflation tends to deny selection boards access to clear differentiation based on performance. To be assured their proper weight, Definitely Promote recommendations must be limited so that fewer officers meet the central board with a Definitely Promote than can be promoted. Said another way, value is associated with limited supply.

**Will I be able to see my promotion recommendation form?**
Yes. You will have access to your promotion recommendation form. Your senior rater will provide you with a copy of the form after review by the evaluation board.

**How will the number of Definitely Promote recommendations for my unit be computed?**
For the BPZ category your senior rater will multiply the total number of the below-the-promotion-zone eligible officers in the wing or equivalent unit by the appropriate allocation percentage, rounding down. For the APZ and IPZ category, your senior rater will multiply only the number of in-the-promotion-zone eligible officers in the wing or equivalent unit by the appropriate percentage, again rounding down. If, for example, there are eight captains in your wing eligible for major IPZ and three eligible APZ, the number of Definitely Promote recommendations available to your senior rater is five (8 x .65). These five recommendations will go to the top performers among the eleven APZ and IPZ officers.

## SOME ADDITIONAL INFORMATION ON OFFICER EVALUATIONS

**Unfavorable Information Files (UIFs) (AFR 35-32).** UIFs provide commanders a repository of substantiated derogatory information concerning the member's personal conduct and duty performance that may form the basis for administrative, personnel, or judicial actions. These files are "For Official Use Only" and are closely controlled at all levels to preclude unauthorized disclosure. UIFs may include these items among others: AF Form 1137, *Unfavorable Information Files Summary*; documentation concerning placement on the control roster; failure to discharge a just financial obligation; misconduct or substandard performance resulting from emotional instability; drug or alcohol abuse; or similar deviations from accepted norms of behavior. UIFs are maintained by the military personnel flight and contain only that unfavorable information that has been verified for file by the individual's commander or higher authority. In addition, a copy of the AF Form 1137 on officers is maintained at MAJCOM level. Exact disposition instructions for the UIF and its contents are in table 35-5, AFM 12-50. Except for documentation concerning court-martial convictions, certain (specified) civil court convictions, drug abuse, records of certain (specified) Article 15 UCMJ actions mandatory for file, and control roster actions, the documentation must be referred to the member for comment. The notification of "intent to file" optional information in the UIF will be sent by the commander to the member for comments.

## WHAT CONDUCT PRODUCES A MORE FAVORABLE RATING?

Of obvious importance to you who seek to obtain good performance reports—and you should—are the factors your rating official weighs. First, read an OPR form. If, with objectivity, you cannot rate yourself highly, you'd better start a regime of self-improvement quickly.

**An Aid to Receipt of Good Performance Reports.** You must earn good performance reports that lead to selection for promotion and preferred assignments.

I. IDENTIFICATION DATA *(Read AFR 36-10 carefully before filling in any item)*

| 1. NAME *(Last, First, Middle Initial)* | 2. SSN *(Include suffix)* | 3. ACTIVE DUTY GRADE | 4. PERMANENT GRADE |
|---|---|---|---|
| Knutson, Charles R. | 000-00-0000FR | 1st Lt | 1st Lt |

| 5. ORGANIZATION, COMMAND, LOCATION AND PAS CODE | 6. ACADEMIC PERIOD | 8. PERIOD OF REPORT FROM | THROUGH |
|---|---|---|---|
| 657th Personnel Research Lab Lackland Air Force Base TX (AFSC) | 36 days | 8 Sep 91 | 14 Jun 92 |
| | 7. LENGTH OF COURSE: 39 weeks | 9. REASON FOR REPORT: ☒ FINAL ☐ ANNUAL ☐ DIRECTED | |

10. NAME AND LOCATION OF SCHOOL OR INSTITUTION
Trinity University, San Antonio, Texas

| 11. NAME OR TITLE OF COURSE | 12. DUTY AFSC |
|---|---|
| Graduate Program in Business | MA |

II. REPORT DATA *(Complete as applicable)*

| 1. COURSE HOURS COMPLETED | 2. COURSE HOURS FAILED | 3. AFSC AWARDED | 4. AERO RATING AWARDED | 5. DEGREE AWARDED |
|---|---|---|---|---|
| 30 | 0 | | | MA |

6. COURSE SUCCESSFULLY COMPLETED *(Final report only)* ☒ YES ☐ NO *(If "NO" give reason)*

| 7. TITLE OF THESIS | 8. ACADEMIC FIELD |
|---|---|
| Job Analysis - Key to Better Management | Business Administration |

9. DISTINGUISHED GRADUATE *(Final report only)* ☒ YES ☐ NO DISTINCTION MADE FOR THIS COURSE

III. COMMENTS *(If applicable or appropriate)*

ACADEMIC/TRAINING ACCOMPLISHMENTS *(Special achievements related to curriculum, research, communication, etc.)*

PROFESSIONAL QUALITIES *(Bearing, appearance, conduct)*

OTHER COMMENTS

Add any other comments not covered elsewhere. Enter explanation if paragraph 7-2e(9) is used in section II of report.

IV. REPORTING OFFICIAL

| NAME, GRADE, SVC, ORGN, LOCATION | DUTY TITLE | SIGNATURE / SSN *(Include suffix)* | DATE |
|---|---|---|---|
| Joseph P. Antonucce, Col, USAF 6570th Personnel Research Lab Lackland AFB TX (AFSC) | Commander | 000-00-0000FR | 14 Jun 1992 |

EDUCATION/TRAINING REPORT, AF FORM 475.

*Forbes Magazine,* a publication for business executives, included the following helpful principles as developed by Rogers & Slade, Management Consultants. Observing these simple truths should help you not only in the execution of your responsibilities but also in getting good performance reports.

*In my relations with those who supervise me, I will—*

- Accept my full share of responsibility.
- Make sure I know what is expected of me.

- Do what is requested in the best manner I know.
- Be agreeable when asked to do something difficult or unpleasant.
- Be honest—and not try to cover up my errors.
- Stand up for my decisions—but admit it promptly if they are shown to be wrong.
- Accept criticism in good spirit and not let a few rebukes get me down.
- Point to needed improvements but make sure my ideas are well thought out and clearly presented.

*In my relations with those under my supervision, I will—*

- Sell the job to be done, and not pull my rank.
- Be firm but reasonable.
- Treat those working under me as human beings—consider their feelings.
- Accept proffered suggestions—or explain why they should not be used.
- Give full job instructions and not pass the buck.
- Be friendly but not intimate—not play favorites.
- Set a good working example—not break rules I expect others to follow.
- Back up my people when they are right and give credit when and where due.

**An Aid to Avoidance of Bad Performance Reports.** Those who have had the opportunity of evaluating thousands of performance reports as they sat on selection boards for promotion or elimination have commented on the patterns that appear among officers whose records are below standard and have offered these tips for avoiding poor performance reports:

- Eliminate any tendency or display of unprofessional conduct, including intemperate use of liquor, questionable sexual practices, and obscenity or vulgarity.
- Avoid generating ill will among seniors, associates, or juniors.
- Avoid a reputation of mediocre or undependable performance of duty.
- Avoid a reputation of being a poor credit risk.

**Summary.** Officers may earn splendid reports that will lead to a successful and envied career by establishing a reputation of finding always a way of "getting things done"; by winning the good will of those with whom they are surrounded, seniors and juniors alike; and by preparing themselves today and tonight for the discharge of the tasks of tomorrow or next week.

## HOW TO WORK FOR AN "SOB"

In times past, readers have often asked for help in the delicate area of how to deal with the difficulties of working under certain officers. The editorial staff considered the matter and decided to attempt to offer something constructive about it. Surely, here was a field in which great good was possible. We invited an officer to write his views. Here is his answer:

*Dear Editor:*

*You asked if I'd write a piece on how to work for an SOB. The mere thought raised wells of sympathy within me for those unfortunates who, as I did in times gone by, now suffer under a hair-shirt boss who is intolerable. How to live with the Grouchy, the Unreasonably Impatient, the Unfair, the Mean and Vicious—the summation of all the SOBs I've served under? My enthusiasm was quickened by the thought that I might be able to help those who had fallen on such evil times as to inherit an SOB as unit commander. Ah, the troubles I've known from SOBs!*

*Well, I took pen in hand and began to cast about among the multitude of my SOB superiors to select the most horrendous one as my opening illustration, so as better to explain how I survived my painful ordeal while retaining my sanity. With elation upon discovering my perfect example, I began to describe old General Blank, the biggest SOB, surely, in all the world. As I wrote, however, I began to recall how, after I grew to know General Blank, I learned of his nerve-shattering war experiences in Asia, of his being finally relieved of his command and sent home more or less in physical collapse. I recalled his singular touchiness about his wife, a nosy young lady who caused no end of trouble within the base, and I wondered whether the great differential in ages between Blank and his young wife—25 years—made him thus sensitive. These and other things about Blank occurred to me. On second thought, I decided he was not my candidate for Senior SOB.*

*When I remembered Major Dumguard, though, I knew I had my prize SOB. Dumguard's extreme impatience, his growled answers, his sudden violent angers over nothing, his indifference toward my problems—these and many other characteristics of a bonded 100-proof, aged in wood SOB came to my mind. Yet, my resolve faded when I remembered Dumguard's young son hanging so long between life and oblivion with spinal meningitis; the deep shock of his wife's death; the fact that he lagged in promotion far behind his colleagues.*

*In fact, I must admit it, I can tell no one how to work for an SOB, because I've never worked for one. I have worked for people who were suffering from illnesses, physical or mental, and who vented symptoms of these on me occasionally. I have worked for people who were bewildered, discouraged, tired, hurt, nervous, miserable, and afraid. These, too, made my life unpleasant. But I see now that these people were not true SOBs. They were human beings in some sort of trouble, people in pain, whether from real or fancied ills. Therefore, I must turn back to you unmarked pages on SOBs. I can't recall a one. Is it possible there aren't any?*

*Very truly yours,*

## A LEGENDARY CLASSIFICATION SYSTEM

A distinguished military leader of the German Army of a past era devised a classification of officers that applies, we had best admit, even to the Air Force. According to this legend, officers fall into only four classes:

- The brilliant and industrious. They make the best staff officers, for their talents provide maximum service to commanders.
- The brilliant and lazy. They are the most valuable and constitute the commanders. Their tendency to avoid troublesome and time-consuming detail enables them to retain the perspective necessary in the art of making decisions. Their plans tend to the simple, the direct, and the most promising for easy success.
- The stupid and lazy. While this group will add little to military luster, they can be used on small tasks that are necessary to be accomplished. At least, they will do no great harm. They can be retained and used.
- The stupid and industrious. Great damage may result from their actions. Attacking the ill-advised with zeal and energy, they may induce a disaster. They are the most dangerous. They must be eliminated!

## OFFICE PERFORMANCE REPORTS—VINTAGE 1813

Extracted from the Adjutant General's School Bulletin, April 1942, and reprinted below are excerpts from an effectiveness report that has been gathering dust these many years. Names of the officers have been changed, and any similarity to persons living or dead is coincidental.

Lower Seneca Town, August 15th, 1813.

Sir:

I forward a list of the officers of the—th Regt. of Infty. arranged agreeable to rank. Annexed thereto you will find all the observations I deem necessary to make.

Respectfully, I am, Sir.
Yo. Obt. Sevt.,
Lewis Cass

—th Regt. Infantry

Alexander Brown—Lt. Col., Comdg.—A good natured man.
Clark Crowell—1st Major—A good man, but no officer.
Jess B. Wadsworth—2nd Major—An excellent officer.
Captain Shaw—A man of whom all unite in speaking ill—A knave despised by all.
Captain Thomas Lord—Indifferent, but promises well.
Captain Rockwell—An officer of capacity, but imprudent and a man of violent passions.

| | |
|---|---|
| Captain Dan I. Ware<br>Captain Parker | Strangers but little known in the regiment. |
| 1st Lt. Jas. Kearns<br>1st Lt. Thomas Dearfoot | Merely good—nothing promising. |
| 1st Lt. Wm. Herring<br>1st Lt. Danl. Land<br>1st Lt. Jas. I. Bryan<br>1st Lt. Robert McKewell | Low, vulgar men, with the exception of Herring. From the meanest walks of life—possessing nothing of the character of officers and gentlemen. |

1st Lt. Robert Cross—Willing enough—has much to learn—with small capacity.
2nd Lt. Nicholas Farmer—A good officer, but drinks hard and disgraces himself and the Service.
2nd Lt. Stewart Berry—An ignorant unoffending fellow.
2nd Lt. Darrow—Just joined the Regiment—of fine appearance.

| | |
|---|---|
| 2nd Lt. Pierce<br>2nd Lt. Thos. G. Slicer<br>2nd Lt. Oliver Warren | Raised from the ranks, but all behave well and promise to make excellent officers. |
| 2nd Lt. Royal Gore<br>2nd Lt. Means<br>2nd Lt. Clew<br>2nd Lt. McLear | All promoted from the ranks, low, vulgar men, without one qualification to recommend them—more fit to carry the hod than the epaulette. |
| 2nd Lt. John Sheaffer<br>2nd Lt. Francis T. Whelan | Promoted from the ranks. Behave well and will make good officers. |

Ensign Behan—The very dregs of the earth. Unfit for anything under heaven. God only knows how the poor thing got an appointment.

| | |
|---|---|
| Ensign John Breen<br>Ensign Byor | Promoted from the ranks—men of no manner and no promise. |

Ensign North—From the ranks. A good young man who does well.

# 14

# USAF Education and Training

*Untutored courage is useless in the face of educated bullets.*

—General George S. Patton, Jr.

"The mission of the United States Air Force is to fly and fight and don't you ever forget it" was the Air Force's motto during the Vietnam War and it remains true today. To do this requires that the Air Force be highly organized; thus it is also a large bureaucracy (see chapters 23 and 24). It must be equipped efficiently, so a close working relationship with science and industry is essential. Its men and women must be highly prepared by education and training, the subjects of this chapter. There are three main components—precommissioning programs, specialty training, and professional military education (PME)—as well as other opportunities to help officers enhance their skills.

## PRECOMMISSIONING PROGRAMS (AFR 53-1)

**The U.S. Air Force Academy (AFACAD).** Since the Air Force Academy graduated its first class in 1958, it has produced 26,000 graduates, nearly 60 percent of whom remain on active duty today and who constitute 15 percent of the USAF officer corps. Enrollment at the school, located in Colorado Springs, is about 4,000 in a four-year college program leading to a bachelor of science degree. Thirty cadets have become Rhodes Scholars and nearly 200 others have earned other prestigious scholarships and fellowships. Those in the Class of 1996 and thereafter will incur a six-year active-duty service commitment (ADSC). The Academy is the only educational institution in the USAF not part of the Air Education and Training Command (AETC). For further details see AFR 53-10.

**Air Force Reserve Officer Training Corps (AFROTC).** Congress originally authorized ROTC on college campuses in 1916, just before America entered World War I. Thirty years later, after World War II, a separate Air ROTC came into being, eventually under the old Continental Air Command (CONAC) and since 1952 under Air University, Maxwell AFB, Alabama, as Air Force ROTC. In its 50-year history, the program has produced 206,351 new officers, nearly 26,000 alone in the decade 1984–93. Graduates constitute 42 percent of today's active-duty officers, about 36,000, and nearly half of active-duty general officers—48 percent—are AFROTC graduates. There are both two- and four-year programs, and in both qualified applicants receive AFROTC scholarships. There are 138 AFROTC detachments on American college and university campuses, with "cross-town" arrangements with more than 600 other institutions. There are 11,500 cadets enrolled nationwide. Besides the college program, Senior AFROTC, there is a Junior AFROTC program that is expanding from 320 high schools in 1993 to more than 600 in 1996, its purpose to inculate citizenship and an appreciation of aerospace power in high school students. For further details on AFROTC, see AFR 45-48.

**Officer Training School (OTS).** Located at Air University, Maxwell AFB, Alabama, OTS is a 12-week officer procurement program that recruits and trains non-AFROTC college graduates, including those from the Airman Education and Commissioning Program, or AECP (see AFR 53-20). It has the capacity to expand output quickly in an emergency and to contract it when the Air Force needs fewer "brown bars." For instance, OTS turned out nearly 3,200 second lieutenants in 1985 but only 350 in 1991. About one fourth of active-duty officers, or 21,000, came from OTS or the one-time Officer Candidate School (OCS). For further details see AFR 53-27.

**Nonline Officer Orientation.** In addition to the three major officer procurement programs described above, the Air Force commissions directly about 1,100 nonline officers, medical professionals, judge advocates, and chaplains, plus a few non-active-duty reservists. They learn how to be Air Force officers at one of three courses at Maxwell AFB, Alabama; the Military Indoctrination for Medical Service Officers Course, the Health Professional Officer Indoctrination Course, or the Air Force Orientation Course. These prepare students for life as an Air Force officer by providing training in leadership, professional knowledge, defense studies, drill and ceremonies, and communication skills. These nonline officers make up most of the 18 percent (15,000 or so) of active-duty officers not commissioned through the Academy, AFROTC, or OTS.

## SPECIALTY TRAINING

Whatever their source of commission, most newly commissioned USAF line officers will go to either flying training or technical training schools, except for those who will learn their skills in on-the-job training, or "OJT."

**Air Force Flying Schools.** All undergraduate flight training is conducted by the Air Training Command. Pilot and navigator training is conducted entirely under military auspices at Air Force bases under the supervision of Headquarters, Air Training Command, Randolph AFB, Texas. Currently, undergraduate pilot training is conducted at Columbus AFB, Mississippi; Laughlin AFB, Texas; Reese AFB, Texas; Vance AFB, Oklahoma; and Sheppard AFB, Texas. Navigators are trained at Mather AFB, California. Fighter training is conducted at Luke AFB, Arizona, and Tyndall AFB, Florida, while Air Mobility Training is conducted at Altus AFB, Oklahoma.

**Air Force Technical Schools.** As the Air Force, along with the world at large, grows increasingly technical in its operations, the need for technically trained officers increases also. The Air Training Command operates a number of Technical Training Schools to which officers may be assigned. Courses are designed to advance the officers' proficiency in their career fields whether jet aircraft maintenance, electronics, missile maintenance and operation, intelligence, or hundreds of other such technological and support field careers. The main centers of such training are at Goodfellow AFB, Keesler AFB, Sheppard AFB, and Lackland AFB. Courses vary in length.

## PROFESSIONAL MILITARY EDUCATION (AFR 53-8)

Education in the discipline of the profession of arms is called Professional Military Education, or PME, and is the systematic acquisition of the theoretical and applied knowledge of that profession. In World War II, the United States surprised the German general staff with the ability of our armed forces to expand quickly from fewer than half a million men in 1940 to a well-organized and well-led force of more than 12 million in 1945. Three principal reasons were the services' excellent PME system between the two world wars; learning from our failures in industrial mobilization in World War I; and an available pool of about 74,000 reserve officers, 77 percent of them commissioned through ROTC.

The primary purpose of Air Force PME today is to train experts in the application of aerospace operations and to provide the ability to participate in joint service operations. The USAF officer PME system consists of three levels of instruction conducted through resident and nonresident programs. Some officers will participate in programs of the National Defense University, the other U.S. services, the U.S. State Department, NATO, foreign countries, and civilian institutions.

The levels of instruction in the Air Force are Primary PME (Squadron Officer School), Intermediate PME (command and staff level course), and Senior PME (war and defense level courses). Air University at Maxwell AFB is the center for Air Force Officer PME programs and is where classes for all three stages are conducted.

**Squadron Officer School (SOS).** SOS is the first level of PME instruction and all active-duty line officers will have the opportunity to attend it in residence. Captains with four to seven years' active commissioned service are eligible to attend and are nominated by their major air commands. They incur an ADSC of one year (see AFR 36-51). The school is a seven-week TDY program conducted six times a year with about 650 officers in each class—3,900 a year. SOS increases a young officer's ability to assume progressively more responsibility in the U.S. Air Force as well as improving professional competence and enhancing dedication to the profession of arms. Officers who have completed SOS also have greater understanding of their professional role, how U.S. forces are employed, leadership and management, and effective communication. Nonline officers are expected to complete SOS by correspondence through the Extension Course Institute (ECI).

**Air Command and Staff College (ACSC).** ACSC is the Air Force's intermediate service school (ISS), a PCS course of ten months attended by about 580 U.S. and foreign officers each year whose performance clearly shows potential for further advancement. Active-duty line officers are chosen by Headquarters USAF Central ISS Designation Boards in a highly competitive selection process. Those eligible are majors with at least three years since their last PME education assignment, at least three years' retainability, three years on station at projected departure date, and compliance with AFR 53-11 weight limits. Graduates incur a three-year ADSC upon completion of ACSC.

The college broadens the knowledge and increases the professional qualifications of future commanders and staff officers, emphasizing combat and combat support operations. ACSC prepares officers to plan and execute warfare at the operational level; improves communications, analytical, and problem-solving skills a staff officer needs; enhances command, leadership, and combat support skills; imparts an understanding of U.S. military power and our national interests; and fosters the understanding needed for joint duty assignments. Each summer ACSC conducts a Reserve Forces Course to update selected Air National Guard and Air Force Reserve majors on the USAF, its doctrine, and its weapon systems. Each academic year selected Air Guard and reserve officers join the resident ACSC class for a week. All midlevel officers not selected for resident ACSC or other ISS should complete one of the associate programs (either by seminar or correspondence) that ACSC administers in conjunction with ECI.

**Air War College (AWC).** AWC is the Air Force's senior service school (SSS). The student body is a carefully selected group of about 255 students, officers, and U.S. government civilians brought together for a ten-and-a-half-month course of graduate-level study. They are joined by officers from the other U.S. services and a number of other nations. Active-duty line officers are selected by annual Headquarters USAF Central SSS Designation Boards in a highly selective process. Students are colonels and lieutenant colonels with less than 23 years' active commissioned service; as with ACSC graduates, they incur a three-year ADSC upon completion. Other requirements are also similar to those for ISS. AWC prepares senior military officers to develop, maintain, and lead the aerospace components of national power to deter conflict and win victory in war. Three times a year selected Air Guard and reserve officers, lieutenant colonels through major generals, join resident AWC students to examine specific issues and capabilities of the total force. The AWC Department of Associate Studies in conjunction with ECI provides seminar and correspondence programs for eligible personnel not selected for resident schooling.

**Joint, Other Services, and Non-DOD PME Courses.** The Goldwater-Nichols Defense Reorganization Act of 1986 established a requirement for the joint specialty officer (JSO). To meet JSO educational requirements, the chairman of the joint chiefs of staff (CJCS), with the services, began a two-phase joint PME process whereby students receive Phase I Joint PME (PJE1) at both ISS and SSS and Phase II Joint PME (PJE2) at the Armed Forces Staff College and at the National Defense University's two senior service schools, the National War College (NWC) and Industrial College of the Armed Forces (ICAF), continuing both phase requirements. The JCS's aim is that AFSC, NWC, and ICAF graduates be used primarily in joint-duty assignments.

*Armed Forces Staff College (AFSC).* Located in Norfolk, Virginia, AFSC has the mission, prescribed by the JCS, preparing selected officers of all services for joint and combined staff duty. The curriculum considers the strategic, doctrinal, and operational concerns of the JCS and the commanders in chief of unified and specified commands, the "CINCS," in the likely environment graduates will encounter. There are two courses a year.

*Industrial College of the Armed Forces (ICAF).* Housed at Fort McNair, D.C., ICAF, a major component of the NDU, is a joint SSS operating under JCS direction. It began as the Army Industrial College after World War I to prevent future failures in military procurement, and it became a joint service school after World War II. It focuses on managing resources for national security: Its mission is to prepare selected officers from all services and senior career civilian governmental officials for positions of high trust in the federal government. Criteria are the same as for AWC, but officers will not attend both.

*National War College (NWC).* Also at Fort McNair, NWC is the only senior service school in the U.S. military educational system with the specific mission of studying national security policy preparation. It prepares selected personnel of the armed forces, State Department, and other U.S. government agencies for the exercise of joint and combined high-level policy, command, and staff functions for planning and carrying out national strategy. Criteria for attendance are the same as for AWC, but officers will not attend both.

*NDU National Security Management Off-Campus Course.* This provides a program for personnel unable to attend the resident school programs, drawing upon the curricula both of ICAF and NWC, but stressing the allocation and management of resources for national security. Eligibility criteria are the same as for the AWC Associate Program.

*Other Service Schools.* A few Air Force officers may be selected to attend the other services' intermediate service schools—Army Command and General Staff College, the College of Naval Command and Staff, or the Marine Corps Command and Staff College—and their senior service schools—the Army War College or the College of Naval Warfare.

*Non-DOD PME Courses.* A few Air Force officers may be selected to attend International PME courses, such as the ISS U.S. Army School of the Americas or the SSS Inter-American Defense College or NATO Defense College. The USAF also participates in a large number of allied PME courses, such as the RAF Staff College or German Staff College (ISS level), or the Royal College of Defense Studies, Canadian National Defense College, or French Air War College (SSS level).

*Civilian PME Courses.* These SSS equivalents for a chosen few are the U.S. State Department Seminar on National and International Affairs and the Harvard University Research Fellow Program.

## OTHER TRAINING AND EDUCATION PROGRAMS

**Air Force Institute of Technology (AFIT).** An AU organization located at Wright-Patterson AFB, Ohio, AFIT conducts scientific, technological, and other specialized education to satisfy Air Force educational requirements. At "Wright-Pat" are the School of Engineering, the School of Civic Engineering, and the School of Systems and Logistics. AFIT's Civil Institutions Directorate oversees Air Force personnel taking full-time a wide variety of graduate programs at civilian universities to meet Air Force needs. These include the outstanding airmen assigned to the Airman Education and Training Program (AECP) to complete their undergraduate college education before earning commissions at OTS.

**Education with Industry.** Selected officers can volunteer to be assigned to civilian industries to study industrial organization, management, and technology so that they can apply this knowledge to their Air Force specialties. AFIT administers this program (see AFCAT 36-223).

**Minutemen Educational Program.** Missile launch officers assigned to Minuteman missile wings can participate in this program, which can lead to a master's degree, with full tuition paid and no ADSC incurred.

**Tuition Assistance.** Most Air Force bases have extensive on-base graduate college programs. Officers may take classes on their own time with the Air Force paying 75 percent of tuition costs. Any ADSC runs concurrently with other obligations.

**Educational Delays.** AFROTC graduates may request an educational delay in reporting to active duty to complete graduate work at their own expense.

**Community College of the Air Force.** The Community College of the Air Force, with 447,504 registrations through June 1994, offers means for individuals to acquire associate in applied science degrees. More than 130,200 degrees have been awarded through the CCAF.

**University Correspondence Courses.** Military personnel may take university correspondence courses. For available courses see catalogues prepared by the Defense Activity for Non-Traditional Education Support (DANTES). See AFR 213-1 and consult your base education services officer.

**U.S. Armed Forces Institute (USAFI).** Since World War II USAFI has offered a wide range of academic and military courses on an off-duty basis to miliary personnel. See your base education services officer.

**Extension Course Institute (ECI).** ECI offers a wide range of correspondence courses to all Air Force personnel, including both PME and technical skills programs.

With all the above offerings, you have no real excuse for not increasing your education and knowledge while in the Air Force.

## SELF-EDUCATION

Self-improvement and study must be a part of the program for any officer who aspires to high success. Attendance at schools and performing the required duties of an assignment are not enough. The working day is short, eight hours or less in many instances. The profitable use of leisure time is an important factor, and healthful, interesting recreation is certainly part of it. The development of skills through selected hobbies may be invaluable. The development of real enjoyment in planned reading will be of great aid to the ambitious officer. Current fiction, biography, and serious books of the day constitute a part of it. The officer must keep abreast of events and be able to talk intelligently with intelligent people, both military and civilian. The study of military history is a most important part of a wise program. An amazing number of officers who have achieved high position have been thorough students of history, with emphasis on military history. Study of contemporary world history should be required. Self-study of selected subjects to broaden a professional career should be included. The *Air University Suggested Professional Reading Guide* provides a systematic program of selective reading (see appendix B).

All officers should become proficient in reading, writing, and speaking at least one foreign language. Officers who choose to plan the use of some small part of their leisure time, not overlooking the need for recreation and enjoyment of family, will gain a material advantage over their peers who plan and act less wisely. There are small things in which officers should be proficient that can be mastered quickly. Ability to type letters and reports so that they have a professional makeup and appearance will get over the frequently encountered obstacle of the lack of competent clerical help, especially in the field. Knowledge of the elements of bookkeeping and accounting will serve all officers well on all manner of assignments.

There are other types of knowledge becoming necessary for officers in this modern technological age. In studying career field requirements, the Air Force Educational Requirements Board recommended certain disciplines that officers should master, either in college or afterward. They include oral and written communication, logic, basic statistics, basic college mathematics, probability theory, introduction to electronic data processing, basic personnel management, and human relations. In most cases, officers will have to pursue these subjects on their own time in an off-duty education program.

The Air Force authorizes attendance for participation at meetings of technical, scientific, professional, or similar organizations when attendance contributes to Air Force missions or programs, and provides a medium for exchanging technical data (AFR 30-9). Other provisions authorize officers to accept graduate fellowships offered by recognized foundations.

## PROFESSIONAL ASSOCIATIONS

Listed below are the names of associations and societies of possible interest to Air Force officers. The list is by no means inclusive.

Air Force Association (AFA), 1501 Lee Highway, Arlington, VA 22209-1198, $21 per year (includes subscription to *Air Force* magazine).

Air Force Historical Foundation (AFHF), 1101 Vermont Ave., Suite 400, Washington, DC 20005, $25 per year (includes subscription to *Air Power History*).

American Military Institute (AMI), Virginia Military Institute, Lexington, VA 24450, $25 per year (includes subscription to *Journal of Military History*).

American Red Cross (ARC), 430 17th and D Sts. NW, Washington, DC 20006.

Armed Forces Communications and Electronics Association (AFCEA), 4400 Fair Lakes Court, Fairfax, VA 22033.

Company of Military Historians (CMH), N. Main St., Westbrook, CT 06948, $30 per year (includes subscription to *Military Collector and Historian*).

Military Order of the World Wars (for all officers), 435 N. Lee St., Alexandria, VA 22314, $30 per year (includes subscription to *Officer Review*).

National Defense Transportation Association (NDTA), 50 South Pickett St., Suite 220, Alexandria, VA 22304-3008, $35 per year (includes subscription to *Defense Transportation Journal*).

National Guard Association of the United States, One Massachusetts Ave. NW, Washington, DC 20001 (includes subscription to *National Guard Magazine*).

National Sojourners, Inc., 8301 E. Boulevard Dr., Alexandria, VA 22308-1399, $30 per year (includes subscription to *The Sojourner*). An organization of officers who are Freemasons.

Reserve Officers Association (ROA), One Constitution Ave. NE, Washington, DC 20002-5624, $25 per year (includes subscription to *The Officer*).

Society of American Military Engineers (SAME), 607 Prince St., Alexandria, VA 22320-2289, $24 per year (includes subscription to *Military Engineer*).

The Retired Officers Association (TROA), 201 N. Washington St., Alexandria, VA 22314-2529, $20 per year (includes subscription to *The Retired Officer*).

## PROFESSIONAL PERIODICALS AND JOURNALS

Following are some of the service and other journals of possible interest to Air Force officers.

*Air Force* magazine (monthly), The Air Force Association, 1501 Lee Highway, Arlington, VA 22209-1198, $21 per year with membership in AFA.

*Air Force Times* (weekly), 6883 Commercial Ave., Springfield, VA 22159-0250, $48 per year.

*Airman* (monthly), USGPO, Washington, DC 20402-5000, official USAF periodical distributed within the Air Force.

*Air Power Journal*, USGPO, Washington, DC 20402-5000, distributed within the Air Force.

*Armed Forces Journal International* (monthly), 2000 L St. NW, Suite 520, Washington, DC 20036, $35 per year.

*Aviation Week and Space Technology*, 1221 Avenue of the Americas, New York, NY 10020, $72 per year.

# 15

# Officer Professional Development

*Victory smiles upon them who anticipate the changes in the character of war, not upon those who wait to adapt themselves after they occur.*

—General Giulio Douhet, *Command of the Air,* 1921

Officer professional development is essential to support the Air Force mission and to provide the professional growth our officers expect. The officer who is most effective at carrying out the mission is one who is professionally prepared to assume the responsibilities that go with a particular rank. The Officer Professional Development Program (ODP) is designed to support Air Force requirements and maintain maximum combat effectiveness while developing a well-rounded, professionally competent officer corps. The officer's professional development must harmonize with long-term Air Force requirements.

## OBJECTIVES OF PROFESSIONAL DEVELOPMENT

Professional development includes actions and experiences that improve an officer's ability to do his or her job and increasingly contribute to the Air Force mission. Professional development starts with concentrating on expertise in one primary skill, broadens throughout one's career, and ends, one hopes, with the officer being a generalist (if not a general!) with both depth and breadth. An officer grows by combining his or her career specialty with ability to lead and to manage in peace and in war. The Air Force offers officers numerous ways to enhance their professional credentials.

## PATH OF PROFESSIONAL DEVELOPMENT

The most important indicator of potential is the way an officer performs daily on the job and develops leadership abilities. That is certainly true for lieutenants, captains, and junior majors. A limited number of captains will serve in lower-level staff assignments, and a significant number of majors will serve in staff jobs at all levels. Nevertheless, a staff job is not a prerequisite for promotion up through lieutenant colonel. A broader range of experience is more important for lieutenant colonels. In general, a demanding staff job as a senior major or lieutenant colonel will enhance one's potential to perform as a colonel or above. Most colonel jobs require staff competence as well as skill in one's specialty and developed leadership talents.

Professional military education (PME) and graduate academic education should parallel and support job requirements. PME should build upon a solid foundation of officership laid during precommissioning programs. The uniqueness of the military profession and the particular values and culture of the military officer corps are the bedrock on which all future professional development is based.

The focus for company grade officers (lieutenants and captains) should be on developing the skills they need, especially leadership and communication. The emphasis for the field grades and of the ISS should shift to the effective management of people and resources, as well as skills needed for staff work. Lieutenant colonels and colonels must understand the elements of aerospace force deployment and the policy considerations that drive them, so that is the role of the highest PME level, the SSS. Successful completion of appropriate PME courses will increase promotion potential. Advanced academic degrees are important to the extent that they enhance the officer's job performance and professional qualifications.

## ROLE OF THE OFFICER EVALUATION SYSTEM (OES)

The OES is an integral part of the OPD with three purposes: (1) to furnish feedback to officers on how well they are doing and advise them on how to improve; (2) to provide a long-term cumulative record of performance and potential; and (3) to provide central selection boards with sound information to help them pick the best-qualified officers for promotion. The OES focuses on performance and is a tool that officers can use both in their professional development and in that of the officers they supervise. See AFR 36-10, *Officer Evaluation System*, and AFP 36-6, *USAF Officer's Guide to the Officer Evaluation System*.

## ROLE OF THE PROMOTION SYSTEM

Objectives of the officer promotion system are to select officers through a fair and competitive process that advances the best qualified officers for positions of increased authority and responsibility and to provide the needed career incentive to attract and maintain an officer corps of high quality. Promotion boards are told that demonstrated leadership abilities and performance of primary duties are of overriding importance and far outweigh all other considerations. Therefore, officers should concentrate on duty performance in their current grade and not on "square-filling" exercises. See AFP 36-89, *Promotion of Active Duty Lists Officers*, and AFP 36-32, *You and Your Promotions—The Air Force Officer Promotion System*.

## ROLE OF THE ASSIGNMENT SYSTEM

According to AFR 36-23, the purpose of the officer assignment system is to fill Air Force requirements. Although one may express preference, officers volunteer only one time—when they take the oath of office. Officers should not concern themselves with mapping out their careers in detail but instead concentrate on their current duty. The only assignment with which the officer should be concerned is the current one, and when available for a new assignment, the one that immediately follows. Qualifications and professional development are the primary factors in making assignments, and commanders play a key role in the process. The assignment system is an integral part of OPD, and officers must realize that assignments are made to fill Air Force needs with the best-qualified officers.

There are some steps officers can take to enhance their careers, however, and in late 1993 the Air Force issued the first two in a new series of career guides for USAF officers. Pilots, for example, can base career growth on a three-legged stool of technical expertise, staff performance, and leadership opportunities. First, after initial training, a pilot should upgrade to a higher skill level as soon as possible. Next, volunteer for an overseas assignment early in your career. Serve an instructor tour, preferably in Air Education and Training Command. Get a master's degree. Upgrade to mission command before being selected for major, which should happen at 11 years' commissioned service. Attend ISS in residence and after graduation serve in a joint-duty staff assignment at a higher headquarters. Pass muster with a return-to-flying board and get a senior squadron job. Earn promotion to lieutenant colonel at 15 years. Head for the Air Staff in a top-level advisory post. Make full colonel at 20 years. Return to a flying wing as operations officer or group commander. Attend War College. Earn selection to brigadier general at 24 years of service.

The Air Force constructed this advice from historical analysis of the current crop of brigadier generals and squadron commanders. More than 90 percent of the brigadiers had attended SSS in residence, earned a master's degree, and were promoted early. Eighty percent had commanded a wing, 70 percent had commanded a squadron, and 40 percent had served on staff at the Pentagon. As for squadron commanders, mostly lieutenant colonels, about 90 percent had served as instructor pilots and earned master's degrees, about 50 percent had been squadron ops officers, and 40 percent had attended ISS in residence. In short, they were groomed for success from the start. With some variations, this advice is applicable to nonrated officers as well.

## PROFESSIONALISM

The ultimate objective of career development is a quality called "professionalism," brought to its highest standard of excellence. All of us readily recognize the meaning of professionalism when we apply the term to a minister, a doctor, a lawyer, or an engineer. What does it mean when applied to an Air Force officer? To assess this, it is first necessary to appreciate the unique scope of an Air Force officer's professionalism—the vast field of knowledge, skill, and comprehension that is encompassed in an Air Force career. The military forces of the United States constitute, incomparably, the most stupendous effort of the American people. Nearly a fifth of the federal budget is spent on our military forces; about 2.5 million people are in the armed services, both active-duty and reserve, plus another 873,000-plus civilians. The complicated, expensive tools of our military forces rest on the entire range of U.S. technology and industry, involving deeply other professional areas, such as medicine, engineering, law, education, and all forms of science. Moreover, the military forces are an integral, crucial part of U.S. diplomacy and international relations: Separation of "peacetime" foreign policy from the existence and strength of U.S. armed forces is permanently outmoded. Finally, the armed forces exert, through their diverse requirements and activities, a major effect on the U.S. economy. Plainly, it is not enough that Air Force officers be expert in particular fields of Air Force operations: They are part of a vast complex that touches all aspects of American life and, therefore, must seek to achieve a professionalism that matches the uniquely multiple strands of responsibility and knowledge that characterize their profession above all others.

Professionalism begins at less lofty levels than the ultimate responsibilities of the top officers of the Air Force. It begins with *sure* skill and knowledge relative to the particular task assigned to Air Force officers. It begins when Air Force officers know how to perform their own job at maximum efficiency, routinely, prudently, smoothly. The reliable sign of the true professional is the calm, seemingly easy performance of tasks under all circumstances, without noise or heroics, without unnecessary risk or extravagant use of resources.

When we looked at the performance of Air Force officers in Vietnam, we saw professionalism on every hand. War is no place for amateurs; it is the professional who counts. The Secretary of the Air Force once asked an Air Force captain in Vietnam to name the single greatest asset of Air Force units operating there. The Secretary had expected the answer to be "superior equipment." But the captain answered: "The professionalism of our personnel; they know their jobs and perform them efficiently, expertly."

Professionalism is expanded and exploited when Air Force officers know how to create professionalism in airmen. This task means teaching, careful supervision, discipline, and morale. It is the mark of officer pros that they have working with them airmen who are also pros.

Because of the vast field of concerns, Air Force officers must steadily increase professional competence through expanding their own knowledge by taking every opportunity to add educational levels, by upgrading basic educational degrees to master or doctorate, by attending military schools, and by reading widely. In particular, Air Force professionals should come to understand the very serious business management aspects of the Air Force, because the net capabilities of the Air Force will always be an expression of the efficiency with which Air Force officers use the resources made available by the Congress. Nearly 75 billion dollars a year—the largest single-purpose expenditure of the nation—is the business responsibility of Air Force officers. This money is used in a thousand ways: as pay, for procurement of equipment and supplies, for construction, for maintenance and operations, and for research and development. The business end of this problem is not only the more than 100,000 contracts with U.S. industry but also the accurate determination of requirements, the formulation of realistic plans, and the efficiency of use of available resources. All Air Force officers participate in this vast business of the Air Force. The Air Force can obtain the most national security from its huge annual budget only when all Air Force officers obtain the most efficient results from their use of their part of the total.

In their fields of career development, all Air Force officers should constantly seek to heighten and broaden their competence so that at each succeeding level of their careers, they will fully deserve the accolade: a professional.

# 16

# The U.S. Air Force as a Lifetime Career

*Today, as always, if a nation is to keep its freedom it must be prepared to risk war.*
—President Lyndon B. Johnson, 1964

The relative attractiveness of a military career is the subject of continuing national debate. It should be. The regular officer corps of our U.S. armed forces constitutes the most important single bulwark of the security of the republic. Those great groups of American professionals—the engineers, the doctors, the lawyers, the business executives—contribute much to the advancement of American civilization. They do not, however, compare with professional military officers in the face of danger. Danger is with us—continuing national danger in an age of monstrous weapons. For this reason, the corps of professional military officers must be of the highest quality. Only *you* know whether you might improve that quality. Furthermore, only *you* know whether a military career appeals to you. If you are undecided, perhaps the following considerations will help in reaching a decision.

Whatever careers people may choose, certain criteria seem to apply to their choices:

- Pay and emoluments.
- Security.
- Advancement possibilities.
- Living conditions.
- Prestige of the career.
- Challenge of the career.
- Associations.
- Retirement benefits.

Rarely do young people deliberately choose a career in which, in their minds, most of the above criteria seem unfavorable. Yet, few career fields offer maximum favors in all of the criteria cited. The engineer who is building a railroad in the upper reaches of the Amazon would not cite living conditions as the basic attractiveness of the work. The wildcat oil prospector would not cite retirement benefits as the forte of that career. The priest would not cite pay. Thus, each career emphasizes some and slights some of these criteria. Just so does the military career. Let's look at it objectively.

## PAY AND EMOLUMENTS

Officers of our armed services receive comparatively good pay and emoluments:

*Medical expenses* are normally a minor item to most officers and their families. The Air Force provides medical attention for officers and their dependents, thus almost eliminating the financial hazard of serious illness. Though officers may suffer extended illnesses, their pay continues in full, except for flight pay.

*Insurance costs* are lower because of the availability of government life insurance and certain survivor benefits.

*Commissaries and base exchanges* offer food and sundries at costs lower than those in the average civilian establishment.

*Travel and transportation* expenses usually match government allowances, although the average officer can suffer a net loss in this regard (see chapter 4).

*Leave with pay* is available to each officer 30 days per year (see chapter 8).

*Travel* to foreign countries and all around the United States is an experience that officers take as a matter of course but one that would cost a shocking amount of money if undertaken privately. Our civilian friends spend many hard-earned dollars globetrotting for pleasure and education (see chapter 22).

## SECURITY

Officers enjoy a relatively high degree of job security. They cannot be separated from the service except by due process of applicable laws. Although physical disability incurred in the first eight years of service results in separation without retirement benefits, important VA benefits accrue. After eight years of service, the officer who becomes physically disabled receives retirement status and pay depending on the degree of disability. For all practical purposes, a regular officer has lifetime security, barring only serious misconduct and incompetence.

Security may seem a pale and lifeless quality to you as a young person contemplating a vigorous career. Yet, with the addition of a family, even the young must give due concern to the sureness of their living income. Officers never grow wealthy on their military pay, but they can enjoy the peace of mind that comes from an assured source of livelihood for themselves and their dependents. As an officer, you can plan a long, stable future with confidence. Realistically considering not only the merits of security in your present job but also the needs of old age and even security for your yet unborn children may convince you that security is a career criterion of sterling quality. (See chapter 17.)

## ADVANCEMENT

For the regular officer, advancement in rank is available at stipulated periods, and the opportunity to advance more rapidly is almost unlimited. You don't need to seek help through special influences. Merit alone will take you upward. Of course, the competition is keen and grows sharper as you reach higher ranks. Nevertheless, you may aspire to any military position to which your personal endowments can carry you.

On the other hand, not every officer can be a general; mathematics points this fact out inexorably. On the contrary, most officers will end even full careers as lieutenant colonels. Therefore, if you correctly assess yourself as no better than average, you cannot reasonably expect to wear stars. The stars are there, however, waiting for the officer with the ability and the will to win them.

Advancement in the Air Force is more than a matter of promotion; it includes also advancement in responsibility. Whereas in some professions advancement takes the form of a steadily increasing standard of income, often these increases of income are not associated with increased responsibility and authority. In some careers, men and women may labor at essentially the same level of responsibility for 12 to 15 years, doing work that grows dull and burdensome. Not so in the Air Force.

## LIVING CONDITIONS

The living conditions of Air Force officers and their families range across a wide spectrum. Not all married officers can expect to have quarters at air bases because not that many quarters yet exist. Consequently, officers may find themselves occupying rental housing in civilian communities adjacent to air bases.

Although housed off the air base, officers and their families usually find the air base the center of their activities. The various facilities of the base, the exchange, the officers' club, swimming pools, golf courses, and social gatherings will probably appeal to you and your family.

Your children may attend schools on the air base or, more probably, will enroll in schools of the adjacent civilian community. Your children's schooling may include numerous shifts among schools in various parts of the world.

Perhaps the most notable "living condition" of an Air Force career is the frequent changes of station. Air Force officers live like nomads; here today, Japan tomorrow, Germany yesteryear. These uprootings are inherent in the life of a career officer. Often they mean temporary (and not so very temporary) separation of the family. Weigh this consideration well before choosing the Air Force as a career, for it arises often.

Hazard is also part of Air Force life. As a member of the Air Force, each officer is subject to being dispatched suddenly into danger. The war in Southwest Asia was stark evidence of this fact. On the other hand, in these days of nuclear-armed intercontinental ballistic missiles, perhaps danger is simply where you find it. Consider, however, that hazard is a greater factor in an Air Force career than it is in almost any civilian vocation.

## PRESTIGE OF THE CAREER

Officers of the Air Force generally hold a place of high respect in the minds of Americans. The career officer is a member of an honorable profession the importance of which is beyond question. The officer is accepted in any social group, is considered an excellent credit risk, and is assumed to be an intelligent and responsible citizen.

These are the basic attributes of prestige in its actual application. Public opinion polls continue to reflect the public's high rating of the military officer in America.

## CHALLENGE OF THE CAREER

Few, if any, career fields offer greater challenge to the individual than does the Air Force. Never before in the history of mankind has so much power been assembled in organized fashion as is represented by the capabilities of the U.S. Air Force. Making ready, or employing if need be, this almost incredible power is a vast job of endless ramifications. The task embraces fully the entire fields of engineering, law, medicine, political science, personnel management, industrial production, research, science, and even advertising. Hardly an aspect of American genius does not reflect itself in the operation of our Air Force. At the same time, the Air Force does not have a single solution for every situation because nothing is static. Events and the progress of science do not permit or tolerate stereotyped procedures. The problems are many, difficult, and urgently in need of solution. If you seek a challenge to your own abilities, you need look no further than an Air Force career.

## CAREER ASSOCIATIONS

Probably the most satisfactory aspect of an Air Force career lies in the associations it offers with a peerless company of fine men and women. The officers of the Air Force and their families are a group whose qualities are unexcelled by any professional corps in the nation. They are honorable people who adhere to a high code of conduct. They are loyal people who serve the nation without stint. They are able people who meet the great tasks of the Air Force and the difficulties of Air Force life with sure competence. They are interesting people who contribute to the knowledge and the culture of the nation from their worldwide experiences. They are, on the whole, good people whom it is good to know. The comradeship of the Air Force has no parallel in civilian professions and, therefore, no yardstick by which to measure its value. It is truly the sparkling attraction of an Air Force career.

Not only does the Air Force career offer fine associations with the people of the Air Force, but also it affords a matchless opportunity to meet and know men and women of every walk of life in this and many other nations. Few civilian Americans compare with the average Air Force officer in the cosmopolitan nature of his or her friendships. Almost any Air Force officer of 20 years' service can name personal friends in every state of the union and in a large number of foreign countries.

## RETIREMENT BENEFITS

Regular officers of the Air Force enjoy excellent retirement prospects. Subject to the approval of the Department of the Air Force, an officer may retire after 20 or 30 years' service (see chapter 17). Retired officers receive a substantial percentage of their active-duty pay and retain privileges of access to air base clubs, commissaries, exchanges, and athletic and medical facilities. Taken together with a reasonable insurance program, these provisions permit a retired officer to live comfortably and in dignity, though not luxuriously.

As an Air Force officer, you may look forward to retirement at an age early enough to permit you to enjoy leisure or embark on another career. So many of our civilian friends must remain at their posts of work until death or crippling disease fells them. On the

THIS IS WHAT THE CAREER IS ALL ABOUT.

other hand, as an Air Force officer, you may retire after 20 years' service at about 42 years of age or at any time thereafter, subject to current laws.

## SUMMARY

Now, you have a reasonably accurate appraisal of career choice criteria as they apply to an Air Force career, the major pros and cons involved. In these days of harsh materialism and bitter cynicism, we sometimes hesitate to utter a sentence resting on idealism. Yet, one last word needs saying. All decent men and women will seek, *must* seek, a way of life that permits them to respect their own work. All honorable people share an innate urge to be useful. The Air Force, standing as it does today between freedom and its implacable enemies, holds open wide a door to you who would feel that your career is one *you* can respect.

# 17

# Retirement

*I have done the state some service, and they know't.*

—Shakespeare, *Othello*

Retirement from the Air Force is an event that, in most cases, ends a long and successful military career and opens the way to a new career or to years of modest leisure. The majority of mandatory retirements of Air Force officers are after 28 years' service, in the grade of lieutenant colonel, and on retirement pay equal to 70 percent of the officer's basic pay as a lieutenant colonel. However, there are many other mandatory or voluntary versions of retirement that will be discussed later in this chapter. Some such retirements are the result of dire physical disability: Dangers inherent in Air Force life, sharpened by wars such as Vietnam, make disability retirements not uncommon. Other early retirements, as after 20 years' service, are voluntarily sought by Air Force officers who wish to shift to a civilian career.

## VOLUNTARY RETIREMENT

**After 20 Years' Service.** Any commissioned officer on the active list of the U.S. Air Force who has completed not less than 20 years' or more than 30 years' active federal service in the armed forces of the United States, at least 10 years of which have been active commissioned service, may in the discretion of the Secretary of the Air Force be retired upon application with annual pay equal to 2½ percent of the annual basic pay of the rank with which retired, multiplied by the number of years of service credited for pay purposes and not to exceed a total of 75 percent of such annual basic pay. For members who entered the service between 7 September 1980 and 31 July 1986, retired pay is determined using a monthly retired pay base (see 10 U.S.C. 1407). In computing the number of years of such service for the purpose of determining the percentage of active-duty annual pay, service credit shall be computed to the nearest whole month actually completed for any portion of a year that is six months or more.

For servicemembers retiring after 1 October 1983, each whole month of active service is credited at the rate of 1/12 of 2½ percent per year. Days less than 30 do not count. For example, the multiplier for 20 years and six months of active service is 51¼ percent. There are also certain save-pay provisions. See AFR 35-7 for those provisions. For servicemembers entering active service after 1 August 1986, the formula is that 1 percent is deducted for each year served less than 30. Thus, the retired member who serves 20 years will receive 40 percent of base pay rather than 50 percent, but at age 62, the original multiplier will be restored (see also the Military Retired Reform Act of 1 July 1987).

**After 30 Years' Service.** An officer who has been 30 years in the service may, upon application, in the discretion of the president, be so retired and placed on the retired list (10 U.S.C. 8918. AFR 35-7).

**Application for Retirement.** Application for retirement will be made by AF Form 1160 over the signature of the officer concerned, as prescribed in AFR 35-7.

**Early Retirement Policy.** The Air Force follows a liberal retirement policy for regular and reserve officers who have a minimum of 20 years' active federal service. At least 10 years of the 20 years' active federal service must have been in a commissioned status. For time-in-grade requirements, see the section on retired grade later in this chapter (10 U.S.C. 1370).

## RETIREMENT FOR PHYSICAL DISABILITY

The Career Compensation Act established a very important departure in remuneration following separation from active service as a result of physical disability. See 10 U.S.C., Chapter 61. No member is retired for physical disability if the disability is less than 30 percent, unless the member has at least 20 years' service.

The provisions of the act that affect disability retirement become less difficult to understand if each is considered separately. The intention is to treat commissioned and enlisted persons, regular and nonregular, on the same basis and to relate the pay given to the degree of disability or the length of service.

All personnel subject to disability retirement fall into one of two groups: (1) regulars and nonregulars called or ordered to active duty for more than 30 days; (2) regulars and nonregulars ordered to active duty, including training duty, for 30 days or less (see 10 U.S.C. 1201, 1202, 1204, and 1205).

The first stage in any proceeding for separation for physical reasons is a finding by the service that members, by reason of a disability, are not qualified to perform their duties. If members are kept on duty, there are, of course, no separation proceedings.

But if a finding is made that the members *cannot* be retained in service, the proceedings enter a second stage. If the disability resulted from "intentional misconduct" or "willful neglect" or was incurred during unauthorized absence, the government gives the members nothing, but merely separates them.

Third, if the disability was *not* due to misconduct or neglect, the next question is: Is the disability 30 percent or more under the VA standard rating? (Loss of an eye or loss of use of a limb and chronic, severe high blood pressure are disabilities of 30 percent or more; loss of one or two fingers or one or two toes, loss of hearing in one ear, or defects of scars that do not seriously interfere with functions are not.)

If the disability is less than 30 percent, and the member has less than 20 years' service, no retirement is given. Instead, the servicemember is given *severance pay,* which is two months' basic active-duty pay for each year of active service, to a maximum of two full years' active pay. Half or more of a year counts as a full year.

From this point, the disposition of disabled personnel in the two groups varies in some respects, depending upon the group to which each person belongs. The three stages in separation proceedings just mentioned are common to all personnel, *except* for one group—the nonregular ordered to active duty, including training duty, for 30 days or less. With this group, the disability normally must result from an injury.

**Types of Retirement.** Two types of retirement are possible. If the disability is obviously permanent, retirement is final. But if the Personnel Evaluation Board (PEB) has any question about the permanency of the disability, the servicemember goes on a "temporary disability retired list."

If *permanently retired,* the servicemember is paid by one of the following pay plans, whichever is more beneficial:

• Two and one-half percent of active-duty basic pay of the rank held at time placed on retired list, multiplied by the number of years of service creditable for pay purposes. (This benefits those of long service whose disabilities may be less than total. A half year or more of service counts for a full 2½ percent of active pay.)

• The same percentage of active-duty pay as the percentage of disability. (This benefits individuals of lesser service who have grave disabilities. Because one cannot retire with less than the 30 percent disability, nor receive more than 75 percent of active pay, the percentage of active pay under this option will run from 30 to 75 percent, depending on degree of disablement.)

The same pay provisions apply while on the *temporary retired list,* except that, in recognition of the adjustments to civilian life and the employment handicaps faced by a person subject to recall to duty, the minimum pay while on the temporary list will be 50 percent of active pay.

For those who entered service after 7 September 1980 and become either permanently or temporarily retired, retired pay will be determined using a monthly retired pay base (see 10 U.S.C. 1407).

Special provisions of the act, which will not be discussed here because of their limited application but which can be read from 10 USC by those interested, provide for (1) basing of retired pay on a temporary rank previously held satisfactorily, (2) recomputing retired pay of disabled persons who incur further disability while on a postretirement active-duty tour, and (3) extending to nonregulars retiring for disability the same commissary, base exchange, military hospital, and other benefits as are enjoyed by retired regulars.

Maximum period on the temporary retired list will be five years. During this period, examinations will be given at least every 18 months, the actual frequency probably depending on the nature of the disability. At the end of the five years, or earlier if one of the examinations definitely settles the permanency of the disability, one of the following things can happen:

• The retirement may be made permanent. The percentage of disability will be recomputed as of time of permanent retirement. Thus, a change in retirement pay may result. Of course, change in pay *will* result if the final pay under the most favorable option is less than the half-pay the person was assured on the temporary list.

• The disability may be found to be less than 30 percent. Retirement pay will be stopped and the person with less than 20 years' service given severance pay.

• The members may be qualified for military duty. If so, their retirement pay will be stopped and they will be, if they desire, reappointed regular or reserve officers or reenlisted, with status as much as possible like that they would have attained had they never left the active list. If they do not consent to return to duty, they are dropped from both active and retired rolls for good.

Persons who have completed 20 years' active service are entitled to retirement even if their disability is less than 30 percent.

Other retirement provisions contained in AFR 35-4 should be examined by armed forces personnel. If you are facing retirement for disability, you should study all methods of compensation—including VA compensation—weighing the income-tax factor, if any, before making a decision.

## STATUTORY AGE RETIREMENT

**At 62 or 64 Years of Age.** Unless retired or separated earlier, all regular commissioned officers (other than officers who are permanent professors or registrar of the United States Air Force Academy) shall be retired on the first day of the month following the month in which they become 62 years of age. Officers who are permanent professors or registrar at the U.S. Air Force Academy shall be retired on the first day of the month following the month in which they become 64 years of age.

The president may defer the retirement of an officer serving in a position that carries a grade above major general, but such a deferment may not extend beyond the first day of the month following the month in which the officer becomes 64 years of age. Not more than ten such deferments of retirement may be in effect at any one time (10 U.S.C. 1251).

## MANDATORY RETIREMENT

**Major Generals.** Unless provided otherwise by some provision of law, all officers in the regular grade of major general in the Regular Air Force shall be retired on the first day of the first month beginning after the date of the fifth anniversary of their appointment in that grade in the Regular Air Force, or on the first day of the month after the month in which they complete 35 years of active commissioned service, whichever is later.

**Brigadier Generals.** Unless provided otherwise by some provision of law, all officers in the regular grade of brigadier general in the Regular Air Force who are not on a list of officers recommended for promotion to the regular grade of major general shall be retired on the first day of the first month beginning after the date of the fifth anniversary of their appointment in that permanent grade in the Regular Air Force, or on the first day of the month after the month in which they complete 30 years of active commissioned service, whichever is later (10 U.S.C. 635).

**Colonels.** Unless provided otherwise by some provision of law, all officers in the regular grade of colonel in the Regular Air Force who are not on a list of officers recommended for promotion to the regular grade of brigadier general shall be retired on the first day of the month after the month in which they complete 30 years of active commissioned service (10 U.S.C. 634).

**Lieutenant Colonels.** Unless provided otherwise by some provision of law, all officers in the regular grade of lieutenant colonel in the Regular Air Force who are not on a list of officers recommended for promotion to the regular grade of colonel shall be retired on the first day of the month after the month in which they complete 28 years of active commissioned service (10 U.S.C. 633).

**Majors, Captains, and First Lieutenants.** Any promotion-list majors, captains, or first lieutenants who have been considered and not recommended by a selection board for permanent promotion will be designated "deferred" officers. If they are not recommended by the next consecutive selection board convened for the selection of officers of that grade, they shall be discharged from the Regular Air Force on the date requested by them and approved by the Secretary of the Air Force, but not later than the first day of the seventh calendar month beginning after the month in which the president approves the report of the last board that did not recommend them for promotion. If they are eligible for retirement under any provision of law in effect on that date, they shall be retired. If on the date on which the officers are to be discharged they are not eligible for retirement under any provision of law and are not within two years of becoming entitled to retirement under some provision of law, they shall be honorably discharged (10 U.S.C. 631-632).

**Deferment of Discharge.** If on the date on which officers are to be discharged as prescribed in the above paragraph for the various grades, the officers have not completed 20 years' service and are not eligible for retirement under any provision of law in effect on that date, but are within two years of becoming entitled to retirement under some provision of law, their date of discharge shall be the date on which they become entitled to retirement, rather than that prescribed above, and they shall be retained on the active list in the permanent grade then held until qualified for retirement and then be retired, unless sooner retired or separated under some other provision of law (10 U.S.C. 632).

**Removal from Active List.** If officers are removed from the active list of the Regular Air Force pursuant to the provisions of AFR 36-2 for failure to achieve such standards of performance as the Secretary of the Air Force may by regulations prescribe and if on the date of removal they are eligible for voluntary retirement under any provision of law then in effect, they shall be retired in the grade and with the retired pay to which they would be entitled if retired upon their own application. If on the date of removal the officers are not eligible for voluntary retirement, they shall be honorably discharged in the grade then held (10 U.S.C. 1186).

## RETIRED GRADE, RANK, AND STATUS

Commissioned officers shall be retired in the highest grade in which they served on active duty satisfactorily, as determined by the Secretary of the Air Force, for not less than six months. In order to be eligible for voluntary retirement in a grade above major or below lieutenant general, commissioned officers must have served on active duty in that grade for not less than three years.

Officers whose lengths of service in the highest grade they held while on active duty do not meet the service-in-grade requirements specified shall be retired in the next lower grade in which they served on active duty satisfactorily for not less than six months. Upon retirement, officers who are serving in or have served in a position of importance and responsibility designated by the president to carry the grade of general or lieutenant general may, at the discretion of the president, be retired, by and with the consent of the Senate, in the highest grade held by them while serving on active duty (10 U.S.C. 1370).

**Physical Disability.** Any officers of the Regular Air Force who may be retired for physical disability determined or incurred while serving under a temporary appointment in a higher grade shall have the rank and receive retired pay computed as otherwise provided by law for officers of such higher grade.

Any officers of the Regular Air Force on the retired list who shall have been placed thereon for reasons other than physical disability shall, if they incur physical disability while serving on active duty under a temporary appointment in a higher grade, be promoted on the retired list to such higher grade and receive retired pay computed as otherwise provided by law for officers of such higher grade retired on account of physical disability incident to service.

Any officers of the Regular Air Force on the retired list who shall have been placed thereon by reason of physical disability shall, if they incur additional physical disability while serving on active duty under a temporary appointment in a higher grade, be promoted on the retired list to such higher grade and receive retired pay computed as provided by law for officers of such higher grade, provided that the Secretary of the Air Force, or such person or persons as designated, shall find that the additional physical disability is incident to service while on active duty in the higher grade and not less than 30 percent permanent.

Any officers of the Regular Air Force on the retired list who shall have been placed thereon for reasons other than physical disability shall, if they incur physical disability while serving on active duty in the same grade as that held by the officers on the retired list, receive retired pay computed as otherwise provided by law for officers of such grade retired on account of physical disability incident to the service.

**Increases of Retired Pay.** Retired pay is increased in accord with rises in the Consumer Price Index. Thus, between June 1977 and December 1990 the pay of retirees doubled. This increase will be the computed percent change adjusted to the nearest $^{1}/_{10}$ of 1 percent (10 U.S.C. 1401(a)).

## MISCELLANEOUS

**Date Retirement Becomes Effective.** Except in cases of officers retired for disability, retirement must be effective on the first day of a month. The last day of a month is their last day of active service, and the following day is their first day of retired status. Retirement for disability is effective on the date specified in the retirement order (5 U.S.C. 8301).

**Government Employment of Officers after Retirement.** In 1964, Congress passed legislation authorizing the federal government to employ retired regular officers on a basis of compensation making it feasible for the retired regular officer to accept such employment. It is now possible for the retired regular officer to receive the full pay of a civilian government job, plus a stipulated portion of retirement pay. Retired military officers may not be hired by the Department of Defense for at least six months after their retirement.

**Residence and Travel Abroad.** Permission to travel and reside in a foreign country is no longer required of retired Air Force personnel, except for personnel who occupied "sensitive" positions or acquired "sensitive" information before retirement.

Officers' requests for retirement at foreign service stations, if otherwise appropriate, normally will be approved by the Department of the Air Force. Such approval will not be given should it become necessary to return them to the United States for hospitalization or other purposes of the government, and they will not be returned to an oversea station solely for the purpose of retirement there. The officers may, however, obtain authority for foreign residence or travel, after retirement, as indicated above.

**Travel of Retired Personnel by Transport.** An important privilege for specified retired personnel is space-available transportation on government-owned aircraft. *Space available* means space unassigned after all space requirement travel assignments have been made and space that would otherwise be unused if not authorized and assigned to the use indicated.

There is a nominal charge to cover subsistence and service.

Applications for space-available travel are to be submitted to the appropriate terminal authority, who acts on them on a first come, first served basis. Consult any transportation officer or personnel officer. Return transportation cannot be assured, and return by commercial transportation may be necessary at personal expense.

**Travel to Home.** Officers of the Regular Air Force are presumed to have no established home. They may select and proceed to a home at government expense, so far as authorized, at any place in the world at which they desire and intend to establish a bona fide home at any time within one year after retirement, provided they do these things:

- Actually proceed thereto and establish a home.
- Submit thereafter a mileage voucher for land travel certifying thereon that such place is home or previously execute such certificate.
- Previously obtain authority of the theater commander in writing in event residence is not within a territory of the United States and meet host government residency rules.
- Previously obtain a passport or statement that passport will be issued from the Department of State if required for residence where retirement is requested.

**Retired Officer Status.** An Air Force officer placed on the retired list is still an officer of the United States (31 Ct. Cl. 35).

**Change in Status after Retirement.** In the absence of any showing of fraud, the retirement of an officer under a particular statute exhausts the power of the president and the Secretary of the Air Force, and the record of executive action cannot be revoked or modified so as to make retirement relate to another statute, even though the case were one to which more than one statute properly applied at the time retirement was accomplished; and, further, the statutes relating to retirement apply only to officers on the active list, and there is no authority for the restoration of a retired officer to the active list for the purpose of being again retired (Sec. 326 (1) Dig. Op. JAG 1912–40; see also AFR 31–3).

**U.S. Air Force Retired Lists.** The Secretary of the Air Force maintains officer retired lists, upon which are placed the names of all commissioned officers of the Regular Air Force and the Air Force Reserve retired from active service.

## RETIREMENT OF AIR NATIONAL GUARD AND AIR FORCE RESERVE OFFICERS

**Retirement for Physical Disability.** The laws governing retirement for physical disability apply equally to all officers on active military duty whether of the Regular Air Force or of the Air Reserve Forces.

**Retirement for Age and Length of Service.** Chapter 67, Title 10, U.S.C., establishes retirement opportunities for AF Reserve and Air National Guard officers who attain age 60 and who satisfy stated requirements of service or service credits described in the law as "points" (see AFR 35-7).

A minimum of 50 points must be earned in any year in order for that year to count for retirement purposes. All points, however, are credited in computing retirement pay, if eligible for retirement. Points accrue and are accredited on the following basis:

• One point for each day of active federal service.

• One point for each drill or period of equivalent instruction, such drills and periods of equivalent instruction to be restricted to those prescribed and authorized by the secretary of the respective service for the year concerned and to conform to the requirements prescribed by other provisions of law.

• Fifteen points for membership in a reserve component for each year of federal service other than active federal service.

All periods of active federal service are counted for retirement purposes. One day of retirement credit is credited for each point earned while on inactive service with a limitation of 60 days for retirement purposes in any year.

The amount of retirement pay is computed at a rate equal to 2½ percent of the active duty annual basic pay (excludes allowances for quarters and rations, hazardous duty pay, and other special pay) officers would receive if serving, at the time granted such pay, on active duty in the highest grade, temporary or permanent, satisfactorily held by them during their entire period of service, multiplied by a number equal to the number of years and any fraction thereof for which retirement credits have been granted. For this purpose, the year is established at 360 days.

Retired pay for members who entered the Air Force after 7 September 1980 is determined using a monthly retired pay base. In computing this pay base, the rates of basic pay to be used are those most favorable to the member (10 U.S.C. 1407 (a)).

Officers of the Air National Guard and AF Reserve should have their own carefully checked and verified record of service establishing their retirement credits properly brought up to date. Advice of regular instructors or their assistants should be solicited in developing this record. Thereafter, they should enter currently all credits earned so that they will be continually informed of their retirement status. This retirement pay does not reduce other retirement benefits, such as that which may accrue from Social Security legislation or civil service retirement pay, nor should it serve to reduce retirement pay earned by participating in retirement programs of corporations or other employers.

## THE RETIRED OFFICERS ASSOCIATION

The Retired Officers Association has as its purpose the aid of retired personnel of the various services and components in every proper and legitimate manner. It is at 201 N. Washington Street, Alexandria, VA 22314. Dues are $20 per year.

# 18

# Voluntary and Involuntary Separations

*The officer should wear his uniform as the judge his ermine, without a stain.*
—Rear Admiral John A. Dahlgren

AFR 36-2 and AFR 36-12 cover separation of officers other than by retirement. Their provisions apply to all officers of any of the components who are serving on active duty.

## INVOLUNTARY SEPARATION

Under the provisions of pertinent sections of Title 10, U.S. Code, as implemented by AFR 36-2, the Air Force may discharge officers for moral or professional dereliction, in interests of national security, or for substandard performance of duty. The following are reasons for initiating action to determine whether a regular or nonregular officer should be retained in the Air Force.

(1) Financial irresponsibility.

(2) Mismanagement of personal or government affairs.

(3) Recurrent misconduct.

(4) Drug or alcohol abuse (see AFR 30-2).

(5) Failure at any school when attendance at the school is at government expense if the failure resulted from factors over which the officer had control.

(6) Failure to conform to prescribed standards of dress, personal appearance, or military deportment.

(7) Defective attitude.

(8) Retention is not clearly consistent with the interests of national security.

(9) Misrepresentation or omission of material facts in official written or oral statements or documents.

(10) Failure to demonstrate acceptable qualities of leadership required of officers of his or her grade.

(11) Failure to demonstrate acceptable standards of professional (including technical) proficiency required of officers of his or her grade.

(12) A progressive falling off of duty performance resulting in an unacceptable standard of efficiency.

(13) Sexual perversion.

(14) A record of marginal service over an extended period of time as indicated by performance reports.

(15) Failure to properly discharge assignments commensurate with grade and experience.

(16) Fear of flying.

Commanders may recommend initiation of action when they determine that action is appropriate. They forward the recommendations through channels to the wing or base commander (or commanders of groups directly subordinate to a major command) for initiation of action if action is appropriate. Commanders above wing or base level or at Headquarters USAF may also initiate action. They initiate action by preparing a letter of notification and forwarding it to the officer concerned.

Officers against whom action is initiated may submit written statements or other documentary evidence they feel should be considered in evaluating their cases, or they may apply for retirement, if eligible, or they may tender their resignations. Upon receipt of the officer's reply to the letter of notification of initiation of action, the major commander determines whether further processing of the case is warranted. If the officer applies for voluntary retirement or tenders resignation, the major commander forwards the application to Headquarters USAF.

If an officer does not apply for voluntary retirement or tender resignation, and if the major commander determines that further action is warranted, the case is referred to a selection board. If the selection board determines that the officer should be required to show cause for retention in the Air Force, the major commander convenes a board of inquiry. The board of inquiry examines witnesses and documentary evidence and then recommends that the officer be retained or removed from active duty with the character of discharge. When the selection board recommends an officer for retention, the major commander may recommend that a reserve officer be released from active duty. The major commander sends the board of inquiry report to Headquarters USAF, where the case is reviewed by a Board of Review and final action is taken by the Secretary of the Air Force. The Air Force Personnel Board at Headquarters USAF considers the cases of certain probationary officers and officers who waive consideration by a board of inquiry. The Secretary of the Air Force takes final action.

A regular or nonregular officer who has completed 5 or more, but less than 20, years of active service immediately before discharge or release from active duty will receive separation pay equal to:

(1) 10 percent of the product of years of active service, and 12 times the monthly basic pay that the officer received at the time of discharge or release from active duty, or $30,000, whichever is less; or,

(2) one-half of the above amount, but in no event more than $15,000, as determined by the Secretary of the Air Force, unless the Secretary determines that the conditions of discharge or separation do not warrant such pay. In determining the number of years of active service for computing separation pay, a part of a year that is six months or

more is counted as a whole year, and a part of a year that is less than six months is disregarded.

**Rights of Officers Required to Show Cause for Retention.** The recorder invites witnesses, both for the officer and for the government, to appear if the legal advisor judges that they are reasonably available and that their testimony can contribute materially to the case.

Officers may apply for voluntary retirement, if eligible, or tender their resignations before the Secretary of the Air Force makes a final decision.

Officers may appear in person before the board of inquiry, may present evidence on their own behalf, may be represented by counsel, and must be allowed access to unclassified records that the legal advisor to the board of inquiry considers relevant to the case.

Officers may be granted such time as is reasonable and necessary to prepare and present their cases before the board of inquiry.

**Involuntary Release of Nonregular Officers.** Air Force policy requires the involuntary release from active duty of nonregular officers not promoted to the next higher temporary grade, due to insufficient retainability for permanent change of station, and because of failure to complete flying or technical training (AFR 36-12).

Except for ROTC Scholarship or AECP graduates whose education was funded at government expense, AFROTC or OTS graduates with less than five years' active duty immediately before date of separation are released from active duty as soon as possible after elimination from undergraduate flying training or technical training, unless the Air Force requires their continued service on active duty. Officers may not receive readjustment pay.

Officers with an established date of separation (DOS) who have less than five years' active duty immediately prior to DOS may be released when they are surplus, when units or bases are moved or deactivated, or when they return to CONUS from an oversea assignment (AFR 36-20 and AFR 36-12).

Officers serving in the grades of second lieutenant, first lieutenant, or captain are released from active duty when they are not promoted to the next higher temporary grade. Second lieutenants are released when they do not qualify for promotion. First lieutenants and captains are released when they are passed over twice.

**Involuntary Discharge of Regular and Nonregular Officers—Failure of Promotion to Their Next Higher Permanent Grade.** Title 10, U.S. Code, requires the involuntary discharge of regular and nonregular first lieutenants, captains and majors who are twice passed over for promotion to their next higher grade and who are not eligible for retirement or for retention to qualify for retirement (AFR 35-7).

Regular and reserve second lieutenants are honorably discharged when they are not qualified for promotion. A regular second lieutenant is discharged as soon as possible. Reserve second lieutenants are discharged as soon as possible after completing three years of promotion service in the grade of second lieutenant if they have fulfilled their military service obligation.

Lieutenant colonels who are not recommended for promotion retire upon completing 28 years' service. See also chapter 17.

**Dates of Separation for New Officers.** Newly commissioned officers have dates of separation of 4 years following their date of commissioning for nonrated officers and 10 years for those engaged in flying training. The Air Force convenes annual selection-in boards that choose a number of officers each year for career reserve status.

## SELECTIVE CONTINUATION PROGRAM

**Captains and Majors.** Officers with the regular grade of captain or major who are subject to discharge or retirement because they were not selected for promotion may, subject to the needs of the service, continue on active duty if they are chosen by a selection board with the approval of the Secretary of the Air Force. Captains may not continue on active duty under this program for a period that extends beyond the last day of the month in which they complete 20 years of active commissioned service unless they are promoted to the regular grade of major. Majors may not continue on active duty under this program for a period that extends beyond the last day of the month in which they complete 24 years of active commissioned service unless they are promoted to the regular grade of lieutenant colonel.

Officers selected for continuation on active duty who are not subsequently promoted or continued on active duty and who are not on a list of officers recommended for continuation or for promotion to the next higher grade shall, unless sooner retired or discharged under another provision of law, be discharged upon the expiration of the period of continued service or, if eligible, be retired. Officers who would otherwise be discharged and who are within two years of qualifying for retirement under some provision of law shall continue on active duty until qualified for retirement under that law, and then be retired.

**Lieutenant Colonels, Colonels, Brigadier Generals, and Major Generals.** Officers with the regular grade of lieutenant colonel, colonel, brigadier general, or major general who are subject to retirement for years of service may, subject to the needs of the service, defer retirement and continue on active duty if chosen by a selection board with the approval of the Secretary of the Air Force.

**Above Major General.** Officers subject to retirement for years of service who are serving in a grade above major general may, subject to the needs of the service, defer retirement and continue on active duty by order of the president.

**Length of Deferral.** Any deferrals of retirement and continuation on active duty under the Selective Continuation Program shall be for a period not to exceed five years, and not to extend beyond the date of the officer's 62d birthday.

**Declining Deferral.** Officers selected for continuation on active duty who decline to continue on active duty shall be discharged, retired, or retained on active duty, as appropriate.

## VOLUNTARY SEPARATION

The right of officers to resign their commissions or to request release from active duty is subject to certain restrictions growing out of their military status. The president or the Secretary of the Air Force may accept a resignation or request for release, as appropriate, through any properly designated office (AFR 36-12).

Normally, a tendered resignation or request for release from extended active duty will be approved. However, an application for separation may be disapproved when an officer is under investigation; is under charges or awaiting result of trial; is absent without leave; is absent in hands of civil authorities; is insane; is in default with respect to public property or funds; is serving under a suspended sentence to dismissal; has an unfulfilled active-duty service obligation or agreement; is serving in time of war or when war is imminent, or in a period of emergency declared by the president or

Congress; or in any other instance where the best interest of the Air Force requires retention.

A resignation or request for release must contain a complete statement of reasons and, when appropriate, documentary evidence to substantiate the reasons given.

**Resignation for Hardship.** Officers may tender their resignations when their retention in the service causes undue hardship to themselves or to members of their family. In such instances, they must include documentary evidence with their application.

**Resignation as Conscientious Objector.** A tender of resignation based on conscientious objection is handled on an individual basis. The Secretary of the Air Force makes the final determination based on the facts and circumstances and the policies set forth in AFR 35-24. The officer must be conscientiously opposed to participation in war in any form; opposition must be founded on training and on a sincere and deeply held belief.

**Resignation in Lieu of Demotion or Elimination from Service.** Officers under consideration for demotion or elimination may tender their resignations in lieu of further proceedings (AFR 36-2 or AFR 36-12).

Presumably, officers who believe their cases are worthy would elect to have the proceedings continue. But if they consider elimination or demotion almost a certainty, and are unwilling to accept demotion, they may choose to resign rather than to submit to the embarrassment of having their shortcomings aired before a board of fellow officers.

**Resignation for the Good of the Service.** A resignation "for the good of the service" is a serious matter. Such resignations are utilized under the following conditions: Officers who are triable by court-martial for their conduct may tender their resignations for the good of the service if charges have not been preferred; or they may tender their resignations for the good of the service in lieu of trial if formal charges have been preferred or if they are under suspended sentence.

The Air Force will not usually accept such a resignation when the offense or conduct is such that a court-martial would result in a punishment more severe than dismissal. For example, an officer accused of fraud that might result in confinement in a penitentiary would not be permitted to resign for the good of the service. Historically, this form of resignation has been used in lieu of trial when an officer is accused of serious transgressions of moral codes or other unofficerlike conduct that would result in no greater sentence than dismissal after a court-martial.

> *"Tender consideration for worthless and incompetent officers is but another name for cruelty toward the brave men who fall sacrifices to these defects of their leaders."*—President Davis to the Confederate Congress, 8 October 1862.

# Part Three • Your Family

# 19

# Social Life in the Air Force

*The value of tradition to the social body is immense. The veneration for practices, or for authority consecrated by long acceptance, has a reserve of strength which cannot be obtained by any novel device.*

—Rear Admiral Alfred Thayer Mahan

Social activities and relationships in the Air Force are almost exactly identical to those of polite society in civilian communities. Although officers and their spouses will find little need for adjustment from their civilian habits with respect to social activities while on duty in the Air Force, there are a few differences. In general, the income of officers is known to all others: There is no place for bluffing or "keeping up with the Joneses." Another difference is the fact that an air base is in itself a *small* community in which everyone knows almost everyone else. This fact makes for tight-knit social relations and close scrutiny by all of each family's activities. In this sense, officers and their families live in goldfish bowls. Bear this notion carefully in mind at all times.

## SOCIAL LIFE ON THE BASE

**How to Be a Good Citizen of the Air Base.** Following is a series of tips that if abided by will tend to make the officer and spouse a helpful unit in air base social life. Strive to be on good terms, if not good friends, with all. Choose your close associates with great care. Do not openly express your personal dislikes of individuals. Do not become a member of a clique. Keep your dinner guests, your running partners, and your tennis matches open to a broad sweep of the families on your air base. Do not attempt to live beyond your means. In repaying your social obligations, do so within your means. If a simple dinner is the best you can do, provide it without excuses. Call on newly arrived families, and offer them your assistance. Don't merely sit there for fifteen minutes making conversation. See what you can do to help. When members of officers' families are ill, visit them, offering books, flowers, or magazines if you can afford them. Take an appropriate part in the community activities of the base.

**Official Calls.** Usually, the commander of an air base will hold a reception or open house, perhaps twice a year, for the new arrivals on the base. The old practice of calling on the commander within twenty-four hours after arrival on the air base has been abandoned. Because of the large flow of officers into air bases in these years, it is obviously impractical for commanders to receive each newly arrived officer individually, as much as they might like to do so. Practices vary among air bases and with different commanders, however, so inquire on arrival what the desires of the commander of your air base or squadron might be.

**Calling Cards.** Calling cards are rarely used by officers nowadays, but if special circumstances require their use, proceed as follows: Officers' calling cards are of the same size normally used by civilians. The complete name is generally used, such as *John Joseph Jones,* although middle initials may be used if desired.

**Social Functions.** Receptions, dinners, dances, teas, and other such social functions are performed in the Air Force in essentially the same manner as in civilian life.

It is a courtesy to your host or hostess to accept or regret invitations as soon as you possibly can. A formal written invitation should be replied to in the same style as received. If regretting an informal invitation, be sure to state clearly a sound reason why you cannot accept it, such as illness in the family, a previously accepted engagement, or military duty.

Often, a reception includes a receiving line. The line is based upon the position taken by the senior officer or honored visitor. Other members of the receiving line form on the left of the senior or honored person in order of rank of the officers with their spouses on their left. An aide or an officer acting in that capacity usually greets the guests and introduces them to the honored personage in the receiving line. The officer precedes the spouse in passing through the line. In order to avoid embarrassment and confusion, be certain to announce your name very clearly to the aide, who may then present you accurately to the receiving line. Greet each person in the receiving line before proceeding into the main area of the reception. In greeting the members of the receiving line, repeat their names, as for example, "Colonel Smith, I am very happy to meet you, sir."

At dinner dances, guests should invite their dinner partners, their hostesses, guests of honor, and houseguests to dance, regardless of dancing ability.

At cocktail parties, circulate as much as possible, conversing with as many people as you can. Do not retire to a corner to tell jokes or discuss flying or talk shop.

Upon leaving a social function, bid your host and hostess farewell, expressing thanks for the hospitality you have received. If you must leave early, explain your reasons.

It is customary to reciprocate an invitation received, regardless of whether you accepted or regretted such invitation. In this connection, you extend to houseguests of officers invitations to social gatherings to which their host has been invited.

*Seating at a Formal Dinner.* The lady of honor at a formal dinner is the lady being honored or the wife of the senior officer present. The lady of honor is always seated at the right of the host, who sits at the head of the table. The lady of next highest rank or honor is at the left of the host. The hostess sits at the foot of the table. The most distinguished (or oldest) gentleman is on the right of the hostess, and the second senior gentleman is on her left. The third senior gentleman sits on the right of the lady of honor. Others are arranged in order of rank, alternating between men and women,

CAPTAIN NOAH MATTHEW JACKSON

AIDE-DE-CAMP TO MAJOR GENERAL SECREST

UNITED STATES AIR FORCE

LIEUTENANT COLONEL AND MRS. NATHAN MENZO NEELY

DEAN STANLEY WILLINGHAM

CAPTAIN

UNITED STATES AIR FORCE

*Mary Alice Weible*

*Captain*

*United States Air Force*

EXAMPLES OF CALLING CARDS.

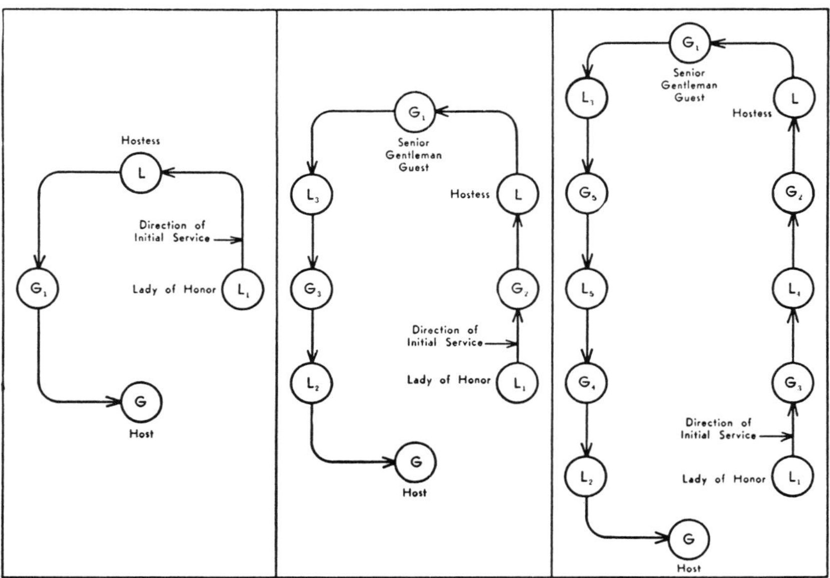


SEATING AND SERVING GUESTS AT DINNER.

and descending in order of rank or honor from the head of the table. The term "rank" in this connection does not necessarily mean military rank, but must be adjudged by the host and hostess in accord with circumstances.

**The Art of Being a Good Houseguest.** Much has been written about the art of being a good host. But all too little has been written about being a good houseguest, and it needs doing. Thoughtlessness or ignorance sometimes plays havoc with cherished friendships. Thoughtfulness will cement and strengthen them. As in all other human relationships, good breeding is shown by a proper regard for the rights of others.

The host and hostess should be informed as nearly as practicable of the exact hour of planned arrival and departure. This practice will enable them to plan your visit and permit them to plan to resume their normal contacts and activities. Particularly annoying are the invited guests who accept an invitation and state only that they will arrive during a day. The host and hostess are left in the dark. Will arrival be morning, afternoon, or evening? Should they remain at home, cancelling other things they have planned in order to be certain to receive the guests upon arrival? Should they plan the evening meal for the guests' presence? Equally troublesome are the guests who neglect to announce a definite time as to departure. The host and hostess will wish to extend all possible consideration to the guests but upon departure will wish to resume other work.

Uncertainty in these routine arrangements is displeasing. Of course, guests who arrive to stay "for a few days" and fail to inform their hosts even as to the day of planned departure until they descend with packed bags to say their farewells pass entirely beyond the pale. One way to do it is a letter, a telegram, or a telephone call that might state: "Thanks for your kind invitation. We accept with pleasure. We plan to arrive at your home soon after four Friday afternoon and must start our return before nine on Monday morning." Houseguests who accept a weekend invitation without making known these simple things have taken a firm and certain step that often will deny their receiving further invitations. Having established these days and dates, bend heaven and earth to keep them.

Guests must adjust to the conditions of the household. They should keep their things picked up and their rooms tidy. The bathroom should be left in at least as good condition as they found it. Guests should take complete care of their rooms and be similarly thoughtful of the bath. Guests in a servantless home should share in the household work to the extent that is welcome or acceptable. In this way, hosts and guests have more uncrowded hours in which to enjoy one another, and the host and hostess are spared excessive strains.

If plans have been made or suggested, guests must show their pleasure in sharing them. Adaptability is the password.

Both host and hostess will require more time to be by themselves in order to take care of personal responsibilities. Make it easy for them to do so. Take a walk, write a letter, go for a long run, or read a book.

An invitation by guests to take the family of their hosts out to dinner is often a welcomed courtesy *but it must not be pressed if once proffered and declined.*

Before departure, be certain no personal belongings are left behind for the hosts to package and mail. A remembrance to the hosts in the form of flowers, candy, or a book, given either before or after departure, is generally most appreciated. A thank-you letter written a day or two after departure is a necessary courtesy. If there is a servant, leave a tip.

Failure to do these things and others that will suggest themselves will subject you to the old saying, "making the hosts twice glad"—glad when the guests arrive and glad when they depart. Doing them may result in future invitations. The essence is regard for the rights and feelings of others.

**The Geography of Military Social Life.** As soon as the officer and family arrive at an air base, they will observe that service personnel fall into one of two categories: the group that lives on the base in government quarters and the group that lives off the base in housing rented or bought in a nearby city. Regardless of which group your family may fall into, you may find that the officers' club at the air base is the center of your social activity. At the officers' club, you can find a seven-day-a-week program of entertainment with nights for bingo, others for dancing, and others for family dinners. Your military social life probably will largely consist of either visiting the quarters of your friends on the base or off the base or attending some kind of entertainment at the officers' club.

## SOCIAL LIFE IN THE CIVILIAN COMMUNITY

Because some married Air Force officers live in civilian communities rather than on air bases, a substantial amount of their social life pertains to their civilian neighbors. In such circumstances, and if they can afford it, officers are well advised to become active participants in the social activities of their communities. The idea that an officer on duty in a foreign country is an ambassador of the United States is well advertised. Less emphasized, but just as important, is the fact that officers living in a civilian community are ambassadors of the Air Force to the American public. Accordingly, Air

Force officers should constantly seek to create a good impression on their civilian neighbors. In the main, this good impression is accomplished through unimpeachable conduct of the officer and family. It is also helpful, however, if officers become members of the churches, societies, and clubs of the civilian community and participate fully in such social life as the neighborhood offers. It is perhaps more important that Air Force officers discharge their social obligations to their civilian neighbors in a manner reflecting credit on the Air Force than it is that they meet these criteria in respect to other Air Force personnel. In a sense, all social niceties can be summed up in the phrase "Be a good neighbor." This notion certainly applies to your civilian friends as well as to your Air Force associates.

## TIPS ON ETIQUETTE

**The Right Words.** Introducing your wife to any man (except chiefs of state and very high church dignitaries): "Mary, this is Colonel Brown."

Introducing your husband to another man: "Colonel Brown, may I present my husband, Jack," or "Jack, this is Lieutenant Black." The correct order is to introduce the junior to the senior or the younger to the older.

Introducing one lady to another: "Mrs. Jones, may I present Mrs. Green," or "Mary, this is Mrs. Green."

Introducing one officer to another: "Major Smith, this is Captain Brown."

Introducing yourself to an officer senior to you: "Sir, may I introduce myself? I am Captain Jones." (Wait for the other to extend a hand.)

Introducing yourself to an officer of equal or lesser rank: "I'm Captain Margaret Jones." (Extend your hand.)

Introducing children or teenagers to adults: "Lieutenant Jones, this is Mary Smith."

Responding to an introduction: "How do you do, Colonel Green?"

Thanking host and hostess on departing a social function: "Thank you for a delightful evening."

If you *must* leave a function noticeably early: "Mrs. (Hostess), I'm sorry I must leave early." (Then give reason, and make it good!)

Gentlemen are introduced or presented to ladies, not the reverse. This holds even though the gentleman may be very distinguished and the lady very young. *Exceptions:* the president of the United States, a royal personage, a church dignitary.

The most common way to make introductions, always in good taste, is to state the names in proper sequence, the lady, the senior, more distinguished, or more elderly first. "General Smith—Captain Jones." "Miss Youthful—Colonel Adams." "Mrs. Elderly Lady—General Cole." Use a rising inflection for the first name pronounced. The more formal method: "General Smith, may I present Captain Jones?"

Acknowledgment of an introduction by saying "How do you do?" is always appropriate.

When men are introduced they shake hands, standing, without reaching across another person, if possible. They may say nothing, just look pleasant or smile, or say a courteous, "It is nice to meet you," or "How do you do?"

When women are introduced to each other, with one sitting, one standing, the seated one rises to greet her hostess, or a very distinguished lady, as an act of respect. This would apply, for example, to the wife of a very senior officer. In the usual case, the seated lady does not rise. The reply to an introduction may be a simple "How do you do?"

When a man is introduced to a woman he does not offer his hand unless the lady

# PROPER DRESS

| Event | Officer, Male | Wife | Officer, Female | Husband |
|---|---|---|---|---|
| *Official call* | Service dress uniform | Afternoon dress or suit* | Service dress uniform | Suit |
| *Informal dinner* | Civilian suit or service dress uniform | Cocktail dress or simple dinner dress | Cocktail dress or simple dinner dress or service dress uniform | Suit |
| *Formal dinner* | Service dress uniform or mess dress uniform or dinner jacket | Dinner dress** | Service dress uniform or mess dress uniform or dinner dress | Dinner jacket |
| *Private cocktail party* | Civilian suit unless a uniform is suggested on the invitation | Cocktail dress or dressy suit | Cocktail dress or dressy suit unless a uniform is suggested on the invitation | Suit |
| | *Note:* If proceeding from a cocktail party to a more formal function, it is proper to wear to the cocktail party appropriate attire for the more formal affair. | | | |
| *Official cocktail party* | Service dress uniform | Cocktail dress or dressy suit | Service dress uniform | Suit |
| *Barbecue or other informal outdoor affair* | Sport coat, no tie | Blouse and skirt or slacks, but no shorts | Blouse and skirt or slacks, but no shorts | Sport coat, no tie |
| *Official reception (not including dinner)* | Service dress uniform or mess dress uniform | Dressy afternoon clothes or cocktail dress | Service dress uniform or mess dress uniform | Suit |
| *Official reception (including dinner)* | Service dress uniform or mess dress uniform | Dinner dress | Service dress uniform or mess dress uniform | Suit or dinner jacket |
| *At home or open house (before 6 P.M.)* | Civilian suit | Afternoon dress or suit | Afternoon dress or civilian suit | Suit |
| *Parades and retreats* | Service dress uniform | Daytime dress or suit* | Service dress uniform | Suit |
| *Private dinner at officers' club* | Civilian suit | Cocktail dress or simple dinner dress | Cocktail dress or simple dinner dress | Suit |

* Hats and gloves have been a military tradition among officers' wives at official daytime occasions, such as a Change of Command or Retirement parade, Official Call, Tea, or Luncheon. This elegant tradition is reviving.

** Traditionally, a dinner dress is a long dress with long- or elbow-length sleeves and a high or scoop neckline (as opposed to a strapless ball gown).

proffers hers. In Europe, men are taught to take the initiative in shaking hands. A woman does not refuse a proffered hand.

A woman or man, introducing husband or wife to another, may say, "This is my husband," or "May I introduce my wife?"

At a social occasion, host and hostess should shake hands with guests in greeting and upon their departure.

Using titles with names:

Major General Black: "General Black."

Brigadier General White: "General White."

Colonel Smith: "Colonel Smith."

Lieutenant Colonel Jones: "Colonel Jones."

First Lieutenant Brown: "Lieutenant Brown."

Second Lieutenant Green: "Lieutenant Green."

**Reaction to Invitations.** Respond to an invitation (1) promptly, and (2) in kind. "Promptly" means within 24 hours. "In kind" means in the same manner as the invitation is received. If received orally, respond orally. If received in an informal note, respond by informal note (unless a telephone RSVP is specified in the invitational note). If the invitation is received in the form of a formal note or card, respond fully, in writing, on formal note paper, and in the third person: "Lieutenant Jones is happy to accept the kind invitation of Colonel and Mrs. Smith to dinner on 3 January 1996 at seven o'clock."

Always explain a regret to an informal invitation; normally, you do not give reason in regretting a formal written invitation. *Do not* regret an invitation issued by your commander unless official duties unavoidably prevent your attendance.

If invited to dinner, and you are a bachelor, inquire of your hosts whether they wish you to escort anyone to the function. After attending a private social function, it is essential to write a note to your hostess (or make a telephone call) thanking her for the entertainment.

Remember to return the courtesy extended to you. It is not necessary that this be in exactly the same form as the courtesy you received. Inviting your recent host and hostess to be your guests at a college football game is a fully satisfactory reciprocation for a dinner.

## THE FORMAL DINING-IN

Certain ceremonies and traditions are part of the Air Force way of life. One of these is the "dining-in," a formal dinner of a unit or organization.

For the convenience of Air Force officers everywhere, we have included material prepared at the Air University at Maxwell Air Force Base for assistance to officers who may desire to hold a dining-in for their units, or whose commanders may have assigned them the duty of making preparations for a dining-in.

The dining-in is a formal dinner function for members of an organization or unit (also see AFP 30–6).

**Background.** The custom of dining-in is a very old tradition in England, but is not exclusively military. It is believed that dining-in began as a custom in the monasteries, was adopted by the early universities, and later spread to the military units of the country when the officers' mess was established.

The late General H. H. Arnold probably started the dining-in within the Army Air Corps when he used to hold his famous "wing-dings." The contacts of U.S. Army Air

Corps personnel with the British and their dinings-in during World War II gave additional impetus for the growth of this custom in the USAF. It was recognized that those occasions provided situations where ceremony, tradition, and good fellowship could play an important part in the life of military organizations.

**Purpose.** The dining-in provides a situation for officers to see how ceremony and tradition play a part in the life of an Air Force unit. It also provides an occasion for officers to meet socially at a formal military function. It is an excellent means of saying farewell to departing officers and welcoming new officers. Further, the dining-in provides an opportunity to recognize individual and unit achievements. All of these are very useful in building high morale and esprit de corps.

**Planning.** Preparation for the dining-in should begin well in advance. Date, location, and speaker should be selected, and reservations made. The dinner should be held in a suitable private place dictated by good taste. Details for the various arrangements should be allocated to individuals and their specific duties outlined. An order of events, or agenda, should be prepared.

**Attendance.** Traditionally, attendance at a dining-in was mandatory, and many commanders still consider this function a mandatory requirement, similar to a commander's call. Other commanders feel that since goal of the dining-in is to bring members closer together, attendance should be voluntary so that those who feel that they were forced to attend will not dampen the spirit and enthusiasm of the others. The decision as to whether a dining-in is voluntary or mandatory appropriately rests with the commander.

Dinings-in are attended by officers assigned to the unit holding the dining-in. They are the "members of the mess." Officers not assigned to the unit or of similar units invited to participate by the commander are not members of the mess, and may attend only if invited as guests. Most dinings-in are held at the officers' club.

There are two types of guests: official guests and personal guests. Official guests are honored guests of the mess. The guest speaker is an official guest. All official guests are seated at the head table and their expenses are shared by the members of the mess. Because of the costs and space at the head table, the number of official guests should be limited.

Personal guests may be either military officers or civilians. They are not seated at the head table, and their expenses are paid by the sponsoring member.

Senior officers from other units and organizations and civic leaders from the local community should be considered when inviting guests. It is a good way to enhance relations between base units and with civilian neighbors.

**Guest Speaker and Other Guests.** The guest speaker should be a military member or a civilian who can be expected to address the mess in an interesting manner on an appropriate subject. The guest speaker should be invited well in advance and advised of what to expect and what is expected of a dining-in guest speaker. Arrangements should be made for the guest speaker and for other invited guests as protocol and custom dictate.

**Dress.** The dress for the dining-in should be the mess dress uniform. Civilian guests usually wear semiformal wear, but business attire may be acceptable. The proper dress for civilians should be clearly stated in the invitation. Retired officers may wear the mess dress or civilian attire.

**Dining-in Customs.** All members of the mess should arrive within 10 minutes after the opening time to meet the guests before dinner is served. When the signal is given for dinner, the members should enter the dining room and stand behind their chairs. There will be no smoking from the time the members enter the dining room until the president of the mess so permits. (Members, unless properly excused, will not leave the mess before the guest of honor and the president have departed.)

The guest of honor and the president of the mess will be the last to join the head table. The president formally opens the mess and continues according to the agenda. The president will remain standing while speaking but will seat the other members of the mess after the toast to the chief of staff has been given.

The president's welcoming remarks, after the invocation, will set the tone for the formal part of the agenda. Guests at the head table are introduced by the president of the mess. Other guests of the mess should be introduced by an appropriate member of the mess.

If there is to be an informal portion of the dining-in, such as some form of entertainment, there should be a distinct break between the formal and informal portions.

Each time the mess is adjourned and reassembled, members should stand behind their chairs until the persons at the head table have left the table or are seated.

At any time after the toast to the chief of staff, a member may ask to be recognized for an appropriate reason. A typical reason may be that a toast has been forgotten. In such a case, the member will stand and ask to be recognized by saying, "Mr. President, I have a point of order." The president will recognize the member by calling rank and name. The member will, in a polite and forthright manner, tell the president that the toast was not proposed. The president will then ask the member who has the floor, or Mr. Vice, to propose the appropriate toast.

During the dining-in each member should try to pay respects to the guest of honor. After the mess is adjourned, members should remain at the dining-in until the guest of honor and the president of the mess have left. If there is to be an extensive delay in their leaving, the president may then decide to allow members to leave. Some unobtrusive signal, such as casing a unit flag, would be an appropriate means of notifying members the dining-in is over. Mr. Vice will be the last member to leave the dining-in.

**Presentation of Awards.** If individual and unit achievements are to be recognized at the dining-in, an appropriate ceremony should be arranged. This ceremony should take place during the formal portion of the dining-in. A convenient time would be immediately preceding the guest of honor's speech. Under no circumstances should any ceremony follow directly after the speech, because this speech should be the highlight of the dining-in.

**Duties of President and Others.** The detailed duties of the president of the mess, the arrangements officer, the host officers, the protocol officer, the mess officer, and Mr. Vice should be specified in advance. For example, the duties of the president of the mess (usually the commander of the unit holding the dining-in) might include these:

- Set the date.
- Determine the location.
- Secure a suitable speaker. In the invitation to the guest speaker, such information as description of the audience, a description of the occasion, and some suggested topic areas will be helpful to the speaker.
- Arrange for a chaplain to give the invocation. Inform the chaplain regarding the invited guests.
- Appoint any or all of the following:

*Arrangements officer.* To work closely with the president in determining the date and location, and in identifying and inviting the guest speaker. He or she is also responsible

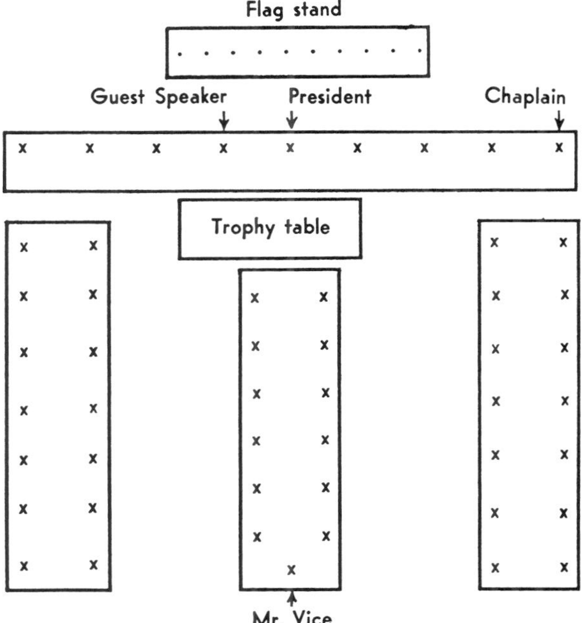


TABLE LAYOUT AND SEATING ARRANGEMENTS.

for the menu, seating, decorations, music and entertainment, billing and reservations, invitations, and the agenda. Other duties include the following: preparing table arrangements, arranging for name cards (head table) and organization identification cards, flags, trophies, public address system, president's gavel and board, dinner chimes at Mr. Vice's place, pencils and pads at head table; seeing that the guest of honor cup is engraved and on hand, and that awards are on hand; and arranging for a photographer. The arrangements officer should not make any final decisions on major aspects of the dining-in without consulting the president.

*Host officers.* To contact designated guests in advance and inform them as to mess customs, dress, place, agenda, and other guests; arrange to meet them on arrival; provide transportation and quarters if needed; introduce guests to president at mess, other guests and members, brief them where they are to sit; when they leave, see that they are escorted to cars and given a farewell on behalf of all members of the mess.

*Mess officer.* To make dining room reservations, select menu, coordinate timing of food service with head waiter to agree with desires of president of mess; arrange for mess charges to be paid; arrange for bar facilities if president so indicates; if steak is to be served, arrange for use of "steak indicators" except at head table, where a waiter should take individual orders.

*Protocol officer.* To prepare invitations to all guests for president's signature, brief and assist the host officers as necessary, prepare biographical sketches, and prepare follow-up correspondence with guest of honor after the dining-in.

• Appoint and brief Mr. Vice (a junior officer selected for wit and ability to speak) on duties.

• Meet all guests before dinner is served.

• Open the mess with one rap of the gavel and close it with two raps.

• When introducing the guests to the mess, leave no room for doubt in the minds of the guests as to when and if they are to acknowledge the introduction. Avoid over-flattering comments.

• When the president desires that a toast be made, the president should call on Mr. Vice. A simple "Mr. Vice" will suffice. (The president will have previously briefed Mr. Vice, who will know which toast is to be proposed.)

**Duties of Mr. Vice.** The president may assign such duties as these:

• Prepare appropriate toasts as directed by the president. Poems and ditties by Mr. Vice are encouraged.

• Be prepared to propose any other toasts the president may call for during the evening.

• Be prepared to help the president resolve unforeseen requirements for toast proposals.

• Sound the dinner chimes at appropriate times.

• Be the last officer to leave the mess.

*Examples of toasts:*

HONORED GUEST SPEAKER:

Most honored guest,
Your words of wisdom we did hear;
And if your footsteps we can follow,
This Air Force, this nation of ours
Will have nothing to fear.
—"TO OUR HONORED GUEST."

We're glad that you have been our guest,
And hope you feel the same.
Your wisdom, be sure, we will embrace,
But for your wit, YOU must take the blame.
—"TO OUR GUEST SPEAKER."

GUESTS:

To our guests from far and wide:
Accept our friendship, joy and pride.
Join our laughter, enjoy our wine,
And may your future ever shine.
—"TO OUR GUESTS."

Honored guests from side to side,
You grace our tables to our pride.
To you honored guests we drink this toast:
We hope you enjoy the evening the most.
—"TO OUR GUESTS."

TO ALL MEMBERS (UNITS):

To you who join our December crowd,
We sing praises long and loud.

Let's take our cups and drink good cheer.
One and all, we're glad you're here.
—"TO OUR MEMBERS."

TO THE OLD AND NEW GUARD:
To those that are leaving
Let all remember
That they, at their beginning,
Were once young and tender,
And to those that now
Hold the future in balance,
Face up to the task
And accept the challenge.
—"TO THE OLD AND NEW."

**Agenda.** The agenda should be prepared to fit the needs of the specific occasion. Here is a sample:

WING DINING-IN
DATE
PLACE

1800—Arrive to meet guests.

1827—Informal period ends. Please move into the dining room upon sounding of dinner bell by Mr. Vice. (Do not take glasses to dining room. Wine is served for toasting.) No smoking.

1830—The Mess is formally opened with one rap of the gavel by the president of the mess. (Remain standing.) (For Air Force units, the commander or senior officer will act as president.)

1833—Invocation by chaplain.

1835—Toast to the president of the United States. (Response: "To the president.") Toasts to the heads of allied nations, if representatives are present. (Response should be the proper one for that particular country and office.) Toast to the chief of staff, USAF, by Mr. Vice. (Response: "To the chief of staff.")

1836—President seats the mess.

1837—Welcoming remarks by the president of the mess.

1840—Introduction of all guests (if guests are present).

1850—Toast by Mr. Vice to our guests, if applicable (guests remain seated). (Response: "Hear, Hear.")

1851—Cocktail, salad, and steak courses are served. Place a steak indicator in front of your place: pink—rare; blue—medium; yellow—well done. Indicators will be on your table in a glass. Dessert, coffee, and cigars as soon as main course is completed. (The mess may smoke when the president lights up.)

1935—Individual achievements recognized and awards presented.

1945—Explanation of unit achievements and award of trophies (if appropriate).

2000—Introduction of the speaker by the president.

2005—Message by speaker.

2025—President calls for toast to speaker.

2026—Closing remarks by president.

2030—President adjourns mess.

2045—Move back to dining room on sounding of bell for entertainment and informal activities. (A previously designated senior officer will act as master of ceremonies for these activities.)

# 20

# Personal Affairs and Aid for Your Dependents

*Man has two supreme loyalties—to country and to family. . . . So long as their families are safe, they will defend their country, believing that by their sacrifice they are safeguarding their families also.*

—Captain B. H. Liddell Hart

All officers of the U.S. Air Force may expect sudden changes of station, either temporary or permanent, or changes in their personal status. Personnel affected by such movements may anticipate months or years of separation from their dependents, during which time they may be unable to properly attend to their personal affairs and welfare.

Efficiency of performance varies in direct ratio to servicemembers' peace of mind and mental stability. No servicemembers want to expose dependents to distress, want, or insecurity. All officers and airmen in the Air Force should arrange their personal affairs so that dependents will be adequately protected and provided for in order to prevent any legal entanglement or embarrassment that could be caused by their absence.

The time to prepare for the sudden separation caused by military transfer is now, while personal matters are moving along in a routine manner, rather than during that turbulent and busy period immediately preceding departure upon a change of station. It is imperative that military personnel keep their personal affairs properly arranged to provide the maximum protection and security for their dependents and that they ensure that dependents have ample knowledge of and receive all rights and benefits to which they are entitled. Because individual preparations are determined by the needs of the individuals concerned, it is impossible to prescribe an exact set of preparations applicable to all personnel in the Air Force. The status of some may require only simple adjustments while others may require complicated and minutely detailed arrangements. To assist all personnel in properly arranging their personal affairs, this chapter sets forth in detail the varied subjects that Air Force personnel should consider in providing for the welfare, protection, and security of their dependents at all times.

Also, the Air Force is acutely conscious of the importance to its members of sound guidance in providing assistance in the solution of personal problems. For this reason, each base has a personal affairs staff. As an aid to individuals, a series of Air Force pamphlets in the 211 series provide a sound approach to all manner of personal problems.

Members of the Air Force who need advice on personal matters should go first to their personal affairs officer, state their problem candidly and completely, and invite guidance. It will be extended willingly, authoritatively, and without cost. The confidence divulged will be protected.

## ALLOTMENTS OF PAY AND DEDUCTIONS

**General.** Allotments of pay may be authorized by all military personnel on active duty wherever serving (see AFM 177-373) to the following people and organizations:

- Individuals or banks for the support of dependents or to savings or checking accounts.
- Life insurance companies for the payment of premiums on life insurance on the life of the allotter.
- Federal savings and loan associations.
- Lending institutions holding loans insured by the Federal Housing Administration or the Housing and Home Finance Agency.
- Air Force Aid Society and American Red Cross for payment of loans made by these organizations to military personnel.

**Authorization, Discontinuances, and Limitations of Allotments.** AF Form 1548 *(Allotment Authorization)* will be executed in duplicate for the purpose of authorizing, reauthorizing, changing, or discontinuing Class S allotments. Class S allotments to a bank for savings (including a checking account) must be made to the credit of one individual only. No allotment for savings (including a checking account) will be made until the allottee has made satisfactory arrangements with the bank for acceptance.

Officers may allot so much of their basic pay, monthly subsistence allowance, and quarters allowance as will leave sufficient balance equal to or greater than the amount of income tax to be withheld in accordance with AFM 177-373 and current Internal Revenue Service regulations.

**Emergency Allotments.** In exceptional cases, when persons in active service have not made adequate provision for the support of certain dependents, the Secretary of the Air Force may act in their behalf to make allotments for the well-being and protection of their dependents. Such allotments may be terminated at the request of the person whose pay is charged therewith (AFM 177-373).

## LEGAL ASSISTANCE PROGRAM (AFR 110-22)

If members of the armed forces have problems of such a nature that the services of an attorney are desirable or necessary, they may go to the nearest legal assistance officer attached to the judge advocate's office on any base. The legal assistance officer (LAO) will counsel, advise, carry on necessary correspondence, negotiate, and draw up any legal papers necessary. The LAO is, by regulation, prohibited from entering a formal appearance in a litigated matter.

**Wills of Air Force Personnel.** *Desirability.* All servicemembers should give consideration to the making of a will, if they have not already done so. Whether a will is necessary or desirable and the form it should take depend on the desires and circumstances of the individual, and the laws of the place of execution and of the probable place of probate. State laws govern the execution and probate of wills, and the requirements in these respects vary considerably among the various states.

When people die without having made a will, they are said to have died "intestate." In such event, the estate is administered and distributed according to the statute of "Descent and Distribution" of the state of legal domicile or, in the case of real property, the state or states in which such real property is located. This law thus, in effect, creates a will for the individual, which is administered by an "administrator" appointed by the court, and the estate is distributed to the family members in the manner prescribed by the statute.

If the manner of distribution so prescribed by law does not meet your desires or needs, you can direct a distribution of your estate according to your wishes by making a will.

*Review of a will.* An executed will should be reviewed from time to time, especially when such events as marriage, birth of children, divorce, or death of a named beneficiary occur. Changes of status such as these often affect the provisions of a will. A will is not effective until death and can be replaced by a new will or changed by a codicil at any time that the testator feels it is necessary. Unless the will is extremely complicated, the use of codicils should be avoided. If the will is replaced by a new will, all copies of the previous will should be destroyed. Whenever circumstances change, officers should review their wills with the aid of legal counsel.

*Safekeeping.* Military personnel, because of their transient status, should not keep the original copy of their wills in their possession. After completion, the original copy of the will should be mailed to the named executor or chief beneficiary for safekeeping or placed in some other secure place where it will be available in the event of death. It is advisable, for reference purposes, to keep a copy of the will, with a notation as to the location of the original will. The principal beneficiary should be advised of the location of the original.

*Emergency will.* In the event of emergencies that necessitate the immediate execution of a will, officers should write out their desires as to the distribution of possessions and have them attested by three competent witnesses. Such a handwritten will should state the full name, grade, service number, and permanent address of the officer, the exact desires as to the distribution of possessions, the name and address of the person desired to be the executor, and the date, place, and circumstances of execution. Such a will should definitely be replaced as soon as possible by one prepared with the aid of legal counsel.

**Power of Attorney.** A power of attorney is a legal instrument whereby you may designate another person to act in your behalf in legal or personal matters. The one executing the power of attorney is usually referred to as the "principal," and the one to whom the authority is given is usually referred to as the "attorney-in-fact" or simply as the "attorney" for the principal. You may grant the authority of a power of attorney to a member of your family or to any other person of legal age and capacity; however, when appointing your attorney-in-fact, you should select somebody in whom you have complete trust and confidence. The authority given in a power of attorney, unlike that of a will, becomes invalid upon the death of the principal.

The power of attorney can be made very general and unlimited in scope, or it can be restricted to certain specific functions, depending on the needs and desires of the principal. A power of attorney may or may not be honored, depending on its acceptance by the individual to whom it may be presented for a transaction in the principal's name. Because the principal is held responsible for the actions of an attorney-in-fact performed within the limits of the power of attorney, it is advisable not to execute power of attorney until a specific need or use for it exists. As a rule, a restricted power of attorney will accomplish the specific needs of the individual.

*Preparation and legal counsel.* The requirements as to preparation of the form and content of a legally effective power of attorney vary considerably under the laws of the various states. For this reason, and in order to properly fulfill the needs and desires of the principal, each power of attorney should be individually prepared under the guidance of legal counsel with due regard to the laws of the state of execution and of the probable place of exercise of the powers granted. Legal counsel should be consulted for the preparation of a power of attorney when the need for such instrument exists.

**Estates.** *Kinds of property.* A person accumulates various types of possessions during a lifetime, which become known collectively as an "estate." This estate may consist of "real estate," which is land and any buildings, constructions, fixtures, and improvements erected thereon or attached thereto; "personalty," which includes all items of personal property, such as clothes, household furnishings, automobiles, money, stocks, bonds, jewelry, and, in general, any property that is not "real estate"; or a combination of both "real estate" and "personalty."

*Importance of joint tenancy.* Air Force personnel, in their arrangements of personal matters for the protection of their dependents, should consider the importance and advantages of arranging title to most of their property by "joint tenancy." In this way, officers will enable the joint tenants to use and control the property during their lifetime and in the event of their death, to obtain full title as survivor without the property being subject to administration through the courts. Property owned in joint tenancy cannot be disposed of by a will if the joint tenants survive. The solution to the officers' problem of providing for the care, welfare, and comfort of dependents in the event of prolonged absence or death can be more effectively accomplished through the establishment of title to property by "joint tenancy" than it can be done by a power of attorney and a will. The rights of control of property by the joint tenant are full and absolute when title is kept in joint tenancy, and upon the death of the officer, the property will pass automatically into full possession of the joint tenant without judicial proceedings. Personal property held in joint tenancy may, however, make it subject to tax because the Soldiers' and Sailors' Relief Act does not protect dependents.

Sound appraisement on the part of the owner concerning the capabilities and integrity of the contemplated joint owner should be exercised, and, in general, it is *not* advisable to establish joint property title with a person of short acquaintance.

Except as limited by state statutes, titles by joint tenancy with right of survivorship can be granted for various types of property. Deeds establishing ownership to real estate, and bills of sale for personal property, such as automobiles, machinery, household goods, or livestock, can be held in joint tenancy with right of survivorship. Joint bank accounts can be opened, and stocks and bonds can be issued to joint owners, with the right of survivorship in each case.

U.S. Savings Bonds can be issued to joint owners with right of survivorship if the purchaser so requests. A savings bond already issued to a single owner (without a designated beneficiary) is part of the estate but can be reissued during his or her lifetime to joint owners upon proper application to the Treasury Department. Bonds issued to a single owner with a designated beneficiary can be cashed only by the owner during his or her lifetime and on death of the owner do not become part of the estate but go directly to the named beneficiary. Such bonds cannot be reissued without the consent of the beneficiary. A bond held in joint ownership can be cashed by either joint owner with or without the consent of the other joint tenant.

*Legal assistance.* Legal advice should be obtained before anybody creates a joint tenancy title on property. Gift, inheritance, or other taxes may often affect the enactment of joint tenancy titles. Competent legal assistance will inform one of the advantages and disadvantages of holding the various kinds of property in joint tenancy and will also facilitate the proper establishment of such an estate with due regard to all applicable laws (see AFR 110-22).

**Safe-Deposit Boxes.** Many banks maintain safe-deposit boxes and rent them to people for a yearly fee that varies with the size of the box. When available, a safe-deposit box in a conveniently located reputable bank or trust company is usually the best place to keep valuable papers such as stocks, bonds, deeds to property, insurance policies, receipts, and a copy of one's will.

**Automobile.** *Title.* The determination as to the proper owner of an automobile is made, not by possession, but by the certificate of title or other evidence of ownership from the state in which the automobile is registered. Most states maintain a bureau of motor vehicles or some other similar agency for this purpose. If the title of the automobile is in the name of one person, such automobile, in the event of the death of the owner, would become part of the estate, subject to that person's will, if executed, or the laws of "Descent and Distribution" of the appropriate state. The actual determination as to disposition of the automobile, pending the result of probate, would rest with the state authorities. Subject to statutory limitations of the state of registration, title to an automobile may be held jointly by a husband and a wife. Under such title, in the event of death of one, the automobile would become the property of the survivor. This method is usually the most effective for providing for the use of and title to the automobile for the spouse in case of prolonged absence or death of the officer. It has its disadvantages, however, in the statutory limitations mentioned above and in the fact that difficulties are sometimes encountered in effecting transfer of the automobile without the presence and signatures of both joint owners, and in the spouse's being subject to personal property taxes in some states.

*Changing of title.* Because state laws govern the transfer of title to an automobile, extreme care should be exercised that all provisions of law relative to such transfer are met. If you want to transfer title to an automobile from yourself to your spouse and you jointly, you should check with the bureau of motor vehicles or other similar agency in the state in which the automobile is registered, requesting the exact procedure necessary to accomplish such action. Upon receipt of the instructions, use the legal assistance facilities in completion of the transfer of title.

*Importance of insurance.* In many cases, an automobile is the most valuable single item of property owned by the officer. It is, therefore, advisable to protect such property with adequate insurance. The insurance policy should cover the owner, the spouse, and all other persons who may have occasion to drive the vehicle. Lack of adequate insurance protection may result in extreme financial, legal, and personal difficulties.

Many states have enacted or are enacting compulsory insurance laws, and strict compliance with these laws is necessary. Officers should not be deceived into a false state of security by possessing only the amount of insurance required by law. In some states, compulsory insurance provides only minimum protection rather than adequate insurance protection.

**Soldiers' and Sailors' Civil Relief Act.** The purpose of the Soldiers' and Sailors' Civil Relief Act is to relieve members of the armed forces from worry over the inability to meet their civil obligations by providing adequate representation for the servicemember during an absence and postponement of certain civil proceedings and transactions until release from such military service. There is nothing in the act that relieves one from the actual payment of the debts or other obligations, but in the event that the servicemember is unable to pay premiums on commercial insurance policies, to pay taxes, or to perform other obligations with reference to right and claims to lands of the United States, certain relief may be afforded by this act. In the event of legal action based on a servicemember's breach of obligation, the relief afforded under this act is within the discretion of the court and depends upon whether the ability of the servicemember to discharge the obligations or to prosecute the action or defense is materially affected by reason of military service.

*Insurance.* The payment of premiums on commercial life insurance may be protected under Article IV of this act.

*Other protections.* In addition to the protection of commercial life insurance, the Soldiers' and Sailors' Civil Relief Act provides arrangements for adequate legal representation and stays of execution for servicemembers on the following legal matters:

- Eviction for nonpayment of rent.
- Court proceedings arising from mortgages, leases, liens, and other contractual obligations.
- Payment of taxes. Tax payment may be deferred in some cases. Officers are not required to pay local taxes in the state where they are stationed unless, by some act of the officers, they become legal residents, provided the officers maintain legal residence in another state and discharge their liability in that state.

*Importance of legal assistance.* This summary of the Soldiers' and Sailors' Civil Relief Act has mentioned only the major points contained in the act. It is very important, therefore, that any officers who are suddenly presented with a tax bill or threatened with legal action of any kind while away from their state of domicile should immediately report the matter to their legal assistance officer, who can then study the case and possibly avert court action through implementation of some of the points of the Soldiers' and Sailors' Civil Relief Act. Too often, people delay in notifying the legal assistance officer of their legal difficulties until the case has already reached the litigation stage, with the result that the legal assistance officer is unable to assist. The importance of prompt notification and use of legal assistance facilities in any legal entanglement cannot be overemphasized.

**Joint Bank Accounts.** *Meaning of joint bank accounts.* A joint bank account is one in which two persons have full authority to perform the functions of depositing and withdrawing funds from the same account. Such an account may be either a savings account or a checking account and is considered to be the joint property of the persons concerned. It is possible in most states to maintain joint accounts, and most banks have a specially prepared contract form setting out the legal status of such account in accordance with the state laws that govern the operations of the bank. Such a contract and the accompanying passbook usually contain a phrase somewhat as follows: "John

Doe and Mary Doe, jointly or either, with rights of survivorship and not as tenants in common."

*Advantages of joint bank accounts.* The chief advantage of a joint account is that the funds are readily available to either or both of the parties at any time. This situation is especially important to Air Force personnel because by maintaining their accounts in such a status, they enable their dependents to obtain the funds therein even though the servicemember is absent for any reason whatsoever. If officers carry bank accounts in their names only, the dependents may be deprived of the use of the money at a time when it is most urgently needed. Another great advantage is that in the event of death of one of the parties, the survivor automatically becomes sole owner of the money in the account, usually without having the funds frozen while the will of the deceased is being probated. Thus, the spouse or other dependents will have the money available at a time when it is urgently needed.

**Allotments to Joint Bank Accounts.** Allotments to a bank for deposit in a savings or checking account must be made to the credit of one person. It is permissible, however, to make an allotment to a bank even though the one to whom the allotment is credited is a party in a joint account. Proper arrangements for acceptance and depositing of the allotment must be made with the bank concerned before initiation of such an allotment (AFM 177-373).

**Credit Unions.** The Air Force encourages and assists the establishment of credit union facilities on Air Force installations as cooperative organizations to stimulate systematic savings and create a source of credit for both provident and productive purposes. One is usually to be found on any good-sized base (AFR 170-17).

## AGENCIES OF ASSISTANCE TO AIR FORCE PERSONNEL AND THEIR DEPENDENTS

**Civilian Health and Medical Program of the Uniformed Services (CHAMPUS).** For families of active-duty personnel, CHAMPUS is extremely important. It provides extensive medical care and hospitalization as a right, not as a mere privilege, and at greatly reduced cost to the individual.

Officers are urged to determine upon arrival at any new station or new residence for family members the place each would go for medical care or hospitalization—civilian facility or service facility. This assessment includes the situation of a son or a daughter away at school or college. Leave nothing to chance, and avoid delay if emergency arises.

The CHAMPUS service provided is of a very high standard. The Air Force provides highly capable direction from the top. Still, not every human ailment or frailty is covered, and not every item of expense is paid by the government. Officers must learn of these exceptions and apply them, if necessary, to their own family situations.

Under CHAMPUS from civilian sources, it is accurate to say that the major portion of the costs are paid by the government for all normal illnesses and needs for surgical care. Partial charges are made, as stated later.

There are definite exclusions for which the government does not pay the costs. In broad terms, these are chronic situations, cosmetic or voluntary surgery, domiciliary situations, treatment of congenital defects, and conditions that are nonacute.

CHAMPUS provides for the inpatient care in civilian hospitals, including outpatient service for spouses and children of active-duty personnel. The legislation authorized both a new civilian hospitalization program and outpatient care from civilian medical facilities for military retirees and their spouses and children and also for the spouses and children of deceased active-duty or retired military personnel.

Separate assistance is available for mentally and physically handicapped spouses and children of active-duty personnel.

Military medical facilities may still be used by dependents and by retirees and their spouses and children on a space-available basis.

*Cost of Civilian Outpatient Care for Spouses and Children of Active-Duty and Retired Personnel and for Retirees.* The charge to family members of active-duty personnel E-4 and below using civilian medical facilities for outpatient care is $50 per year per person (but not more than $100 per family) *and* 20 percent of the remaining outpatient cost. Above E-4 the rate is $150 per person and $300 per family.

The charge to retired personnel and to their spouses and children using civilian medical facilities for outpatient care is also $150 per person (but not more than $300 per family unit) *and* 25 percent of the remaining outpatient cost.

*Cost of Civilian Hospital Care.* For spouses and children of active-duty military personnel receiving inpatient care in a civilian hospital, there is a basic charge of $7.10 per day, or the first $25 of the hospital cost, whichever is greater. One must obtain a certificate of nonavailability from the nearest military medical facility.

The charge to retired personnel and to their spouses and children (and to the dependents of deceased military personnel) receiving inpatient care in a civilian hospital is 25 percent of the cost (the government pays 75 percent of the allowable charges, including physicians' fees).

*Note:* Retirees and their dependents who become eligible for Social Security Medicare at age 65 will no longer be entitled to the civilian hospitalization and civilian outpatient care provided in CHAMPUS. They will continue to be eligible for space-available care in military facilities.

*Identification.* When applying for any kind of medical care—at a service or civilian facility or from a civilian physician—dependents are required to present their identification and privilege cards (DD Form 1173) as proof of their eligibility for medical care. If an unauthorized person uses this card to obtain medical care, a fine of up to $10,000 and imprisonment for up to five years may be imposed on the offender. Dependents who allow others to use their cards unlawfully may be subject to the same penalties.

*Caution:* Ask civilian physicians whether they participate in CHAMPUS. If not, seek other physicians. You may identify those in your community who do participate by inquiring of the American Medical Association, the Medical Bureau, or similar offices in your area. Under service regulations, understood by participating civilian physicians, the government will pay for authorized care with the understanding that there will be no additional charge above those authorized to the dependent or sponsor for that care. (There have been instances of physicians who have asked and collected from patients sums in addition to the charges they have agreed to accept.)

**Dental Care Provided to Service Families.** Dental treatment is provided to hospital inpatients who are hospitalized for other authorized care, but only when required as a necessary part of the treatment of the basic medical or surgical condition for which hospitalized. Outpatient treatment of fractures, dislocations, lacerations, and other wounds that are legitimately cared for by dentists may also be paid for. Authorized dental care does not include artificial teeth, bridges, fillings, teeth straightening, or prolonged treatment of the gums.

At armed forces and U.S. Public Health Service medical facilities, dental care is provided as follows:

- In the United States: (1) In an emergency, to relieve pain and undue suffering. Permanent fillings, bridges, and dentures are not authorized. (2) If required for treatment of a medical or surgical condition. (3) In areas designated "remote" on a facilities-available basis.
- Outside the United States: On a facilities-available basis.

In 1987, Congress established the Uniformed Services Active Duty Dependents Dental Plan (DDP), a dental insurance program for spouses and children of active-duty personnel. The cost is shared by the government and the servicemember. It is a comprehensive program requiring monthly payroll deductions for insurance premium payment, with the amount based on numbers of eligible dependents. Only servicemembers serving on EAD for 24 months or longer may enroll family members. Dependents are enrolled automatically when they are entered into the DEERS system. For specific details of covered benefits and related information, consult the DDP Program Evidence of Coverage (EOC) booklet or AFR 168-19.

## FAMILY SERVICES PROGRAM

At each Air Force base, an organization exists to aid Air Force personnel and their families in meeting personal problems. The organization consists of volunteers, usually the spouses of Air Force officers and airmen stationed at the air base.

**The Family Services Center.** The focus of operations is known as the family services center, which is an office or a building located on the base.

The activities of the family services program include providing assistance to Air Force families in respect to such matters as these:

- Information concerning the air base and its adjoining community.
- Information concerning housing on and off base.
- Thrift shops.
- Nurseries.
- Other air base services and facilities.

The family services center provides help to families in the event of an emergency or casualty by arranging for transportation, baby-sitters, necessary shopping, and other assistance. The center usually maintains a loan service of household utensils sufficient to meet minimum needs of a family awaiting the arrival of their household goods. At many bases, an FSC welcoming committee member calls on newly arrived personnel to offer aid in any degree needed. The family services center operates an indoctrination course to inform spouses of Air Force personnel of essential facts concerning allotments, insurance, Social Security, retirements, casualty benefits, and the like.

## AIR FORCE AID SOCIETY (AFR 211-1)

**Mission.** The Air Force Aid Society (AFAS) is the emergency relief organization for the U.S. Air Force. Its mission is to improve the morale and welfare of Air Force personnel and their dependents by providing financial assistance in times of emergency. The aid society augments the relief available to the servicemember through the American Red Cross and it is not intended that the aid society will compete with or replace the work of the American Red Cross because the congressional charter of the American Red Cross makes it the primary relief organization for the armed forces.

**Eligibility.** The following classes of individuals are eligible for assistance:

• USAF personnel on active duty and USAF personnel retired from active duty for length of service or disability and their dependents.

• Dependents of recently deceased USAF personnel who died while on active duty or after they were retired from active duty for length of service or disability.

• AF Reserve and Air National Guard personnel on full-time active duty with the USAF for at least 90 days, and their dependents. (Does not include tours of active duty for training or attendance at service academies or Armed Forces Preparatory School.)

• Army, Navy, and Marine personnel and their dependents may receive assistance through the Air Force Aid Society when an AER or NRS office is not readily accessible and it is not feasible to refer the applicant to the Red Cross.

Eligible dependents are the spouse and minor children of Air Force personnel. Parents who are wholly dependent upon the servicemember may be considered eligible dependents. The existence of a Class D allotment to a relative other than the spouse or child of an airman is acceptable as reasonable evidence of an airman's acceptance of responsibility to support the relative. The existence of a voluntary allotment in an amount constituting substantial support, regular maintenance as a member of an officer's household, or other reliable indication of true dependency will be accepted as evidence that an officer's dependent is eligible for AFAS assistance.

**Assistance.** Aid society assistance is rendered in the form of non-interest-bearing loans or cash grants or combinations of both. Assistance may be obtained by those entitled to it by contacting the aid society officer at any Air Force installation or by writing to the Air Force Personnel Center, Randolph AFB, TX 78150-5001. Persons eligible for assistance who are not connected with or living at or near an Air Force base should make application for assistance from the aid society through their local chapter of the American Red Cross.

The Air Force Aid Society is a charitable organization. It receives no government funds that can be used for relief purposes. The income of the aid society comes from gifts and contributions, royalties from books and songs given to the aid society, legacies, and interest on the invested capital. The limited resources of the aid society and the very large number of persons eligible under its charter for assistance make it mandatory for aid society assistance to be limited to cases of emergency only and also make it essential that aid society assistance be restricted to those cases that do not rightfully belong to some other welfare organization.

## AMERICAN RED CROSS (AFR 211-11)

Consistent with the congressional charter of the American National Red Cross, the Red Cross has been charged with the primary responsibility of a broad program of volunteer aid to military personnel and their dependents. The Air Force Aid Society coordinates its functions with the American Red Cross in such a manner as to avoid duplication of effort in providing for the welfare of military personnel and their dependents. The American Red Cross carries out its responsibilities through personnel assigned to military establishments and through the home service program of local Red Cross chapters.

## AIR FORCE CHAPLAINS (AFR 265-1)

**Religious Services.** *Marriage.* The chaplain is authorized to perform the marriage rite, provided that all local laws are met and proper legal permission is obtained in each case. Persons contemplating marriage are urged to confer with the chaplain of their faith in order to ensure that proper arrangements are made for the marriage.

*Funerals.* The commander or his representative will assist in making funeral arrangements, and the chaplain will conduct appropriate burial services at the interment of members of the military service, active and retired, and for their families, when requested. If the families of personnel who die in the United States request transportation of the body to a home burial ground instead of permitting burial in a post or national cemetery, they will normally be expected to provide a clergyman for the burial services because the chaplain's other duties preclude absence from the unit for an extended period.

*Other Services.* Chaplains conduct such other services as are required for the religious guidance of the members of each faith. In this manner, Air Force personnel are afforded every opportunity to attend their individual religious services.

**Conferences and Retreats.** Chaplains, assisted by civilian religious leaders, are authorized to conduct religious conferences and retreats for Air Force personnel. For the purpose of attending such conferences and retreats, Air Force personnel may be placed on temporary duty. These may be conducted at either military or civilian locations.

## PERSONAL AFFAIRS OFFICER (AFR 211-3)

**Casualty Assistance.** The personal affairs officer assists and advises the dependents of deceased servicemembers of the various benefits and privileges to which they are entitled. Such advice includes information regarding six months' death gratuity, dependents' compensation, arrears in pay, personal effects, family allowance, burial flag, settlement of government life insurance, and burial allowance. The personal affairs officer is also in a position to refer the dependents to related agencies in regard to civil-service preference, Social Security benefits, states' benefits, transportation of dependents and household goods, and issuance of grave markers.

**Other Assistance.** Personal affairs officers advise military personnel and their dependents as to their rights in securing benefits from the government and as to sources of information and procedures, but are strictly forbidden by law from acting as an agent or attorney for such persons other than in the discharge of their official duties. In their capacity as advisor to military personnel and their dependents, personal affairs officers maintain liaison with the American Red Cross director, the Air Force Aid Society officer, and other agencies, in order that they may tactfully bring to the attention of these organizations instances of personnel and their families who are in financial need or in need of other assistance.

## SCHOLARSHIPS AND CONCESSIONS FOR DEPENDENTS OF AIR FORCE PERSONNEL

**Air Force Educational Assistance Program.** Through the use of Central Welfare funds, this program provides for merit scholarships and long-term, interest-free loans to dependent children of active-duty personnel.

The scholarship aspect provides for up to 30 four-year scholarships annually. Recipients are selected from among those achieving the highest scores on qualifying tests. The loan provision stipulates only that a recipient must have the academic aptitude necessary to assure a "reasonable chance" of completing college. Loans may be continued on a yearly basis throughout the normal four-year academic program, provided academic progress is satisfactory and there is still a need. Loans must be repaid within 10 years of completion of the schooling.

**Air Force Aid Society.** *The General Henry H. Arnold Student Loan Program.* Those eligible for this program are children (including stepchildren and legally adopted children) of an Air Force member in any of the following categories:

- Active member of the Air Force.
- Selected Reserve (either Air National Guard or Air Force Reserve).
- USAF Reserve and National Guard on continuous active duty during the entire school term for which assistance is requested.
- Retired because of length of active-duty service, disability, or attainment of age 60 (reserve component).
- Deceased while on active duty or in retired status.

Additionally, the applicant must be a U.S. citizen enrolled and in good standing at or accepted for admission to an approved educational institution on a full-time basis.

Applicants or interested persons who desire additional information should write to the Director, Air Force Aid Society, National Headquarters, 1735 N. Lynn St., Arlington, VA 22209.

**The Rockefeller Foundation.** Veterans who desire to continue their education may receive assistance through an emergency fellowship granted by the Rockefeller Foundation. Those receiving educational benefits under the GI Bill may receive supplemental aid through the foundation, while those veterans who are ineligible for GI Bill assistance may apply for the full cost of education. All inquiries regarding assistance by the Rockefeller Foundation should be addressed to the organization at 1133 Avenue of the Americas, New York, NY 10036.

**Other Sources of Scholarships.** Many states, universities, colleges, and junior colleges offer scholarships or concessions to children of service personnel. Requests for information regarding such policies should be made to local state authorities or to the institution the applicant wishes to attend.

## APPOINTMENT TO THE FEDERAL SERVICE ACADEMIES

The president is authorized to appoint a limited number of cadets from the United States at large to be selected from sons and daughters of members of the armed services who were killed or died in service as the result of wounds, injuries, or disease received or aggravated in active service. All such appointees must be otherwise qualified and will be selected in order of merit as established by competitive examination.

Sons and daughters of persons who have been awarded the Medal of Honor, if otherwise qualified, may be appointed by the president as cadets from the United States at large to the federal service academies.

## IN-SERVICE HOUSING LOANS

If officers have been on extended active duty for at least two years, they may finance the purchase of a home by an FHA loan. The law provides a system of mortgage insurance that enables the officers to more easily build or purchase homes. It authorizes the FHA to insure loans up to 97 percent of an appraised value. In addition, the Air

Force will pay ½ of 1 percent of the mortgage insurance premium monthly. This amount is the premium the FHA receives for guaranteeing the mortgage, and during the life of the loan, it amounts to a substantial sum.

## PAY, ALLOWANCES, AND ALLOTMENTS OF PERSONNEL REPORTED MISSING

**Pay and Allowances.** All personnel who are in active service and who are officially determined to be absent in a status of missing are entitled, for the period they are officially carried or determined to be in such status, to have credited to their accounts the same pay and allowances entitled at the beginning of such period of absence or to which they may become entitled thereafter. Such entitlement shall terminate upon the date of receipt by the Department of the Air Force of evidence that the servicemember is dead or upon the date of death prescribed or determined. Such entitlement, however, shall not terminate upon expiration of term of service during absence, and in case of death during absence shall not terminate earlier than the dates stated herein. No pay and allowances accrue to such missing persons for any period during which they may be officially determined absent from their posts of duty without authority, and they shall be indebted to the government for any payments from amounts credited to their account for such period of absence (AFM 177-373).

**Allotments.** Allotments instituted before the absence of a missing person who is entitled to accrued pay and allowances will continue to be paid regularly for a period of 12 months from the date of absence. In the absence of an allotment for support of dependents or payment of insurance premiums, or if an existing allotment is insufficient for its purposes, the Secretary of the Air Force can direct that adequate allotments be instituted. Information listed on DD Form 93 *(Record of Emergency Data)* will be used as a guide in such determinations. The total of all allotments, however, may not exceed the total pay and allowances to which the missing person is entitled.

When the 12 months' period from date of commencement of absence is about to expire in the case of a missing person, the Secretary of the Air Force shall cause a full review of the case to be made. Following such review and when the 12 months' period has expired, the Secretary of the Air Force is authorized to make a finding of death, or if the person is for any reason assumed to be living, to direct the continuance of the person's missing status. When a finding of death is made it shall include the date upon which death shall be presumed to have occurred for purposes of termination of entitlement to accrual of pay and allowances, settlement of accounts, and payment of death gratuities. Such date shall be the day following the day of expiration of the 12 months' period or in cases where the missing status has been extended, a day to be determined by the Secretary of the Air Force.

Any new allotment or increases in allotments authorized by the Secretary of the Air Force for the well-being of dependents or the payment of insurance may be terminated by the missing person upon return to duty status.

Application by dependents for the initiation of new allotments or changes of existing allotments should be filed with the AF Accounting and Finance Center, Denver, CO 80279, on the prescribed form, which may be obtained at military installations, or from chapters of the American Red Cross. Applications in any form may be accepted if they satisfactorily establish the identity, relationship, and dependency of the applicant and the need for the increase of allotment requested. The application must indicate allotments and family allowances, if any, being paid to the dependents on whose behalf the application is submitted. It must also include or be accompanied by evidence establishing the need for the allotment or increase requested. The specific amount needed and the date the allotment or increase is desired to be effective must be stated.

## BENEFITS AFTER SEPARATION

During the period of military service, all servicemembers accrue certain rights and privileges under various public laws that will be available to them after discharge or release from active duty. The administration and payment of these benefits are the responsibility of the Department of Veterans Affairs (VA). Entitlement to benefits varies with length, time, and type of service as well as disabilities incurred in service. In all cases in which veterans desire to apply for one or more of these statutory benefits, they should obtain all necessary information from the nearest VA installation. An extract from VA Pamphlet 27-82-2, *A Summary of Department of Veterans Affairs Benefits* March 1991, follows.

**Montgomery G.I. Bill—Active Duty.** The Montgomery G.I. Bill—Active Duty program provides education benefits for individuals entering military service after 30 June 1985. Servicemembers will have their basic pay reduced $100 a month for the first 12 months of their service unless they specifically elect not to participate in the program. The money is nonrefundable.

Servicemembers who were eligible for the noncontributory G.I. Bill benefits as of 31 December 1989 who served three years of continuous active duty after 30 June 1985, as well as those who served two years on active duty followed by four years of satisfactory participation in the Selected Reserve after 30 June 1985, may also be eligible but will not have their basic pay reduced. These persons must have been on active duty on 19 October 1984 and continued without a break in service through the individual's qualifying period.

Servicemembers who after 31 December 1976 received a commission as an officer from the service academies or ROTC scholarship programs are not eligible.

The basic entitlement portion provides assistance for 36 months based on three years of continuous active duty. Individuals who serve an additional five years may receive a supplemental benefit for 36 months plus a supplemental discretionary kicker.

An individual must serve at least two years of continuous active duty if the initial period of service is less than three years or if applying as a servicemember, or serve at least three years if the initial period is three years or more. If the individual does not complete the required service, the veteran must have been discharged for a service-connected disability, for hardship, for a preexisting medical condition, or have been involuntarily separated due to a reduction in force. If the individual is released for the convenience of the government, the servicemember must have served at least 20 months of an obligation of less than three years, or 30 months of an obligation of three years or longer.

When the veteran completes the obligation period of active duty, he or she must be discharged with an honorable discharge. Before completing the obligated period of service the individual must have met the requirements of a secondary-school diploma or an equivalent certificate.

Eligibility will end after 10 years, beginning on the date of release from active duty or on the last day on which the individual becomes entitled, whichever is later. This date may be extended if you are unable to train due to disability.

Benefits (currently up to $350 monthly) are payable for attendance at institutions of higher learning, noncollege degree programs, apprenticeships or on-the-job training, and pursuit of correspondence training. Veterans may pursue refresher and remedial and deficiency courses and qualify for tutorial assistance.

*Educational Institutions within the United States.* Institutions providing education at the elementary school level or above may be approved for training. These may include public or private elementary or secondary schools; vocational or business schools; colleges; universities; professional, scientific, or technical institutions; or on-the-job and apprenticeship programs as well as cooperative or farm cooperative programs. Servicemembers may obtain information on approval of courses or schools through their local VA office.

*Educational institutions outside the United States.* VA benefits are authorized only for college and graduate school. The Secretary of the Air Force, at his discretion, may deny or discontinue the educational assistance of any veteran in a foreign educational institution if he finds that such enrollment is not in the best interest of the veteran or the government.

*Counseling.* Servicemembers can receive counseling from professionally qualified counselors. Counseling can assist individuals in a number of ways:

- Choosing a suitable educational or vocational objective.
- Seeing how to make the best use of the training or experience he or she now has to get a good job.
- Dealing with personal problems that keep a person from doing his or her best in school or at work.

Counseling is available upon request. Once a request is received, a convenient time and place will be arranged.

*Change of Program.* A change of program may be approved by VA. A change from one program to another when the first is a prerequisite to the second is not considered a change of program.

*Apprenticeship or Other On-the-Job Training.* Eligible veterans may pursue, on a full-time basis only, an approved program of apprenticeship or other training on the job. Apprenticeships must meet the standards published by the U.S. Secretary of Labor, and all apprenticeship or on-the-job training programs must be approved by a state approving agency or VA.

When an individual begins an apprenticeship or other on-the-job training, the wages received from the employer will be at least one half of the wages paid for the job for which the person is being trained. Wages will be increased at regular intervals. The amount of wages paid by the employer will not affect the VA training allowance.

*Tutorial Assistance.* Persons enrolled in a postsecondary program on a half-time-or-more basis may receive a special allowance for individual tutoring. To qualify, the student must show that he or she has a deficiency in a particular area, making tutoring necessary, and that the tutor is considered qualified by the school.

*Work-Study Program.* Students may earn an additional allowance from VA under the work-study program. To be eligible, the student must be enrolled in a three-quarter or full-time program of education or training under Vocational Rehabilitation, VEAP, the Survivors' and Dependents' Education Program, or the Montgomery G.I. Bill—Active Duty program. VA attempts to capitalize on the student's major area of study so that the work performed will be a practical extension of his or her education. The total number of hours a student may work each semester may not exceed 25 times the number of weeks in the enrollment period. A student who agrees to work fewer hours gets a proportionally lesser amount. Students will be paid 40 percent of the amount of the work-study agreement in advance. The hours are to be worked during or between enrollment periods during a semester or other applicable enrollment period. VA will pay at the same rate as the federal hourly minimum wage or the applicable state minimum wage, whichever is greater.

*Restrictions.* VA cannot pay educational assistance or special training allowances to persons on active duty with the armed forces or the Public Health Service whose education or training costs are being paid by the federal government. This bar also applies to persons receiving education or training under the Government Employees' Training Act and being paid their full salary during that period.

**Montgomery G.I. Bill—Selected Reserve.** This educational entitlement program is available for members of the Selected Reserve, including the National Guard; those who, after 30 June 1985, enlist, reenlist, or extend an enlistment in the Selected Reserve for a period of six years or more; and those who are appointed or are serving as a reserve officer and agree to serve in the Selected Reserve for not less than six years in addition to any other period of obligated Selected Reserve service after 30 June 1985.

To receive benefits, an individual must complete his or her initial period of active-duty training. In addition, a reservist must have completed the requirements for a high school diploma or the equivalent before completing initial active duty. Educational assistance is payable for the pursuit of an undergraduate degree or noncollege degree program at an institution of higher learning. Reservists who have a six-year commitment in the Selected Reserve after 30 September 1990 may pursue noncollege degree programs at a vocational school, cooperative training, or apprenticeship or on-the-job training. The reserve member must continue to satisfactorily participate in the Selected Reserve.

An eligible reservist is entitled to a maximum of 36 months of educational assistance. Eligibility will end 10 years from the date eligibility began or the date of separation from the Selected Reserve, whichever is earlier. This date may be extended if the Reservist is unable to train due to a service-connected disability.

A reservist who fails to participate satisfactorily in the Selected Reserve is no longer eligible for education assistance and may be required to repay a portion of the education benefits received.

Counseling services are provided to assist eligible servicemembers and reservists.

**Vocational Rehabilitation for Service-Disabled Veterans.** *Eligibility and Entitlement.* For an individual to be entitled to vocational rehabilitation, he or she must have a disability or disabilities that VA has rated at least 20 percent compensable or have filed an original application for vocational rehabilitation before 1 November 1990 if the service-connected disability is rated less than 20 percent compensable. In addition, VA must find that the veteran has an employment handicap, and the veteran must be within his or her period of eligibility. The basic period of eligibility is generally 12 years following the date the person is notified of entitlement to VA compensation for disability. This period may be adjusted if the veteran is unable to train for a period as a result of medical conditions. The 12-year period may also be extended if the individual has a serious employment handicap and needs additional time to complete a rehabilitation program.

*Training and Other Rehabilitation Services.* VA provides evaluation and counseling to assist veterans in the development of a comprehensive rehabilitation plan designed to suit their particular needs. An initial evaluation will establish eligibility and entitlement and determine whether there is a need for extended evaluation, independent living services, educational or vocational training, or employment assistance.

If a veteran has a serious disability, he or she may receive services under an extended evaluation program to determine and improve training potential. Generally, an extended evaluation may not exceed 12 months, but longer periods are possible.

If an individual enters a training program, VA may authorize up to 48 months or more in colleges and universities, vocational schools, and on-the-farm, on-the-job, or apprenticeship programs, as well as special rehabilitation facilities. VA pays the full cost of tuition, books, fees, supplies, and equipment.

While in training, if a veteran has unexpected financial problems, VA may be able to provide a no-interest loan to help him or her through the period of difficulty. VA can also arrange for tutoring services to assist in completion of the training program.

After training is completed, VA will help the veteran find a suitable job. This employment assistance may be provided for up to 18 months. An individual may be eligible for employment assistance as a total program or in addition to training. A veteran may also qualify for job assistance if he or she took part in the VA or state rehabilitation program at some earlier time and is otherwise eligible for and entitled to assistance under the vocational rehabilitation program.

*Subsistence Allowance.* While an individual is taking part in training or in extended evaluation, he or she may receive a subsistence allowance in addition to disability compensation or military retired pay. This subsistence allowance may continue for two months following completion of training to provide financial support during the initial period of search for and adjustment to employment.

**Loan Guaranty Benefits.** Eligible veterans and service personnel may obtain GI loans made by private lenders for a home, manufactured home and/or lot, or certain types of condominiums. An existing VA loan on a home owned by a veteran may be refinanced in order to lower the interest rate. Recorded liens may also be refinanced on property owned and occupied by the veteran as the veteran's home. Such loans are also available to unmarried surviving spouses of service personnel who died on active duty or as a result of service-connected disabilities. Spouses of service personnel who have been missing in action for more than 90 days, captured in line of duty by a hostile force, or forcibly detained or interned in line of duty by a foreign government or power are eligible for home loans. VA direct loans are available to certain eligible veterans with permanent and total service-connected disabilities only to supplement a grant to acquire a specially adapted home. Entitlement to loan guaranty benefits is available until used.

VA loans for which commitments were made prior to 1 March 1988 are usually freely assumable, but individuals should protect themselves by obtaining a release of liability from VA before completing a sale by assumption. For loans after that date it is unlawful to allow assumption without the prior approval of the loan holder or VA.

Individuals are eligible for VA financing if their service falls within any of the following categories:

*Wartime Service.* Personnel who served any time during the Vietnam Era (5 August 1964 to 7 May 1975) or the Persian Gulf War period (2 August 1990 and ending by presidential proclamation) must have served at least 90 days on active duty and have been discharged or released under other than dishonorable conditions. Those who served less than 90 days may be eligible if discharged because of a service-connected disability.

*Service after 16 October 1981.* Officers separated from service that began after this date must have met one of the following criteria:

• Completed 24 months of continuous active duty or the full period (at least 181 days) for which they were called or ordered to active duty, and have been discharged or released under conditions other than dishonorable.

• Completed at least 181 days of active duty and been discharged or released from active duty under section 1171 "early out" or 1173 "hardship" of title 10, U.S. Code, or have been determined to have a compensable service-connected disability.

• Been discharged for a service-connected disability.

*Active-Duty Service Personnel.* Members now on active duty are eligible after having served on continuous active status for at least 181 days (90 days if you served during the Persian Gulf War), regardless of when service began.

Under certain conditions, a servicemember may be eligible to use the benefit more than once if he or she can meet the requirements for restoration of entitlement or substitution of entitlement. The local VA office can provide specifics concerning these requirements.

If you do not have a Certificate of Eligibility for Loan Guaranty Benefits and wish to obtain one, complete VA Form 26-1880, *Request for Determination of Eligibility and Available Loan Guaranty Entitlement*, and send it along with the required supporting documents to VA.

Accurate determinations of eligibility can be made only by VA. You should not obligate yourself for the purchase of a home, condominium, or manufactured home solely on the basis of this information. Before undertaking any such obligations, contact VA directly concerning your eligibility for the benefit.

*Specially Adapted Homes.* Veterans may be entitled under certain conditions to a VA grant for a home specially adapted to their needs.

To be eligible for this grant an individual must have a service-connected disability entitling him or her to compensation for permanent and total disability due to one of the following reasons:

• The loss or loss of use of both lower extremities, such as to preclude locomotion without the aid of braces, crutches, canes, or a wheelchair.

• Disability that includes blindness in both eyes having only light perception, plus loss or loss of use of one lower extremity.

• The loss or loss of use of one lower extremity together with residuals of organic disease or injury, or the loss or loss of use of one upper extremity, which so affects the functions of balance or propulsion as to preclude locomotion without the aid of braces, crutches, canes, or a wheelchair.

If eligible, a veteran may use this grant to pay part of the cost of building or buying a specially adapted home or to remodel an existing dwelling for his or her special needs. If the person already owns such a home, the grant may be used to reduce the mortgage balance.

*Special Home Adaptations.* A veteran may be entitled under certain conditions to a VA grant for special adaptations to an existing home.

To be eligible for this grant he or she must have a service-connected disability entitling him or her to compensation for permanent and total disability due to blindness in both eyes with 5/200 visual acuity or less, or anatomical loss or loss of use of both hands.

If eligible, an individual may use this grant to pay the cost of acquiring necessary adaptations to his or her residence or to purchase a residence that has already been adapted with special features that are determined to be reasonably necessary because of the disability.

**Compensation for Disability.** VA pays compensation to servicemembers who are disabled by injury or disease incurred in or aggravated by active service in line of duty. Payments are based on the degree of disability.

VA pays additional money for dependents if the member's service-connected disabilities are evaluated by VA as 30 percent or more disabling. In addition, if the servicemember is 30 percent or more disabled and his or her spouse is in need of regular aid and attendance, an increased dependency allowance is payable for the spouse.

Special monthly compensation rates may be authorized for veterans whose service-connected disabilities are very severe and meet certain statutory requirements. These special rates apply, for example, for blinded veterans and those who have lost limbs or the use of limbs.

**Non-service-connected Pension.** Veterans having served at least 90 days on active duty in the armed forces with one day beginning or ending during a period of war who have become permanently and totally disabled and are unable to maintain substantially gainful employment may be eligible for VA's non-service-connected disability pension. VA does not pay pension if the veteran's estate and that of his or her spouse and dependent children is so large that it is reasonable that the veteran use some of it for living expenses or if the veteran's income exceeds the applicable limit in the law.

**Annual Clothing Allowance.** VA pays an annual clothing allowance to persons who are entitled to receive disability compensation for a condition that requires the wearing or use of one or more prosthetic or orthopedic appliances that are determined by VA to wear out or tear clothing, or the use of medicine that will stain the patient's outer clothing.

**VA Medical Care.** VA provides hospital or outpatient care when needed for all service-connected medical or compensated dental conditions. VA gives treatment at one of the many VA medical centers or clinics, or, under certain circumstances, VA may pay for outpatient care by a hometown doctor or dentist. Generally, VA cannot authorize payment for services of hometown doctors or dentists not approved in advance.

Certain persons who were administratively discharged under other than honorable conditions may be furnished health care for any disability incurred or aggravated during active-duty service in line of duty.

Hospital care in VA facilities is provided to any veteran who is rated service connected; is retired from active duty for a disability incurred or aggravated while in military service; is in receipt of VA pension; is eligible for Medicaid; is a former POW; is in need of care for a condition possibly related to exposure to dioxin or other toxic substance (such as Agent Orange) while in Vietnam 5 August 1964 through 7 May 1975; is in need of care for a condition possibly related to exposure to ionizing radiation from participating in nuclear tests or in the American occupation of Hiroshima or Nagasaki, Japan, between 11 September 1945 and 1 July 1946; or has an income below $19,408 for veterans with no dependents, below $23,290 for a veteran with a spouse ($1,330 added for each additional dependent) (mandatory category). Veterans with incomes in excess of these amounts may be furnished hospital care in VA facilities on a space-available basis if they agree to pay VA a copayment (discretionary category). (Income amounts listed above will be adjusted 1 January of each year by the same percent VA pension rates are increased.)

Hospital care is not available to veterans where the entire period of service was active duty for training, unless the individual was disabled from a disease or injury incurred or aggravated in line of duty. In this case, the person is eligible for medical services on the same basis as other veterans with service-incurred diseases or disabilities.

Outpatient medical services will be furnished, without limitation, to the following:

- Any veteran, for service-connected disabilities.
- A veteran with a combined service-connected disability rating of 50 percent or more for any medical disability.
- A veteran for the injury suffered as a result of VA hospitalization.
- Any veteran in a VA-approved vocational rehabilitation program.
- Any veteran in one of the following groups, on a pre- or posthospital care or ambulatory care basis to obviate the need for hospitalization (until the patient's condition is stabilized or the patient is admitted): (1) Any veteran rated 30 percent or 40 percent service-connected (for treatment of their nonservice-connected conditions); (2) Any veteran whose annual income does not exceed the maximum applicable rate of pension for a veteran in need of regular aid and attendance. Note: The veteran's income must be lower than that level that will qualify him or her for the mandatory category of hospital care.

Outpatient medical services may be furnished, without limitation, to the extent resources and facilities are available to the following:

- Any veteran who is a former prisoner of war.
- Any World War I or Mexican Border Period veteran.
- Any veteran receiving aid and attendance or housebound pension benefit.
- Any veteran in one of the following groups, on a pre- or posthospital care or ambulatory care basis to obviate the need for hospitalization (until the patient's condition is stabilized or the patient is admitted): (1) Any veteran exposed to a toxic substance in a herbicide or defoliant used for military purposes in Vietnam or to radiation as a consequence of participation in the test of a nuclear device or of service with the occupation forces of Hiroshima or Nagasaki, Japan, prior to 1 July 1946; (2) Any veteran identified in the mandatory category for hospitalization purposes whose income is more than the pension rate of a veteran in need of regular aid and attendance; (3) Any veteran identified in the discretionary category for inpatient purposes.

As part of outpatient medical treatment, a veteran may be eligible for home health services necessary or appropriate for the effective and economical treatment of disabilities. These services include some home improvements and structural alterations.

Those who are Vietnam-era veterans or who served in a theater of combat operations after 2 August 1990 may also obtain readjustment counseling and follow-up mental health services to facilitate adjustment to civilian life.

Those who need a prosthetic appliance may be eligible if they are receiving hospital or domiciliary care or meet the basic requirements for outpatient treatment.

Veterans who are blind in both eyes and entitled to compensation for any service-connected disability; in receipt of increased pension based on the need for aid and attendance; former POWs; or veterans of the Mexican Border Period or World War I may receive approved electronic and mechanical aids for the blind and their necessary repair and replacement, and a guide dog, including cost of training to use the dog and the cost of the dog's medical attention.

*Dental Care.* You may apply for and be authorized to receive a one-time episode of dental treatment from VA if you meet the following criteria: have not been dishonorably discharged; served on active duty for a period of not less than 180 days (90 days for Persian Gulf War veterans); and applied for dental care within 90 days after discharge. In addition, your military discharge certificate must not state that you were provided a complete dental examination (including dental x rays) and all appropriate dental treatment indicated by the examination was provided within 90 days prior to discharge.

Individuals may apply for dental care at any time and be eligible to receive treatment if they meet the following criteria:

- Have service-connected compensable dental disabilities.
- Have service-connected noncompensable dental disabilities adjudicated as resulting from combat wounds or service injuries.
- Have service-connected noncompensable dental conditions and were a prisoner of war for a period of less than 90 days.
- Were a prisoner of war for more than 90 days.
- Have non-service-connected dental conditions that are determined by VA to be associated with or aggravating a service-connected medical problem.
- Have service-connected disabilities rated at 100 percent.

For eligible veterans who are pursuing a vocational rehabilitation course, dental treatment may be provided to avoid interruption of the training program.

If you received dental treatment while hospitalized in a VA medical center, that treatment may continue on an outpatient basis if it is professionally determined to be reasonably necessary.

*Alcohol and Other Drug Dependence Treatment.* VA has a program for the treatment of veterans for alcoholism and other drug dependence. Veterans who have such a problem should contact the nearest VA medical center or outpatient clinic.

*CHAMPVA (Civilian Health and Medical Program of the Department of Veterans Affairs).* Medical care is available to the spouse or child of a veteran who has a total permanent service-connected disability. Medical care is also available to a surviving spouse or child in the event of a servicemember's death if the servicemember dies of a service-connected disability or at the time of death has a total and permanent service-connected disability, or dies on active duty, in line of duty. This applies only when the applicant does not have entitlement to similar care under CHAMPUS (Civilian Health and Medical Program of the Uniformed Services) or Medicare.

CHAMPVA cost-shares only certain medical bills. The beneficiary pays the full bill for any care that is not covered by CHAMPVA. For care that is covered, the beneficiary still pays for part of the bills. How much the beneficiary pays depends on whether the provider's rates are compatible with the CHAMPVA determined allowable cost, and if they agree to accept the CHAMPVA rate as their full fee for the care provided. For outpatient care, there is a yearly deductible of $50 for one person or $100 for a family. The beneficiary pays the provider for the first $50 (or, for a family, $100) worth of medical bills in a calendar year. Then, after the deductible is met, CHAMPVA pays 75 percent of the allowable charge for each medical bill. CHAMPVA began a new system of paying civilian hospitals for inpatient care. Under the system, called "diagnosis-related groups" (DRGs), most hospitals in 48 states, the District of Columbia, and Puerto Rico will be paid a fixed rate for inpatient services, regardless of how much the care actually costs. The DRG amounts paid for inpatient services are based generally on national averages of costs for specific services. The beneficiary pays 25 percent of inpatient care plus anything over the allowable charge.

**Automobiles or Other Conveyances.** If you are a veteran or active-duty applicant with service-connected loss, or permanent loss of use, of one or both hands or feet, or permanent impairment of vision of both eyes to a certain prescribed degree, you may receive a grant from VA toward the purchase price of an automobile or other conveyance. VA also provides for the purchase, replacement, and maintenance of automobile adaptive equipment. The grant is paid directly to the seller after the purchase is authorized by VA and the automobile or conveyance has been accepted by the veteran or his or her representative. Service-connected ankylosis of one or both knees or hips qualifies the claimant for adaptive equipment only.

**SGLI (Servicemen's Group Life Insurance) and VGLI (Veterans' Group Life Insurance).** SGLI was established in September 1965 to provide group insurance coverage for members on active duty in the uniformed services. Coverage has been extended to Ready Reservists, Retired Reservists, members of the National Guard, ROTC members while engaged in authorized training, and service academy personnel. Initially maximum coverage was for $10,000. Subsequent legislation increased maximum insurance coverage to $200,000.

VGLI was established in August 1974 to provide for the conversion of SGLI to five-year nonrenewable term insurance. The program provides for the replacement of SGLI with VGLI in an amount equal to or less than the amount of SGLI the member had in force at separation from service.

Application and payment for VGLI must be made to the OSGLI (Office of Servicemen's Group Life Insurance) within 120 days following separation. If application is not made within 120 days, you can submit it within one year from the date SGLI coverage terminated, but you must be in acceptable health. If you were totally disabled at the time of separation, there is a limited extension, not to exceed one year, of the 120-day filing period.

Effective 1 January 1986, members of the IRR (Individual Ready Reserve) and ING (Inactive National Guard) are also eligible to purchase VGLI. Application must be made to OSGLI within 120 days of entry into the IRR or ING. Applications will also be accepted for up to one year beyond the 120 days, but you must be in acceptable health. Individuals who remain in the IRR or ING throughout the five-year VGLI period may renew their coverage for subsequent five-year periods, provided they remain in the IRR or ING.

Any former member insured under VGLI who may again become eligible for SGLI is automatically insured under the SGLI program. You may participate in both plans as long as the combined amount of SGLI and VGLI does not exceed $200,000 at any time.

The SGLI-VGLI program is supervised by VA and administered by OSGLI. For more information contact any VA office or OSGLI at 213 Washington Street, Newark, NJ 07102.

**Burial Benefits.** *Reimbursement of Burial Expenses.* VA will pay a $300 burial and funeral expense allowance for deceased veterans who were, at the time of death, entitled to receive pension or compensation, or would have been entitled to receive compensation but for the receipt of military retired pay. Eligibility is also established when death occurs in a VA facility or in a contract nursing home to which the deceased was properly admitted. In addition, VA will pay a $150 plot or interment allowance if the requirements for the burial allowance are met, or if the deceased was discharged from active duty because of disability that was incurred or aggravated in line of duty. The plot allowance is not payable if the veteran is buried in a national cemetery. If the veteran is buried without charge for the cost of a plot or interment in a state-owned cemetery, used solely for burying persons eligible for burial in a national cemetery, the $150 plot allowance may be paid to the state. For veterans who die of a service-connected disability, VA will pay a burial allowance up to $1,500 in lieu of other burial benefits. Claim for nonservice-connected burial allowance must be filed within two years after burial or cremation. There is no time limit for filing a claim for service-connected benefits.

*Burial Flag.* VA will issue an American flag to drape the casket of an eligible veteran who was discharged under conditions other than dishonorable. VA will also issue a flag for a veteran who is missing in action and is later presumed dead. After the funeral service, the flag may be given to the next of kin or close friend or associate of the deceased. Flags are issued at any VA office, VA national cemetery, and most local post offices.

*Interment in National Cemeteries.* VA operates the National Cemetery System. The interment of a deceased veteran of wartime or peacetime service and any person who died in the active military, air, or naval service, whose service (other than for training) terminated other than dishonorably, will be authorized in any cemetery in which grave space is available. Deceased spouses, minor children, and certain adult dependent children of an eligible veteran are also eligible. Persons originally enlisting in military service after 7 September 1980 and all other people entering military service after 16 October 1981 who do not complete 24 months of continuous active duty, or the full period for which the person was called or ordered to active duty, are generally not eligible for burial in a national cemetery. There is no charge for a grave in a national cemetery. A headstone or marker with appropriate inscription for each decedent buried in a grave will be provided by the government. Application for burial can be made by the next of kin or their funeral director, only at the time of death of the veteran (or that of an eligible dependent) by contacting the director of the national cemetery where burial is desired.

*Transportation of Deceased Veteran to a National Cemetery.* VA may pay the cost of transportation of a deceased veteran for burial in a national cemetery when (1) the veteran dies of a service-connected disability; or (2) the veteran was in receipt of (but for the receipt of retired pay or disability pension would have been entitled to) disability compensation. Payment shall not exceed the cost of transportation to the national cemetery nearest the veteran's last place of residence in which burial space is available.

*Headstones or Markers.* VA will furnish, upon request, at no charge to the applicant, a government monument to mark the grave of an eligible veteran buried in a national, military post or base, state veterans', or private cemetery. Monuments are also provided for the eligible dependents of veterans who are buried in national, military post or base cemeteries, or state veterans' cemeteries. Dependents buried in private cemeteries are not eligible for a monument.

Memorial monuments are provided for eligible, individual veterans whose remains are not recovered or identified, buried at sea, or are otherwise unavailable for interment. The monuments bear an *"In Memory of"* inscription as their first line.

The grave of a veteran must be *unmarked* in order for a monument to be furnished at government expense. Monuments are not provided for placement within the United States for a veteran buried in a marked grave in an overseas location.

*Eligibility.* The following are eligible for burial benefits:

• Veterans of wartime and peacetime service prior to 7 September 1980 who were discharged from active military service under conditions other than dishonorable. Service after 7 September 1980 must be for a minimum of 24 months or have special circumstances.

• Persons whose deaths occurred while serving in the U.S. Armed Forces.

• Veterans' dependents who are buried in national, military post or base cemeteries or in state veterans' cemeteries. (Divorce or remarriage terminates eligibility for the nonveteran spouse.)

**Death Benefits.** *Educational Assistance for Dependents.* If a servicemember is permanently and completely disabled from service-connected causes, should die as a result of service, or should die while completely disabled from service-connected causes, VA will pay a monthly allowance to help educate his or her spouse and each son or daughter. These payments are usually provided for children between the ages of 18 and 26, and their marriage is not a bar to this benefit. A surviving spouse's remarriage terminates entitlement. In some instances, handicapped children may begin a special vocational or restorative course as early as age 14. Spouses and children of service personnel who are currently missing in action, captured in line of duty, or forcibly detained in line of duty by a foreign power for more than 90 days are also eligible for these educational benefits. An eligible person may have his or her eligibility date extended due to a disability.

Educational and vocational counseling services are available on request to assist eligible dependents in career or job planning, and in developing an educational plan.

*Montgomery GI Bill—Active Duty Death Benefit.* A death benefit may be payable to a designated survivor if the servicemember's death is in service and is service connected. The servicemember must have been eligible for the Montgomery GI Bill at the time of death or would have been eligible. VA will pay an amount equal to the participant's actual military pay reduction less any education benefits previously paid or any accrued benefits paid.

*DIC (Dependency and Indemnity Compensation).* Payments are authorized for surviving spouses, children, and parents of service personnel or veterans who died on or after 1 January 1957 from any of the following: (1) a disease or injury incurred or aggravated in line of duty while on active duty or active duty for training or (2) an injury incurred or aggravated in line of duty while on inactive duty training. Benefits also may be paid to surviving spouses and children of veterans whose death was not related to military service but who immediately before death suffered total service-connected disability for ten or more years or continuously since discharge for not less than five years.

The basic rate of payment for a surviving spouse is determined by the military grade of the deceased veteran. There may be additional payments for children under age 18 and for spouses in need of aid and attendance or those permanently housebound because of disability. Children of the veteran may be eligible for DIC in their own right when the surviving spouse is ineligible for any reason.

Children who are determined to have become helpless prior to age 18 or those between the ages of 18 and 23 who are attending an approved course of instruction may continue to receive benefits with the amount dependent upon whether a surviving spouse is also entitled.

Monthly payments to dependent parents depend on income and marital status.

Parents may also be paid additional monthly amounts if in need of regular aid and attendance.

*Reinstated Entitlement Program for Survivors (REPS).* REPS pays benefits similar to Social Security benefits after Social Security payments cease for some surviving spouses and some unmarried children over age 18 and attending school. To be eligible for REPS benefits, the survivors must have entitlement based on a veteran's service-connected death that occurred prior to 13 August 1981 or based on a later death resulting from service-connected disability acquired before 13 August 1981.

In these limited cases, a surviving spouse who no longer qualified for Social Security as a parent of a child under age 16 may qualify for REPS payments if a child between the ages of 16 and 18 is in the spouse's custody. A child over age 18 and less than 22 may qualify for payments when attending a full-time course of education. The educational course must be approved and be a post-secondary course.

*Non-service-connected Death Pension.* VA's death pension may be paid to eligible surviving spouses and children of veterans who had 90 days or more of wartime service or who had less than 90 days of wartime service but were separated from such service for a service-connected disability, who have died of causes not related to their service. For payment of death pension, the term "veteran" includes a person who has completed at least two years' honorable service but whose death in such service was not in the line of duty.

Surviving spouses and unmarried children under age 18, or until age 23 if attending an approved course of instruction, may be eligible for pension if their income does not exceed certain limits. Children who become permanently incapable of self-support because of physical or mental disability before age 18 may receive pension as long as the disability remains and they do not marry. Pension is not payable to persons whose estates are so large that it is reasonable that they use some of it for living expenses.

An additional allowance is payable to a surviving spouse who is a patient in a nursing home or otherwise determined to be in need of regular aid and attendance or who is permanently housebound because of a disability.

Surviving spouses and children who were entitled to benefits under the death pension program that existed prior to 1 January 1979 may continue to receive pension at the rate in effect as of 31 December 1978, provided their incomes do not exceed the applicable limit. They may also elect to be covered by the current Improved Pension program if it is to their advantage. However, election is final.

**Presidential Memorial Certificates.** The president expresses the nation's gratitude for the veteran's honorable service in the armed forces by providing a memorial certificate bearing the president's signature to the next of kin and other family members of deceased veterans. This program was initiated in 1962 by President John F. Kennedy and has been continued by all subsequent presidents. Eligible recipients may include next of kin, other related persons, and friends of the veteran. A certificate awarded to one eligible person does not preclude issuance to other family members or friends. VA initiates a request on a family's behalf when a recently deceased veteran's survivor files a claim for benefits or notifies a VA regional office of a veteran's death. Eligible persons also may obtain a certificate with a written request to any VA regional office, enclosing a copy of any document that verifies the veteran's honorable military service.

**Other Benefits.** *Civil Service Preference Certificates.* VA will issue civil service preference certificates to eligible veterans seeking government employment. To be eligible, discharge must have been under honorable conditions from a period of active service in the armed forces, or the veteran must have incurred a service-connected disability during any period of service. Under certain conditions certificates may be issued to the veteran's spouse, surviving spouse, or mother.

*Exchange and Commissary Privileges.* Honorably discharged veterans with a 100 percent service-connected disability and their dependents are entitled to exchange and commissary store privileges. Also covered are unmarried surviving spouses of veterans who were rated 100 percent service-connected disabled at time of death. Certification of disability and assistance with DD Form 1172, *Application for Uniformed Services Identification and Privilege Card*, may be obtained from VA regional offices.

*State Benefits.* Many states offer benefits to veterans that are independent of federal benefits. These benefits differ from state to state. Often the eligibility is dependent on the state being the place of residency or home of record at the time of enlistment. For information, consult your local telephone directory under state government or call the VA toll-free number.

## VOTING

**Voting Assistance.** Air Force personnel are encouraged to exercise the privilege of voting in federal, state, and primary elections. In order to encourage and assist eligible airmen to vote, the Department of Defense maintains liaison with the various state election authorities to obtain current voting information, which, through Air Force channels, is promptly disseminated to all Air Force installations for the information of all personnel. Voting officers are available at squadron level to answer pertinent questions concerning forthcoming elections in the servicemember's state of domicile and to provide printed postcard applications for state absentee ballots, which are transmitted airmail, postage free, to the appropriate state. Every effort is made to ensure that all personnel are protected against coercion of any sort in making their political choices and to maintain the integrity and secrecy of the ballots cast (see AFPs 211-4 and 211-19).

**Responsibility.** Although the Air Force provides information and assistance concerning elections and voting procedures, the actual decision to vote rests with the individual servicemember. Voting must be entirely voluntary, and no servicemember will be required or ordered to participate in political elections.

**Determination of Eligibility.** The determination of eligibility and the specification of requirements for voting are completely governed by the appropriate state. In order to vote, all servicemembers must meet such requirements and must be declared eligible to vote by the state in which they desire to exercise their voting privilege.

## PERSONAL AFFAIRS RECORD

It is very important that you prepare and keep up to date a record of your personal affairs and property. Both you and your family will probably have more than one occasion to refer to such a record during your military service.

Fill in your record carefully and completely and then, if you wish, make as many copies of your record as you will need for your family or for other persons whom you wish to trust with such information. Be sure you consider each item and make the record as complete and accurate as possible.

Remember, keep your record up to date, as changes or additions occur, by amending the original record or preparing a completely new record, and send copies to whomever you give copies of the original record.

*Start now* to get the necessary information and to prepare your record, *and don't stop* until it is complete.

---

*Note:* For more detailed information, see Jonathan P. Tomes, *Servicemember's Legal Guide,* 2nd ed., Stackpole Books, 1992; P. J. Budahn, *Veteran's Guide to Benefits,* Stackpole Books, 1994.

# 21

# A Security Program for Your Family

*He that hath wife and children hath given hostages to fortune.*

—Sir Francis Bacon

Very few officers entering extended active duty with the Air Force are interested in the aftermath of their own deaths. Consequently, some do not give serious attention to the question of life insurance and estate planning. Yet every person, regardless of profession, should study these problems with utmost care. Generally speaking, it is only through life insurance programs and wise investment of savings that most of us can hope to provide adequately for the care of those we leave behind.

## ESSENTIALS

The basic essential of a family security program, including life insurance and investments, is to provide an adequate estate for those who are dependent upon the officer. There are literally a hundred different variations of insurance, some inexpensive, some very expensive. Never lose sight of the basic fact that the primary object of life insurance is to provide for the well-being of dependents after your own death. Everything else is incidental. There are insurance policies that promise a rich dividend to you at some selected age. These are called endowment policies. If you can afford them over and above adequate protection for your family against the ever present contingency of your own death, well and good. First, however, see to it that your insurance program gives your family a reasonable chance for an acceptable standard of living after you have died.

**Timing.** It will take no belaboring of the point to convince you, as an intelligent officer, that the time to take out insurance policies is at the earliest age you can afford them. All types of policies involve increased premiums with increased age. Do not become "insurance poor," but *complete* your insurance program as soon as your personal finances permit, certainly while you are a major. Remember that insurance is paid off in dollars, which are subject to inflation; in other words, the purchasing power of insurance dollars may become less and less with passing years. Therefore, along with your insurance program and throughout your active service, you should follow a sound investment program in investment trusts or common stocks.

**Educational Policies.** Educational policies are designed to produce a given amount of money (say $20,000) for the education of one of your children. Such a policy matures and is payable to you at a stipulated age of your child or is payable to your child at the time of your death. These are worthwhile policies, but they are relatively expensive.

**Ordinary Life Insurance.** This form of life insurance obtained from a reputable commercial company is often called straight life insurance. Although it does have a cash surrender value that you can use in circumstances of acute financial stress, its main characteristic is that it provides a high level of financial security for your family at a low cost. You may use the proceeds of such a policy to serve the purposes of educational and endowment policies when protection is no longer needed.

**Term Insurance.** You will hear that term insurance is far cheaper than ordinary or straight life insurance. So it is, for a limited period. After a few years, however, term policies must be renewed *at the increased age of the applicant.* Thus, by the time you are 45 years of age, your so-called cheap term insurance may have become prohibitive in price. Moreover, upon retirement or later, you may become uninsurable because of physical disability or age. If, however, your need for insurance or for additional insurance is temporary, you may find term insurance best meets this special need.

**Servicemen's Group Life Insurance (SGLI).** Congress approved in 1965 a group life insurance program for all members of the armed forces. This program authorizes $200,000 life insurance to any person on active duty. The benefits of this insurance will be paid to the beneficiary named by the servicemember (spouse, children, parents, next of kin, or executor) with minimum limitation as to place or manner of death.

The SGLI program costs the servicemember $16 per month, with premium payments deducted from monthly pay and additional costs met by the government. This monthly premium is automatically deducted from your pay unless, in writing, you decline to have coverage or wish to have a lesser amount of coverage. The insurance is valid until 120 days after termination of active duty; within that 120 days, you may convert the insurance into a commercial life insurance policy *without physical examination* if desired. While coverage under this program is optional, its advantages to Air Force members are so obvious and considerable that it should not be necessary to urge it upon you. In no other way can you obtain so much life insurance so inexpensively. For further information, see AFR 211-23, *Servicemen's Group Life Insurance and Veteran's Group Life Insurance*.

**Group Insurance Association.** You should also consider the advantages of certain group-plan term policies, especially those designed specifically for the needs of officers, such as those offered by the Armed Forces Relief and Benefit Association.

**Seek Competent Advice.** In developing your personal insurance program, seek the advice of a competent estate planner. Insurance agents of reputable agencies are capable of guiding you accurately and expertly to the proper solution of your insurance problems. They are salespeople and are interested in their commissions. For the most part, however, they will give you the facts. It is your duty to your dependents to know these facts. AFPs 211-40 and 211-41 are good source material.

## DETERMINING A TOTAL SURVIVOR BENEFIT GOAL

Computing or estimating the amount and duration of the monthly income that your survivors should have is a very individual problem. You should think it out in consideration of your own set of circumstances. Discuss it with your spouse or other beneficiary, and use logical analysis to make a decision based on the answers to the following very searching and very personal questions:

**Protection.** At the time of the analysis, is the spouse qualified in some art, trade, or profession, so that he or she could recover promptly to supply all or a major portion of income requirements? Or is he or she untrained for a specific vocation? Consider present age, health, and the spouse's wishes. At what age should it be considered that he or she would be unable to provide a part of the required income or would not wish to do so?

When there are children to be protected, their age must be considered, with costs of support and education. If there are physical or mental frailties these factors must be evaluated. On the average, how much income per month will be required for the support and education of the children and for how many years?

**Clean-up Fund.** In the event of the sudden death of the head of the family, how much cash will be needed at once to pay up current bills, installment accounts, and other obligations? Under this heading should be included the expense as it can be estimated of establishing the survivors in a permanent location with the special and heavy costs this task includes.

**Present Worth of Estate.** Most service families have a tangible net worth that increases through the years preceding retirement. Omit for the present consideration items of personal property that may have material value, but that would not be sold or of themselves add to income. What is the total upon which survivors could depend for living income from the present family estate? This amount is the primary base upon which to build the ultimate program.

An annual reevaluation of this personal estate in an objective manner as would be done by a banker or the trustees of an estate is necessary.

**Survivor Benefits.** Each individual should study carefully the potential income that would be received by the family in event of death. This study should be repeated every few years because laws and conditions change. For example, how much would the spouse receive as the death gratuity (six months' pay but not in excess of $6,000)? How much per month from VA Dependency and Indemnity Compensation or pension? How much from Social Security? How much from insurance policies? How much from the Survivor Benefit Plan? Consideration of these potential benefits to the family will almost invariably lead to the conclusion that the income provided is insufficient. A sound program of additional insurance and investment in stocks or bonds will be the method chosen by most officers to close the gap. Obviously, the sooner such additional programs are begun, the more time is available to spread their cost and to allow for appreciation of investments. Whatever you decide to do, *begin early* (see AFP 211-15).

**Death Gratuity.** Upon the death of an active-duty (but NOT a retired) servicemember, there is paid a death gratuity of six months' pay, up to a maximum of $6,000. There is also a provision that the gratuity is payable if a member or former member dies of a service-connected cause within 120 days after discharge or release from active duty or active duty for training. The gratuity includes base and longevity pay, special incentive and hazard pay, but not rental or subsistence allowances. It is not taxable.

Death gratuity will be paid to the surviving spouse or, if there is no surviving spouse, to the surviving children in equal shares. If there is neither spouse nor children, the member may designate one or more parents, brothers, or sisters. If the member has no surviving spouse or children and has not designated a beneficiary, payment will be made to the parents in equal shares or, if there are no surviving parents, to the surviving brothers and sisters in equal shares. No other person will be entitled to the death gratuity.

**Arrears of Pay.** Upon the death of an Air Force officer, the spouse is entitled to receive whatever arrears of pay would have been due to the officer, provided that the spouse is the beneficiary designated on DD Form 93, *Record of Emergency Data*. The Air Force Finance Center will furnish the beneficiary the proper forms for application for arrears of pay (DD Form 397).

**Accrued Leave Payments.** In 1965, authorization was established to pay to survivors of military personnel who die with accrued leave unused and not otherwise compensated for an amount corresponding to base pay for the number of days of accrued leave on record, up to a maximum of 60 days. Thus, the survivors of Air Force officers could receive as much as two months' base pay in addition to other survivor benefits.

## DEPENDENCY AND INDEMNITY COMPENSATION

The Survivors Dependency and Indemnity Compensation Act of 1974 provides for compensation to survivors for the loss of an officer or soldier whose death is attributable to military service. All *service-connected deaths* that occur in peace or wartime in the line of duty qualify the eligible survivors for the Dependency and Indemnity Compensation (DIC). Retired officers' survivors may qualify also providing the VA rules the death to have been from service-connected causes. As amended in 1986, the Act now provides monthly payments to an unremarried widowed spouse in 1994 of $769. Thus, the higher the pay grade of the deceased member, the higher the compensation payable to the member's survivors. Once established, however, the DIC rate is fixed. Rate increases are only by separate congressional action. DIC payments are not authorized to the survivors of a retired officer whose death is not service-connected. (A small pension may be paid to the widow or widower, as discussed later, provided her or his income is below a stated minimum.) This gap must receive consideration in developing a total family security plan.

Compensations may be increased for widows and widowers with children under 18 or with a child over 18 who is incapable of self-support. An additional sum may be awarded for each child between 18 and 23 who attends a VA-approved school. All such compensations are income tax-free. The officer's surviving children will receive compensations should the spouse die. Dependent parents likewise qualify for compensations. Your finance officer or any VA office can assist you in computing the various possible compensations and pensions for your particular family situation.

## PAY AND SIX-MONTHS' DEATH GRATUITY

At the time of a servicemember's death, there will be pay due for a month or a fractional part of a month. The spouse receives this arrears in pay upon claim to the nearest accounting and finance center.

In addition to the arrears in pay, a death gratuity is payable to the survivors of a servicemember who dies while on active duty, active duty for training, or inactive duty training (weekly drills), or of a retired servicemember who dies of a service-connected disability within 120 days after separation from the active list. The amount of this gratuity is six months' basic pay, with a minimum of $800 and a maximum of $6,000. In practice, military pay rates have increased so much since these limits were established that the six months' gratuity is now $6,000 for all members.

These payments should be included in the determination of assets and benefits in an individual's estate security plan.

## SURVIVOR BENEFIT PLAN (SBP)

The Survivor Benefit Plan (SBP) became effective in September 1972. It allows members of the uniformed services to elect to receive a reduced retirement pay in order to provide annuities for their survivors, for another person with an insurable interest in the servicemember, or, under certain conditions, for an ex-spouse. Under SBP, the federal government pays a substantial portion of the overall cost. Participation in the SBP is open to all future retirees, including members of the reserve forces when they attain age 60 and become entitled to retired or retainer pay. Present retirees have previously been afforded the opportunity to participate.

Under SBP, future retirees may elect to leave up to 55 percent of their retired pay to their selected annuitants. Participation in SBP is automatic at the 55 percent rate for those still on active duty who have a spouse or children. Prior to retirement, the member may fill out an election form electing a reduced coverage, or the member may decline to participate. However, the spouse must concur in the election of reduced or no coverage. The minimum base amount of retired pay upon which SBP is based was initially set at $300 per month; but beginning in October 1985, the minimum base amount was raised by the same percentage factor as any increase in active-duty pay. Effective with the 1 January 1994 pay raise, the minimum base amount for SBP is $400.

Costs for spouse-only coverage under SBP are 2½ percent of the minimum base amount, plus 10 percent of the remainder. Thus, a member entitled to $1,000 per month in retired pay, who desires to leave 55 percent ($550) to his or her spouse, pays $76.15 per month ($7.95 for the first $318 and $68.20 for the remaining $682). Note that the cost is based upon the total retired pay used to compute the SBP annuity and not upon the amount of the annuity. Extension of the coverage for a child or children costs about ½ of 1 percent of the annuity amount per month. In the above example, this extended coverage would cost the member approximately $2.75 per month.

There are a number of points about the SBP that deserve careful consideration. Most decisions are irrevocable, but deductions under the plan cease during any month in which there is no eligible beneficiary. Further, the coverage may be switched to a new spouse if the retiree remarries. An important advantage of SBP is that the amount of coverage is tied to the Consumer Price Index (CPI). Whenever retired pay is adjusted on the basis of the CPI, the amount selected by the retiree as an annuity base, the deduction from retired pay covering the adjusted base, and the annuity payable to selected beneficiaries will be adjusted accordingly. The plan thus provides for automatic cost-of-living adjustments. The plan also contains a provision that when the beneficiary becomes eligible for Social Security survivor benefits, the SBP payments will be permanently reduced by the amount to which the beneficiary is entitled from Social Security, based solely upon the member's military pay, up to a maximum of 40 percent of the SBP payment. However, there is no offset if the surviving spouse is working and has earnings that are too high for Social Security payments to be paid. Neither is there an offset if the spouse is receiving Social Security payments based upon his or her own earnings rather than a widow's or widower's benefit based upon the military member's earnings. In 1985, the law was changed to eliminate the Social Security offset and replace it with a two-tiered system in which the survivor receives 55 percent of the base amount of retired pay until age 62, at which time the amount drops to 35 percent of the base amount of retired pay, which continues for the life of the survivor. Retirees after 1 October 1985 are enrolled in the two-tiered system. The annuity of the survivor of a member who retired prior to 1 October 1985 will be recomputed when the survivor reaches age 62. After that time, the annuity will be either that computed under the older offset system or the newer two-tiered system, whichever is greater.

The plan also provides that if a retiree dies of a service-connected cause, as a result of which survivors are entitled to DIC payments (see Dependency and Indemnity Compensation earlier in this chapter), the SBP payment will be reduced so that the total of the two payments—DIC and SBP—will be equal to the full amount otherwise payable under SBP. Thus, the total income to the survivors from SBP, DIC, and Social Security can equal or be slightly higher than the SBP income alone, depending upon the extent of the offset for Social Security. On the other hand, since SBP (as well as Social Security) is tied to the Consumer Price Index, the retired member also is assured that the spending power provided through SBP will remain relatively constant regardless of the effect of inflation.

It is apparent that participation in SBP has definite advantages and, perhaps, disadvantages that call for study, obtaining advice, and care in deciding if coverage is desired and in selecting the amount. SBP is not necessarily a panacea for all military retirees, but it deserves careful consideration as a benefit accruing to you as a result of military service, which is available for use in planning your estate.

## SOCIAL SECURITY

Military personnel accrue Social Security benefits for active service as an important element of their overall security program. Participation is mandatory. Under the Social Security program, your base pay is taxed at a prescribed rate. The maximum taxable earnings are increased as average wage levels rise. At the same time, the benefits payable also increase. The amount of the benefit received from Social Security will depend upon the Average Monthly Earnings (AME) and the number of years of credit that have been accrued. The benefit of most general interest is the monthly income that an officer and eligible members of the officer's family attain when the officer reaches age 65. (Reduced benefits may be selected for ages 62, 63, and 64, as well.) Payments are provided for disabled officers and for their spouses and children. Monthly income is provided for an officer's widow or widower with children under 18 years of age, or for children alone, or for the widow or widower at age 60, or for dependent parents. These important benefits, then, supplement other insurance-type security programs. Application for benefits may be made at any Social Security office.

Note: It is important that you ensure that the Social Security Administration has credited you with the correct contributions. This may be accomplished by requesting the status of your account at approximately three-year intervals. Postcard-type forms are available at any Social Security office to use for this request.

## PENSION FOR DEPENDENTS OF RETIRED PERSONNEL AND VETERANS WHOSE DEATHS WERE NOT SERVICE CONNECTED

A modest survivor pension may be payable to dependents of veterans or retired personnel when retirement was for a reason other than physical disability or death occurred for reason other than a service-connected cause. But the spouse and children of the veteran or retired individual are the only eligibles.

The following payments are not considered income as to death pension payments:

- Government life insurance proceeds and, in some cases, commercial life insurance proceeds.
- The six months' death gratuity.
- Donations from public or private relief or welfare organizations.
- Payments of pension, compensation, and dependency compensation of the VA.
- Survivor Benefit Plan.
- Lump-sum Social Security death payments.
- Payments to a person under public or private retirement annuity, endowment, or similar plans or programs equal to that person's contributions.
- Proceeds of a fire insurance policy.
- Amounts equal to amounts paid by a spouse or a child of a deceased veteran for just debts, the expenses of the last illness, and the expenses of burial that are not reimbursed by the VA.

For pension and other benefit rates, consult your personal affairs officer.

## MUTUAL INSURANCE ASSOCIATIONS FOR SERVICEMEMBERS

There are mutual associations of officers of the military service that have very material importance. Eligible officers may assume with confidence that these organizations are well and carefully administered and that the services provided are tailored to fit military requirements.

**The Army and Air Force Mutual Aid Association.** 468 Sheridan Ave., Fort Myer, Arlington, VA 22111-5002. This association has served officers since 1879.

**The Armed Forces Relief and Benefit Association.** This nonprofit service organization offers group life insurance with its attendant low cost to supplement an officer's permanent program. Membership is open to regular officers and to reserve officers on extended active duty.

Rates are *very low* because it is group insurance. At death, the insurance may be paid in a lump sum or part in lump sum, part in installments, all in installments, or as an annuity.

While this insurance is limited to active officers, there is provision for conversion to other forms of insurance with the John Hancock Mutual Life Insurance Company, one of the underwriters of the program.

Address: The Armed Forces Benefit Association
909 N. Washington St.
Alexandria, VA 22314-1556

**Air Force Association Life Insurance.** This plan provides term insurance at low rates, convertible to commercial insurance without physical examination on separation from the service.

Address: AFA Insurance Division
1501 Lee Highway
Arlington, VA 22209-1198

**United Services Automobile Association.** This association was founded to provide automobile insurance at cost for officers and warrant officers of the armed services. In addition to automobile insurance, it also makes available a valuable household goods/personal effects policy. Both are arranged to meet the specific conditions of officers.

*Eligibility.* Policies may be obtained by active and retired officers; Advanced ROTC, OTS/OCS, and academy cadets; those in certain precommissioning programs; warrant officers of the several services; officers and warrant officers of National Guard and reserve components when ordered to extended active federal duty; and the spouses of such deceased officers and warrant officers, so long as their status is not changed by remarriage.

*Automobile Coverage.* The automobile coverage is broad and similar in scope to policies offered by commercial companies. Its policies cover throughout the United States and in many foreign countries. Shipment coverage is provided upon request.

*Household Goods and Personal Effects Policy.* The association also offers insurance on personal effects and household goods against the hazards of fire, transportation, theft, windstorm, flood, earthquake, and many other perils. There is no adjustment of premium because of relocation of goods. Coverage is worldwide.

Address: United Services Automobile Association
USAA Building, San Antonio, TX 78288

**Armed Forces Insurance.** This group offers insurance against fire losses to personal and household effects regardless of station or duty and at actual cost to members. Coverage is worldwide and applies automatically for damage by named hazards to property wherever located, in government or civilian storage, in use, or in transit. Coverage A provides protection against loss from fire, lightning, smoke, flood, earthquake, explosion, hail, or windstorm or while being transported by common or public carrier, including U.S. government vehicles, vessels, or aircraft. Exceptions include automobiles or other gasoline-propelled machines, animals, boats, some types of collections, and loss or damage due to hostile or warlike action. It does not protect against loss in parcel post or mail. An additional coverage B against theft, pilferage, sabotage, and so on is also available. Premium rates are very low. Settlements are prompt and fair to all concerned.

Eligibility for membership includes any commissioned or warrant officer of the regular services or of the reserve components on active duty, except that a reserve member must have signified, by contract, an intent to remain on active duty for a period not less than three years. The spouse of a deceased member is permitted to continue the insurance in his or her name until remarriage or death.

Address: Armed Forces Insurance
P.O. Box G
Fort Leavenworth, KS 66027

# 22

# Oversea Movement of Your Family and Life Overseas

*Travel teaches tolerance.*

—Benjamin Disraeli

Air Force officers must expect to spend about three years out of every ten at an oversea station. Depending on where the officers are assigned, they may go alone to an oversea assignment, leaving their families behind in the United States for some months, the period varying with different oversea stations. This separation of officers and their families is the result of the limited housing available at oversea bases. On arrival in the oversea area, officers sign up on a priority list for family housing. This list is governed by the length of the period of separation that has occurred. In some oversea areas, officers are permitted to obtain for themselves private rental housing, but this housing must be approved by the oversea command before it can be used as a basis for dependent travel.

## ACTION BEFORE DEPARTURE

When alerted for an oversea move, officers are counseled on travel procedures and tour elections. When dependent travel is authorized, an advance application for concurrent travel should be submitted if the officers intend to move dependents overseas.

Official orders of the Department of the Air Force assigning officers to an oversea command prescribe the timing, the method of transportation, and other essential information about the journey. At the outset the officers should have prepared at least twenty copies of orders, for they will need to file them on many occasions incident to movement, pay, travel allowances, shipment of personal property, and other matters en route and after arrival.

Upon receipt of orders, the officers should report at once to the base administrative officer, transportation officer, finance officer, supply officer, and surgeon, receiving from them detailed instructions, which they must be certain to understand and follow to the letter. The officers must set their official and personal houses in order so that no dangling, unfinished official or personal business will arise at the last minute before departure or after departure. All personal bills or obligations must be paid, or definite arrangements made to defer payment.

At every step, the officers must bear in mind that their spouses, if not authorized to travel concurrently, will have need for certain documents in connection with later movement to the oversea area. The officers must therefore ensure that the spouses have all necessary documents, such as titles to automobiles, copies of officers' orders, insurance policies, inventories of household goods, children's school records, birth certificates, and the like. The officers should leave with the spouses signed copies of DD Form 1299, *Application for Shipment and/or Storage of Personal Property*, together with 20 copies of the officers' travel orders. The officers must also ensure that the spouses have sufficient money (an allotment may be indicated) to cover family needs during the period of separation, including the period of movement overseas.

**Record of Expenses.** The officer and spouse should, from the beginning of all actions connected with the oversea movement, maintain a record of out-of-pocket expenses incurred. Military dependents are reimbursed for out-of-pocket expenses, such as taxi fares, tips, passport fees, visa fees, and other items during transfers. The list of reimbursable expenses is a long and complicated one. Therefore, the wise officer and spouse will maintain a record of *all* expenses of any type and after arrival at the oversea station consult with the finance officer as to which of these items will result in reimbursement. These reimbursements are in addition to per diem or other direct travel allowances authorized.

**Applications for Nonconcurrent Dependent Travel.** If concurrent travel was not approved, upon arrival at the assigned station overseas officers may apply through their commanders for dependent travel authorization. Approval of applications for dependent travel is given when the oversea commanders concerned can ensure that adequate family housing, either government or private, will be available for the dependents upon their arrival. The officers must have at least 12 months remaining on their tours to move dependents overseas at government expense.

**Receipt of Passport Authorization.** After the officer's application for dependent travel is approved by the oversea commander, a letter authorizing the dependents to apply for a no-fee passport is furnished to them.

**Application for No-Fee Passport.** Upon receipt of passport authorization, dependents should make application for a no-fee passport through the military personnel flight (MPF) at the sponsor's base of assignment. When making application, dependents must present these documents:

- A birth certificate for each member of the family going overseas.
- Two identical photographs not smaller than 2″ x 2″ and taken full face and without hat.
- Proof of American citizenship if not native born.

**Photographs.** Individuals are required to obtain separate no-fee passports, regardless of age, and, accordingly, individual photographs are required.

**Processing Passport.** The application for passport is then forwarded for processing to the Passport Division, Department of State, Washington, DC 20520. Upon issuance, the passport is forwarded to the appropriate aerial port of embarkation, where it will be given to the dependents upon their arrival. Upon receipt of the processed passport, the appropriate port of embarkation will, at the time the dependent's priority number comes up, issue port call to the dependent.

**Warning.** Upon receipt of authorization, dependents should apply for passport with the least possible delay. Dependents who delay applying, following receipt of passport authorization, may deny themselves an earlier port call. In this regard, it is important that dependents have their birth certificates and citizenship evidence on hand so that the passport application is not delayed.

The appropriate aerial port of embarkation will not issue a port call until the passport has been received. If the passport is obtained through nonmilitary channels or if it is inadvertently sent directly to the dependent, it must be dispatched immediately to the appropriate aerial port of embarkation.

**Dependents' Travel Orders.** At the appropriate time, the oversea command will issue to the officer's dependents a letter of instructions similar to the one shown below.

**SAMPLE LETTER OF INSTRUCTIONS TO BE FORWARDED TO DEPENDENTS TRAVELING UNACCOMPANIED BY THEIR SPONSOR**

(Suggest sponsor's aid in composition so that only pertinent facts are included.)

Dear. . . . . . . . . . . . . . . . . . . . . . . . . . . . . . . .: (date)

Inclosed are copies of Special Order No. . . . . . . . . . . . . . . . . . . . . . . . . . . . . . . . . . . . . . . . . . . . . . ., this headquarters, dated . . . . . . . . . . . . . . . . . . . . . . ., covering your transportation from the United States to join your sponsor in this area. The Air Force base indicated in these orders has also been advised of your impending travel and is prepared to assist you in any way possible. You should contact the MPF at the base for assistance. For your information, however, there are certain things we would like to acquaint you with in order to enable you to travel with a minimum of delay and maximum of efficiency. These are:

*a.* MEDICAL REQUIREMENTS: If you are pregnant, you are requested to furnish the Transportation Officer at the base designated to handle your movement a confirming statement from the attending physician as to expected date of birth of child. Prior to departure from the United States you will likewise be required to be immunized against . . . . . . . . . . . . . . . . . . . . . . . . . . . These inoculations may be received at any military installation. A private physician may administer inoculations, but must furnish you with a certificate for presentation to proper authorities. You are required to complete AF Form 1466, *Medical and Educational Clearance for Dependent Oversea Travel*, before travel is authorized. If this has not been obtained, you are urged to make an appointment with the nearest Air Force medical facility at your earliest convenience. Medical reports and recommendations from civilian physicians may be provided. However, the certificate must be signed and approved by an Air Force medical services evaluator. In some cases, it may be necessary to report in person for further evaluation or examination before clearance can be issued. The purpose is to assure that adequate and necessary care is available in the area of assignment.

*b.* TRANSPORTATION: (Use applicable subparagraph.) (1) Your sponsor is serving in an "administrative weight restricted" oversea area. Shipment of household goods, not to exceed _______ pounds, is authorized. In addition to household goods, shipment of unaccompanied baggage is authorized. This shipment will not exceed 350 pounds per dependent 12 years of age and older and 175 pounds per dependent under 12 years of age.

(2) Your sponsor is serving in a "full JTR weight" oversea area. Shipment of household goods, not to exceed _______ pounds, is authorized. Part of the shipment may be shipped as unaccompanied baggage. This shipment will not exceed 350 pounds per dependent 12 years of age and older and 175 pounds per dependent under 12 years of age. A "free checkable" baggage allowance, which is normally 66 pounds, is authorized for you and each of your dependents for your travel by air. You should check with the transportation office to determine actual number of pounds authorized in your case. Shipment of your automobile (is) (is not) authorized. Delivery of the automobile to a military water port is your responsibility. This must be accomplished at your own expense. The Transportation Officer will furnish you with information regarding your household goods, automobile, and personal travel. The Transportation Officer also makes all necessary arrangements for the shipment of your baggage and household goods. You will be provided with the required transportation requests to enable you to proceed to the proper point of departure from the United States. It is imperative that you travel only during the period indicated in the attached orders. Do not report to the commercial gateway before the time specified in the reservation confirmation furnished by the personnel processing you for oversea movement. (Personally procured travel performed via foreign flag carrier is not reimbursable unless a statement is provided that a U.S. certificated carrier was not available.)

*c. (Any additional information deemed necessary for the orderly movement of the individuals should be included in additional paragraphs. Information relative to clothing that should be worn or accompany the individual, what to expect after arrival in the oversea area, instructions on applying for passports and visas if necessary, and related items should be included.)*

*d.* If there are any questions relative to your travel to this area that have not been covered, it is suggested that the outbound assignments unit in the MPF of the base designated to handle your movement be queried. He is equipped to provide you with advice and assistance as needed.

*e.* Transportation has been scheduled for you during (the month indicated in orders). It is important that you travel during (the month indicated in orders). In the event an unforeseen emergency requires you to travel in a month other than indicated, request you advise the outbound assignments unit in the MPF at (the designated base), who will advise the overseas order writing agency.

Sincerely,

The following paragraph is suggested for inclusion under c above if alien spouse or alien adopted children are involved.

*c.* Also inclosed is DD Form 1278, *Certificate of Overseas Assignment to File Petition for Naturalization*, which will serve as your authority to file your petition for naturalization. This form should be filed with your application for petition for naturalization if you have not already filed with the nearest office of the Immigration and Naturalization Service. If you have already filed your application, this form should be forwarded immediately to the appropriate I&NS Office. As soon as citizenship is granted, you should immediately file an application for passport.

(Reference AFR 10–4, volume I, chapter 8, for list of CONUS Air Force activities capable of providing support to unaccompanied dependents.)

Note that the letter of instructions provides that the officer's dependents should make contact with the MPF at the nearest air base. The MPF will make application for the family's flight reservations. In due course, the MPF will inform the officer's dependents of the exact time, date, and flight number of the reservation for air travel. The MPF will further assist the officer's dependents in carrying out all necessary preparations for oversea movement.

**Immunizations Required.** All dependents transported overseas at government expense are required to receive certain immunizations before departure from the United States. At the present time, the immunizations required for entry into the oversea commands are these:

- *Adults.* Tetanus.
- *Children.* Pediatric immunizations up to date.

If immunizations are obtained from a private physician, a complete record should be maintained. Also, dependents are advised that immunization requirements may change without notice and that current information in this regard may be obtained from the nearest armed forces medical facility. The dependent's record of immunization must be on Public Health Service Form 731 (Yellow). Others will not be accepted.

**Shipment of Household Goods.** The officer's spouse should consult with the base transportation officer concerning the disposition of household goods. Specific recommendations concerning items of household goods to be shipped to a particular foreign country are in the numbered AF pamphlets in the 216 series pertaining to that country. This information will doubtless be reinforced by letters from the officer overseas informing the spouse of conditions there. The transportation officer will arrange for storage of all or any portion of the family's household goods in commercial facilities located in the general vicinity of the base. Decisions must therefore be made as to what, if any, items of household goods should be left in storage in the United States. Other household goods will be shipped to the oversea base by any of several surface modes as designated by the transportation officer and will be in transit about two months. Some oversea commands limit the weight of household goods that can be shipped to about 2,000 pounds. Check with the transportation officer.

## ACTIONS ON RECEIPT OF PORT CALL

When the family has received its port call, that is, information as to the exact time for reporting to the aerial port of embarkation (APOE), final decisions must be made on the following points:

• The exact time, as designated by the officer's spouse, for household goods to be picked up by the commercial carriers for delivery to the oversea base of assignment, or to the commercial storage facility as designated by the transportation officer.

• What shall be shipped as *unaccompanied baggage.* Unaccompanied baggage is authorized to the extent of 600 pounds per dependent. This baggage may include such items as clothes, pots and pans, light housekeeping items, and collapsible items, such as cribs, playpens, and baby carriages when necessary for the care and comfort of an infant. It may be expected that the unaccompanied baggage will arrive in the oversea area about one week after the arrival of the dependents. Unaccompanied baggage must be placed in strong containers, such as trunks, which may weigh no more than 300 pounds per container and be of no greater volume than 15 cubic feet.

• What shall be carried as *hand baggage.* In these cases, 66 pounds per person is authorized. This baggage will go with the traveler on the same aircraft and must be taken to the APOE by the traveler.

• What to do about the *automobile.* If the dependent's orders authorized the shipment of a privately owned vehicle (POV), the officer's spouse should drive the car directly to the aerial port of embarkation where arrangements can be made, for a modest fee, to have the car delivered to the surface port of shipment for vehicles.

It is at this time that the officer's spouse will be required to present the certificate of title to the automobile or, if a lien is held on the car, authorization from the holder of the lien permitting the car to be taken out of the United States.

If the privately owned vehicle is to be delivered directly to the port of shipment, the dependent asks the transportation officer at the air base which port of shipment will receive and ship the car. The car is then delivered by the dependent to that port of shipment. Depending upon the oversea area to which the dependent is going, one of the following ports of shipment for automobiles will be applicable: Bayonne, N.J., Baltimore, Norfolk, Cape Canaveral, New Orleans, Seattle, Oakland, or San Pedro.

**Movement to the APOE.** The mode of travel of the family to the APOE is determined by whether or not a POV is to be shipped overseas. If travel is to be by automobile, the spouse should make reservations ahead of time for necessary overnight stops at hotels or motels.

If travel is to be by commercial means, transportation requests should be secured from the transportation officer and reservations made for travel to the APOE.

**Arrival at the APOE.** The officer's spouse should arrange to arrive a few hours before the specified time of the flight. It is not necessary, nor is it desirable, that the family arrive the day preceding the specified date of departure for overseas. If circumstances make it necessary, however, overnight facilities can be provided at the APOE. On arriving at the APOE, the dependents should proceed directly to the processing point. The processing-out procedure will require about one hour. At this time, copies of orders must be shown, and immunization records will be checked. Hand baggage will be tagged, weighed, and loaded on the aircraft. The spouse should keep in hand only those items absolutely necessary during the course of the flight, such as toiletries and infant needs (diapers and formula). The spouse should carry only about $150 in cash; any additional funds should be in the form of travelers' checks.

**The Flight Overseas.** Travel in an Air Mobility Command (AMC) aircraft is virtually identical to travel in a commercial airliner. Meals are served and facilities for warming babies' bottles and food are available. If the flight makes a stop en route, a snack bar and a small BX facility will be found at hand. If a delay is extended, the hand baggage loaded aboard the airplane will be made available to the passengers. Individuals should wear warm, comfortable clothes.

**Arrival at Destination.** The AMC flight on which the dependents travel will take them to some central point near their final destination, such as Frankfurt or Tokyo. At this point, it is necessary to claim hand baggage checked aboard the AMC flight. If it is necessary for the dependents to remain overnight before continuing their journey, transient hotel facilities will be made available to them. Transportation to such transient facilities will be provided by the Air Force. Further travel will be by staff car, bus, or train in most cases. Arrangements for this will have been made by the authorities at the AMC terminal overseas. Upon landing at the AMC terminal overseas, the family will be informed of the means of further travel and the schedule of such travel. Necessary intermediate transportation, such as from the AMC terminal to the rail station, will be provided by the Air Force. On arrival at the final destination, the family should be met by the officer or the officer's agent.

**Movement of POV.** The privately owned vehicle (POV) turned in for shipment at the APOE will move via surface vessels to a seaport in the area to which the family is traveling. The automobile will be about one month in transit. It will arrive at such a port as Bremerhaven in Germany or Yokohama in Japan, where it must be picked up by the officer or the officer's agent. The government does not transport the automobile from the seaport to the duty station of the officer. The officer will be notified by the port authorities of the arrival of the automobile. Usually, the officer can obtain a pass to cover absence while accepting delivery of the automobile.

**Traveling on Tourist Passports.** Authorized dependent travel at the expense of the government is the only travel plan fully endorsed by the Department of the Air Force. Dependents choosing to travel on *tourist passports* for the purpose of visiting their sponsors at oversea bases do so as civilian tourists, traveling commercially and at no expense to the government. It is strongly recommended that dependents electing to travel in the status of civilians fully inform their sponsors of their plans before performing such travel. AFR 36-20, *Officer Assignments*, stipulates that the sponsor will serve a longer tour if dependents join the sponsor in the theater at any time in any status, *except* for those dependents traveling in tourist status whose entry has been approved by the Air Force major commander concerned.

**Shipment of Pets to Oversea Areas.** Certain pets may be shipped at the owner's risk and at no expense to the government through the appropriate port of embarkation on surface carriers belonging to the Military Sea Transportation Service, provided that all requirements are met and that space is available.

**Exchange Facilities Overseas.** Air Force personnel preparing for oversea assignments should *not* assume that they must take with them all things needed for a three-year tour. The exchanges overseas are excellent. They are prepared to meet every conceivable need from clothing (adults, children, and infants) to washing machines, stereos, and automobiles. Virtually everything needed or even desired by an Air Force family can be obtained in the exchanges. Moreover, the local economy of such countries as Germany, Italy, Japan, and England offer many supplementary sources from which family needs can be met, although at increased prices. The exchanges, however, are complete in themselves because oversea exchanges are allowed to stock and sell to military personnel items denied to exchanges in the United States.

**Commissaries Overseas.** Like the exchanges, military commissaries overseas meet all food needs. Military families who buy foods at the local markets do so merely because they prefer that course. The commissary can and does meet all normal needs. Food prices in the oversea commissaries are comparable to those in military facilities in the United States.

**Medical Care Overseas.** The family need not be concerned regarding adequate medical care overseas for adults or children, including prenatal treatment. Excellent clinics are available in all areas, and a general military hospital will be found in the vicinity. Optical and dental services are available for dependents in the military facilities. Do not buy extra sets of glasses for dependents before going overseas. At the oversea clinic, the cost is far less.

**Schools Overseas.** Grade school and high school facilities are provided in all established commands. Standards are closely supervised. Considering the intangible values to be derived by travel and life in an oversea land for a span of a few years, most parents consider that their children have been benefited by the experience. In the unusual case where children's schools are not provided under military control, parents should learn about facilities used by American citizens in the area or explore the possibilities for instruction by mail with home tutoring. Unless there are very unusual circumstances indeed, there is no strong reason for Air Force families to be separated merely because of the school situation of their children, because educational facilities for our children have been provided in a manner that has been acceptable to most parents.

**Movement of Dependent Students to and from Oversea Areas.** Bona fide student dependents of military personnel stationed outside the continental United States are authorized transportation on a space-available basis to the port of embarkation in the United States to attend school in the United States and between the United States and an oversea port to spend their summer vacations with their families. Only one round trip per year is authorized and normally will be taken during the summer vacation period. Dependents who pass the age of 21 years while engaged in full-time undergraduate study will be authorized the same transportation.

The following procedures will apply:

- The military sponsor overseas will be responsible for requesting a travel authorization from the oversea installation.
- The oversea installation will issue the necessary travel authorizations and will forward the authorizations to the student dependent.
- If movement is to be by AMC, the students will be directed to report to the APOE serving the particular oversea area for movement on a space-available basis. (The student should be prepared for a possible delay at the APOE of several days.)

**Postal Service.** The Army-Air Force Postal Service provides mail service overseas for Air Force and Army personnel for all commands, bases, and stations. Postal rates are identical to those in the continental United States. Air mail, registry service, and parcel post service are provided.

**Merchandise Subject to U.S. Customs.** Service overseas provides an opportunity for the purchase of merchandise made in foreign lands, such as cameras from Germany, pearl necklaces from Japan, and objects of art peculiar to the country or station. Items are often sold for prices materially lower than the cost of similar items in the

United States, such as the perfumes of France. The officer and spouse who make a real study of these possibilities, purchase wisely, and avoid the purchase of merchandise that will be undesired upon their return to the United States may acquire unusual possessions they will cherish throughout their lives.

All such purchases should be made with due regard to customs regulations. The laws and regulations governing the entry of merchandise purchased abroad into the United States are quite liberal and, surprisingly, far more liberal than is the common understanding. The entry or attempt at entry of merchandise purchased abroad without the required customs declaration is an evasion of the law. It is smuggling. It is subject to severe penalties provided in the laws. It is not smart to smuggle. It is much smarter to inform yourself as to what can be brought into the United States openly and legally. For articles of personal use and enjoyment in a household, the quantity authorized for free entry may prove to be entirely sufficient.

**Housing in Oversea Areas.** The character of housing available to officers overseas varies considerably among the oversea areas. Government quarters are, however, generally adequate, and some are excellent. Although the standard of government quarters in any oversea area approximates that of quarters on air bases in the United States, there are exceptions. Therefore, read the current AF 216 series pamphlet on the particular foreign country of interest.

Private housing is an entirely different proposition. The standards may be quite low in such matters as electricity available, effectiveness of the plumbing systems, and heating. The price of private housing is often very high for what the Air Force officer would consider an acceptable house. The cost of utilities in general is two or three times that in the United States. On the other hand, officers who are authorized to find housing on the local economy may receive a station allowance that partly compensates for the increased costs encountered. The amount of the COLA (cost of living allowance) varies with oversea stations. As a general matter, it is possible to obtain household help at fairly reasonable rates.

**Travel and Recreation Opportunities in Oversea Areas.** One of the great attractions of life overseas is the opportunity provided to travel in foreign countries and to take advantage of the recreational facilities available. In Europe, U.S. military personnel may travel about among the interesting countries of this Old World during short periods of leave. By using the facilities of the various U.S. military installations sprinkled over Europe, it is possible to visit a vast number of interesting places at a reasonable cost. In the Orient, distances become a problem, but nonetheless it is possible for officers to make arrangements to visit countries other than the one to which they are assigned. In Europe and in Japan, facilities for sports of all kinds are not only available, but also close at hand. Where the oversea station is somewhat isolated, such as Korea, it will be found that arrangements have been made to accommodate sports enthusiasts of all types.

## LEARNING THE LANGUAGE

Headquarters USAF once announced as a goal that all officers will become proficient in at least one foreign language. Officers going overseas are obviously in a much better position to meet this requirement within a foreign environment than are their peers who stay at home. It is an opportunity that should not be passed up, especially since foreign language proficiency has been stated officially to be a professional qualification improving the officer's career potential. Off-duty classes, mixing with the host people, and study of the local culture and government are methods that should be used. Even if the language is a difficult one, the officer and family should learn at least the phrases of courtesy and of the social amenities. They will carry you a long way.

## LIVING CONDITIONS OVERSEAS

Each foreign country presents the Air Force officer and family with new and sometimes startling living conditions. Conditions vary widely among countries. Therefore, each foreign station must be studied separately; generalizations are worthless and misleading. Officers and their spouses who are on orders to a foreign country should read the appropriate information pamphlet (AFP 216 series) before making *any* decision regarding the forthcoming foreign service tour. Furniture, housing, cost of living, clothes, pets, currency, operation of appliances, and a thousand other considerations are covered in the Air Force pamphlet relative to each country, but it does not usually cover individual bases specifically. Most of the usual blunders will be avoided if the pamphlet is read carefully. These are available through the personal affairs officer or at the family services center of your base.

After consulting the appropriate Air Force pamphlet on life in the particular country to which the family is going, the following points should be considered:

• Will your electric equipment work on the current (voltage and cycle) in the oversea area? In the case of voltage, a 220-volt system can be reduced to 110 volts by use of a transformer available at the oversea exchange. A 50-cycle current is more difficult. In general, if the current is 50 cycles (as in France) it would be better to omit shipment of stereo equipment and electric clocks, but these items can be adapted to 50-cycle by a competent electrical repairman. Your refrigerators, washing machines, deep freezes, and small electrical appliances will operate satisfactorily on the 50-cycle system.

• Don't stock up. You will find all necessary items available overseas, and in many cases, available in forms and at prices preferable to the situation in the United States.

As an observation applicable to life in almost all oversea areas, it is possible to say this: You will find the situation not at all difficult, not nearly as "different" as you might have thought. Therefore, relax. You are not going to the moon, but rather, in most cases, to highly civilized and industrialized countries whose cultures were 1,000 years old when America was discovered.

**Armed Forces Hostess Association.** An information service of unique value is provided by the Armed Forces Hostess Association, Room 1A-736, The Pentagon, Washington, DC 20310-3133 (703) 697-3180/6857. This is a volunteer association of military wives of all services, who will provide you on request considerable information on your oversea base, including appliances, climate, schools, clothing, travel, shipment of pets, and other helpful tips. State Department post reports, MAAGs, and missions reports are available also. Include your rank, specific location (APO if possible) and date of departure.

## TOURS OF DUTY

The Air Force seeks to ensure equitable distribution of oversea assignments to its personnel. See AFR 36-20 for the policies and length of oversea tours. While the policy is on a "first to return, first to go" basis, officers will understand that manning tables and specific requirements must influence actual selections, and that lengths of tours may change with the military situation.

## CLAIMS FOR DAMAGED GOODS

When the officer's household goods are delivered at the new station, occasionally items are missing or damaged. Claims for damaged goods are processed by the claims office, which is a branch of the base legal office (also referred to as the staff judge advocate office). General information about processing a claim is also provided by personnel in the transportation office when servicemembers make initial arrangements to have their items delivered to their new residence.

Part Four • Your Air Force

# 23

# The Departments of Defense and the Air Force

*We must effectively discharge our responsibility to be absolutely certain that the future integrity and combat capability of the Air Force are maintained. How well you fulfill this responsibility will determine to a large extent the future security of our nation.*
—General Curtis E. LeMay, former Chief of Staff, USAF

The U.S. Constitution establishes the basic principle that the armed forces be under civilian control. By giving the president the position of commander in chief, the Constitution provides the basic institutional framework for military organization. This chapter outlines the organization of the Air Force and its role in national defense.

## THE COMMANDER IN CHIEF

Following World War II, an increasing need to integrate military policy with national policy compelled the president to assume a much more active role as commander in chief of the armed forces. As commander in chief, the president has the final word of command authority, but, as head of the executive branch, is subject to the "checks and balances" system of the legislative and judicial branches. The heavy demands of domestic and foreign duties require the president to delegate authority broadly and wisely. Responsibility for national defense matters is delegated to the Office of the Secretary of Defense (OSD) and to the Department of Defense (DOD).

## THE DEPARTMENT OF DEFENSE

The basic purpose of the National Security Act of 1947, and its later amendments, was to establish the Department of Defense. This department, which directly affects more than 3.3 million employees and their

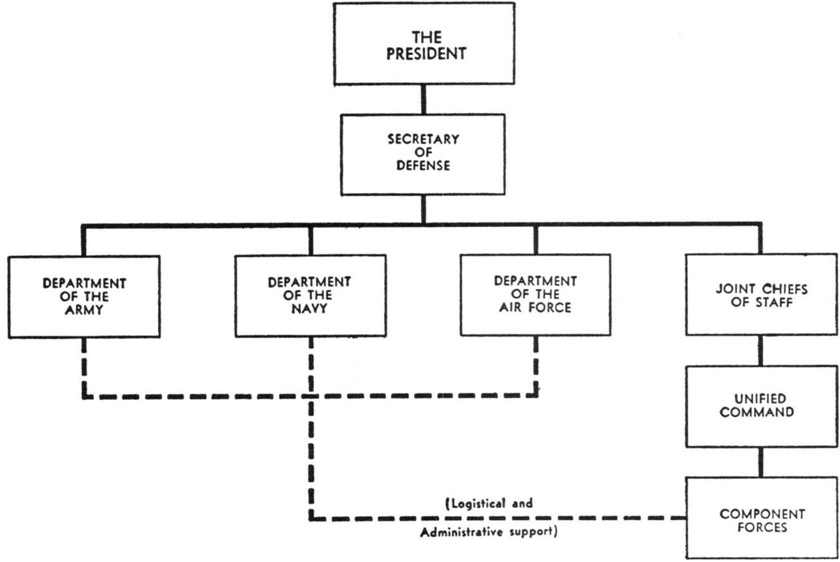


ARMED FORCES COMMAND LINES.

families, establishes policies and procedures for the government relating to national security. It includes the Office of the Secretary of Defense; the Joint Chiefs of Staff (JCS); the Departments of the Army, the Navy (including the U.S. Marine Corps), and the Air Force; unified, specified, and combined commands; defense agencies; and DOD field activities. As the civilian head of the DOD, the secretary of defense reports directly to the president.

**Office of the Secretary of Defense.** The president appoints the secretary of defense, with the advice and consent of the Senate. As the principal assistant to the president for military matters, the secretary has the authority to exercise direction and control over all elements of the DOD. The line of operational command flows from the secretary of defense *through* the JCS directly to the specified and unified commanders. The JCS is *not* in the chain of command. The secretary also delegates authority. For example, the responsibility for strategic and tactical planning is given to the JCS. The military departments have responsibility for training, administrative, and logistic support of the unified and specified commands.

In the performance of his demanding duties, the secretary requires the help of many assistants, chief of whom is the deputy secretary of defense. When considering matters requiring a long-range view, and in formulating broad defense policy, a number of advisory bodies and individual advisors also assist the secretary of defense. The most important policy advisory body working directly with the secretary of defense is the Armed Forces Policy Council.

*The Armed Forces Policy Council* advises the secretary of defense on matters of broad policy relating to the armed forces and considers and reports on any other matters that, in the opinion of the secretary, need attention. The council consists of the

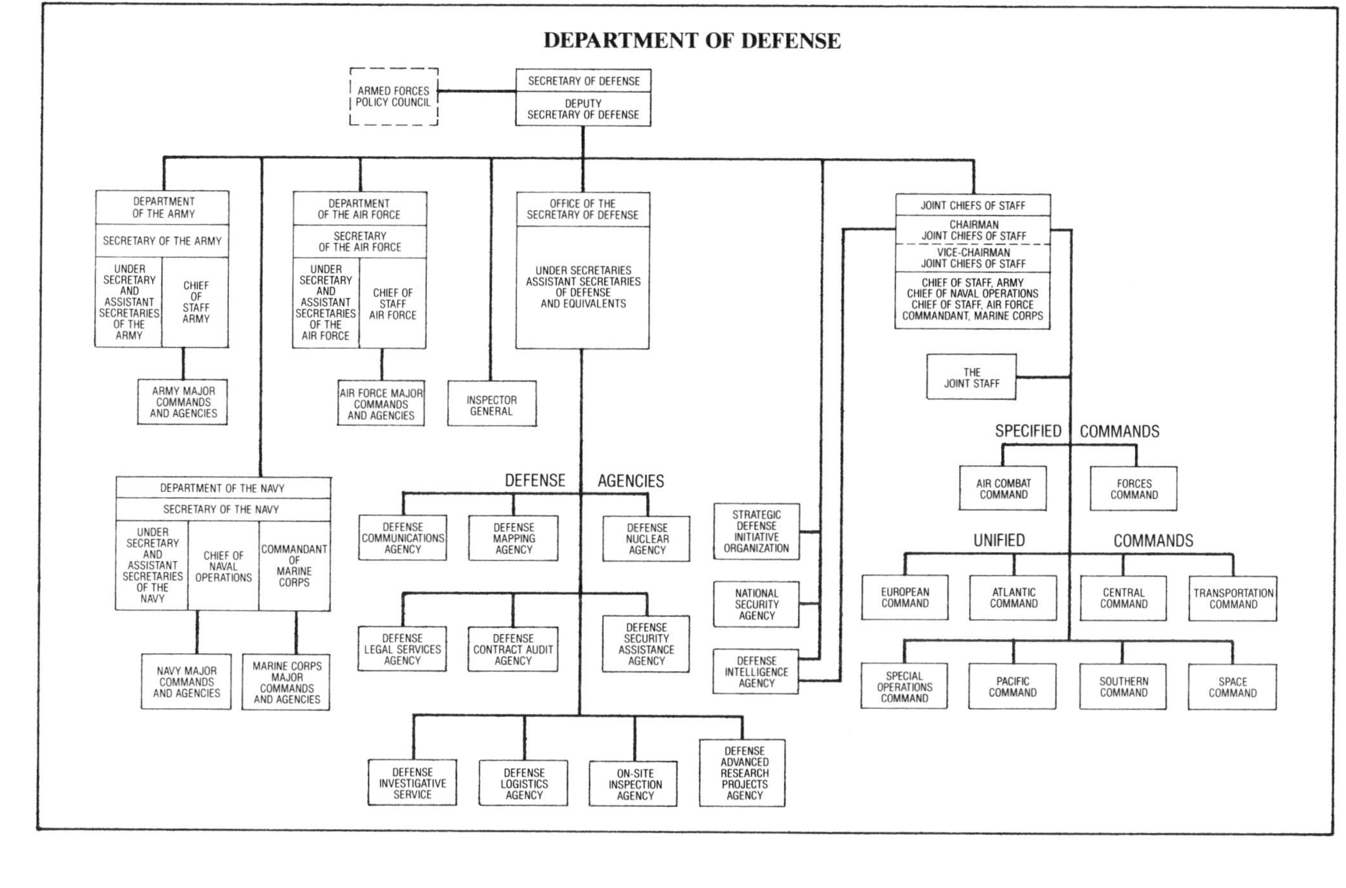
DEPARTMENT OF DEFENSE
ARMED FORCES POLICY COUNCIL
SECRETARY OF DEFENSE
DEPUTY SECRETARY OF DEFENSE
DEPARTMENT OF THE ARMY
SECRETARY OF THE ARMY
UNDER SECRETARY AND ASSISTANT SECRETARIES OF THE ARMY
CHIEF OF STAFF ARMY
ARMY MAJOR COMMANDS AND AGENCIES
DEPARTMENT OF THE AIR FORCE
SECRETARY OF THE AIR FORCE
UNDER SECRETARY AND ASSISTANT SECRETARIES OF THE AIR FORCE
CHIEF OF STAFF AIR FORCE
AIR FORCE MAJOR COMMANDS AND AGENCIES
INSPECTOR GENERAL
OFFICE OF THE SECRETARY OF DEFENSE
UNDER SECRETARIES ASSISTANT SECRETARIES OF DEFENSE AND EQUIVALENTS
JOINT CHIEFS OF STAFF
CHAIRMAN JOINT CHIEFS OF STAFF
VICE-CHAIRMAN JOINT CHIEFS OF STAFF
CHIEF OF STAFF, ARMY
CHIEF OF NAVAL OPERATIONS
CHIEF OF STAFF, AIR FORCE
COMMANDANT, MARINE CORPS
THE JOINT STAFF
SPECIFIED COMMANDS
AIR COMBAT COMMAND
FORCES COMMAND
UNIFIED COMMANDS
EUROPEAN COMMAND
ATLANTIC COMMAND
CENTRAL COMMAND
TRANSPORTATION COMMAND
SPECIAL OPERATIONS COMMAND
PACIFIC COMMAND
SOUTHERN COMMAND
SPACE COMMAND
DEPARTMENT OF THE NAVY
SECRETARY OF THE NAVY
UNDER SECRETARY AND ASSISTANT SECRETARIES OF THE NAVY
CHIEF OF NAVAL OPERATIONS
COMMANDANT OF MARINE CORPS
NAVY MAJOR COMMANDS AND AGENCIES
MARINE CORPS MAJOR COMMANDS AND AGENCIES
DEFENSE AGENCIES
DEFENSE COMMUNICATIONS AGENCY
DEFENSE MAPPING AGENCY
DEFENSE NUCLEAR AGENCY
DEFENSE LEGAL SERVICES AGENCY
DEFENSE CONTRACT AUDIT AGENCY
DEFENSE SECURITY ASSISTANCE AGENCY
DEFENSE INVESTIGATIVE SERVICE
DEFENSE LOGISTICS AGENCY
ON-SITE INSPECTION AGENCY
DEFENSE ADVANCED RESEARCH PROJECTS AGENCY
STRATEGIC DEFENSE INITIATIVE ORGANIZATION
NATIONAL SECURITY AGENCY
DEFENSE INTELLIGENCE AGENCY

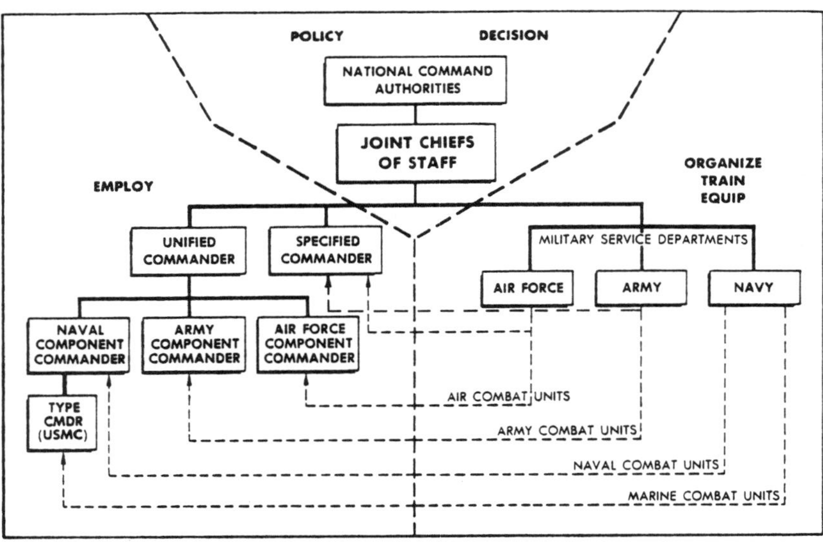


COMMAND RELATIONSHIPS.

secretary of defense (chairman); the deputy secretary of defense; the secretaries of the Army, the Navy, and the Air Force; the chairman of the Joint Chiefs of Staff; the undersecretaries of defense; the Army and Air Force chiefs of staff; the chief of naval operations; and the commandant of the Marine Corps. Officials of the DOD and other departments and agencies in the executive branch may be invited to attend appropriate meetings of the council.

**Undersecretaries of Defense.** Two undersecretaries of defense (one for policy, the other for acquisition) assist the secretary of defense. The undersecretary of defense for policy is the senior advisor to the secretary of defense on all matters concerning political-military affairs, arms limitations negotiations, and the integration of departmental plans and policies with overall national security objectives.

The undersecretary of defense for acquisition supervises the performance of the entire DOD acquisition system. This includes setting policy for acquisition matters, including contracting, research and development, atomic energy, production, construction, logistics, developmental testing, and procurement.

The secretary of defense receives staff assistance through a number of special agencies. These include the Defense Intelligence Agency, the Defense Investigative Service, and the Defense Logistics Agency. These agencies, as well as others, provide special skills, expertise, and advice to the secretary of defense.

**Joint Chiefs of Staff.** The chairman of the Joint Chiefs of Staff is the principal military advisor to the president, the National Security Council, and the secretary of defense. Subject to the authority and direction of the president and the secretary of defense, members of the JCS serve as advisors and military staff to the unified and specified commanders. The JCS prepares strategic plans and provides for the strategic direction of the armed forces. It reviews the plans and programs of unified and specified commands, reviews major personnel and logistic requirements of the armed forces, and establishes unified doctrine. The JCS is also responsible for the assignment of logistic responsibilities to the military services, for the formulation of policies for joint training, and for coordinating military education.

The members of the JCS consist of the chairman; the chief of staff, U.S. Army; the chief of naval operations; the chief of staff, U.S. Air Force; and the commandant of the Marine Corps. The chairman of the JCS serves as a member of, and presides over, the JCS and furnishes the recommendations and views of the JCS to the president, the National Security Council, or the secretary of defense. Other members of the JCS may also provide advice to these bodies, when requested. If a member disagrees with an opinion of the chairman, the chairman presents that advice with his own.

When the chairman is not present, the vice chairman of the JCS serves as chairman. The vice chairman may participate in all meetings of the JCS but may not vote on a matter before the JCS except when acting as chairman. JCS duties take precedence over all other duties; therefore, as the military heads of their respective services, JCS members delegate appropriate duties to their vice chiefs of staff, but retain responsibility.

The Joint Staff supports the JCS. The Defense Intelligence Agency provides intelligence support, over which the JCS has operational control. The Joint Staff is composed of officers in approximately equal numbers from all the services. The Joint Staff neither operates nor is organized as an overall armed forces general staff, and it has no executive authority. It performs such duties as the JCS prescribes. However, the Joint Staff is structured in such a way that it is responsible for many key agencies within the DOD. One of the agencies most vital to military success is the National Military Command System.

**National Military Command and Control.** The National Military Command System provides our command authorities with all the information they need to make decisions and the means to transmit those decisions to subordinate levels. At the peak of its communication system is the National Military Command Center (NMCC). The NMCC receives data from various command and control centers of the unified and specified commands. It also receives data from such defense agencies as the National Security Agency and the Defense Intelligence Agency. Members of the Joint Staff analyze and process this information and pass pertinent messages on through the State Department Operations Center and the National Indications Center of the Central Intelligence Agency to the Situation Room in the White House. Like the Pentagon itself, the NMCC is a soft target for intercontinental ballistic missiles. To ensure command and control survivability under all-out nuclear attack, the NMCC has Alternate NMCC.

**Unified, Specified, and Combined Commands.** The president, with the advice and assistance of the chairman of the JCS, through the secretary of defense, establishes unified and specified commands for the performance of military missions.

A *unified command* has a broad, continuing mission and is under a single commander. The unified commands are the U.S. Strategic Command, U.S. Atlantic Command, U.S. European Command, U.S. Pacific Command, U.S. Southern Command, U.S. Central Command, U.S. Space Command, U.S. Special Operations Command, and U.S. Transportation Command. Unified commands also consist of significant assigned components of two or more services and are normally organized on a geographical basis. A component consists of the component commander and those individuals, organizations, or installations under the military command that have been assigned to the unified command. Other individuals, organizations, or installations may operate directly under the component commander.

A *specified command* also has a broad continuing mission but normally consists of forces from only one service and is functionally oriented. It may include units and staff representation from other services. If the allocation of such staffs or units is to be major or of long duration, it will be established as a unified command. There are two specified commands: Air Combat Command and Air Mobility Command.

The secretary of defense assigns the military mission to unified and specified commands. The commander of a unified or specified command deploys, directs, controls and coordinates the action of the command's forces; conducts joint training exercises; and controls certain support functions. The unified or specified commander is responsible to both the secretary of defense and the president. The component commanders or the commanders of subordinate commands exercise operational command. After a force has been assigned to a unified command, it cannot be transferred except by authority of the secretary of defense or under special procedures of that office with the approval of the president. All units not assigned to a unified or specified command remain with their respective services.

Each military service furnishes administrative and logistic support for its forces assigned to a unified command. The individual services continue to issue assignment orders, logistic support orders, personnel change orders, and similar documents. DOD agencies such as the Defense Logistics Agency and the Defense Communications Agency perform certain logistic and administrative support functions. Even though the individual services furnish logistic support to their respective components of the unified command, a unified commander can exercise directive authority in order to ensure effectiveness and economy of operations.

The logistic authority of unified commands expands under wartime conditions and when critical situations make it necessary. Unified commanders have authorization to use the facilities and supplies of all forces assigned to their commands as necessary to accomplish their wartime missions. Achieving maximum effectiveness from our armed forces requires that the efforts of all the services be integrated closely. The authority of the president and the secretary of defense maintains unity of effort; the secretaries of the military departments and the JCS exercise this authority.

The capability of a unified commander can expand through the formation of either a *subordinate unified command* or a *joint task force* (JTF). Each is composed of joint forces under a single commander. The primary difference between the two lies in the scope of the operation. The subordinate unified command has a continuing mission and command arrangement. Specific time, place, and mission are the limits of a JTF.

Another structure within the DOD is the *combined command*, which consists of forces from more than one nation. The Air Force Space Command is part of one such combined command—the North American Air Defense Command, which includes Canadian forces. The U.S. European and U.S. Atlantic Commands contribute forces to NATO. Combined commands operate similarly to unified commands, except that command is much less structured in combined commands. Units from the member nations retain their national identities, and much negotiation between nations is necessary to make the command function effectively.

**The Military Departments.** Although operational command rests with the DOD, the military departments—the Army, the Navy (including the Marine Corps and, in wartime, the Coast Guard), and the Air Force—continue as separate agencies. Although service secretaries are not responsible for military operations, they assist the secretary of defense in managing the administrative, training, and logistic functions of the military departments. Except in operational matters, the secretary of defense issues orders to a service through its secretary. The service secretaries are responsible for the economy and efficiency with which their departments operate.

The traditional roles and mission of each branch of service are commonly referred to as "functions." In addition to specific combat roles, they furnish operational forces to unified and specified commands. The secretary of defense and the JCS established the functions of the armed forces in the Key West Agreement, which was revised in 1953 and again in 1958. The general functions of the armed forces are the following:

- Support and defend the Constitution of the United States against all enemies, foreign and domestic.
- Ensure, by timely and effective military action, the security of the United States, its possessions, and areas vital to its interests.
- Uphold and advance the national policies and interests of the United States.
- Safeguard the internal security of the United States.

In addition to the general functions, the military services also have some specific functions they share. These include the following:

- Preparing forces and establishing reserves of equipment and supplies for the effective prosecution of war, and planning for the expansion of peacetime components to meet the needs of war.
- Maintaining, in readiness, mobile reserve forces that are properly organized, trained, and equipped for employment in an emergency.
- Providing adequate, timely, and reliable department intelligence for use within the DOD.
- Organizing, training, and equipping interoperable forces for assignment to unified or specified commands.
- Providing, as directed, administrative and logistic support to the headquarters of unified and specified commands, including direct support of the development and acquisition of command and control systems for those headquarters.
- Preparing and submitting (to the secretary of defense) budgets for their respective departments, and justifying (before Congress) budget requests as approved by the secretary of defense.
- Administering the funds made available for maintaining, equipping, and training the forces of their respective departments, including those assigned to unified and specified commands.
- Conducting research; developing tactics, techniques, and organization; and developing and procuring weapons, equipment, and supplies.
- Developing, supplying, equipping, and maintaining bases and other installations, including lines of communication. Providing administrative and logistical support for all forces and bases.
- Providing, as directed, such forces, military missions, and detachments for service in foreign countries as may be required to support the national interests of the United States.
- Assisting in training and equipping the military forces of foreign nations.
- Assisting each other in accomplishing their respective functions, including the provision of personnel, intelligence, training, facilities, equipment, supplies, and services.
- Preparing and submitting, in accordance with other military departments, mobilization information to the JCS.

Each service develops and trains its forces to perform the primary functions that support the efforts of the other services. Carrying out their primary functions helps to accomplish overall military objectives. The assignment of collateral functions may not be used as the basis for additional force requirements.

## THE DEPARTMENT OF THE AIR FORCE

The Air Force is responsible for preparation of air forces necessary for the effective prosecution of war and military operations short of war, except as otherwise assigned. In accordance with integrated joint mobilization plans, the Air Force is also responsible for expansion of its peacetime components to meet the needs of war. The *primary functions* of the Air Force include the following:

- To organize, train, equip, and provide forces for the conduct of prompt and sustained combat operations in the air—specifically, forces to defend the United States against air attack in accordance with doctrines established by the JCS; to gain and maintain general air supremacy; to defeat enemy air forces; to conduct space operations; to control vital air areas; and to establish local air superiority except as otherwise assigned herein.
- To organize, train, equip, and provide forces for appropriate air and missile defense and space control operations, including the provision of forces as required for strategic defense of the United States, in accordance with joint doctrines.
- To organize, train, equip, and provide forces for strategic air and missile warfare.
- To organize, train, equip, and provide forces for joint amphibious, space, and airborne operations, in coordination with other military services, in accordance with joint doctrines.
- To organize, train, equip, and provide forces or close air and air logistic support to the Army and other forces as directed, including airlift, air support, resupply of airborne operations, aerial photography, tactical air reconnaissance, and air interdiction of enemy land forces and communications.
- To organize, train, equip, and provide forces for air transport for the armed forces, except as otherwise assigned.
- To develop, in coordination with the other services, doctrines, procedures, and equipment for air defense from land areas, including the United States.
- To organize, train, equip, and provide forces to furnish aerial imagery for use by the Army and other agencies as directed, including aerial imagery for cartographic purposes.
- To develop, in coordination with the other services, tactics, techniques, and equipment of interest to the Air Force, and not provided for elsewhere, for amphibious operations.
- To develop, in coordination with the other services, doctrines, procedures, and equipment employed by USAF forces in airborne operations.
- To provide launch and space support for the DOD, except as otherwise assigned.
- To develop, in coordination with the other services, doctrines, procedures, and equipment employed by USAF forces in the conduct of space operations.
- To organize, train, equip, and provide land-based tanker forces for in-flight refueling support of strategic operations and deployments of aircraft of armed forces and Air Force tactical operations, except as otherwise assigned.
- To organize, train, equip, and provide forces, as directed, to operate air lines of communications.
- To organize, train, equip, and provide forces for the support and conduct of special operations.

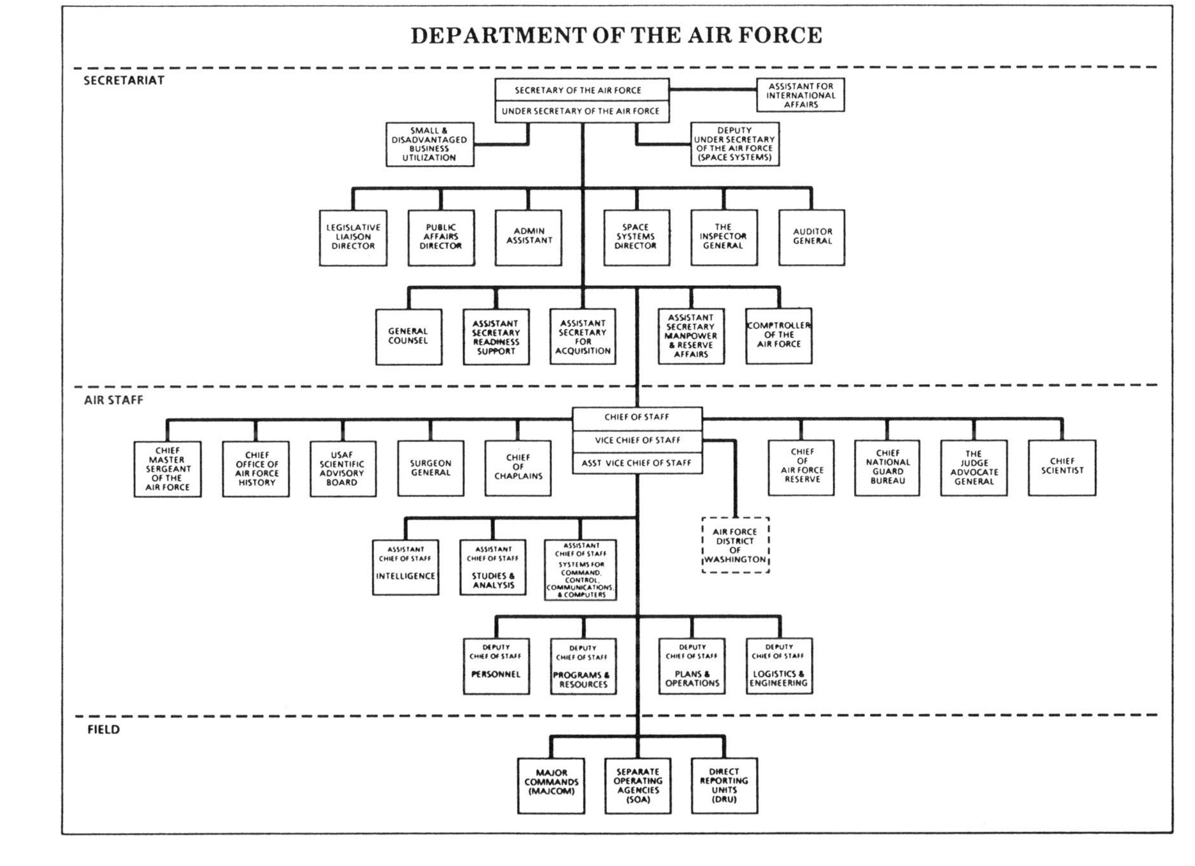

DEPARTMENT OF THE AIR FORCE
SECRETARIAT
SECRETARY OF THE AIR FORCE
UNDER SECRETARY OF THE AIR FORCE
ASSISTANT FOR INTERNATIONAL AFFAIRS
SMALL & DISADVANTAGED BUSINESS UTILIZATION
DEPUTY UNDER SECRETARY OF THE AIR FORCE (SPACE SYSTEMS)
LEGISLATIVE LIAISON DIRECTOR
PUBLIC AFFAIRS DIRECTOR
ADMIN ASSISTANT
SPACE SYSTEMS DIRECTOR
THE INSPECTOR GENERAL
AUDITOR GENERAL
GENERAL COUNSEL
ASSISTANT SECRETARY READINESS SUPPORT
ASSISTANT SECRETARY FOR ACQUISITION
ASSISTANT SECRETARY MANPOWER & RESERVE AFFAIRS
COMPTROLLER OF THE AIR FORCE
AIR STAFF
CHIEF OF STAFF
VICE CHIEF OF STAFF
ASST VICE CHIEF OF STAFF
CHIEF MASTER SERGEANT OF THE AIR FORCE
CHIEF OFFICE OF AIR FORCE HISTORY
USAF SCIENTIFIC ADVISORY BOARD
SURGEON GENERAL
CHIEF OF CHAPLAINS
CHIEF OF AIR FORCE RESERVE
CHIEF NATIONAL GUARD BUREAU
THE JUDGE ADVOCATE GENERAL
CHIEF SCIENTIST
AIR FORCE DISTRICT OF WASHINGTON
ASSISTANT CHIEF OF STAFF INTELLIGENCE
ASSISTANT CHIEF OF STAFF STUDIES & ANALYSIS
ASSISTANT CHIEF OF STAFF SYSTEMS FOR COMMAND, CONTROL, COMMUNICATIONS, & COMPUTERS
DEPUTY CHIEF OF STAFF PERSONNEL
DEPUTY CHIEF OF STAFF PROGRAMS & RESOURCES
DEPUTY CHIEF OF STAFF PLANS & OPERATIONS
DEPUTY CHIEF OF STAFF LOGISTICS & ENGINEERING
FIELD
MAJOR COMMANDS (MAJCOM)
SEPARATE OPERATING AGENCIES (SOA)
DIRECT REPORTING UNITS (DRU)

• To organize, train, equip, and provide forces for the support and conduct of psychological operations.

• To provide equipment, forces, procedures, and doctrine necessary for the effective prosecution of electronic warfare operations and, as directed, support of other forces.

*Collateral functions* of the Air Force include conducting the following:

• Surface sea surveillance and antisurface ship warfare through air operations.

• Antisubmarine and antiair warfare operations to protect sea lines of communications.

• Aerial minelaying operations.

• Air-to-air refueling in support of naval campaigns.

Air Force responsibilities *in support of space operations* include the following:

• Organizing, training, equipping, and providing forces to support space operations.

• Developing, in coordination with the other military services, tactics, techniques, and equipment employed by USAF forces for use in space operations.

• Conducting individual and unit training of Air Force space operations forces.

• Participating with the other services in joint space operations, training, and exercises as mutually agreed to by the services concerned, or as directed by competent authority.

*Other responsibilities* of the Air Force include the following:

• With respect to amphibious operations, the Air Force will develop, in coordination with the other services, tactics, techniques, and equipment of interest to the Air Force and not provided for by the Navy and the Marine Corps.

• With respect to airborne operations, the Air Force has specific responsibility to provide USAF forces for air movement of troops, supplies, and equipment in joint airborne operations, including parachute and aircraft landings; and to develop tactics and techniques employed by USAF forces in the air movement of troops, supplies, and equipment.

• With respect to close air support of ground forces, the Air Force has specific responsibility for developing, in coordination with the other services, doctrines and procedures, except as provided for in Navy responsibilities for amphibious operations and in responsibilities for the Marine Corps.

## COMMON SERVICE FUNCTIONS

The Army, Navy, Air Force, and Marine Corps, under their respective secretaries, are responsible for the following functions:

• Determining service force requirements and making recommendations concerning those requirements to support national security objectives and strategy and meet operational requirements of unified and specified combatant commands.

• Planning for use of the intrinsic capabilities of the other services' resources that may be made available.

• Recommending to the JCS the assignment and deployment of forces to unified and specified combatant commands established by the president through the secretary of defense.

• Administering service forces.

• Providing logistic support for service forces, including procurement, distribution, supply, equipment, and maintenance, unless otherwise directed by the secretary of defense.

• Developing doctrines, procedures, tactics, and techniques employed by service forces.

• Conducting operational testing and evaluation.

• Providing for training for joint operations and exercises in support of unified and specified combatant command operational requirements, including the following:

— Development of service training, doctrines, procedures, tactics, techniques, and methods of organization in accordance with policies and procedures established in service publications.

— Development and preparation of service publications to support the conduct of joint training.

— Determination of service requirements to enhance the effectiveness of joint training.

— Support of joint training directed by commanders of the unified and specified combatant commands and conduct of such additional joint training as is mutually agreed upon by the services concerned.

— Operating organic land vehicles, aircraft, and ships or craft.

— Consulting and coordinating with the other services on all matters of joint concern.

— Participating with the other services in the development of the doctrines, procedures, tactics, techniques, training, publications, and equipment for joint operations that are the primary responsibility of one of the services.

The forces developed and trained to perform the primary functions hereafter will be employed to support and supplement other military service forces in carrying out their primary functions, wherever and whenever such participation results in increased effectiveness and contributes to the accomplishment of overall military objectives. As for collateral functions, while the assignment of such functions may establish further justification for stated force requirements, such assignment will not be used as the sole basis for establishing additional force requirements.

The Department of the Air Force is made up of the Office of the Secretary of the Air Force, Air Staff, and USAF field units.

The U.S. Air Force is organized on a functional basis in the U.S. (or, "Z.I."—Zone of the Interior) and on a geographic basis overseas by major commands (MAJCOMs), as well as a number of field operating agencies (FOAs) and direct reporting units (DRUs). As of 1994 there are eight MAJCOMs, 38 FOAs, and three DRUs.

## MAJOR COMMANDS

**Air Combat Command (ACC).** Headquarters: Langley AFB, Virginia. ACC is the USAF's principal offensive war machine. It operates all USAF bombers and CONUS-based fighter and attack aircraft; organizes, trains, equips, and maintains combat-ready forces for joint operations; and provides nuclear forces to the joint U.S. Strategic Command. It has 253,831 total personnel (active duty, Air Reserve forces, and civilian) and 1,223 aircraft of all types in 34 wings and two bomb groups in four numbered Air Forces—the 1st, 8th, 9th, and 12th—on 32 CONUS and two oversea bases.

**Air Education and Training Command (AETC).** Headquarters: Randolph AFB, Texas. It recruits, trains, and educates USAF enlisted and officer personnel, providing basic military training, initial and advanced technical training, and officer and flying training. AETC also provides military graduate and professional continuing education. It has 64,598 total personnel, plus 398,816 students a year. It has 1,444 aircraft in nine flying wings, seven specialized units, and five technical training units under the 2d and 19th Air Forces, plus the Air University, all located mainly on 19 CONUS bases.

**Air Force Materiel Command (AFMC).** Headquarters: Wright-Patterson AFB, Ohio. It manages the research, development, test, acquisition, and sustainment of weapon systems; produces and acquires advanced systems; and operates major product, test, logistics, specialized centers, laboratories, and schools at 17 locations. It has 124,337 total personnel.

**Air Force Space Command (AFSPC).** Headquarters: Peterson AFB, Colorado. It operates and tests USAF ICBM force for joint U.S. Strategic Command, ground-based missile warning radars, sensors and satellites, national space-launch facilities, and worldwide space surveillance radars and optical systems, and provides command and control for DOD satellites and ballistic missile warning to NORAD and joint U.S. Space Command. It has 41,168 personnel, 550 ICBMs, and 41 satellite systems, organized into two numbered air forces—the 14th and the 20th—ten wings, and three groups. AFSPC has more than 50 units worldwide.

**Air Force Special Operations Command (AFSOC).** Headquarters: Hurlburt Field, Florida. It is the air component of the U.S. Special Operations Command, a unified command. As such, it deploys specialized airpower, delivering special operations combat power anywhere, anytime. It provides unconventional warfare, direct action, special reconnaissance, counterterrorism, and foreign internal defense support to the unified commands. It has 11,554 total personnel and 138 specialized aircraft (such as the AC-130, MC-130, MH-53, and MH-60) in one CONUS wing and two overseas groups. AFSOC also operates a school and a test center.

**Air Mobility Command (AMC).** Headquarters: Scott AFB, Illinois. It provides rapid global airlift and air refueling for U.S. armed forces, is the USAF component of the U.S. Transportation Command, and in wartime provides forces to theater commands. It has 118,718 total personnel and flies 914 aircraft in 14 wings stationed on 14 bases in two numbered air forces, the 15th and the 21st.

**Pacific Air Forces (PACAF).** Headquarters: Hickam AFB, Hawaii. It plans, conducts, and coordinates offensive and defensive air operations in the Pacific and Asian theaters and organizes, trains, equips, and maintains resources to conduct air operations. Its 47,110 total personnel keep 331 aircraft flying in 10 wings on 9 overseas bases. There are four numbered air forces, the 5th, 7th, 11th, and 13th.

**U.S. Air Forces in Europe (USAFE).** Headquarters: Ramstein AB, Germany. It plans, conducts, coordinates, and supports air and space operations to achieve U.S. national and NATO objectives. To do so it supports U.S. military plans and operations in Europe, the Mediterranean, the Middle East, and Africa. It has 39,189 personnel and 220 aircraft, organized into 12 wings and 5 groups operating at 17 installations in 7 Allied countries. There are 3 numbered air forces: 3d, 16th, and 17th.

## SUBCOMMANDS AND LOWER LEVELS OF COMMAND

Below the MAJCOMs are the following levels of command, in descending order: numbered air force, air division, wing, group, squadron, and flight.

**Numbered Air Force (NAF).** Normally an operations-oriented agency, an NAF controls two or more air divisions or units of comparable strength. Its wings may be assigned to air divisions or directly under the NAF headquarters. NAFs are organized primarily on a geographic basis, but can also be functionally oriented (that is, perform a specific mission). There is no specific staff organization for an NAF. The NAF headquarters consists of the commander, a functional staff, and directorates.

**Wing.** An *operational wing* normally has two or more operational squadrons. When an operational wing has the primary mission on a base, it is usually responsible for maintaining and operating the base and has a combat support or air base group assigned for this purpose. As a host wing, an operational wing becomes the lowest level capable of sustained and completely independent operation; it contains all the elements needed for performing a mission. It is self-supporting in the functional areas of materiel, maintenance, supply, and munitions necessary to conduct operations. When an operational wing is a tenant, it has the same operational capacity, but must depend on a host command for logistic support.

An *air base*, or *combat support*, wing has a support, rather than an operational, mission. It is responsible for maintaining and operating a base and for supporting operational units. A specialized mission wing does not usually have aircraft or missiles assigned to it and is involved in a specialized area such as intelligence or weather. This kind of wing may be either a host or tenant on a base. Wing headquarters commands and controls its units, supervises training, and when host, directs the operation of the air base on which it is located.

**Group.** The group is a flexible unit composed of two or more squadrons whose functions may be operational, support, or administrative in nature. A group may control squadrons having identical, similar, or different missions, but all are directed toward the common mission of the wing. A group is designated by number and, whenever possible, takes the number of the wing to which it is assigned. There are three types of groups:

The *operational* group exercises control over two or more squadrons, at least one having an operational mission. It is used at a small base where no other support for the squadrons with an operational mission is available. To provide this support, the group has one or more support squadrons. An operational group is not usually subordinate to an operational wing.

The *combat support,* or *air base,* group's primary mission is to operate and maintain a base and to provide base support and services to the organizations located on the base. These groups have functional squadrons where required for proper discipline and control. Combat support groups operate bases that support tactical or strategic units. Air base groups operate bases that support other types of organizations.

The *support* group exists in a support command. Its primary mission is directly related to the command mission. It may or may not have the additional responsibility of operating a base.

**Squadron.** A squadron is the basic unit in the Air Force. It is used to designate the mission units in operational commands. It is also used as the unit for functional entities such as civil engineering, security police, and transportation. In addition, important segments of large functional entities such as organizational maintenance are normally squadrons. Regardless of the functional area that uses it, a squadron has a vital mission.

**Flight.** There are two types of flights. The Air Force uses numerically designated flights primarily where there is a need for small mission elements to be incorporated into an organized unit. This is the lowest unit level in the Air Force. Alphabetically designated flights are components of squadrons and consist of several elements with identical missions. These flights are not units and are equivalent to branches. Flights A, B, C, and D of a security police squadron would be one example.

## FIELD OPERATING AGENCIES

Field Operating Agencies (FOAs) are Air Force subdivisions that carry out field activities under operational control of Headquarters USAF staff agencies, providing specialized services as their names indicate. There are 38 of them.

**Air Force Audit Agency.** Headquarters: Washington, D.C. Provides internal audit evaluations for all levels of Air Force management.

**Air Force Base Conversion Agency.** Headquarters: Arlington, Virginia. Provides management for Air Force bases in CONUS as they are closed by congressional acts.

**Air Force Center for Environmental Excellence.** Headquarters: Brooks AFB, Texas. Provides USAF commanders with environmental remediation and facilities design.

**Air Force Civil Engineer Support Agency.** Headquarters: Tyndall, AFB, Florida. Provides technical and professional engineering support to the Air Force.

**Air Force Civilian Personnel Management Center.** Headquarters: Randolph AFB, Texas. Manages, operates, and supports USAF civilian personnel programs and systems.

**Air Force Combat Operations Staff.** Headquarters: Washington, D.C. Supports the USAF chief of staff and deputy chief of staff for plans and operations in the Air Force Operations Support Center 24 hours a day.

**Air Force Command, Control, Communications, and Computer Agency.** Headquarters: Scott AFB, Illinois. Develops and validates $C^4$ architectures, technical standards, requirements, policies, procedures, and solutions.

**Air Force Cost Analysis Agency.** Headquarters: Arlington, Virginia. Conducts Component Cost Analyses (CCAs) for major weapon system acquisition programs and automated information systems.

**Air Force Doctrine Center.** Headquarters: Langley AFB, Virginia. Develops and publishes basic and operational doctrine for the USAF.

**Air Force Flight Standards Agency.** Headquarters: Andrews AFB, Maryland. Sets standards for global integrated flight operations in peace and war to advance safe flight operations.

**Air Force Frequency Management Agency.** Headquarters: Arlington, Virginia. Develops USAF policy and procedures for radio frequency spectrum management.

**Air Force Historical Research Agency.** Headquarters: Maxwell AFB, Alabama. Serves as the repository for all Air Force historical documents, maintaining the largest collection of documents on U.S. military aviation in the world.

**Air Force Inspection Agency.** Headquarters: Kirtland AFB, New Mexico. Provides Air Force leaders with assessments of readiness, discipline, and management effectiveness.

**Air Force Legal Services Agency.** Headquarters: Bolling AFB, D.C. Provides civil and military legal services to the USAF and its personnel.

**Air Force Logistics Management Agency.** Headquarters: Maxwell AFB Gunter Annex, Alabama. Develops new or improved concepts to enhance logistics effectiveness.

**Air Force Management Engineering Agency.** Headquarters: Randolph AFB, Texas. Works with air staff and MAJCOMs to achieve improvement through process reengineering.

**Air Force Medical Operations Agency.** Headquarters: Bolling AFB, D.C. Directs programs for the Air Force Medical Service.

**Air Force Military Personnel Center.** Headquarters: Randolph AFB, Texas. Executes USAF personnel programs and policies.

**Air Force News Agency.** Headquarters: Kelly AFB, Texas. Gathers, packages, and disseminates electronic and printed news and information.

**Air Force Office of Special Investigations.** Headquarters: Bolling AFB, D.C. Provides criminal investigative and counterintelligence information and services to commanders.

**Air Force Personnel Operations Agency.** Headquarters: Washington, D.C. Executes personnel programs in the D.C. area.

**Air Force Program Executive Office.** Headquarters: Washington, D.C. Manages and accounts for USAF acquisition programs.

**Air Force Real Estate Agency.** Headquarters: Bolling AFB, D.C. Acquires, manages, and disposes of property worldwide.

**Air Force Reserve.** Headquarters: Washington, D.C. Supports the active-duty force.

**Air Force Review Boards Agency.** Headquarters: Washington, D.C. Manages various military and civilian appellate processes for the Secretary of the Air Force.

**Air Force Safety Agency.** Headquarters: Kirtland AFB, New Mexico. Executes USAF safety and nuclear surety policies, plans, and programs.

**Air Force Security Police Agency.** Headquarters: Kirtland AFB, New Mexico. Provides expertise for security of nuclear weapons and weapons systems, information security, law enforcement, air base defense, and antiterrorism.

**Air Force Services Agency.** Headquarters: Randolph AFB, Texas. Assists the chief of staff on morale, welfare, recreation, and services activities.

**Air Force Studies and Analyses Agency.** Headquarters: Washington, D.C. Provides analyses, simulation, and modelling tools to assess force-structure options and acquisition decisions for the secretariat and air staff.

**Air Force Technical Applications Center.** Headquarters: Patrick AFB, Florida. Monitors compliance with nuclear treaties.

**Air Intelligence Agency.** Headquarters: Kelly AFB, Texas. Provides direct intelligence, security, electronic combat, foreign technology, and treaty-monitoring support to national decisionmakers and field air component commanders.

**Air National Guard.** Headquarters: Washington, D.C. Provides air defense of CONUS, and under federal jurisdiction enforces federal authority, suppresses insurrections, and serves in the national defense.

**Air Reserve Personnel Center.** Headquarters: Denver, Colorado. Provides personnel services and administrative support to members of the Air Reserve Forces.

**Air Weather Service.** Headquarters: Scott AFB, Illinois. Provides central weather, climatological, and space support to the Air Force and Army.

**Center for Air Force History.** Headquarters: Washington, D.C. Researches, writes, and publishes books and other studies on Air Force history.

**Joint Services Survival, Evasion, Resistance, and Escape Agency.** Headquarters: Fort Belvoir, Virginia. Serves as secretary of defense executive agent for DOD Code of Combat/SERE-related training and DOD POW/MIA programs.

**7th Communications Group.** Headquarters: Washington, D.C. Provides communications and computer support to the Pentagon.

## DIRECT REPORTING UNITS

Direct Reporting Units (DRUs) are directly subordinate to Headquarters, USAF.

**Air Force District of Washington.** Headquarters: Bolling AFB, D.C. Supports USAF units in the capital area. It is "housekeeper" for Headquarters, USAF.

**Air Force Operations Test and Evaluations Center.** Headquarters: Kirtland AFB, New Mexico. Conducts operational testing and evaluation of new or modified weapon systems or components.

**USAF Academy.** Headquarters: Colorado Springs, Colorado. Educates potential Air Force officers.

# 24

# The Air Reserve Forces

*The reservist is twice the citizen.*

—Sir Winston Churchill

The Air Reserve forces are the *Air National Guard* and the *Air Force Reserve.* All our reserve forces are placed in one of three categories: Ready Reserve, Standby Reserve, and Retired Reserve. This reserve force is close to 450,000 men and women and uses an annual budget of well over $4 billion (AFR 45 series).

## THE READY RESERVE

Ready Reserve means that portion of our reserve forces that can be ordered to active duty under conditions short of a congressional declaration of war or national emergency. The total Ready Reserve, including the Guard, is just over 265,000 people. The *Air National Guard* is a Ready Reserve force composed entirely of units organized and trained to be used as units, 118,000 strong. The Ready Reserve portion of the *Air Force Reserve* includes not only this type of unit but also individual reservists assigned to specific mobilization positions with regular Air Force organizations and other individuals earmarked as attrition replacements. There are 146,000 total in the Ready Reserve (81,000 paid and 65,000 unpaid), many of whom were sent to the Persian Gulf in 1990 and 1991. Some have since served in Somalia and Bosnia.

## THE STANDBY RESERVE

In addition to the Ready Reserve, there is within the Air Force Reserve a Standby Reserve that can be ordered to active duty *only* when Congress declares war, or national emergency, as some were for the Gulf

War. This totals about 17,000 people. Some of these Standby Reservists would not be available because of critical needs of the government or the civilian community as a whole.

Although a number of Standby Reservists participate in correspondence courses or train with Ready Reserve units, the majority of them would need refresher training in order to function effectively in their Air Force specialties.

## WHY AIR RESERVE FORCES?

First, the question of why we have reserve units. One reason is that the Constitution and the Congress say that we will. But another very good reason is that reserve units provide an economical way to maintain a surge expansion capability for the Air Force during peacetime.

The reserves—even the Standby and Retired Reserves—provide the Air Force a strong base of grass roots community support. They are an effective influence in favor of Air Force recruiting as well. By talking about the Air Force, the reservists help to interest young people in Air Force careers.

The primary reason for reserves is wartime support. Until a few years ago, the Air Force, like the other U.S. military services, traditionally had relied on its reserve components to supply the extra manpower and capability needed for wartime expansion.

Under current concepts for their use, the "Ready Now" reserves are very much a part of our deterrent strength. Their readiness and usefulness are vital to the Air Force mission and, therefore, to the security of the nation. When the Air Force says its reserves are "Ready Now," it means that they can fight today. They can be and have been called up in hours. Call the roll: the Korean War, the 1961 Berlin Crisis, the 1962 Cuban Missile Crisis, the Vietnam War, Grenada, Panama, and the Persian Gulf War, just to name the big ones.

The use of reserve forces to help keep the peace is sometimes thought to be a new concept. But it really isn't. The idea of the citizen-soldier was born as a "ready now" concept. As far back as 1607, the citizens of the Virginia Colony formed a local militia called the "Train Band." As rapidly as their populations could support them, the train bands were formed in other nearby colonial settlements. The members of these organizations were not professional soldiers. They were farmers, weavers, silversmiths, and merchants. Their military obligation was a 24-hour-a-day affair, and there was hardly a period from 1622 until after the American Revolution when some of the members of the "train band" were not serving as soldiers on a full-time basis. There was no active establishment; the citizen-soldiers were the sole defense of their community.

Our country and economy grew, however, as our population grew, and a standing military force became a necessity if only to prevent constant disruption of the more and more complex national structure. With the oceans as effective barriers to sudden attack, our citizen-soldiers had time on their side and could become, in fact, reserves—to be called upon only when the size and strength of the regular establishment had to be increased for war.

This, then, became the pattern for our military forces: an active-duty establishment strong enough to fend off the first attack, and a reserve that could be mobilized and trained to expand the regular force to war-winning size.

But military weapons and concepts of war are constantly changing. Today, our Air National Guard and Air Force Reserve are much more than just a wartime mobilization force. They are, truly, an integral and vital part of our total aerospace power in being.

## COMPOSITION OF AIR RESERVE FORCES

To give you an idea of how large a part they play in the Air Force plan, we have 152 flying squadrons—93 in the Air National Guard and 59 in the Air Force Reserve flying 2,196 aircraft (1,653 Guard and 543 Reserve).

Additionally, we have a wide variety of nonflying units—communications, medical, aerial port squadrons, and many other types. Altogether there are some 195,872 Air Guardsmen and reservists in the ready-to-go flying and nonflying organizations. All have specific tasks to perform in the war and contingency plans of the major commands. Each major command of the Regular Air Force gets a sizable augmentation force from the reserve.

Air Combat Command, for example, has a reserve force consisting of 49 fighter units and 26 airlift units.

Air Mobility Command gets 12 airlift, 18 airlift associate, and 22 air refueling units.

Special Operations Command has two units.

Pacific Air Forces have one fighter unit, one airlift unit, and one tanker unit.

Reserve medical units of various kinds are also distributed among the commands.

Air Force missions and responsibilities are so broad in scope and of such variety that they can be accomplished only by a completely responsive, instantly reacting, and highly flexible force. They can be accomplished only through the full use of all resources available to the total Air Force, reserve as well as regular.

## AIR RESERVE FORCES TRAINING

Realistic training for wartime readiness is now par for the course for reserve units and personnel. Airlift units carry high-priority cargo while training their personnel in airlift skills. Fighter and reconnaissance units take the place of regular units in support of joint Army-Air Force exercises and maneuvers. Air Defense units fly air alert intercept missions under active Air Force control.

Management has been improved to give Air Force combat commands responsibility for supervising and training and operational inspection of those reserve units that would be assigned to them in wartime. Standards of performance are identical for regular and reserve units. Each aircrew, regardless of component, is required to meet the same rigid requirements as regular Air Force crews before it can be designated combat ready.

The operations room of a good reserve outfit is almost indistinguishable from that of a good regular outfit—except perhaps on weekdays. Our reserve combat crews receive the normal 48 inactive duty training periods and 15 days of active duty each year plus 36 additional flying training periods. Even this is not enough for all flying requirements, and reserve personnel engage in training whenever they can get time off from their jobs—because these part-time airmen have to meet exactly the same training requirements that the full-time Air Force crews must meet. And meet them they do. They pass their operational readiness inspections exactly like active force units. Some of the reserve units pass with exceptionally high scores and beat out the regulars!

How is this possible with a part-time operation? A great deal of the reserve success is due to the stability of personnel. It takes a while longer to train reservists, but the reserves do not have the problem of annual turnover that plagues regular units.

Another asset, and an extremely important one, is the technician program. The air technicians of the Guard and the Air Reserve technicians of the reserve have a dual status: They are full-time employees in a civilian capacity, as well as being reservists who train with the units on weekends and during annual active duty. In other words, they wear two hats. They make up about 14 percent of the total reserve personnel strength, and provide a permanent, hard-core base of skill and experience, not only for the day-to-day maintenance and operating functions but also for training younger personnel. This valuable resource of experience is augmented by a handful of active Air Force advisors who assist in training and assure standardization with the requirements of the gaining commands of the Regular Air Force.

## COLD WAR USES OF AIR RESERVE FORCES

The rather revolutionary Air Force concepts for reserve forces first proved their validity in the fall of 1961. During the Berlin crisis, the president ordered to active duty 36 Air National Guard and Air Force Reserve flying squadrons and an Air National Guard tactical control group—a total of some 27,000 reservists. Very soon after they reported to active duty, 10 fighter squadrons, a reconnaissance squadron, and a complete radar tactical control group were on duty in Europe.

Hardly had the units recalled for Berlin returned to their homes when a new trouble spot appeared. On 22 October 1962, President Kennedy alerted the world on the existence of a Soviet buildup of offensive missiles in Cuba. Late on the night of 27 October, 24 Air Force Reserve troop carrier squadrons and supporting units were ordered to active duty, 400 aircraft and some 15,000 personnel in all.

This recall was the swiftest reserve mobilization since the American Revolution and the battles of Lexington and Concord. Ninety-three percent of the men in these units reported for duty the next morning. Their aircraft were operationally ready, and they could have flown a combat mission that day. Secretary of Defense McNamara called it "a fantastic performance." "This," he said, "is the standard of performance that has been built into the Air Force's Reserve and Guard programs."

But the story of our part in the Cuban crisis was more than the story of the mobilized units. Many units and thousands of individuals who were not ordered to active duty practically came on duty anyway—voluntarily. Air National Guard fighter squadrons that might have been needed were at a peak of readiness. Air Force Reserve recovery units at civilian airfields and unused airstrips supported aircraft dispersal operations of SAC, TAC, and ADC on a purely voluntary basis. The commander of the Strategic Air Command expressed personal thanks to the reservists for the support they gave SAC forces.

Air National Guard C-97 squadrons and Air Force Reserve C-124 squadrons fitted their overwater training flights into the worldwide system of Military Airlift Command, flying essential cargo and filling gaps left by active forces concentration on direct support of Cuban crisis actions.

Even before the mobilization for Cuba, Air Force Reserve troop carrier units had airlifted close to a million pounds of essential defense materiel to Florida to support the buildup.

Twice in little more than a year, the Air Reserve forces proved their effectiveness as a part of our nation's deterrent strength. Twice, their quick response helped to prevent open hostilities. Twice, they demonstrated the validity of the Air Force's "total force" policy of using "Ready Now" reserves.

In 1965, reservists responded within hours to the emergency airlift requirement dubbed "Power Pack" to evacuate U.S. citizens and foreign nationals from the Dominican Republic.

By the end of June, reservists had flown 1,747 missions, carried 5,115 passengers, and airlifted more than 4,000 tons of cargo, logging almost 16,000 flying hours.

In the summer of 1966, the ANG was flying 200 cargo trips a month in support of the Military Airlift Command—half of them in direct support of Southeast Asia operations. Eighteen thousand Guardsmen were involved.

Air Reserve forces contributed heavily to our fighting posture in the Vietnam War. All units were brought to top readiness. Additionally, reserve forces transport aircraft were used on training missions to supplement regular airlift to Vietnam.

In 1973, the AFR flew 300 missions in support of Israel during the Israeli-Egyptian war. Air Reserve forces saw active service in the Grenada and Panama operations, then on a larger scale in the Persian Gulf War, and more recently in Latin America, Bosnia, Russia, Kenya, and Somalia.

## OTHER CONTRIBUTIONS OF THE AIR RESERVE FORCES

There is also a day-to-day payoff that comes from our reserve forces. The in-being capability of today's citizen-airmen pays real dividends in productive effort for the Air Force in peacetime as well as in crisis. The reservists are a valuable asset to their gaining commands. In recent years, the reserve forces provided more than half of all the Air Force support for Army airborne training and air-dropped more than 100,000 paratroopers.

The reserve airlift squadrons need oversea training flights to develop proper standards of operational readiness. The extra airlift of cargo they provide is clear profit for the nation. To give an idea of the size of this profit during one year, 16 Air National Guard airlift squadrons airlifted more than 12 million pounds of MAC cargo overseas. In fact, in this and other programs, the Air Reserve forces provided nearly half of the total Air Force requirement for strategic airlift crews in recent years, and 60 percent of the tactical airlift.

Another contribution of the reserves is to air defense. Each of the ten Air National Guard fighter-interceptor units keeps two aircraft and four aircrews on runway alert around the clock. In Hawaii, the Air National Guard fighter squadron and two radar squadrons are the principal air defense of the island state.

Some nonpay reservists are assigned to flights in which they all have the same profession. These units also help the Air Force in its day-by-day mission. Judge advocate general area representatives receive training credit for performing legal work at Air Force installations too small to have their own JAG section. Research and development flights provide special project assistance that would require costly consultant services otherwise.

These are only a few of the peacetime benefits that come as a by-product of Reserve training. This kind of realistic training helps to maintain the high degree of responsiveness and quick reaction capability that added so effectively to our strength in Berlin, in Cuba, in Southeast Asia, and in the Persian Gulf War.

## BASIC FUNCTION OF THE AIR RESERVE FORCES

As General LeMay, then Air Force chief of staff, stated during the Berlin crisis, "It is pretty obvious that the regular establishment forces can't do all the job—today or in the future. I see a continuing need for Ready Reserve forces that can pitch in and help the active units."

In peacetime, the Air National Guard is commanded by the governors of the various states; it is supported by the Air Force through the National Guard Bureau, under Air Force policies and regulations. It is trained under the supervision of the gaining commands, who also have the inspection responsibility. Thirty states also have state guards as backup to their National Guard units.

The Air Force Reserve is a direct reporting unit of the Air Force and has the same gaining command relationship as the Guard.

Both components are governed by Air Force policies, regulations, and training directives, and both are responsive to training standards and performance requirements prescribed by the gaining command.

The Air Force program for reserve forces is unique. It puts into practice the concept of reliance on a "ready now" augmentation force. As General LeMay told the Congress in 1964: *"The Air Force thinks of the Air National Guard and the Air Force Reserve in the same manner as it does of its regular units. As nearly as possible, we expect the same rapid response from them. They are subjected to identical readiness tests. We need a 'Ready Now' combat capability in the Air Reserve forces because we depend on them to augment the active force in times of crisis."*

## CIVIL AIR PATROL (AFR 46-4)

Although the Civil Air Patrol (CAP) is not a part of the military service, it has been an auxiliary of the U.S. Air Force since 1948 and deserves mention here. CAP was formed in December 1941 under the Office of Civilian Defense to enlist and train civilian volunteers to aid in the national defense, as was the case with the Ground Observer Corps (GOC). In May 1943, CAP was transferred to the War Department for the rest of World War II. CAP civilian volunteers in light aircraft flew numerous support and emergency missions during the war. In 1946 Congress established it as a nonprofit civilian corporation to encourage American citizens to help develop aviation, to provide aviation education and training to senior and cadet members, and to assist in meeting local and national emergencies.

To do so, CAP conducts a national program of aerospace education, runs a comprehensive cadet program (AFR 46-3), carries on a comprehensive senior training program, maintains an emergency service capability, assists governmental agencies in emergency operations, conducts a flight management program, maintains nationwide communications service, and aids in Air Force recruiting. It also flies half of the U.S. Customs Service passive surveillance missions. Members are either cadets aged 13 to 18 or senior members over 18. They wear Air Force uniforms and have a grade structure similar to the Air Force's, but wear distinctive CAP insignia.

CAP National Headquarters is at Maxwell AFB, Alabama, supported by CAP-USAF, an active duty cadre. There are 52 wings—for each state, the District of Columbia, and the Commonwealth of Puerto Rico. Wings may be subdivided into groups, squadrons, and flights. CAP is governed by a national board headed by a civilian national commander; the executive director is a senior active-duty Air Force officer. CAP has 43,000 senior members, 30,000 cadet members, flies 8,500 (including 570 corporate) aircraft, and operates 32,000 radios. For further information, write to Director of Public Affairs, Headquarters CAP, Maxwell AFB, AL 36112.

# Appendix A

# USAF Bases

*Air power is a thunderbolt launched from an egg-shell invisibly tethered to a base.*
—Herman Nickerson, Arms and Policy, 1945

## MAJOR INSTALLATIONS

**Altus AFB,** Okla. 73523-5000; within Altus city limits. Phone (405) 482-8100; DSN 866-1110. AETC base. 97th Air Mobility Wing; 457th Operations Gp. (AMC). Base activated Jan. 1943; inactivated May 1945; reactivated Jan. 1953. Area 4,095 acres, plus 818 leased. Runway 13,440 ft. Altitude 1,376 ft. Military 3,326; civilians 739; approx. 300 TDY students (officer and enlisted) in training per month. Payroll $138 million. Housing: 148 officer, 652 NCO, 296 VAQ, 160 VOQ, 14 TLF. 15-bed hospital.

**Andersen AFB,** Guam, APO AP 96542-5000; 2 mi. N of Yigo. DSN 366-1110. PACAF base. Hq. 13th Air Force. Host unit: 633d Air Base Wing. No aircraft assigned. Tenant unit: 605th Military Airlift Support Sqdn.; 44th Aerial Port Sqdn. (AFRES); 254th Air Base Gp. (ANG); Det. 5, 750th Space Gp.; Det. 602, Air Force Office of Special Investigations (AFOSI). Navy VRC-50 Fleet Logistics Support Sqdn., C-130, S-3, C-2 operations. Andersen serves as a logistic support and staging base for aircraft operating in the Pacific and Indian Oceans. Base activated late 1944; named for Gen. James Roy Andersen, lost at sea between Kwajalein and Hawaii Feb. 26, 1946. General Andersen was the Chief of Staff, Hq. Army Air Forces, Pacific Ocean Areas. Area: 20,504 acres. Runways (north) 10,555 ft. and (south) 11,182 ft. Altitude 612 ft. Military 2,521; civilians 650. Payroll $102 million. Housing: 249 officer, 1,508 enlisted. Unaccompanied housing: 30 officer, 1,056 enlisted. Transient housing: 110 VOQ, 54 VAQ, 18 TLF. One USAF clinic and one Navy hospital on island.

**Andrews AFB,** Md. 20331-5000; 11 mi. SE of Washington, D.C. Phone (301) 981-1110; DSN 858-1110. AMC base. Home of Air Force One and

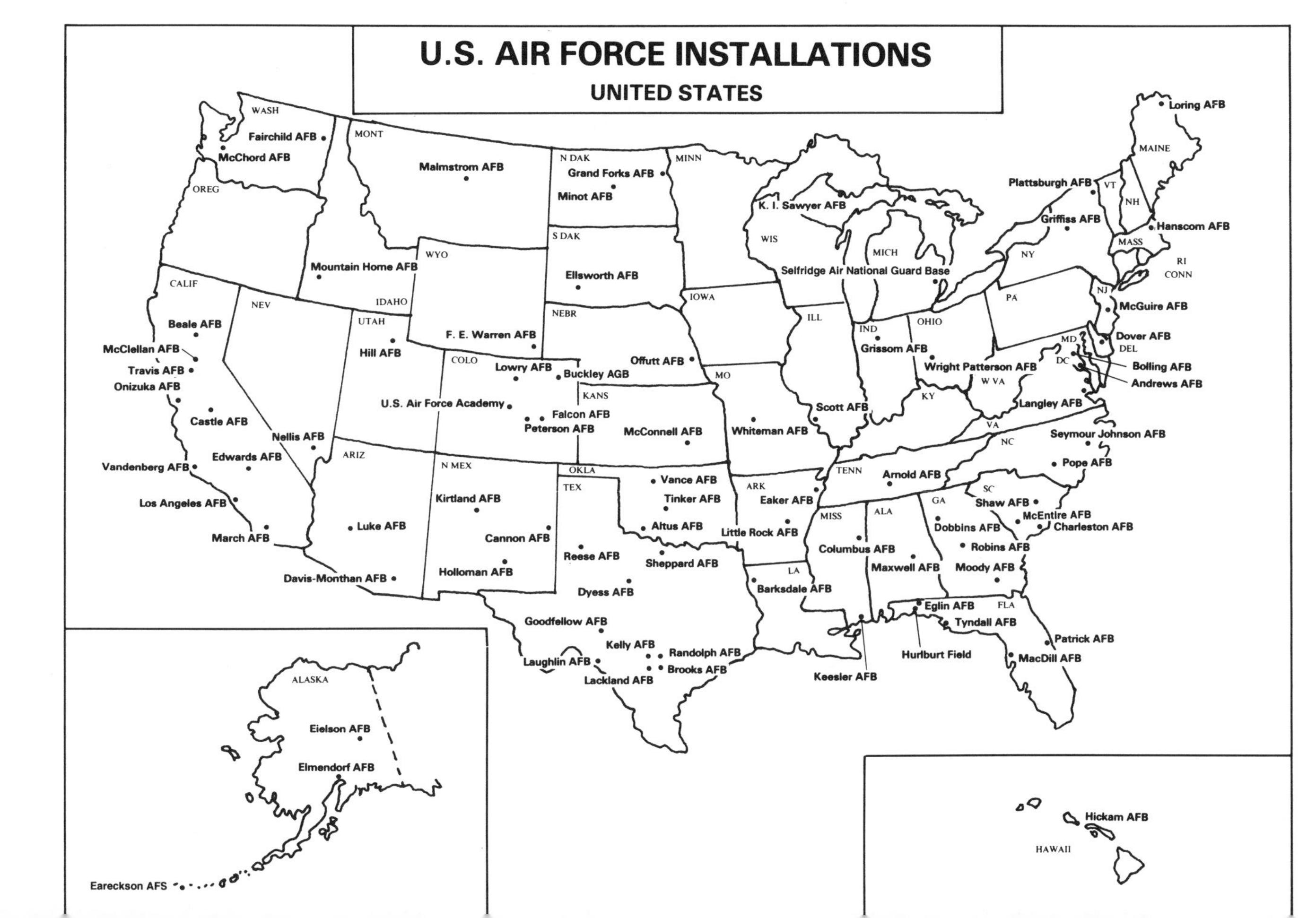
U.S. AIR FORCE INSTALLATIONS
UNITED STATES
WASH
Fairchild AFB
McChord AFB
OREG
MONT
Malmstrom AFB
N DAK
Grand Forks AFB
Minot AFB
MINN
S DAK
Ellsworth AFB
WYO
Mountain Home AFB
IDAHO
CALIF
NEV
UTAH
Hill AFB
F. E. Warren AFB
NEBR
Offutt AFB
IOWA
WIS
K. I. Sawyer AFB
MICH
Selfridge Air National Guard Base
ILL
IND
OHIO
Grissom AFB
Wright Patterson AFB
Beale AFB
McClellan AFB
Travis AFB
Onizuka AFB
Castle AFB
Nellis AFB
Edwards AFB
Vandenberg AFB
Los Angeles AFB
March AFB
COLO
Lowry AFB
Buckley AGB
U.S. Air Force Academy
Falcon AFB
Peterson AFB
KANS
McConnell AFB
MO
Whiteman AFB
Scott AFB
KY
W VA
ARIZ
Luke AFB
Davis-Monthan AFB
N MEX
Kirtland AFB
Cannon AFB
Holloman AFB
OKLA
Vance AFB
Tinker AFB
Altus AFB
TEX
Reese AFB
Sheppard AFB
Dyess AFB
Goodfellow AFB
Kelly AFB
Randolph AFB
Brooks AFB
Laughlin AFB
Lackland AFB
ARK
Eaker AFB
Little Rock AFB
LA
Barksdale AFB
MISS
Columbus AFB
Keesler AFB
TENN
Arnold AFB
ALA
Maxwell AFB
GA
Dobbins AFB
Robins AFB
Moody AFB
FLA
Eglin AFB
Tyndall AFB
Hurlburt Field
Patrick AFB
MacDill AFB
SC
Shaw AFB
McEntire AFB
Charleston AFB
NC
Seymour Johnson AFB
Pope AFB
VA
Langley AFB
MD
DC
Bolling AFB
Andrews AFB
DEL
Dover AFB
NJ
McGuire AFB
PA
NY
Plattsburgh AFB
Griffiss AFB
VT
NH
MAINE
Loring AFB
MASS
Hanscom AFB
RI
CONN
ALASKA
Eielson AFB
Elmendorf AFB
Eareckson AFS
HAWAII
Hickam AFB

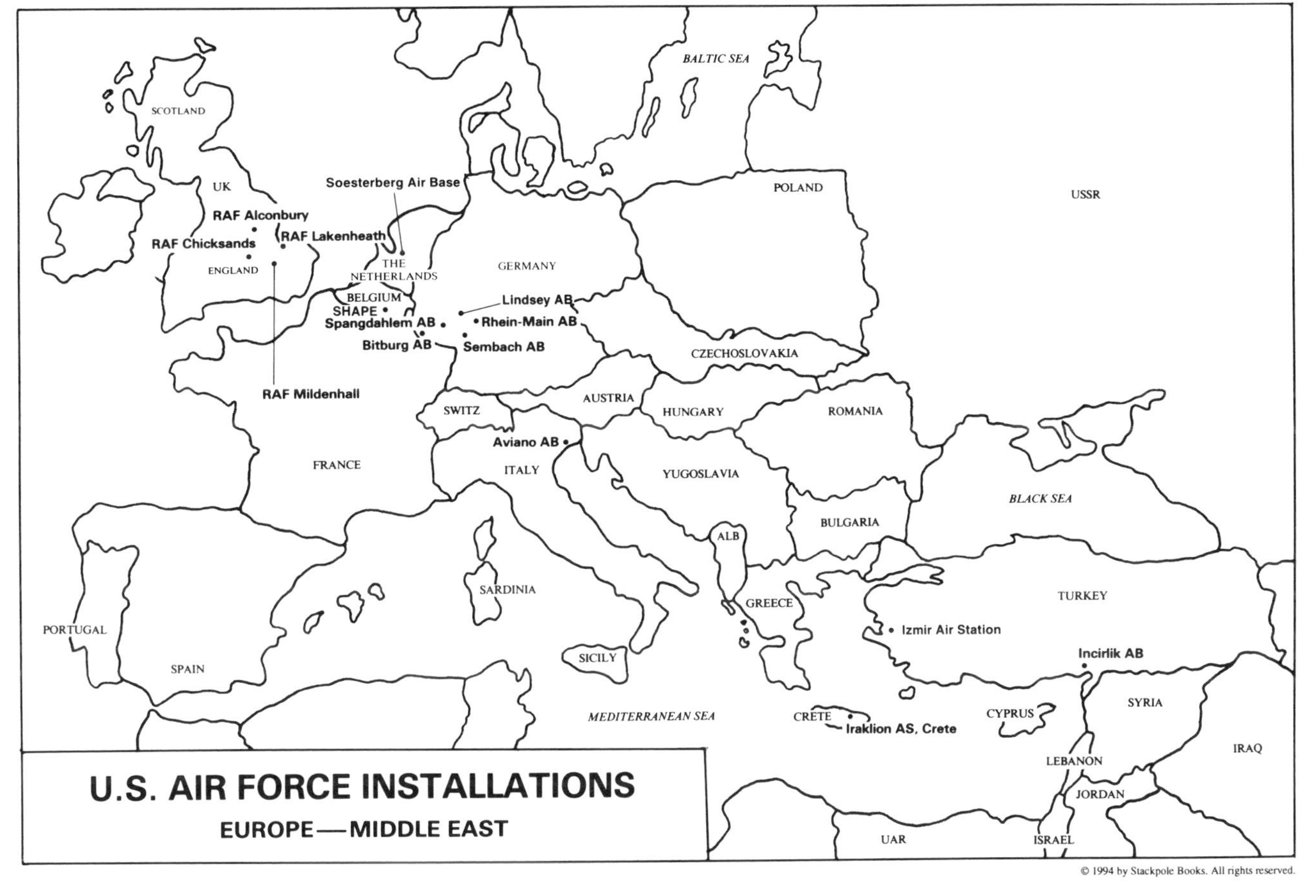

U.S. AIR FORCE INSTALLATIONS
EUROPE—MIDDLE EAST
SCOTLAND
UK
RAF Alconbury
RAF Chicksands
RAF Lakenheath
ENGLAND
RAF Mildenhall
Soesterberg Air Base
THE NETHERLANDS
BELGIUM
SHAPE
Spangdahlem AB
Bitburg AB
Lindsey AB
Rhein-Main AB
Sembach AB
GERMANY
BALTIC SEA
POLAND
USSR
CZECHOSLOVAKIA
AUSTRIA
SWITZ
HUNGARY
ROMANIA
Aviano AB
FRANCE
ITALY
YUGOSLAVIA
BLACK SEA
BULGARIA
ALB
PORTUGAL
SPAIN
SARDINIA
GREECE
TURKEY
Izmir Air Station
Incirlik AB
SICILY
MEDITERRANEAN SEA
CRETE
Iraklion AS, Crete
CYPRUS
SYRIA
IRAQ
LEBANON
JORDAN
UAR
ISRAEL

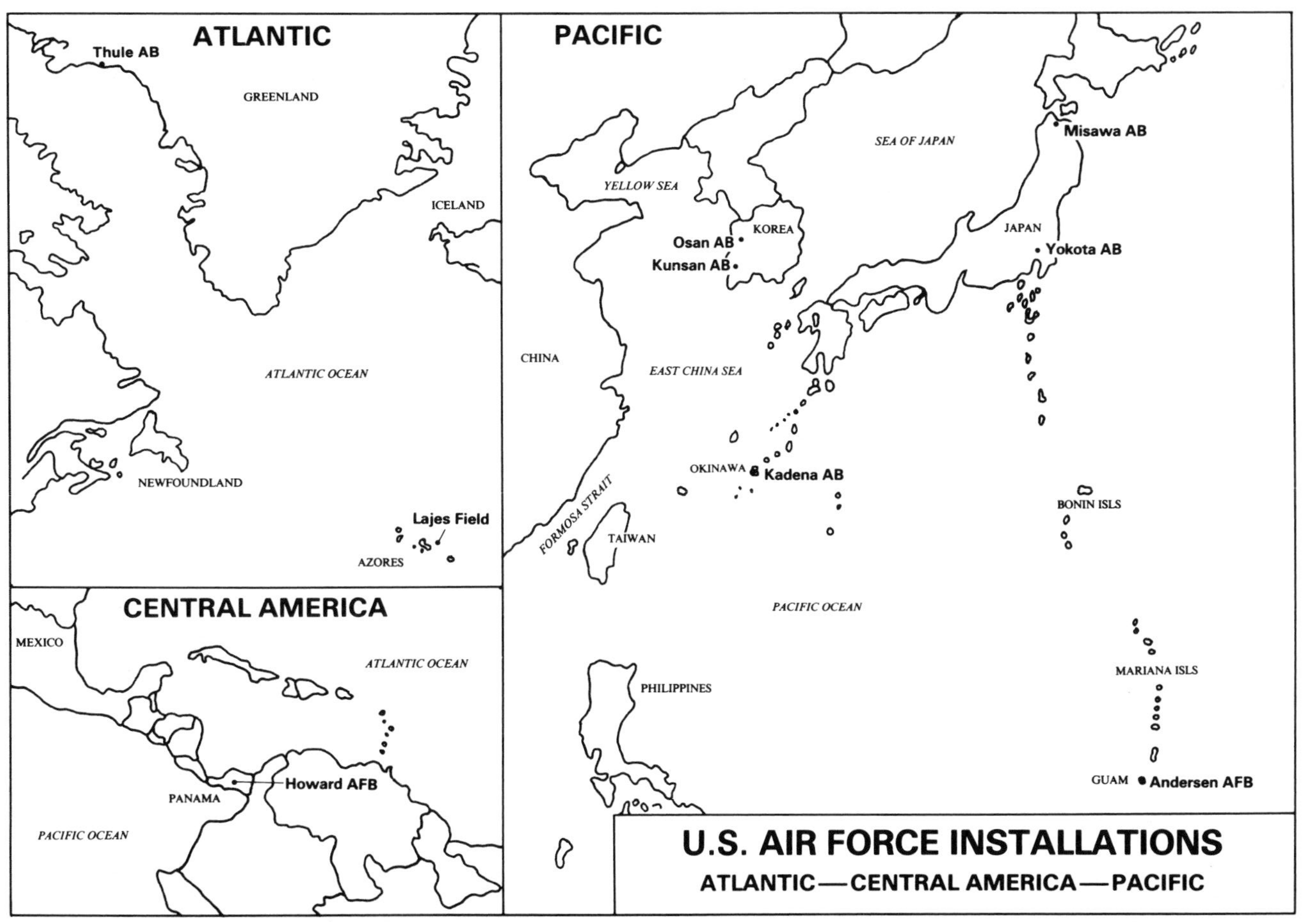


# U.S. AIR FORCE INSTALLATIONS

## ATLANTIC—CENTRAL AMERICA—PACIFIC

gateway to the nation's capital. Host wing is 89th Airlift Wing. Responsible for presidential support and base operations. It supports all branches of service, several major commands, and federal agencies. The wing also hosts Det. 302, AFOSI; Air Force District of Washington Contracting Office; Air National Guard Readiness Center (ANGRC); 113th Fighter Wing (D.C. ANG); 459th Airlift Wing (AFRES); Det. 9, Combat Camera (1st CTCS); Naval Air Facility; Marine Aircraft Gp. 49, Det. A. Base activated May 1943; named for Lt. Gen. Frank M. Andrews, military air pioneer and WW II commander of the European theater, killed in aircraft accident May 3, 1943, in Iceland. Area 7,550 acres (incl. easements). Runways 9,300 ft. and 9,755 ft. Altitude 281 ft. Military 10,009; civilians 3,201. Payroll $402.8 million. Housing: 377 officer, 1,755 NCO, 177 trailer spaces, 974 UEQ, 326 transient (incl. 69 temporary living quarters for incoming personnel, 21 DV suites, 180 VOQ, 56 VAQ). 235-bed hospital.

**Arnold AFB,** Tenn. 37389; approx. 7 mi. SE of Manchester. Phone (615) 454-3000; DSN 340-5011. AFMC base. Site of Arnold Engineering Development Center, the world's largest complex of wind tunnels, jet and rocket engine test cells, space simulation chambers, and hyperballistic ranges. AEDC supports the acquisition of new aerospace systems by conducting research, development, and evaluation testing for DoD, other government agencies, and commercial aerospace firms. Base dedicated June 25, 1951; named for Gen. H. H. "Hap" Arnold, wartime Chief of the AAF. Area 40,118 acres. Runway 6,000 ft. Altitude 1,100 ft. Military 118; civilians 288; contract employees 3,252. Payroll $183.6 million. Housing: 23 officer, 17 NCO, 45 transient. Medical aid station.

**Aviano AB,** Italy, APO AE 09601; adjacent to Aviano, 50 mi. N of Venice. Phone (commercial, from CONUS) 011-39-434-667111; DSN 632-1110. USAFE base. 31st Fighter Wing (formerly 401st FW) supports USAFE and NATO. The unit began flying F-16C/D aircraft in Apr. 1994. In event of war in Europe, the unit will exercise command and control of a variety of deployed weapon systems. It also provides administrative and logistical support to 50 off-base units at 31 locations throughout Italy. Aviano is the only USAF tactical air base in Italy. Originally an Italian flying school, which opened in 1939; the Air Force began operation in 1954. Area 1,140 acres. Runway 8,596 ft. Altitude 413 ft. Military 2,592; civilians 730. Payroll $79 million. 175 govt.-leased housing units. 490 billeting spaces (including contracted spaces), 496 dorm bed spaces. Clinic.

**Barksdale AFB,** La. 71110-5000; in Bossier City. Phone (318) 456-2252; DSN 781-1110. ACC base. Hq. 8th Air Force; 2d Bomb Wing, B-52H and T-37 operations; 458th Operations Gp. (AMC), KC-10 operations; 1st Electronic Combat Range Gp.; Det. 1,307th Civil Engineering Sqdn. RED HORSE; 49th Test Sqdn.; 98th Air Refueling Gp. (AFRES), KC-135 and KC-10 operations; 917th Wing (AFRES), B-52 and A-10 operations. 8th Air Force Museum. Base activated Feb. 2, 1933; named for Lt. Eugene H. Barksdale, WW I airman killed in Aug. 1926 crash near Wright Field, Ohio. Area 22,000 acres (18,000 acres reserved for recreation). Runway 11,756 ft. Altitude 166 ft. Military 7,428; civilians 1,193. Payroll $169 million. Housing: 105 officer, 324 NCO, 154 transient, 1,488 UEQ, 24 TLF, 72 VOQ, 58 VAQ. 40-bed hospital.

**Beale AFB,** Calif. 95903-5000; 13 mi. E of Marysville. Phone (916) 634-3000; DSN 368-1110. ACC base. 9th Reconnaissance Wing; 7th Space Warning Sqdn. (AFSPC). Aircraft include U-2 reconnaissance aircraft, KC-135 Stratotankers, and T-38 Talon trainers. Originally US Army's Camp Beale. Became Air Force installation Apr. 1948; became AFB in Nov. 1951; named for Brig. Gen. E.F. Beale, Indian agent in California prior to Civil War. Area 22,944 acres. Runway 12,000 ft. Altitude 113 ft. Military 3,452; civilians 762. Payroll $95.7 million. Housing: 206 officer, 1,503 enlisted, 18 transient. 25-bed hospital.

**Bitburg AB,** Germany, APO AE 09132-5000; 15 mi. N of Trier. Phone (commercial, from CONUS) 011-49-6561-61-1110; DSN 453-1110. USAFE base. 36th Fighter Wing with two fighter squadrons flying F-15C/D Eagles. Base activated 1952. Area 1,735 acres. Runway 8,221 ft. Altitude 1,228 ft. Military 3,400; civilians 1,125. Payroll $25 million. Housing: 75 officer, 1,128 NCO, 32 VOQ, 190 VAQ, 70 TLF. 20-bed hospital. Base was scheduled to be partially returned to the host government in Sept. 1994.

**Bolling AFB,** D.C. 20332-5000; 3 mi. S of US Capitol. Phone (202) 545-6700; DSN 227-0101. Air Force District of Washington. 1100th Air Base Gp.; 1100th Medical Sqdn.; 1100th National Capital Region Support Gp. (Pentagon); US Air Force Honor Guard; US Air Force Band; Air Force Office of Scientific Research (AFMC); Air Force Chief of Chaplains; Air Force Surgeon General; Center for Air Force History; Hq. Air Force Office of Special Investigations; Defense Intelligence Agency. Activated Oct. 1917; named for Col. Raynal C. Bolling, first high-ranking Air Service officer killed in WW I. Area 604 acres. No runway. Military 1,355; civilians 925. Payroll $50 million. (Personnel and payroll apply to AFDW only.) Housing: 285 officer, 1,100 NCO, 220 transient. Clinic.

**Brooks AFB,** Tex. 78235; in SE San Antonio. Phone (210) 536-1110; DSN 240-1110. AFMC base. Human Systems Center; USAF School of Aerospace Medicine (AFMC); Armstrong Laboratory, Human Systems Program Office; 648th Air Base Gp. Associate units include 615th School Sqdn. (Systems Acquisition School); Air Force Medical Support Agency; 68th Intelligence Sqdn.; Air Force Center for Environmental Excellence; Medical Systems Implementation and Training Element. Base activated Dec. 8, 1917; named for Cadet Sidney J. Brooks, Jr., killed Nov. 13, 1917, on his commissioning flight. Area 1,310 acres. Runway length NA. Altitude 600 ft. Military 1,833; civilians 1,532. Payroll $100 million. Housing: 70 officer, 100 NCO. Clinic.

**Cannon AFB,** N.M. 88103-5000; 7 mi. W of Clovis. Phone (505) 784-3311; DSN 681-1110. ACC base. 27th Fighter Wing, only USAF base with EF-111A/F-111E/F fighter operations. Base activated Aug. 1942; named for Gen. John K. Cannon, WW II commander of all Allied air forces in the Mediterranean theater and former commander, Tactical Air Command. Area 25,663 acres. Runways 10,400 ft. and 8,000 ft. Altitude 4,295 ft. Military 5,200; civilians 920. Payroll $131.5 million. Housing: 143 officer, 1,217 enlisted, 90 transient (20 VAQ, 20 VOQ, 6 DV, 44 TLF). 20-bed hospital.

**Castle AFB,** Calif. 95342-5000; 7 mi. NW of Merced. Phone (209) 726-2011; DSN 347-1110. ACC base. 93d Bomb Wing; 398th Operations Gp. (AETC), conducts training of all ACC B-52 and AMC KC-135 aircrews; Castle Air Museum. Base activated Sept. 1941; named for Brig. Gen. Frederick W. Castle, WW II B-17 pilot and Medal of Honor recipient. Area 3,200 acres. Runway 13,300 ft. Altitude 186 ft. Military 3,824; civilians 1,114. Payroll $125 million. Housing: 98 officer, 895 enlisted, 392 transient (incl. 60 VAQ, 272 VOQ, 12 family quarters, 24 DVQ). 9-bed hospital. Base scheduled to close Sept. 30, 1995.

**Charleston AFB,** S.C. 29404-5000; in North Charleston, 10 mi. from downtown Charleston. Phone (803) 566-6000; DSN 673-2100. AMC base. Joint-use airfield. 437th Airlift Wing; 315th AW (AFRES Assoc.); Det. 1,177th Fighter Gp. (ANG); Det. 17, Site Activation Task Force; Field Training Det. 317; Det. 719, AFOSI; 1st Combat Camera

Sqdn. Base activated Oct. 1942; inactivated March 1946; reactivated Aug. 1953. Area 6,235 acres (incl. auxiliary airfield). Runway length NA. Altitude 45 ft. Military 7,846 (incl. AFRES); civilians 1,701. Payroll $170 million. Housing: 127 officer, 850 NCO, 1,636 dormitory spaces, 75 trailer spaces, 535 transient (7 DV suites, 128 VOQ, 400 VAQ). Medical clinic.

**Columbus AFB,** Miss. 39701-1000; 10 mi. NW of Columbus. Phone (601) 434-7322; DSN 742-1110. AETC base. 14th Flying Training Wing, undergraduate pilot training and introduction to fighter fundamentals. Base activated 1941 for pilot training. Area 6,025 acres. Runways 6,300 ft., 8,000 ft., and 12,000 ft. Altitude 214 ft. Military 1,415; civilians 1,362. Payroll $82 million. Housing: 302 officer, 436 NCO, 67 transient. 7-bed hospital.

**Davis-Monthan AFB,** Ariz. 85707-5000; within Tucson city limits. Phone (602) 750-3900; DSN 361-1110. ACC base. 355th Wing; Hq. 12th Air Force; A-10 combat crew training; OA-10 and FAC training and operations; 41st and 43d Electronic Combat Sqdns., EC-130H electronic operations; 71st Special Operations Sqdn. (AFRES), MH-60G Pave Hawk helicopter operations; Det. 1, 120th Fighter Gp. (Mont. ANG), F-16 air defense operations. Also site of AFMC's Aerospace Maintenance and Regeneration Center, storage location for excess DoD aerospace vehicles. Base activated 1927; named for two local early aviators: 1st Lt. Samuel H. Davis, killed Dec. 28, 1921, and 2d Lt. Oscar Monthan, killed Mar. 27, 1924. Area 11,000 acres. Runway 13,645 ft. Altitude 2,620 ft. Military 5,155; civilians 1,369. Payroll $174.1 million. Housing: 133 officer, 1,106 enlisted, 518 transient (334 VAQ, 168 VOQ, 16 TLF). 35-bed hospital.

**Dover AFB,** Del. 19902-7219; 3 mi. SE of Dover. Phone (302) 677-3000; DSN 445-3000. AMC base. 436th Airlift Wing; 512th AW (AFRES Assoc.). Dover operates the largest aerial port facility on the East Coast. Base activated Dec. 1941; inactivated 1946; reactivated Feb. 1951. Area 3,908 acres. Runway 12,900 ft. Altitude 28 ft. Military 7,115; civilians 1,302. Payroll $140 million. Housing: 108 officer, 1,448 enlisted, 686 transient (512 VAQ, 160 VOQ, 14 TLF). 20-bed hospital.

**Dyess AFB,** Tex. 79607-1960; WSW border of Abilene. Phone (915) 696-0212; DSN 461-1110. ACC base. 7th Wing, two B-1B squadrons (one operational, one training); one KC-135 squadron attached to 43d ARW at Malmstrom AFB, Mont.; two C-130 squadrons; five T-38s. First base to activate an operational B-1B wing. Conducts all B-1 combat crew training for the Air Force. First B-1B arrived June 1985; wing met initial operational capability Oct. 1986. Base activated Apr. 1942; deactivated Dec. 1945; reactivated as Abilene AFB Sept. 1955. In Dec. 1956, renamed for Lt. Col. William E. Dyess, WW II fighter pilot who escaped from a Japanese prison camp, killed in P-38 crash at Burbank, Calif., Dec. 1943. Area 6,405 acres. Runway 13,500 ft. Altitude 1,789 ft. Military 5,013; civilians 693. Payroll $181 million. Housing: 142 officer, 848 enlisted, 131 VAQ/VOQ, 40 TLF. 20-bed hospital.

**Edwards AFB,** Calif. 93524; 20 mi. E of Rosamond. Phone (805) 277-1110; DSN 527-1110. AFMC base. Site of Air Force Flight Test Center (AFFTC), which conducts developmental and follow-on testing and evaluation of manned and unmanned aircraft and related avionics flight-control and weapon systems. AFFTC also operates the USAF Test Pilot School, which trains test pilots, flight-test engineers, and flight-test navigators. Also site of Phillips Laboratory's Astronautics Directorate, US Army Aviation Engineering Flight Activity, NASA's Ames Dryden Flight Research Facility, Jet Propulsion Laboratory's test facility, and secondary landing site for space shuttle missions. Base activities began in Sept. 1933. Originally Muroc Army Air Field; renamed for Capt. Glen W. Edwards, killed June 5, 1948, in crash of a YB-49 "Flying Wing." Area 301,000 acres. Twenty-one runways from 4,000 to 39,000 ft. Altitude 2,302 ft. Military 4,667 (incl. associate units); government and contract civilians 10,490. Payroll $260 million (incl. associate units and contractors). Housing: 629 officer (incl. BOQ), 2,384 enlisted (incl. 765 dormitory spaces and 191 BNCOQ), 161 transient (49 VAQ, 42 VOQ, 9 SNOQ, 10 VIP/VOQ, 51 TLF), 188 trailer spaces. 15-bed hospital.

**Eglin AFB,** Fla. 32542; 2 mi. SW of the twin cities of Niceville and Valparaiso; 7 mi. NE of Fort Walton Beach. Phone (904) 882-1110; DSN 872-1110. AFMC base. Eglin is the nation's largest air force base in terms of land area, covering an area roughly two-thirds the size of Rhode Island. Host unit: Air Force Development Test Center. Associate units: Aeronautical Systems Center, Eglin, and Armament Directorate of Wright Laboratory (AFMC); 33d Fighter Wing; Air Warfare Center; Hq. 646th Communications-Computer Systems Gp.; 919th Special Operations Wing (AFRES); 20th Space Surveillance Sqdn.; 55th Special Operations Sqdn.; 9th Special Operations Sqdn.; 655th Special Operations Maintenance Sqdn.; 728th Tactical Control Sqdn.; US Army Ranger Training Battalion; a US Navy Explosive Ordnance Disposal School; Air Force Armament Museum. Base activated 1935; named for Lt. Col. Frederick I. Eglin, WW I flyer killed in aircraft accident Jan. 1, 1937. Area 463,452 acres. Runways 10,000 ft. and 12,000 ft. Altitude 85 ft. Military 8,429; civilians 4,199 (excl. Hurlburt Field). Payroll $452.4 million (excl. Hurlburt Field). Housing: 263 officer, 2,071 enlisted, 1,200 unaccompanied enlisted units (dorm rooms), 226 trailer spaces (officer and enlisted), 88 family transient. 105-bed USAF regional hospital. AFMC clinic at Hurlburt Field.

**Eielson AFB,** Alaska 99702-5000; 26 mi. SE of Fairbanks. Phone (907) 377-1178; DSN (317) 377-1110. PACAF base. Host unit: 354th Fighter Wing, F-16C/D fighter operations and OA-10 forward air control operations. Cope Thunder exercises assigned in 1992 increased the base population by 126 permanent party military and civilians and 2,000 temporary duty members. Arctic Survival School (AETC); 168th Air Refueling Gp. (ANG). Base activated Oct. 1944; named for Carl Ben Eielson, Arctic aviation pioneer who died Nov. 1929. Area 23,500 acres. Runway length NA. Altitude 534 ft. Military 3,500; civilians 1,384. Payroll $135.1 million. Housing: 140 officer, 1,227 enlisted. Unaccompanied housing: 2 officer, 767 enlisted, 118 VOQ, 152 VAQ. Clinic.

**Ellsworth AFB,** S.D. 57706-5000; 12 mi. ENE of Rapid City. Phone (605) 385-1000; DSN 675-1000. ACC base. Host unit: 28th Bomb Wing, two B-1B squadrons. Associate units: 44th Missile Wing, inactivated July 4, 1994, following removal of all 150 Minuteman II ICBMs. 99th Wing, Air Force's focal point for strategic tactics development and bomber crew training. AMC's 28th Air Refueling Sqdn., KC-135R, being reassigned in mid-1994. South Dakota Air and Space Museum. Base activated in July 1942 as Rapid City Army Air Base; renamed June 13, 1953, for Brig. Gen. Richard E. Ellsworth, killed Mar. 18, 1953, in crash of RB-36 in Newfoundland, Canada. Area 10,632 acres. Runway 13,497 ft. Altitude 3,286 ft. Military 5,200; civilians 580. Payroll $101 million. Housing: 301 officer, 1,783 enlisted, 232 transient units (6 DV, 78 VOQ, 57 VAQ, 48 crew quarters, 43 TLF). 25-bed hospital.

**Elmendorf AFB,** Alaska 99506-5000; bordering Anchorage. Phone (907) 552-1110; DSN (317) 552-1110. PACAF base. Hq. Alaskan Command; Hq. 11th Air Force (PACAF); Hq. Alaskan NORAD Region. Host unit: 3d Wing, F-15/F-15E fighter and C-130, C-12 airlift operations, E-3 airborne warning and control operations, and 3d Medical Center. Tenant units: 11th Air Control Wing (PACAF); Alaskan NORAD Region Operations

Control Center; Rescue Coordination Center (ANG); 381st Air Intelligence Sqdn.; 616th Airlift Support Sqdn. (AMC); plus varied US Army, Navy, and Marine activities. Base activated July 1940; named for Capt. Hugh Elmendorf, killed Jan. 13, 1933, at Wright Field, Ohio, while flight-testing a new pursuit plane. Area 13,130 acres. Runways 7,500 ft. and 10,000 ft. Altitude 213 ft. Military 6,300; civilians 2,425. Payroll $225 million. Housing: 196 officer, 1,480 NCO, 94 temporary lodging units, 94 VOQ, 301 VAQ, 1,126 UEQ. 110-bed hospital.

**Fairchild AFB,** Wash. 99011-5000; 12 mi. WSW of Spokane. Phone (509) 247-1212; DSN 657-1212. ACC base. The base changed from ACC to AMC July 1, 1994, to become the air refueling hub for the western US. Host unit: 92d Bomb Wing. Tenant units: 453d Operations Gp. (AMC); 366th Crew Training Gp. (Survival School, AETC); 141st Air Refueling Wing (ANG); Det. 1, 6th Space Operations Sqdn. (AFSPC). Base activated in Jan. 1942; named for Gen. Muir S. Fairchild, USAF Vice Chief of Staff at his death in 1950. Area 4,543 acres. Runway 13,901 ft. Altitude 2,462 ft. Military 4,246; civilians 1,914. Payroll $136.9 million. Housing: 180 officer, 1,244 NCO, 26 TLF, 1,280 BAQ, 35 VOQ, 61 VAQ. 30-bed hospital.

**Falcon AFB,** Colo. 80912-5000; 10 mi. E of Colorado Springs. Phone (719) 550-4113; DSN 560-1110. AFSPC base. Host unit: 50th Space Wing. Tenant units: 73d Space Gp.; Air Force Space Forecast Center; Ballistic Missile Defense Organization National Test Facility; Air Force Space Warfare Center. Base activated Sept. 26, 1985. Area 3,840 acres. Runway length NA. Altitude 6,267 ft. Military active-duty 2,000; civilians 300; contractors 2,000. No housing or transient quarters. Medical aid station and dental clinic.

**Francis E. Warren AFB,** Wyo. 82005-5000; adjacent to Cheyenne. Phone (307) 775-1110; DSN 481-1110. AFSPC base. Hq. 20th Air Force. 90th Missile Wing, UH-1; 37th Air Rescue Flight. Base activated as Fort D. A. Russell July 4, 1867; under Army jurisdiction until 1947, when reassigned to USAF. Base renamed in 1930 for Francis Emory Warren, Wyoming senator and first state governor. Area 5,866 acres, plus 50 Peacekeeper and 150 Minuteman III missile sites distributed over 12,600 sq. mi. in Wyoming, Colorado, and Nebraska. Runway length NA. Altitude 6,142 ft. Military 3,494; civilians 594. Payroll $112.1 million. Housing: 114 officer, 717 enlisted, 36 transient. 20-bed hospital.

**Goodfellow AFB,** Tex. 76908-5000; 2 mi. SE of San Angelo. Phone (915) 654-3217; DSN 477-3217. AETC base. The 17th Training Wing provides technical training for all Air Force members entering intelligence career fields; provides cryptologic training for members of the other military services, civilian intelligence agencies, and foreign military services; and trains all US Air Force, Army, and Marine Corps personnel in fire protection and rescue. Major units include 17th Training Wing; 8th Space Warning Sqdn. (AFSPC) at Eldorado AFS, the location of Southwest Pave Paws radar site; Goodfellow NCO Academy; 344th Military Intelligence Battalion (US Army); Naval Technical Training Center Detachment; US Marine Corps Detachment. Base activated in Jan. 1941; named for Lt. John J. Goodfellow, Jr., WW I fighter pilot killed in combat Sept. 14, 1918. Area 1,136 acres. No runway. Altitude 1,877 ft. Military 2,900; civilians 625. Payroll $121 million. Housing: 18 officer, 271 NCO, 949 transient (804 VAQ, 116 VOQ, 29 TLF). Clinic.

**Grand Forks AFB,** N.D. 58205-5000; 16 mi. W of Grand Forks. Phone (701) 747-3000; DSN 362-1110. AMC base. 319th Air Refueling Wing (KC-135R and C-12F); 321st

Missile Wing (Minuteman III, UH-1); 319th Bomb Gp. (B-1B and T-38A). Home of the first of AMC's core air refueling wings. B-1Bs scheduled to depart for other bomber bases in summer 1994. Base activated 1956; named after the city of Grand Forks, whose citizens bought the property for the Air Force. Area 5,422 acres. Missile complex covers an additional 7,500 sq. mi. Runway 12,350 ft. Altitude 911 ft. Military 4,780; civilians 739. Payroll $133 million. Housing: 384 officer, 1,887 NCO, 1,135 dormitory, 137 transient. 15-bed hospital.

**Griffiss AFB,** N.Y. 13441-5000; 1 mi. NE of Rome. Phone (315) 330-1110; DSN 587-1110. ACC base. 416th Bomb Wing (slated for inactivation in Sept. 1995); Rome Laboratory (AFMC); 485th Engineering Installation Gp. (scheduled to move to Hill AFB, Utah, in 1995); Northeast Air Defense Sector; 509th Air Refueling Sqdn. (AMC) (will inactivate in early 1995). Base activated Feb. 1, 1942; named for Lt. Col. Townsend E. Griffiss, killed in aircraft accident Feb. 15, 1942 (the first US airman to lose his life in Europe during WW II while in the line of duty). Area 3,896 acres. Runway 11,820 ft. Altitude 504 ft. Military 4,229; civilians 2,686. Payroll $312.5 million. Housing: 169 officer, 566 NCO, 50 trailers, 109 transient. 20-bed hospital.

**Grissom AFB,** Ind. 46971-5000; 7 mi. S of Peru. Phone (317) 688-5211; DSN 928-1110. AMC base. As of Oct. 1, 1994, becomes a Reserve base. 305th Air Refueling Wing; 434th Wing (AFRES). Activated Jan. 1943 for Navy flight training; reactivated June 1954 as Bunker Hill AFB; renamed May 1968 for Lt. Col Virgil I. "Gus" Grissom, killed Jan. 27, 1967, at Cape Kennedy, Fla., with astronauts Edward White and Roger Chaffee in Apollo capsule fire. Area 3,181 acres. Runway 12,500 ft. Altitude 800 ft. Military 2,405; civilians 825. Payroll $8.8 million. Housing: 144 officer, 972 NCO, 198 transient. Clinic, dispensary status.

**Gunter AFB** (see Maxwell AFB, Gunter Annex).

**Hanscom AFB,** Mass. 01731-5000; 17 mi. NW of Boston. Phone (617) 377-4441; DSN 478-5980. AFMC base. Hq. Electronic Systems Center (AFMC) manages development and acquisition of $C^4$ systems. Also site of Geophysics Directorate of Phillips Laboratory (AFMC), center for research and exploratory development in the terrestrial, atmospheric, and space environments, as well as five divisions of Rome Laboratory's Directorate of Electromagnetics and Reliability. Base has no flying mission; transient USAF aircraft use runways of Laurence G. Hanscom Field, state-operated airfield adjoining the base. Base named for Laurence G. Hanscom, a pre–WW II advocate of private aviation, killed in a lightplane accident in 1941. Area 846 acres. Runway length NA. Altitude 133 ft. Military 2,299; civilians 2,195. Payroll $217 million. Housing: 386 officer, 472 NCO, 35-unit TLF, 754 BOQ/VOQ. Clinic.

**Hickam AFB,** Hawaii 96853-5000; 9 mi. W of Honolulu. Phone (808) 471-7110 (Oahu military operator); DSN 471-7110. PACAF base. Hq. Pacific Air Forces. Host unit: 15th Air Base Wing, supporting Air Force units and installations in Hawaii and throughout the Pacific. Major tenant units include 154th Composite Gp. (ANG); 619th Airlift Support Gp. (AMC). Base activated in Sept. 1938; named for Lt. Col. Horace M. Hickam, air pioneer killed in crash Nov. 5, 1934, at Fort Crockett, Tex. Area 2,761 acres. Runway length NA. Altitude sea level. Military 3,341; civilians 1,389. Payroll $118.3 million. Housing: 400 officer, 2,200 enlisted. Unaccompanied housing: 24 officer, 1,016 enlisted, 266 VOQ, 234 VAQ. Clinic.

**Hill AFB,** Utah 84056-5990; 8 mi. S of Ogden. Phone (801) 777-7221; DSN 458-1110. AFMC base. Hq. Ogden Air Logistics Center. Contributes to Integrated Weapon System Management and logistics support for silo-based ICBMs (Minuteman and Peacekeeper); F-4, F-16, and C-130 aircraft; conventional munitions, including Maverick air-to-ground missiles and laser, infrared, and electro-optical guided bombs; and other aerospace components, such as landing gear, photographic and reconnaissance equipment, and training devices. Technology center for software and photonics. Other units include 545th Test Gp. (AFMC), which manages the Utah Test and Training Range; 388th Fighter Wing (ACC); and 419th Fighter Wing (AFRES). Hill Aerospace Museum. Base activated in Nov. 1940; named for Maj. Ployer P. Hill, killed Oct. 30, 1935, while test-flying the first B-17. Area 6,698 acres; manages 962,076 acres. Runway 13,500 ft. Altitude 4,788 ft. Military 4,700; civilians 11,700. Payroll $580 million. Housing: 179 officer, 966 NCO, 45 transient. 35-bed hospital.

**Holloman AFB,** N.M. 88330-5000; 8 mi. SW of Alamogordo. Phone (505) 475-6511; DSN 867-1110. ACC base. 49th Fighter Wing, F-117 Stealth fighter operations (7th, 8th, and 9th Fighter Sqdns.); F-4E aircrew training (20th Fighter Sqdn. and 1st German Air Force Training Sqdn.); AT-38B aircrew training (435th Fighter Sqdn.); HH-60 helicopters (48th Rescue Sqdn.); and 83d Air Control Sqdn. Included in the base's more than 30 associate units are the 46th Test Gp. (AFMC); 4th Space Warning Sqdn. (AFSPC); and Det. 1, 82d Aerial Target Sqdn. (QF-106 drone operations). Base activated in 1942; named for Col. George Holloman, guided-missile pioneer. Area 59,000 acres. Runways 10,575 ft., 12,131 ft., and 8,054 ft. with 7,044 ft. overrun. Altitude 4,093 ft. Military 4,775; civilians 1,700. Payroll $203 million. Housing: 191 officer, 1,310 NCO, 310 transient (70 VAQ, 190 VOQ, 50 TLF). 15-bed hospital.

**Howard AFB/Albrook AFS,** Panama, APO AA 34001-5000. DSN 284-9805. ACC base. With headquarters at Howard, 24th Wing represents USAF in operations throughout Latin America. 24th Wing is an ACC unit reporting to 12th Air Force, Davis-Monthan AFB, Ariz. Major tenants: 617th Airlift Support Sqdn.; 33d Intelligence Sqdn. Howard established in 1928 as a military post, known as Bruja Point Military Reservation; later named for Maj. Charles Harold Howard. Military 2,256; civilians 734. Payroll $40.1 million. Housing: 256 officer, 918 enlisted.

**Hurlburt Field,** Fla. 32544-5000; 5 mi. W of Fort Walton Beach. Phone (904) 882-1110; DSN 579-1110. AFSOC base. Home of Air Force Special Operations Command, the focal point for all USAF special operations matters. Major tenant: 16th Special Operations Wing, equipped with MC-130E (Combat Talon I), MC-130H (Combat Talon II), AC-130H (Spectre Gunship), and MH-53J (Pave Low), MH-60G (Pave Hawk), and HC-130P/N (Combat Shadow, located at Eglin AFB). Other tenants include 505th Command and Control Evaluation Gp., which includes the USAF Air Ground Operations School, USAF Battle Staff Training School (Blue Flag), and the 727th Aircraft Control Sqdn. (T); 720th Special Tactics Gp.; 23d Special Tactics Sqdn.; Joint Warfare Center; USAF Special Operations School; Special Missions Operational Test and Evaluation Center; 823d Civil Engineering Sqdn. RED HORSE; Det. 1, 335th Technical Training Sqdn.; Det. 4, Air Weather Service; Det. 8, 1st Combat Camera Sqdn.; Field Training Det. 327; and Det. 309, AFOSI. Base activated in 1943; named for Lt. Donald W. Hurlburt, WW II pilot killed Oct. 1, 1943, in a crash at nearby Eglin Field Military Reservation. Area 6,600 acres. Runway length NA. Altitude 38 ft. Military 6,700; civilians 483. Payroll NA. Housing: 48 officer, 632 enlisted, transient 258 VOQ/VAQ, 24 TLF. Medical clinic at Hurlburt, 145-bed hospital at Eglin Regional Hospital 12 mi. away.

**Incirlik AB,** Turkey, APO AE 09824; 10 mi. E of Adana. Phone (commercial, from CONUS) 011-90-71-221774 through 221780; DSN 676-1110. USAFE base. Host unit:

39th Wing, supports rotational weapons training deployments for USAFE fighter aircraft. Also home for 628th Airlift Support Sqdn., which provides a full aerial port operation. Base activated in May 1954; present unit began operations in Mar. 1966. Incirlik, in Turkish, means fig orchard. Area 3,400 acres. Runway length NA. Altitude 240 ft. Military 2,094; civilians 2,055. Payroll $31.2 million. Housing: 950 units, 59 BOQ, 293 TLF, 212 VAQ, 315 VOQ, 419 dorm rooms. Regional hospital.

**Kadena AB,** Japan, APO AP 96368-5000; 15 mi. N of Naha, Okinawa. Phone (commercial, from CONUS) 011-81-98938-1111; DSN 630-1110. PACAF base. Host organization: 18th Wing (12th, 44th, 67th Fighter Sqdns.), F-15C/D operations; 909th Air Refueling Sqdn., KC-135 operations; 961st Airborne Warning and Control Sqdn., E-3 operations; 33d Rescue Sqdn., HH-3/HH-60 operations; Western Pacific Rescue Coordination Center; 353d Special Operations Gp. (AFSOC), MC-130 and HC-130 operations; 82d Reconnaissance Sqdn. (ACC); 390th Intelligence Sqdn.; 603d Airlift Support Gp. (AMC). Base named for city of Kadena, Japan. Area 15,000 acres. Runway length NA. Military 7,100; appropriated fund civilians 3,200; nonappropriated fund civilians, including contractors, 10,000. Payroll $300 million. Housing: 900 officer, 3,100 enlisted, 125 temporary lodging units. Unaccompanied housing: 300 officer, 2,425 enlisted, 275 VOQ, 275 VAQ. Clinic. US Naval Hospital at Camp Lester.

**Keesler AFB,** Miss. 39534-5000; located in Biloxi. Phone (601) 377-1110; DSN 597-1110. AETC base. 81st Training Wing (avionics, communications, electronics, radar systems, computer and command-and-control systems, personnel, weather, and administrative courses); Keesler Medical Center. Hosts AFRES weather reconnaissance squadron; AFRES tactical airlift unit; ACC airborne command-and-control squadron; AFMC engineering installation group; Keesler NCO Academy. Base activated June 12, 1941; named for 2d Lt. Samuel R. Keesler, Jr., a native Mississippian and WW I aerial observer killed in action Oct. 9, 1918, near Verdun, France. Area 3,546 acres. Runway 5,600 ft. Altitude 26 ft. Military 8,500; civilians 2,109. Payroll $297 million. Housing: 287 officer, 1,666 NCO, 49 trailer spaces, 2,122 transient (366 VOQ, 1,756 VAQ). 250-bed hospital.

**Keflavik Naval Air Station,** Iceland, APO AE 09725; 3 miles SW of Keflavik. Phone (commercial, from CONUS) 011-354-25-2000, DSN 450-2000. The 35th Wing (ACC) encompasses the 56th Rescue Sqdn., 57th Fighter Sqdn., and 932d Air Control Sqdn. As the only permanent USAF presence in the North Atlantic, the 35th Wing's force of F-15 fighters and HH-60 Pave Hawk helicopters provides air defense for Iceland and air superiority for NATO's western flank as the air component of the Iceland Defense Force, a subunified command reporting to CINCUSACOM. Area 21,322 acres. Runway 6,963 ft. Altitude 171 ft. Military 1,308, civilians 66. 17-bed Naval hospital.

**Kelly AFB,** Tex. 78241-5000; 5 mi. SW of San Antonio. Phone (210) 925-1110; DSN 945-1110. AFMC base. Hq. San Antonio Air Logistics Center provides logistics management, procurement, and systems support for such Defense Department aircraft as the C-5A/B, C-17, C-9, T-37, and T-38, and for such foreign-operated aircraft as the OV-10, A-37, F-5, and C-47. As a specialized repair activity, San Antonio ALC modernizes and performs heavy depot maintenance on the entire fleet of C-5s and performs a significant work load on the T-38 fleet. The ALC also overhauls F100, TF39, and T58 engines and manages more than seventy-five percent of the USAF engine inventory, fuel and lubricants used by the Air Force and NASA, and nuclear weapons. Other major units on base include the Air Intelligence Agency, Air Force Electronic Warfare Center, Joint Electronic Warfare Center, Air Force News Agency, Defense Commissary

Agency, 433d Airlift Wing (AFRES), 149th Fighter Gp. (ANG), Defense Reutilization and Marketing Office, Air Force Audit Agency Office, Defense Distribution Depot, and Defense Information Services Organization. Dating from Nov. 21, 1916, Kelly AFB is the oldest continuously active air base in the US. Named for Lt. George E. M. Kelly, first Army pilot to lose his life in a military aircraft, killed May 10, 1911. Area 4,660 acres. Runway 11,550 ft. Altitude 689 ft. Military 4,900; civilians 16,500. Payroll $680 million. Housing: 45 officer, 368 NCO. Clinic.

**Kirtland AFB,** N.M. 87117-5605; SE quadrant of Albuquerque. Phone (505) 846-0011; DSN 246-0011. AFMC base. Hq. 377th Air Base Wing. Major agencies and units include 58th Special Operations Wing (AETC); Air Force Operational Test and Evaluation Center; Phillips Laboratory; 150th Fighter Gp. (ANG); Field Command's Defense Nuclear Agency; Sandia National Laboratories; Lovelace Biomedical and Environmental Research Institute; Department of Energy's Albuquerque Operations Office; Kirtland NCO Academy; 898th Aviation Depot Sqdn.; Air Force Security Police Agency; Air Force Directorate of Nuclear Surety; Interservice Nuclear Weapons School; Air Force Inspection Agency; Air Force Safety Agency. These agencies furnish nuclear, advanced weapons, and space research, development, and testing; advanced helicopter training and search-and-rescue operations; pararescue training; and operational test and evaluation. Other major units include AFMC Nuclear Support Office; Albuquerque Seismological Laboratory; University of New Mexico Civil Engineering Research Facility. Base activated Jan. 1941; named for Col. Roy C. Kirtland, air pioneer and commandant of Langley Field in the 1930s, who died May 2, 1941. Area 52,678 acres. Runway 19,375 ft. Altitude 5,352 ft. Military 6,240; civilians 14,260. Payroll $764 million. Housing: 2,122 homes. VAQ/VOQ: 130 officer, 180 enlisted. Air Force/Department of Veterans Affairs joint medical center located outside base gates.

**K. I. Sawyer AFB,** Mich. 49843-5000; 21 mi. S of Marquette. Phone (906) 372-6511; DSN 472-6511. ACC base. 410th Bomb Wing; Defense Reutilization and Marketing Office; Det. 205, AFOSI. Base activated 1956; named for Kenneth Ingalls Sawyer, former county commissioner of Marquette who proposed site for county airport, died in 1944. Area 5,214 acres. Runway 12,370 ft. Altitude 1,220 ft. Military 3,000; civilians 900. Payroll $95.9 million. Housing: 203 officer, 1,378 NCOQ, 9 SNCOQ, 199 trailer spaces, 754 single-room BNCOQ, 18 BOQ, 112 transient (35 fully furnished TLF, 35 VAQ, 30 VOQ, 3 DVQ, 9 SNCO DV). 15-bed hospital. Scheduled to close Sept. 30, 1995.

**Kunsan AB,** Republic of Korea, APO AP 96264-5000; 8 mi. SW of Kunsan City. Phone (commercial, from CONUS) 011-82-654-470-1110; DSN 782-1110. PACAF base. Host unit: 8th Fighter Wing, F-16C/D operations, home of the "Wolf Pack." The 8th FW converted to the F-16 Fighting Falcon in Sept. 1981, making it the first active overseas F-16 wing. Base built by Japanese in 1938. Area 2,174 acres. Runway length NA. Altitude 29 ft. Military 2,521; US civilians 35; local nationals 537. Payroll $31.4 million. Unaccompanied housing: 263 officer, 3,697 enlisted, 46 VOQ, 120 VAQ. 6-bed hospital.

**Lackland AFB,** Tex. 78235-5000; 8 mi. SW of San Antonio. Phone (210) 671-1110; DSN 473-1110. AETC base. The 37th Training Wing provides basic military training and skills training for all enlisted Air Force and Air Reserve Component members. Joint service training for Air Force, Navy, and Marine personnel. Primary and advanced training is provided in transportation. Air Force recruiters are also trained at Lackland. The base is the home of the Inter-American Air Forces Academy and Defense Language Institute English Language Center. Wilford Hall Medical Center, the Air Force's largest medical facility, with 1,009 beds, handles patient care and conducts medical education and clinical research. Base activated 1941; named for Brig. Gen. Frank D. Lackland, early commandant of Kelly Field flying school, who died in 1943. Area 6,726 acres (incl. 3,973 acres at Lackland Training Annex). No runway. Altitude 745 ft. Military 7,000; civilians 3,700; students 8,000. Payroll $624.7 million. Housing: 103 officer, 621 NCO, 3,435 transient, plus 158 TLF units.

**Lajes Field,** Azores, Portugal, APO AE 09720-5000; Terceira Island, 900 mi. W of Portugal. DSN 725-1410. ACC base. Host unit: 65th Air Base Wing. Base provides en route support for AMC, USAF, USN, USMC, third-nation, and other authorized aircraft crossing the Atlantic. Tenant units: US Forces Azores; Army 1324th Medium Port Command Azores; Naval Security Gp. Activity Azores (deactivates in June 1994); 650th Airlift Support Sqdn.; Det. 3, Air Force European Broadcasting Sqdn. US operations began at Lajes Field in 1946. Area 1,148 acres. Runway 10,865 ft. Altitude 180 ft. Military 1,246; civilians 1,287. Payroll $39.9 million. Housing: 99 officer, 390 enlisted, 30 TLF, 178 VOQ, 701 VAQ, 6 DVQ, 4 senior NCO. Seven-bed hospital.

**Langley AFB,** Va. 23665-5000; 3 mi. N of Hampton. Phone (804) 764-9990; DSN 574-1110. ACC base. Hq. Air Combat Command. Host unit: 1st Fighter Wing, F-15 fighter operations. Associate units: 2d Aircraft Delivery Gp. (ACC); 480th Intelligence Gp.; 1912th Computer Systems Gp. (ACC); Air Combat Command Heritage of America Band; Det. 1, 158th Fighter Gp. (ANG); US Army TRADOC Flight Det.; Army/USAF Center for Low-Intensity Conflict; Air Force Doctrine Center; Air Force Rescue Coordination Center; 548th Air Intelligence Gp. (ACC). Base activated Dec. 30, 1916. Langley is one of the oldest continuously active air bases in the US. Named for aviation pioneer and scientist Samuel Pierpont Langley, who died in 1906. NASA's Langley Research Center is adjacent to the base. Area 3,974 acres. Runway 10,000 ft. Altitude 10 ft. Military 8,767; civilians 2,710. Payroll $400 million. Housing: 384 officer, 1,250 NCO, 417 transient (216 VAQ, 101 VOQ, 100 TLF). 50-bed hospital.

**Laughlin AFB,** Tex. 78843-5000; 6 mi. E of Del Rio. Phone (210) 298-3511; DSN 732-1110. AETC base. 47th Flying Training Wing, undergraduate pilot training. Base activated Oct. 1942; named for 1st Lt. Jack T. Laughlin, Del Rio native, B-17 pilot killed over Java Jan. 29, 1942. Area 5,239 acres. Runways 6,300 ft., 8,310 ft., and 8,850 ft. Altitude 1,080 ft. Military 1,209; civilians 1,232. Payroll $71.5 million. Housing: 599 units, 54 trailer spaces, 62 transient, 24 TLF. Hospital.

**Laurence G. Hanscom AFB** (see Hanscom AFB).

**Little Rock AFB,** Ark. 72099-5000; 17 mi. NE of Little Rock. Phone (501) 988-3131; DSN 731-1110. ACC base. 314th Airlift Wing, only C-130 training base in DoD, training crew members from all branches of service and some foreign countries. Tenants include 189th Airlift Gp. (ANG); 96th Mobile Aerial Port Sqdn.; 348th USAF Recruiting Sqdn.; Ground Combat Readiness Evaluation Sqdn.; Det. 251, AFOSI; Det. 310, 373d Field Training Sqdn.; Det. 234, Air Force Audit Agency. Base activated 1955. Area 11,373 acres. Runway length NA. Altitude 310 ft. Military 6,692; civilians 521. Payroll $133 million. Housing: 140 officer, 1,395 enlisted, 17 single-occupancy dormitories house 960 people, 348 transient (148 VAQ, 200 VOQ). 25-bed hospital.

**Loring AFB,** Me. 04751-5000; 4 mi. W of Limestone. Phone (207) 999-1110; DSN 920-1110. ACC base. 42d Bomb Wing was activated here Feb. 25, 1953, as Limestone AFB; renamed for Maj. Charles J. Loring, Jr., F-80 pilot killed Nov. 22, 1952, in North

Korea and posthumously awarded Medal of Honor. Area 8,702 acres. Runway 12,100 ft. Altitude 756 ft. Military 700; civilians 650. Payroll $60 million. Housing: 291 officer, 1,457 enlisted, 90 transient, 11 VIP. Medical aid station. Base was scheduled to close Sept. 30, 1994.

**Los Angeles AFB,** Calif. 90009-2960; in South Bay Los Angeles, city of El Segundo, 3 mi. S of Los Angeles IAP. Phone (310) 363-1110; DSN 833-1110. AFMC base. Headquarters of AFMC's Space and Missile Systems Center, which manages the design, development, acquisition, launch, and on-orbit checkout of DoD's space program and shares rocket booster launch with Air Force Space Command. Support unit is 655th Air Base Sqdn. Area 96 acres at Los Angeles AFB and 96 acres at Fort MacArthur Annex and Pacific Crest/Heights housing areas. No runway. Altitude 95 ft. Military 1,812; civilians 1,258. Payroll $150 million. Housing at Fort MacArthur Annex: 574 townhouses, 56 senior enlisted quarters, 29 VOQ, 4 DVQ, 22 TLF. Clinic, commissary, child-care center, and Air Force Family Support Center.

**Lowry AFB,** Colo. 80230-5000; on border between Denver and Aurora. Phone (303) 676-1110; DSN 926-1110. AETC base. Lowry Training Center conducts training in avionics, munitions, logistics, services, and combat camera fields. Other major organizations include the Defense Finance and Accounting Service—Denver Center; Air Reserve Personnel Center, which will remain open in a cantonment area after Sept. 30, 1994. Base activated Oct. 1, 1937; named for 1st Lt. Francis B. Lowry, killed in action Sept. 26, 1918, near Crepion, France, while on a photoreconnaissance mission. Area 1,688 acres. Runway length NA. Altitude 5,400 ft. Military 4,293; civilians 3,805. Payroll $243.3 million. Housing: 71 officer, 791 NCO, 525 VOQ, 1,196 VAQ, 40 TLF. USAF clinic on base will close July 1, 1994. Fitzsimons Army Medical Center 15 minutes away. Base was scheduled to close Sept. 30, 1994.

**Luke AFB,** Ariz. 85309-5000; 20 mi. WNW of downtown Phoenix. Phone (602) 856-7411; DSN 853-1110. AETC base. 58th Fighter Wing, F-15E and F-16 operations; 944th Fighter Gp. (AFRES), F-16 operations; 607th Air Control Sqdn., forward air control operations. Luke, the largest fighter training base in the world, conducts USAF and allied aircrew training in the F-15E and F-16. Base activated 1941; named for 2d Lt. Frank Luke, Jr., observation balloon-busting ace of WW I and first American aviator to receive the Medal of Honor, killed in action Sept. 29, 1918, near Murvaux, France. Area 4,197 acres, plus 2.7-million-acre range at Gila Bend, Ariz. Runways 10,000 ft. and 9,910 ft. Altitude 1,090 ft. Military 5,526; civilians 1,400. Payroll $171 million. Housing: 95 officer, 779 enlisted, 301 transient (137 VOQ, 124 VAQ, 40 TLF). 40-bed hospital.

**MacDill AFB,** Fla. 33621-5000; adjacent to Tampa city limits. Phone (813) 828-1110; DSN 968-1110. ACC base. 6th Air Base Wing; Hq. US Special Operations Command; Hq. US Central Command; and Joint Communications Support Element. The 6th ABW's mission is to operate the air base for the United States' warfighting commands. Base activated Apr. 15, 1941; named for Col. Leslie MacDill, killed in an aircraft accident Nov. 8, 1938, near Washington, D.C. Area 2,319 acres. Runway length NA. Altitude 6 ft. Military 3,922; civilians 2,094. Payroll $162 million. Housing: 130 officer, 674 enlisted, 323 transient (139 VAQ, 137 VOQ, 24 TLF, 23 DVQ). 65-bed hospital.

**Malmstrom AFB,** Mont. 59402-5000; 1.5 mi. E of Great Falls. Phone (406) 731-1110; DSN 632-1110. AMC base. 43d Air Refueling Wing; 341st Missile Wing (AFSPC). Base activated Dec. 15, 1942; named for Col. Einar A. Malmstrom, WW II fighter commander killed in air accident Aug. 21, 1954. Site of SAC's first Minuteman wing. Area 4,137 acres, plus about 24,000 sq. mi. of missile complex. Runway length NA. Altitude 3,525 ft. Military 4,251; civilians 527. Payroll $165.6 million. Housing: 258 officer, 1,148 enlisted, 105 transient. Clinic.

**March AFB,** Calif. 92518-5000; 9 mi. SE of Riverside. Phone (909) 655-1110; DSN 947-1110. AMC base. 722d Air Refueling Wing; Southwest Air Defense Sector; 722d Medical Gp.; Det. 1, 144th Fighter Wing (ANG); 452d Air Refueling Wing (AFRES); 445th Airlift Wing (AFRES) (inactivated Apr. 1, 1994); 163d Air Refueling Gp. (ANG); Customs Aviation Operations Center West. Base activated Mar. 1, 1918; named for 2d Lt. Peyton C. March, Jr., who died in Texas of crash injuries Feb. 18, 1918. Area 6,848 acres. Runway 13,300 ft. Altitude 1,530 ft. Military 6,824; civilians 1,676. Payroll $164 million. Housing: 107 officer, 803 NCO, 172 transient. 80-bed hospital. Scheduled to realign to an AFRES/ANG base in 1996.

**Maxwell AFB,** Ala. 36112-5000; 1 mi. WNW of Montgomery. Phone (205) 953-1110; DSN 493-1110. AETC base. 502d Air Base Wing. Hq. Air University. Air War College; Air Command and Staff College; Air Force Quality Institute; Air University Library; College of Aerospace Doctrine, Research, and Education; Air Force Reserve Officers Training Corps; Officer Training School; Ira C. Eaker College for Professional Development; Hq. Civil Air Patrol–USAF; Squadron Officer School; and Air Force Institute of Technology (at Wright-Patterson AFB, Ohio). Associate units: 908th Airlift Gp. (AFRES); Air Force Medical Management Engineering Team; and Air Force Historical Research Agency. Air University conducts professional military, graduate, and professional continuing education for precommissioned and commissioned officers, enlisted personnel, and civilians to prepare them for command, staff, leadership, and management responsibilities. Base activated 1918; named for 2d Lt. William C. Maxwell, killed in air accident Aug. 12, 1920, in the Philippines. Area 2,524 acres. Runway 7,000 ft. Altitude 168 ft. Military 3,189; civilians 1,648. Payroll $324 million. Housing: 295 officer, 361 enlisted, 276 junior enlisted, 1,478 transient (1,349 VOQ, 91 VAQ, 38 TLF). 40-bed hospital.

**Maxwell AFB, Gunter Annex,** Ala. 36114; 4 mi. NE of Montgomery. Phone (205) 416-1110; DSN 596-1110. AETC base. Under Hq. Air University: College for Enlisted Professional Military Education (includes USAF Senior NCO Academy); Extension Course Institute; Standard Systems Center (AFMC); Air Force Logistics Management Agency. Activated Aug. 27, 1940; named for William A. Gunter, longtime mayor of Montgomery and airpower advocate who died in 1940. Area 368 acres. No runway. Altitude 220 ft. Military 1,395; civilians 868. Payroll included in Maxwell entry. Housing: 104 officer, 220 enlisted, 152 junior enlisted, 463 transient (209 VOQ, 251 VAQ, 3 TLF).

**McChord AFB,** Wash. 98438-5000; 10 mi. S of Tacoma. Phone (206) 984-1910; DSN 984-1110. AMC base. Host unit is 62d Airlift Wing. Major tenants include 446th Airlift Wing (AFRES Assoc.); Northwest Air Defense Sector; 354th Fighter Sqdn., A-10 Thunderbolt II. The 62d AW operates the C-141 StarLifter and is responsible for strategic airlift of personnel and cargo worldwide, on short notice, in support of national objectives. Base is adjacent to Fort Lewis, its primary customer. Base activated May 5, 1938; named for Col. William C. McChord, killed Aug. 18, 1937, while attempting a forced landing at Maidens, Va. Area 4,616 acres. Runway 10,100 ft. Altitude 323 ft. Military 4,661; civilians 1,708. Payroll $200.2 million. Housing: 117 officer, 722 NCO, 744 transient. Dispensary. Madigan Army Medical Center is the newest regional DoD hospital, located 4 mi. SE, with 414 beds.

**McClellan AFB,** Calif. 95652-5000; 9 mi. NE of Sacramento. Phone (916) 643-2111; DSN 633-1110. AFMC base. Hq. Sacramento Air Logistics Center provides logistics management, procurement, maintenance, and distribution support for F/EF-111 and A-10, and, as a second source, for the F-15 and KC-135 weapon systems. The ALC is also program manager for the F-117A Stealth fighter and will be the support center for the F-22 (Advanced Tactical Fighter). Other responsibilities include more than 200 electronic systems and programs and eight space systems; technology centers for very-high-speed integrated circuits, fiber optics, and advanced composites. The ALC has unique capability for robotic non-destructive inspection using X-ray and neutron radiography on F-111-sized aircraft. Other major units include Defense Depot–McClellan; Defense Information Systems Organization—McClellan; 1849th Electronics Installation Sqdn.; Technical Operations Division, Air Force Technical Applications Center; 4th Air Force (AFRES); US Coast Guard Air Station, Sacramento (DOT). Named for Maj. Hezekiah McClellan, pioneer in Arctic aeronautical experiments, killed in crash May 25, 1936. Area 3,763 acres. Runway 10,600 ft. Military 3,000; civilians 11,000. Payroll $580 million. Housing: 100 officer, 564 enlisted, 19 transient. 652d Medical Gp. clinic also controls 652d Medical Gp. Hospital located at Mather AFB.

**McConnell AFB,** Kan. 67221-5000; SE corner of Wichita. Phone (316) 652-6100; DSN 743-1110. AMC base. 22d Air Refueling Wing; 384th Bomb Gp.; 184th Bomb Gp. (ANG). Base activated June 5, 1951; named for Capt. Fred J. McConnell, WW II B-24 pilot who died in crash of a private plane Oct. 25, 1945, and for his brother, 2d Lt. Thomas L. McConnell, also a WW II B-24 pilot, killed July 10, 1943, during an attack on Bougainville. Area 3,113 acres. Runway 12,000 ft. Altitude 1,371 ft. Military 3,091; civilians 331. Payroll $111 million. Housing: 123 officer, 364 NCO, 97 transient (45 VOQ, 31 VAQ, 21 TLF).

**McGuire AFB,** N.J. 08641-5000; 18 mi. SE of Trenton. Phone (609) 724-1100; DSN 440-1100. AMC base. 438th Airlift Wing; Hq. 21st Air Force; N.J. ANG; N.J. Civil Air Patrol; 108th Air Refueling Wing (ANG); 514th Airlift Wing (AFRES Assoc.); McGuire NCO Academy (AETC). Base adjoins Army's Fort Dix; formerly Fort Dix AAB. Activated as AFB 1949; named for Maj. Thomas B. McGuire, Jr., P-38 pilot, second leading US ace of WW II, recipient of Medal of Honor, killed in action Jan. 7, 1945, in the Philippines. Area 3,597 acres. Runways 7,124 ft. and 10,000 ft. Altitude 133 ft. Military 9,558 (incl. AFRES and ANG); civilians 1,657. Payroll $202 million. Housing: 193 officer, 1,560 NCO, 962 transient (210 VOQ, 752 VAQ). 250-bed hospital at Fort Dix.

**Minot AFB,** N.D. 58705-5000; 13 mi. N of Minot. Phone (701) 723-1110; DSN 453-1110. ACC base. 5th Bomb Wing (B-52H); 906th Air Refueling Sqdn./Air Mobility Command (KC-135R); 91st Missile Wing, Minuteman III operations (AFSPC); CPT Flight/23d Bomb Sqdn. (T-38A); 54th Rescue Flight/91st Operations Gp. (HH-1H). Base activated Jan. 1957; named after the city of Minot, whose citizens donated $50,000 toward purchase of the land for the Air Force. Area 5,085 acres, plus additional 19,324 acres for missile sites. Runway 13,300 ft. Altitude 1,668 ft. Military 4,823; civilians 1,036. Payroll $109 million (military only). Housing: 427 officer, 1,737 enlisted, 295 junior enlisted. 45-bed hospital.

**Misawa AB,** Japan, APO AP 96319-5000; within Misawa city limits. Phone (commercial, from CONUS) 011-81-176-53-5181. DSN 226-1110. PACAF base; joint service base. Host unit: 432d Fighter Wing, F-16C/D operations. Tenant units: 301st Intelligence Sqdn.; Naval Air Facility; Naval Security Gp. Activity; US Army field station; Company "E," US Marine Support Battalion. Base occupied by US forces Sept. 1945. Area 3,865 acres. Runway 10,000 ft. Altitude 119 ft. Military 5,176 (total US forces); US civilians 122; local nationals 804. Payroll $166 million. Housing: 335 officer, 1,835 enlisted, 20 temporary lodging units. Unaccompanied housing: 120 officer, 1,711 enlisted, 158 transient (96 VOQ, 62 VAQ). Unaccompanied Navy housing: 108 officer (transient), 855 enlisted (336 permanent party, 519 transient). 25-bed hospital.

**Moody AFB,** Ga. 31699-5000; 10 mi. NNE of Valdosta. Phone (912) 333-4211; DSN 460-1110. ACC base. 347th Fighter Wing, F-16C/D (LANTIRN-equipped) fighter operations, becoming composite wing; 71st Air Control Sqdn.; 336th USAF Recruiting Sqdn.; Det. 717, AFOSI; Field Training Det. 322. Base activated in June 1941; named for Maj. George P. Moody, killed May 5, 1941, while test-flying a Beech AT-10. Area 6,050 acres. Runway 8,000 ft. Altitude 233 ft. Military 4,000; civilians 700. Payroll $81 million. Housing: 36 officer, 268 enlisted, 79 transient (34 VAQ, 33 VOQ, 12 TLF), 39 trailer spaces. 15-bed hospital.

**Mountain Home AFB,** Idaho 83648-5000; 10 mi. SW of Mountain Home. Phone (208) 828-2111; DSN 728-2111. ACC base. 366th Wing, USAF's first air intervention composite wing, with F-16C attack, F-15E interdiction, F-15C air-superiority, and KC-135R air refueling aircraft prepared to deploy rapidly worldwide and perform composite air intervention operations. Base activated in Aug. 1943. Area 9,112 acres. Runway 13,500 ft. Altitude 3,000 ft. Military 3,362; civilians 1,130. Payroll $91 million. Housing: 246 officer, 1,271 enlisted, 263 transient (180 VAQ, 45 VOQ, 38 TLF). 20-bed hospital.

**Nellis AFB,** Nev. 89191-5000; 8 mi. NE of Las Vegas. Phone (702) 652-1110; DSN 682-1110. ACC base. USAF Weapons and Tactics Center, A-10, F-15, F-15E, F-16, and F-4G; 57th Fighter Wing; USAF Weapons School; USAF Combat Rescue School; USAF Air Demonstration Sqdn. (Thunderbirds); 57th Operations Gp.; 414th Training Sqdn. (Red Flag); 549th Joint Training Sqdn. (Air Warrior); 57th Test Gp., including 422d Test and Evaluation Sqdn.; 57th Logistics Gp.; 547th Adversary Threat Sqdn.; 561st Fighter Sqdn. (Wild Weasels); 66th Rescue Sqdn. (HH-60); 554th Medical Gp.; 554th Support Gp.; 820th Civil Engineering Sqdn. RED HORSE; 896th Aviation Depot Sqdn. (AFMC). Base activated in July 1941 as AAF Flexible Gunnery School. Closed in 1947. Reopened in 1949 and named for 1st Lt. William H. Nellis, WW II P-47 fighter pilot, killed Dec. 27, 1944, in Europe. Range restricted area 3.5 million acres plus 12,000 sq. mi. of airspace. Runways 10,051 ft. and 10,119 ft. Altitude 1,868 ft. Military 7,200; civilians 2,000. Payroll NA. Housing: 107 officer, 1,275 enlisted, 100 trailer spaces, 737 transient (193 VOQ, 484 VAQ, 60 TLF). 129-bed joint Air Force/Department of Veterans Affairs hospital opened mid-1994.

**Newark AFB,** Ohio 43057-5990; 1 mi. SW of Newark. Phone (614) 522-2171; DSN 346-7000. AFMC base. Aerospace Guidance and Meteorology Center repairs inertial guidance and navigation systems for most Air Force missiles and aircraft as well as a variety of inertial systems for other branches of the armed forces. Also manages the Air Force's worldwide measurement and calibration program, providing the link between the National Institutes of Science and Technology and the Air Force's 130 precision measurement equipment laboratories at bases around the world. Four tenant units. Activated as an Air Force station Nov. 7, 1962. Area 10–20 acres. No runway. Military 80; civilians 1,500. Payroll $80 million. Base is scheduled for closure, date to be determined.

**Offutt AFB,** Neb. 68113-5000; 8 mi. S of Omaha. Phone (402) 294-1110; DSN 271-1110. ACC base. Hq. US Strategic Command. 55th Wing; Strategic Joint Intelligence Center; Hq. Strategic Communications-Computer Center; Air Force Global Weather Central; 6th Space Operations Sqdn. (AFSPC); National Emergency Airborne Command Post (NEACP); Air Combat Command Heartland of America Band. Base activated 1896 as Army's Fort Crook; landing field named for 1st Lt. Jarvis J. Offutt, WW I pilot who died Aug. 13, 1918, from injuries received at Valheureux, France. Area 4,060 acres (incl. housing area and off-base sites). Runway 11,700 ft. Altitude 1,048 ft. Military 10,100; civilians 2,200. Payroll $475 million. Housing: 513 officer, 2,137 enlisted, 80 VAQ, 171 VOQ, 60 TLF. 60-bed hospital.

**Osan AB,** Republic of Korea, APO AP 96278-5000; 38 mi. S of Seoul. Phone (commercial, from CONUS) 011-82-333-661-1110; DSN 784-4110. PACAF base. Hq. 7th Air Force. Host unit: 51st Fighter Wing, F-16C/D, C-12F, and OA-10A operations. Tenant units: 303d Intelligence Sqdn.; 611th Airlift Support Sqdn.; 554th Civil Engineering Sqdn. RED HORSE (PACAF). Originally designated K-55; runway opened Dec. 1952. Renamed Osan AB in 1956 for nearby town that was the scene of first fighting between US and North Korean forces in July 1950. Area 1,674 acres. Runway 9,000 ft. Altitude 38 ft. Military 5,766; US civilians 208; local nationals 778. Payroll NA. Housing: 153 officer, 59 enlisted, 16 TLF. Unaccompanied housing: 355 officer, 5,656 enlisted, 70 VOQ, 400 VAQ. 30-bed hospital.

**Patrick AFB,** Fla. 32925-5000; 2 mi. S of Cocoa Beach. Phone (407) 494-1110; DSN 854-1110. AFSPC base. Operated by the 45th Space Wing in support of DoD, NASA, and other agency missile and space programs. Major tenants: Defense Equal Opportunity Management Institute; Air Force Technical Applications Center; 41st Rescue Sqdn.; 71st Rescue Sqdn.; 301st Rescue Sqdn. (ANG); 741st Consolidated Aircraft Maintenance Sqdn.; and the Joint Task Force for Joint STARS at Melbourne Regional Airport, Fla. Besides host responsibilities for Patrick AFB and Cape Canaveral AFS, 45th Space Wing also oversees operations at tracking stations on Antigua and Ascension Islands. Patrick has supported more than 3,000 space launches from Cape Canaveral since 1950. Base activated 1940. Named for Maj. Gen. Mason M. Patrick, Chief of AEF's Air Service in WW I and Chief of the Air Service/Air Corps, 1921–27. Area 2,341 acres. Runway 9,000 ft. Altitude 9 ft. Military 2,700; civilians 1,900. Payroll $155 million (military, Civil Service). Housing: 136 officer, 1,230 NCO. 15-bed hospital.

**Peterson AFB,** Colo. 80914-5000; at eastern edge of Colorado Springs. Phone (719) 556-7321; DSN 834-7011. AFSPC base. Hq. Air Force Space Command. Host unit: 21st Space Wing (AFSPC). Provides support to Hq. North American Aerospace Defense Command; Hq. US Space Command; Hq. Army Space Command; 302d Airlift Wing (AFRES). Edward J. Peterson Air & Space Museum. Base activated 1942; named for 1st Lt. Edward J. Peterson, killed Aug. 8, 1942, in aircraft crash at the base. Area 1,277 acres. Runway length NA. Altitude 6,200 ft. Military active-duty 3,100; reserves 1,350; civilians 1,700. Payroll $206 million. Housing: 107 officer, 384 NCO, 217 transient (75 VOQ, 102 VAQ, 40 TLF). Clinic.

**Plattsburgh AFB,** N.Y. 12903-5000; adjacent to Plattsburgh. Phone (518) 565-5000; DSN 689-5000. AMC base. 380th Air Refueling Wing, tanker operations with KC-135; Det. 203, OLA 373d Field Training Sqdn. One of the oldest active military installations in the US, established 1812; AFB since 1955. Area 4,879 acres. Runway 11,758 ft. Altitude 235 ft. Military 2,218; civilians 792. Payroll $75.1 million. Housing: 218 officer, 1,421 NCO, 132 transient (60 VAQ, 49 VOQ, 23 TLF). 8-bed hospital. Scheduled to close Sept. 30, 1995.

**Pope AFB,** N.C. 28308-5000; 12 mi. NNW of Fayetteville. Phone (910) 394-0001; DSN 486-1110. ACC base. 23d Wing. 624th Airlift Support Gp. (AMC); 1st Aeromedical Evacuation Sqdn.; 23d Combat Control Sqdn.; 53d Mobile Aerial Port Sqdn. (AFRES); Det. 3, MACOS (Combat Control School); 18th Air Support Gp.; 1724th Special Tactics Sqdn. (AFSOC). Base adjoins Army's Fort Bragg and provides intratheater airlift and close air support for airborne forces and other personnel, equipment, and supplies. Base activated 1919; named after 1st Lt. Harley H. Pope, WW I flyer, killed Jan. 7, 1917, when his JN-4 "Jenny" crashed into the Cape Fear River near Fayetteville. Area 1,750 acres. Runway 7,500 ft. Altitude 218 ft. Military 4,700; civilians 719. Payroll $172 million. Housing: 459 units, 1,208 dormitory spaces, 268 transient (144 officer, 116 enlisted, 8 TLF). Clinic.

**RAF Alconbury,** United Kingdom, APO AE 09470; 3 mi. NW of Huntingdon; 60 mi. N of London. Phone (commercial, from CONUS) 011-44-480-82-3000; DSN 223-1110. Royal Air Force base. 10th Air Base Wing (USAFE) is host unit and maintains tribase complex; 352d Special Operations Gp. (AFSOC) flies MC-130 Combat Talon, HC-130 Combat Shadow tanker, and MH-53J Pave Low helicopter; Joint Analysis Center (EUCOM) provides intelligence to US and NATO leaders from base at nearby RAF Molesworth. Initially activated in 1938; first used by US forces in Sept. 1942. Area 2,954 acres. Runway length NA. Altitude 160 ft. Military 3,000; civilians 1,250. Payroll $122 million. Housing: 79 officer, 767 enlisted, 250 govt.-leased units (enlisted only), 1,187 dorm spaces. Clinic. Wing will inactivate and 352d SOG will transfer to 100th Air Refueling Wing, RAF Mildenhall, UK, in FY 1995.

**RAF Lakenheath,** United Kingdom, APO AE 09464-5000; 70 mi. NE of London; 25 mi. from Cambridge. Phone (commercial, from CONUS) 011-44-638-52-3000; DSN 226-1110. Royal Air Force base. 48th Fighter Wing (USAFE) flies the F-15E and the F-15C/D and trains for and conducts air operations in support of NATO. Base activated in 1941; 48th FW began operations at RAF Lakenheath in Jan. 1960. Named after nearby village. Area 2,226 acres. Runway length 9,000 ft. Altitude 32 ft. Military 4,480; civilians 2,025. Payroll $169 million. Housing: 1,024 units, 1,065 govt.-leased housing, 161 billeting spaces. Regional medical center.

**RAF Mildenhall,** United Kingdom, APO AE 09459-5000; 30 mi. NE of Cambridge. Phone (commercial, from CONUS) 011-44-638-54-3000; DSN 238-1110. Royal Air Force base. Hq. 3d Air Force (USAFE). 100th Air Refueling Wing (USAFE), KC-135R and European Tanker Task Force operations, regional logistics support. Associate units include 627th Airlift Support Sqdn. (AMC); 922d Reconnaissance Sqdn. (ACC); 488th Intelligence Sqdn.; Naval Air Facility. Base activated in 1934; US presence began in July 1950. Named after nearby village. Area 1,144 acres. Runway length NA. Altitude 33 ft. Military 3,492; DoD civilians 193. Payroll NA. Housing: 40 officer, 79 enlisted; govt.-leased housing shared with RAF Lakenheath; 452 transient (40 TLF, 216 VOQ, 196 VAQ). Medical annex.

**RAF Upper Heyford,** United Kingdom, APO AE 09466; 13 mi. N of Oxford. Phone (commercial, from CONUS) 011-44-869-232331; DSN 263-1110. Royal Air Force base. 20th Fighter Wing was redesignated the 620th Air Base Wing in Jan. 1994. The base, originally scheduled to be placed in standby status, will be returned to the host government by Sept. 30, 1994.

**Ramstein AB,** Germany, APO AE 09094-5000; adjacent to Ramstein; 10 mi. W of Kaiserslautern. Phone (commercial, from CONUS) 011-49-6371-113; DSN 480-1110. USAFE base. Hq. USAFE; Hq. Allied Air Forces Central Europe (NATO). Host unit: 86th Wing, F-16C/D, C-20/21, CT-43, UH-1N, and C-9. The wing commander also serves as commander of the Kaiserslautern Military Community, the largest concentration of US citizens outside the US. Base activated and US presence began in 1953. Area 5,292 acres. Runway length NA. Altitude 782 ft. Military 8,330; civilians 3,612. Payroll $435.3 million. Housing: 5,155 units, govt.-leased units 519, billeting units 1,078. Both the

512th and 526th Fighter Sqdns. are scheduled to inactivate. In Apr. 1994, the F-16s began moving to Aviano AB, Italy. Twelve C-130s from the 37th Airlift Sqdn. at Rhein-Main AB, Germany, moved to Ramstein in Oct. 1994.

**Randolph AFB,** Tex. 78150-5000; 17 mi. ENE of San Antonio. Phone (210) 652-1110; DSN 487-1110. AETC base. Hq. Air Education and Training Command; Hq. 19th Air Force; 12th Flying Training Wing; T-37, T-38, AT-38, and T-1 pilot instructor training; T-43 undergraduate navigator training and T-3 flight screening at Hondo, Tex.; Hq. Air Force Military Personnel Center; Hq. Air Force Management Engineering Agency; Hq. Air Force Services Agency; USAF Occupational Measurement Sqdn.; Air Force Civilian Personnel Management Center; Hq. USAF Recruiting Service. Base activated June 1930; named for Capt. William M. Randolph, killed Feb. 17 1928, when his AT-4 crashed on takeoff at Gorman, Tex. Area 5,003 acres. Two runways, each 8,350 ft. Altitude 761 ft. Military 5,364; civilians 4,302. Payroll $346 million. Housing: 181 officer, 838 NCO, 561 transient (173 VAQ, 358 VOQ, 30 TLF). Clinic.

**Reese AFB,** Tex. 79489-5000; adjacent to Lubbock. Phone (806) 885-4511; DSN 838-1110. AETC base. 64th Flying Training Wing, specialized undergraduate pilot training. Base activated 1942; named for 1st Lt. Augustus F. Reese, Jr., P-38 fighter pilot killed during a train-strafing mission at Cagliari, Sardinia, May 14, 1943. Area 3,953 acres. Runways 6,500 ft., 10,500 ft., and 10,500 ft. Altitude 3,338 ft. Military 1,192; civilians 617. Payroll $50.5 million. Housing: 148 officer, 250 NCO, 63 transient (8 suites, 25 TLF, 14 VOQ, 16 VAQ). Clinic.

**Rhein-Main AB,** Germany, APO AE 09097-5000; 5 mi. S of Frankfurt. Phone (commercial, from CONUS) 011-49-69-699-1110; DSN 330-1110. USAFE base. Host unit: 435th Airlift Wing. Largest combined cargo and passenger terminal in the Air Force. Shares runways with the busiest commercial airport on the Continent. The 37th Airlift Sqdn. flies C-130E aircraft in support of DoD and European theater airlift requirements. Other major units include 362d Airlift Gp.; On-Site Inspection Agency—Europe; Army's 21st Replacement Battalion. Base activated July 1936; US forces began operations Mar. 1945. Named after the confluence of the Rhein and Main rivers west of Frankfurt. Area 923 acres. Runway length NA. Altitude 365 ft. Military 3,546; civilians 1,051. Payroll NA. Housing, on-base, govt.-owned: 152 officer, 490 enlisted; off-base, govt.-owned and -leased: 602 units. 268 rooms/531 beds at base hotel, 176 rooms/278 beds VAQ. Clinic. Was scheduled for partial return to host government in Oct. 1994.

**Robins AFB,** Ga. 31098; 15 mi. SSE of Macon at Warner Robins. Phone (912) 926-1110; DSN 468-1110. AFMC base. Hq. Warner Robins Air Logistics Center provides worldwide logistics management for the F-15 air-superiority fighter, C-130 and C-141 cargo aircraft, helicopters, missiles, and remotely piloted vehicles. Other management responsibilities include the LANTIRN system, JTIDS, E-3 AWACS avionics, most Air Force airborne electronic warfare equipment, airborne communications equipment, airborne bomb- and gun-directing systems, fire-fighting equipment, general-purpose vehicles, and the Worldwide Military Command and Control System. Warner Robins is the lead ALC for the National Aerospace Plane technology and demonstration program. In Apr. 1991, Robins AFB was selected as the US main operating base for the E-8 Joint STARS aircraft. Other major units include Hq. Air Force Reserve (AFRES); 653d Air Base Gp.; 19th Air Refueling Wing; 5th Combat Communications Gp. (ACC); 653d Communications-Computer Systems Gp. (AFMC); 9th Space Warning Sqdn. (AFSPC). Base activated Mar. 1942; named for Brig. Gen. Augustine Warner Robins, an early chief of the Materiel Division of the Air Corps, who died June 16, 1940. Area more than 8,700 acres. Runway 12,000 ft. Altitude 294 ft. Military approx. 4,400;

civilians approx. 12,500. Payroll $698.9 million. Housing: 245 officer, 1,149 NCO, 40 TLF, 137 VOQ. 20-bed hospital.

**Sawyer AFB** (see K.I. Sawyer AFB).

**Scott AFB,** Ill. 62225-5000; 6 mi. ENE of Belleville. Phone (618) 256-1110; DSN 576-1110. AMC base. 375th Airlift Wing; Hq. Air Mobility Command; Hq. Air Force $C^4$ Agency (an FOA); Hq. US Transportation Command; Hq. Air Weather Service; Environmental Technical Applications Center; USAF Medical Center, Scott; 932d Aeromedical Airlift Gp. (AFRES Assoc.) Base activated June 14, 1917; named for Cpl. Frank S. Scott, the first enlisted man to die in an aircraft accident, killed Sept. 28, 1912, in one of the Wright B Flyers at College Park, Md. Area 3,000 acres. Runway 7,061 ft. Altitude 453 ft. Military 6,600; civilians 3,550. Payroll $300 million. Housing: 309 officer, 1,392 NCO, plus 104 spaces for privately owned trailers, 300 transient. 120-bed hospital; 100-bed aeromedical staging facility.

**Sembach AB,** Germany. APO AE 09130-5000; 9 mi. NE of Kaiserslautern. Phone (commercial, from CONUS) 011-49-6302-67-113; DSN 496-1110. USAFE base. Hq. 17th Air Force (USAFE). Host unit: 601st Air Base Wing. Major associate units include USAFE Air Ground Operations School; 601st Regional Support Gp.; Defense Commercial Communications Office; 1st Combat Communications Sqdn. Base activated 1930; US presence began July 1953. Named after a nearby farming community. Area 862 acres. Runway length NA. Altitude 1,037 ft. Military 2,617; civilians 600. Payroll $72.8 million. Housing: 74 officer, 420 enlisted. Billeting: 73 officers, 330 enlisted, 4 chief master sergeant suites. Clinic. Base scheduled for partial return to host government in Sept. 1995.

**Seymour Johnson AFB,** N.C. 27531-5000; within city limits of Goldsboro. Phone (919) 736-5400; DSN 488-1110. ACC base. 4th Wing, F-15E fighter, KC-10 tanker, and T-38 operations; 916th Air Refueling Gp. (AFRES), KC-10 operations. Base activated June 12, 1942; named for Navy Lt. Seymour A. Johnson, Goldsboro native, killed Mar. 5, 1941, in aircraft accident in Maryland. Area 3,233 acres. Runway 11,758 ft. Altitude 109 ft. Military 4,570; civilians 1,185. Payroll $149.2 million. Housing: 154 officer, 1,544 enlisted, 122 transient (56 VAQ, 39 VOQ, 27 TLF). 15-bed hospital.

**Shaw AFB,** S.C. 29152-5000; 10 mi. WNW of Sumter. Phone (803) 668-8110; DSN 965-1110. ACC base. 20th Fighter Wing, F-16 fighter operations and A/OA-10 close air support/forward air control operations; Hq. 9th Air Force. Base activated Aug. 30, 1941; named for 2d Lt. Ervin D. Shaw, one of the first Americans to see air action in WW I, killed in France July 9, 1918, when his Bristol fighter was shot down during a reconnaissance mission. Area 3,363 acres; supports another 13,000 acres. Runways 10,000 ft. and 8,000 ft. Altitude 244 ft. Military 6,000; civilians 1,100. Payroll $167 million. Housing: 170 officer, 1,534 enlisted, 294 transient (164 VAQ, 90 VOQ, 40 TLF). 40-bed hospital.

**Sheppard AFB,** Tex. 76311-5000; 4 mi. N of Wichita Falls. Phone (817) 676-2511; DSN 736-1001. AETC base. The 82d Training Wing includes the 396th Technical Training Gp., which conducts courses in aircraft maintenance, civil engineering, communication, and comptroller and instructor training; the 82d Medical Training Gp., which provides training in biomedical sciences, dentistry, health service administration, medical readiness, medicine, nursing, and the Physician Assistant Training Program; the 82d Field Training Gp., which provides training on specific weapon systems at 46 field training detachments and 18 operating locations worldwide; the 82d Support Gp.; the

82d Medical Gp.; and the 82d Logistics Gp. The 82d Technical Training Gp. is scheduled to be activated in 1994. The 80th Flying Training Wing conducts T-37 and T-38 undergraduate pilot training and instructor pilot training for 12 nations in the Euro-NATO Joint Jet Pilot Training Program. The 80th FTW also conducts introduction to fighter fundamentals with AT-38 aircraft. Base activated June 14, 1941; named for US Sen. Morris E. Sheppard of Texas, who died Apr. 9, 1941. Area 5,486 acres. Runways 7,100 ft., 8,800 ft., and 13,100 ft. Altitude 1,015 ft. Military 7,639; civilians 3,464. Payroll $276 million. Housing: 199 officer, 1,193 NCO, 2,636 transient (1,493 VAQ, 65 TLF, 151 UOQ, 624 UEQ, 303 VOQ). 90-bed hospital.

**Soesterberg AB,** the Netherlands, APO AE 09719; 3 mi. from Zeist; 26 mi. from Amsterdam. Phone (commercial, from CONUS) 011-31-3463-58199; DSN 363-8199. Royal Netherlands air base. 32d Fighter Gp. (USAFE). Base activated 1913; US presence began 1954. Area 515 acres. Runway 8,300 ft. Altitude 66 ft. 33 VAQ, 6 VOQ. Clinic. US military will withdraw from Soesterberg and the 32d Fighter Gp. will inactivate Sept. 30, 1994.

**Spangdahlem AB,** Germany, APO AE 09126-5000; 8 mi. E of Bitburg; 20 mi. NE of Trier. Phone (commercial, from CONUS) 011-49-6565-61-1110; DSN 452-1110. USAFE base. 52d Fighter Wing flies F-16s, F-15s, and A-10s. Base activated and US presence began in 1953. Named after local town. Area 1,282 acres. Runway 10,000 ft. Altitude 1,196 ft. Military 4,600; civilians 600. Payroll $168 million. Housing: 43 officer, 615 enlisted, 500 govt.-leased units, 1,110 billeting spaces.

**Tinker AFB,** Okla. 73145-5990; 8 mi. SE of Oklahoma City. Phone (405) 732-7321; DSN 884-1110. AFMC base. Hq. Oklahoma City Air Logistics Center furnishes logistics support for bombers, jet engines, instruments, and electronics. Other major units include 552d Air Control Wing; 507th Air Refueling Gp. (AFRES); Navy Strategic Communications Wing ONE. Base activated Mar. 1942; named for Maj. Gen. Clarence L. Tinker, whose LB-30 (an early model B-24) went down at sea southwest of Midway Island June 7, 1942. Area 4,885 acres. Runway length NA. Altitude 1,291 ft. Military 6,768; civilians 11,926. Payroll $765 million. Housing: 108 officer, 622 NCO. 22-bed hospital.

**Travis AFB,** Calif. 94535-5000; 50 mi. NE of San Francisco at Fairfield. Phone (707) 424-5000; DSN 837-1110. AMC base. Hq. 15th Air Force; 60th Airlift Wing; 349th Airlift Wing (AFRES Assoc.); David Grant Medical Center; Air Force Band in Blue; Air Museum. Primary mission of 60th AW is strategic airlift. Base activated May 17, 1943; named for Brig. Gen. Robert F. Travis, killed Aug. 5, 1950, in a B-29 accident. Area 6,258 acres. Two runways, each approximately 11,000 ft. Altitude 62 ft. Military 12,082; civilians 3,517. Payroll $407 million. Housing: 372 officer, 2,092 enlisted, 3,546 enlisted dormitory spaces, 823 transient (79 TLF, 203 VOQ, 541 VAQ). 298-bed hospital (acute care), 75 aeromedical staging flight beds, 52 dental treatment rooms.

**Tyndall AFB,** Fla. 32403-5000; 12 mi. E of Panama City. Phone (904) 283-1113; DSN 523-1113. AETC base. 325th Fighter Wing, F-15 operations. The 325th FW provides training for all USAF F-15 air-to-air pilots and maintains readiness for 72 aircraft and assigned operations and support personnel for combat units worldwide. Associate units include Hq. 1st Air Force; Southeast Air Defense Sector; 475th Weapons Evaluation Gp.; Air Force Civil Engineer Support Agency; 331st Technical Training Sqdn.; and 17th Crew Training Sqdn. (USAF Water Survival School). Base activated Dec. 7, 1941; named for 1st Lt. Frank B. Tyndall, WW I fighter pilot killed July 15, 1930, in a P-1 crash.

Area 29,115 acres. Runway length NA. Altitude 18 ft. Military 5,233; civilians 1,787. Payroll $170 million. Housing: 1,069 family units. 35-bed hospital.

**US Air Force Academy,** Colo. 80840-5025; N of Colorado Springs. Phone (719) 472-1818; DSN 259-3110. Direct Reporting Unit. Established Apr. 1, 1954. First class entered Lowry AFB, Colo., July 1955. Moved to permanent location Aug. 1958. Tenant units include Frank J. Seiler Research Lab (AFMC); DoD Medical Exam Review Board. Aircraft flown: T-41, Cessna 150 (cadet flying team), UV-18 (Det. 1, Peterson AFB), 126E (sailplane), ASK-21 (sailplane), SGS-2-33A (glider), TG-7A (motor glider), and T-3A (enhanced flight screener). Area 18,325 acres. Runways 2,500 ft., 3,500 ft., and 4,500 ft. Altitude 7,280 ft. Military 2,795; cadets 4,100; Preparatory School students 196; civilians 1,745. Payroll $298 million. Housing: 620 officer, 609 enlisted, 78 transient, 25 temporary family quarters. 65-bed hospital.

**Vance AFB,** Okla. 73705-5000; 3 mi. SSW of Enid. Phone (405) 237-2121; DSN 940-7110. AETC base. 71st Flying Training Wing, undergraduate pilot training. Base activated Nov. 1941; named for Lt. Col. Leon R. Vance, Jr., Enid native, 1939 West Point graduate, and Medal of Honor recipient, killed July 26, 1944, when air-evac plane returning to the US went down in the Atlantic near Iceland. Area 4,394 acres. Runways 5,000 ft., 9,200 ft., and 9,200 ft. Altitude 1,007 ft. Military 812; civilians 1,326 (approx. 1,200 contract employees). Payroll $108.2 million. Housing: 131 officer, 98 enlisted, 36 transient, 10 TLF. Clinic.

**Vandenberg AFB,** Calif. 93437-5000; 8 mi. NNW of Lompoc. Phone (805) 734-8252 (ext. 6-1611); DSN 276-1110. AFSPC base. Host unit: 30th Space Wing, conducts polar-orbiting space launches and supports research and development tests for DoD, USAF, and NASA space, ballistic missile, and aeronautical systems. The 30th SPW furnishes facilities and essential services to more than 60 aerospace contractors on base. Originally Army's Camp Cooke. Activated Oct. 1941. Base taken over by USAF June 7, 1957; renamed for Gen. Hoyt S. Vandenberg, USAF's second Chief of Staff. Area 98,400 acres. Runway length NA. Altitude 400 ft. Military 3,349; civilians 1,294; civilian contractors 3,835. Payroll $126.4 million (military and civilians); $132.4 million (contractors). Housing: 494 officer, 1,499 NCO, 172 trailer spaces, 400 transient. 45-bed hospital.

**Warren AFB** (see Francis E. Warren AFB).

**Whiteman AFB,** Mo. 65305-5000; 2 mi. S of Knob Noster. Phone (816) 687-1110; DSN 975-6123. ACC base. The 509th Bomb Wing is the base's host unit and was activated Apr. 1, 1993. It received its first of 20 B-2 bombers Dec. 17, 1993. The 351st Missile Wing is a tenant unit and is currently deactivating its 150 Minuteman II ICBMs. 442d Fighter Wing (AFRES). Base activated in 1942; named for Sedalia resident 2d Lt. George A. Whiteman, first pilot to die in aerial combat during the attack on Pearl Harbor. Area 4,627 acres, plus missile complex of about 6,000 sq. mi. Runway 12,400 ft. Altitude 869 ft. Military 3,793; civilians 440. Payroll data NA. Housing: 195 officer, 775 enlisted, 137 transient (12 three-bdrm. guest houses, 53 VAQ, 68 VOQ, 4 DVQ). 30-bed hospital.

**Wright-Patterson AFB,** Ohio 45433; 10 mi. ENE of Dayton. Phone (513) 257-1110; DSN 787-1110. AFMC base. Hq. Air Force Materiel Command; Hq. Aeronautical Systems Center (AFMC); Wright Laboratory; Air Force Institute of Technology (AETC); Wright-Patterson Medical Center; 645th Air Base Wing (AFMC); 906th Fighter Gp. (AFRES) (inactivated Oct. 1, 1994); 907th Airlift Gp. (AFRES); approximately 70 other

DoD activities and government agencies. Originally separate, Wright Field and Patterson Field were merged and redesignated Wright-Patterson AFB Jan. 13, 1948. Named for aviation pioneers Orville and Wilbur Wright and for 1st Lt. Frank S. Patterson, killed June 19, 1918, in the crash of a DH-4. The Wright brothers did much of their early flying on Huffman Prairie, now in Area C of present base. The prairie recently became part of the Aviation Heritage National Historic Park and is open to the public. Area 8,145 acres. Runway 19,600 ft. Altitude 824 ft. Military 9,026; civilians 15,974. Payroll (for FY 1992) $986 million. Housing: 732 officer, 1,629 NCO. 301-bed hospital.

**Yokota AB,** Japan, APO AP 96328-5000; approx. 28 mi. W of Tokyo. Phone (commercial, from CONUS) 011-81-0425-2511, ext. 7020; DSN 225-7020. PACAF base. Hq. US Forces, Japan; Hq. 5th Air Force, 316th ALSG (AMC). Host unit: 374th Airlift Wing (PACAF), C-130, UH-1N, C-9, and C-21 operations. Primary aerial port in Japan. Base opened as Tama Army Air Field by Japanese in 1940. Area 1,750 acres. Runway 12,000 ft. Altitude 457 ft. Military 4,412; US civilians 901; local nationals 1,424. Payroll $156 million. Housing: 574 officer, 1,876 enlisted, 53 TLF. Unaccompanied housing: 232 officer, 1,330 enlisted, 57 SNOQ, 229 VOQ, 190 VAQ. 30-bed hospital.

## MINOR INSTALLATIONS

In addition to the installations listed above, the Air Force has a number of minor installations. These Air Force stations (AFS) and air stations (AS) perform various missions, including air defense and missile warning. Here is a listing of such installations with state (or APO), ZIP code, and major command. When an installation can be reached by a general-purpose DSN number, that number is listed. In some cases, the designation air base (AB) is used.

**Avon Park AFS,** Fla. 33825 (ACC) . . . . . . . . . . . . . . . . . . . . . . . . . . . . . DSN 968-1110
**Cape Canaveral AFS,** Fla. 32925-5000 (AFSPC) . . . . . . . . . . . . . . . . . DSN 467-1110
**Cape Cod AFS,** Mass. 02561-9314 (AFSPC) . . . . . . . . . . . . . . . . . . . . . DSN 557-2202
**Cavalier AFS,** N.D. 58220-5000 (AFSPC) . . . . . . . . . . . . . . . . . . . . . . . DSN 330-3292
**Cheyenne Mountain AFS,** Colo. 80914-5515 (AFSPC) . . . . . . . . . . . . . DSN 268-1011[a]
**Clear AFS,** Alaska APO AP 99704 (AFSPC) . . . . . . . . . . . . . . . . . . . . . DSN 585-6416
**Decimomannu AB** (Italy), APO AE 09606 (USAFE) . . . . . . . . . . . . . . . DSN 621-9267
**Duke Field AFS,** Fla. 32542-6005 (AFSOC) . . . . . . . . . . . . . . . . . . . . . . DSN 875-1110
**Eareckson AFS** (formerly Shemya AFB),
Alaska APO AP 96512-5000 (PACAF) . . . . . . . . . . . . . . . . . . . . . . . DSN 317-392-3000
**Eldorado AFS,** Tex. 76936-5000 (AFSPC) . . . . . . . . . . . . . . . . . . . . . . . DSN 477-4220
**Galena Airport,** Alaska APO AP 96510 (PACAF) . . . . . . . . . . . . . . cmcl. 907-446-3311
**Gila Bend Air Force Auxiliary Field,** Ariz. 85337-5000 (AETC) . . . . . . DSN 853-5220
**Indian Springs Air Force Auxiliary Field,** Nev. 89018-5000 (ACC) . . . DSN 682-6201
**Izmir AS** (Turkey), APO AE 09821 (USAFE) . . . . . . . . . . . . . . . . . . . . . DSN 675-1110
**King Salmon Airport,** Alaska APO AP 96513 (PACAF) . . . . . . . . . cmcl. 907-721-3301
**New Boston AFS,** N.H. 03031-5000 (AFSPC) . . . . . . . . . . . . . . . . . . . DSN 881-1550
**Onizuka AFS,** Calif. 94088-3430 (AFSPC) . . . . . . . . . . . . . . . . . . . . . . . DSN 561-3110[a]
**Pirinclik AS** (Turkey), APO AE 09825 (USAFE) . . . . . . . . . . . . . . . . . . DSN 679-1110
**RAF Chicksands** (UK), APO AE 09465-5000 (USAFE) . . . . . . . . . . . . . DSN 234-1110
**RAF Croughton** (UK), APO AE 09494 (USAFE) . . . . . . . . . . . . . . . . . . DSN 236-1110
**RAF Fairford** (UK), APO AE 09456 (USAFE) . . . . . . . . . . . . . . . . . . . . . DSN 247-1110
**Richards-Gebaur AFB,** Mo. 64030-5000 (AFRES) . . . . . . . . . . . . . . . . . DSN 463-1110

**San Vito dei Normanni AS** (Italy), APO AE 09605 (USAFE) .......... DSN 622-1110
**Thule AB** (Greenland), APO AE 09704-5000 (AFSPC)
(ask for Thule operator) .......................................... DSN 834-1211
**Torrejon AB,** APO AE 09641 (USAFE) ............................ DSN 723-8367
**22d Wing North Bay** (Canada), APO AE 09732 (ACC) .............. DSN 628-2660
**Woomera AS** (Australia), APO AP 96552 (AFSPC) ................. DSN 626-1636
[a]Became minor installation July 1, 1994

## ANG AND AFRES BASES

Note: This section of the Guide consolidates major Air National Guard (ANG) and Air Force Reserve (AFRES) bases into a single listing. Most ANG locations are listed according to the airports whose facilities they share. AFRES units are listed by the names of their bases and are designated as AFRES facilities. There are, in addition, some ANG and AFRES units located on active-duty bases. These may be found in the "Major Installations" section.

**Allen C. Thompson Field,** Miss. 39208-0810; 7 mi. E of Jackson. Phone (601) 939-3633; DSN 731-9210. 172d Airlift Gp. (ANG). ANG area 116 acres. Runway length NA. Altitude 346 ft. Military 1,198, full-time personnel 316. Payroll $16.4 million. Six-bed dispensary.

**Alpena County Regional Airport,** Mich. 49707; 7 mi. W of Alpena. Phone (517) 354-6291; DSN 741-3500. Training site detachment. Facilities used by ANG and AFRES units for annual field training and by Army National Guard (ARNG) and Marine Corps Reserve for special training. Area 610 acres. Runway length NA. Altitude 689 ft. Military 69, civilian full-time support 69. Payroll $2.2 million. Housing: 1,500 personnel. 14-bed hospital. Dispensary.

**Anchorage,** Alaska (Kulis ANGB at Anchorage International Airport) 99502. Phone (907) 249-1208; DSN 626-1208. 176th Composite Gp. (ANG); 144th Airlift Sqdn. (ANG) and 210th Air Rescue Sqdn. (ANG). Base named for Lt. Albert Kulis, killed in training flight in 1954. Area 129 acres. Runway length NA. Altitude 124 ft. Military 1,094, full-time personnel 422. Payroll $19.3 million. Six-bed hospital.

**Atlanta,** Ga. (McCollum ANG Station, Kennesaw, Ga.) 30144; 27 mi. N of Atlanta, 10 mi. from Dobbins ARB. Phone (404) 422-2500; DSN 925-2500. 129th Control Sqdn. and 118th Control Sqdn. (ANG). Area 13 acres. Runway length NA. Altitude 1,060 ft. Military 355, full-time personnel 47. Payroll disbursed through Dobbins ARB.

**Atlantic City Airport,** N.J. 08232-9500; 10 mi. W of Atlantic City. Phone (609) 645-6000; DSN 455-6000. 177th Fighter Gp. (ANG). Area 286 acres. Runway length NA. Altitude 76 ft. Military 1,015, full-time support 383. Payroll $14.3 million.

**Baltimore,** Md. (Martin State Airport) 21220-2899; 8 mi. E of Baltimore. Phone (301) 687-6270; DSN 243-6210. 175th Fighter Gp. (ANG); 135th Airlift Gp. (ANG). Area 175 acres. Runway length NA. Altitude 24 ft. Military 1,890, full-time personnel 520. Payroll $20.1 million. Clinic.

**Bangor International Airport,** Me. 04401-3099; 4 mi. NW of Bangor. Phone (207) 990-7700; DSN 698-7700. 101st Air Refueling Wg. (ANG); 776th Radar Sqdn. (ACC). Area 457 acres. Runway length NA. Altitude 192 ft. Military 1,026, full-time personnel 385, Title 5 civilians 25. Payroll $16.2 million. Small BX.

**Barnes Municipal Airport,** Mass. 01085; 3 mi. N of Westfield. Phone (413) 568-9151; DSN 636-1210/11. 104th Fighter Gp. (ANG). Area 134 acres. Runway length NA. Altitude 270 ft. Military 1,046, full-time personnel 309. Payroll $14.3 million.

**Bergstrom ARS,** Tex. 78719-2557; 7 mi. SE of Austin. Phone (512) 389-0444; DSN 685-1110. AFRES base. 924th Fighter Group, F-16 operations; Hq. 10th Air Force (AFRES); Ground Combat Readiness Center (AFRES). Area 450 acres. Runway length NA. Altitude 541 ft. Reservists 1,200, civilians 350. Activated as a base Sept. 22, 1942. Named for Capt. John A. E. Bergstrom, first Austin serviceman killed in WW II, who died Dec. 8, 1941, at Clark Field, the Philippines. City of Austin converting base to new airport, due to open in 1998. Runway 12,250 ft. Housing: 209 VAQ, 122 VOQ. No BX or commissary facilities available.

**Birmingham Airport,** Ala. 35217. Phone (205) 841-9200; DSN 694-2210. 117th Reconnaissance Wing (ANG). Area 86 acres. Runway length NA. Altitude 650 ft. Military 1,204, full-time personnel 344. Payroll $17.6 million.

**Boise Air Terminal,** Idaho (Gowen Field) 83707; 6 mi. S of Boise. Phone (208) 389-5011; DSN 941-5011. 124th Fighter Gp. (ANG). Also host to ARNG (Army field training site) and Marine Corps Reserve. Airport named for Lt. Paul R. Gowen, killed in B-10 crash in Panama July 11, 1938. Area 1,994 acres. Runway length NA. Altitude 2,858 ft. Military 1,511, full-time personnel 537. Payroll $16.2 million. Limited transient facilities available during ARNG camps.

**Bradley International Airport,** Windsor Locks, Conn. 06026-5000; 15 mi. N of Hartford at East Granby. Phone (203) 623-8291; DSN 636-8310. 103d Fighter Gp. (ANG); ARNG aviation battalion. Base named for Lt. Eugene M. Bradley, killed in P-40 crash in Aug. 1941. Area 126 acres. Runway length NA. Altitude 173 ft. Military 996, full-time personnel 310. Payroll $14.1 million.

**Buckley ANGB,** Colo. 80011; 8 mi. E of Denver. Phone (303) 366-5363; DSN 877-9011. 140th Fighter Wing (ANG); 154th Tactical Control Gp.; Hq. Colorado ANG; 227th Air Traffic Control Flt. (ANG); and 240th Civil Engineering Flt. (ANG). Also host to Navy Reserve, Marine Corps Reserve, ARNG, and Air Force units. Base activated Apr. 1, 1942, as a gunnery training facility. ANG assumed control from US Navy in 1959. Base named for Lt. John H. Buckley, National Guardsman, killed in France Sept. 27, 1918. Area 3,832 acres. Runway length NA. Altitude 5,663 ft. Military 1,436, full-time personnel 364, Title 5 civilians 257. Payroll $26.8 million. Dispensary.

**Burlington International Airport,** Vt. 05401; 3 mi. E of Burlington. Phone (802) 658-0770; DSN 220-5210. 158th Fighter Gp. (ANG). Area 241 acres. Runway length NA. Altitude 371 ft. Military 995, full-time personnel 398. Payroll $14.3 million.

**Capital Municipal Airport,** Ill. 63707-5000; 2 mi. NW of Springfield. Phone (217) 753-8850; DSN 892-8210. 183d Fighter Gp. (ANG). Area 206 acres. Runway length NA. Altitude 592 ft. Military 1,168, full-time personnel 336. Payroll $14.1 million. Dispensary.

**Carswell ARB,** Tex. 76127-6200; 7 mi. WNW of downtown Fort Worth. Phone (817) 782-5000; DSN 739-1110. AFRES base. 301st Fighter Wing (AFRES), F-16 operations. Base activated Aug. 1942; named Jan. 30, 1948, for Maj. Horace S. Carswell, Jr., native of Forth Worth, WW II B-24 pilot and posthumous Medal of Honor recipient. Area approximately 322 acres. Runway 12,000 ft. Altitude 650 ft. Military 8, civilians 575, Reservists 1,400. Payroll $24.7 million. Housing: 0. Lodging: 142 VOQ, 10 VIP.

**Channel Islands ANG Station,** Point Mugu, Calif. 93041-4001. Phone (805) 986-8000; DSN 893-7000. 146th Airlift Wing (ANG). Area 86 acres. Runway length NA. Altitude 12 ft. Military 1,506, full-time personnel 369. Payroll $18.2 million.

**Charlotte/Douglas International Airport,** Charlotte, N.C. 28208. Phone (704) 391-4100; DSN 583-9210. 145th Airlift Gp. (ANG). Area 79 acres. Runway length NA. Altitude 749 ft. Military 1,284, full-time personnel 332. Payroll $17.1 million. Clinic.

**Cheyenne Municipal Airport,** Cheyenne Wyo. 82001. Phone (307) 772-6201; DSN 943-6201. 153d Airlift Gp. (ANG). Area 71 acres. Runway length NA. Altitude 6,156 ft. Military 1,025, full-time personnel 266. Payroll $11.7 million.

**Dannelly Field,** Ala. 36196; 7 mi. SW of Montgomery. Phone (205) 284-7210; DSN 742-9210. 187th Fighter Gp. (ANG). Base hosts 232d Combat Communications Sqdn. Field named for Ens. Clarence Dannelly, Navy pilot killed at Pensacola, Fla., during WW II. Area 51 acres. Runway length NA. Altitude 221 ft. Military 1,053, full-time personnel 346. Payroll $18.1 million. Dispensary.

**Des Moines International Airport,** Iowa 50321; in city of Des Moines. Phone (515) 287-9210; DSN 939-8210. 132d Fighter Wing (ANG). Area 113 acres. Runway length NA. Altitude 957 ft. Military 1,091, full-time personnel 344. Payroll $14.2 million.

**Dobbins ARB,** Ga. (Marietta) 30069-5000; 16 mi. NW of Atlanta. Phone (404) 421-5000; DSN 925-1110. AFRES base. Hq. 14th Air Force (AFRES); 94th Airlift Wing (AFRES); 116th Fighter Wing (ANG); 151st Military Intelligence Battalion (ARNG); 345th Medical Company (USAR). Base activated 1943. Named for Capt. Charles Dobbins, WW II pilot killed in action near Sicily. Area 1,656 acres (ANG 55 acres). Runway length NA. Altitude 1,068 ft. AFRES: active-duty 50, civilians 1,050, Reservists 2,011. Payroll $87 million. ANG: military 1,213, full-time personnel 134. Payroll $4.2 million. USAR: active-duty 16, Reservists 69. Housing: 5 NCO, VOQ, VAQ. Dispensary. NAS Atlanta, Lockheed Aeronautical Systems Co./Defense Plant 6 adjoin Dobbins ARB and use airfield facilities.

**Duluth International Airport,** Minn. 55811-5000; 5 mi. NW of Duluth. Phone (218) 727-6886; DSN 825-7210. 148th Fighter Gp. (ANG). Area 329 acres. Runway length NA. Altitude 1,429 ft. Military 1,009, full-time personnel 379 (plus 24 civilians). Payroll $16.3 million.

**Eastern West Virginia Regional Airport/Shepherd Field,** W. Va. 25401; 4 mi. S of Martinsburg. Phone (304) 267-5100; DSN 242-9210. 167th Airlift Gp. (ANG). Area 349 acres. Runway length NA. Altitude 556 ft. Military 1,269, full-time personnel 295. Payroll $13.8 million. Dispensary.

**Ellington Field,** Tex. 77034-5586; a City of Houston Airport 17 mi. SE of downtown Houston. Phone (713) 929-2221; DSN 954-2221. 147th Fighter Gp. (ANG). Other tenants include NASA Flight Operations, US Coast Guard, ARNG, FAA. Base named for Lt. Eric L. Ellington, pilot killed in Nov. 1913. Area 213 acres. Runway length NA. Altitude 40 ft. Military 1,025, full-time personnel 418. Payroll $18.1 million.

**Forbes Field,** Kan. 66619-5000; 2 mi. S of Topeka. Phone (913) 862-1234; DSN 720-1234. 190th Air Refueling Gp. (ANG). Area 200 acres. Runway length NA. Altitude 1,079 ft. Military 978, full-time personnel 346 (plus 40 civilians). Payroll $14.7 million.

**Fort Smith Municipal Airport,** Ark. 72906. Phone (501) 648-5210; DSN 962-8210. 188th Fighter Gp. (ANG). Area 98 acres. Runway length NA. Altitude 468 ft. Military 1,048, full-time personnel 301. Payroll $12.2 million.

**Fort Wayne International Airport,** Ind. 46809-5000; 5 mi. SSW of Fort Wayne. Phone (219) 478-3210; DSN 786-1210. 122d Fighter Wing (ANG). Area 139 acres. Runway length NA. Altitude 800 ft. Military 1,328, full-time personnel 365. Payroll $15.7 million.

**Francis S. Gabreski Airport,** Westhampton Beach, N.Y. 11978-1294. Phone (516) 288-7300; DSN 456-7410. 106th Rescue Gp. (ANG). Named for Col. Francis S. Gabreski, third leading USAAF/USAF ace of all time. Area 70 acres. Runway length NA. Altitude 67 ft. Military 793, full-time personnel 270. Payroll $12.7 million.

**Fresno Air Terminal,** Calif. 93727-2199; 5 mi. NE of Fresno. Phone (209) 454-5155; DSN 949-9210. 144th Fighter Wing (ANG). Area 127 acres. Runway length NA. Altitude 332 ft. Military 1,004, full-time personnel 395. Payroll $16 million.

**General Mitchell International Airport/ARS,** Wis. 53207-6299; 3 mi. S of Milwaukee. AFRES base. Runway 9,690 ft. Altitude 723 ft. ANG and AFRES have separate telephone lines and facilities. ANG (414) 747-4410; DSN 580-8410. 128th Air Refueling Gp. (ANG). ANG area 111 acres. Military 999, full-time personnel 334. Payroll $14.6 million. AFRES phone (414) 482-5000; DSN 950-5000. 440th Airlift Wing (AFRES). AFRES area 103 acres. Full-time personnel and civilians 350, Reservists 1,183. Payroll $18.9 million.

**Greater Peoria Airport,** Ill. 61607-1498; 7 mi. SW of Peoria. Phone (309) 633-3000; DSN 724-4210. 182d Fighter Gp. (ANG). Area 386 acres. Runway length NA. Altitude 624 ft. Military 1,018, full-time personnel 266. Payroll $10.9 million. Dispensary.

**Great Falls International Airport,** Mont. 59401-5000; 5 mi. SW of Great Falls. Phone (406) 727-4650; DSN 279-2301. 120th Fighter Gp. (ANG). Area 139 acres. Runway length NA. Altitude 3,674 ft. Military 1,019, full-time personnel 392. Payroll $17.1 million. Dispensary.

**Gulfport-Biloxi Regional Airport,** Miss. 39501; within city limits of Gulfport. Phone (601) 868-6200; DSN 363-8200. Training site; also host to 255th Tactical Control Sqdn. (ANG); ARNG Transportation Repair Shop; and 173d Civil Engineering Flt. An air-to-ground gunnery range is located 70 mi. N of site. Area 214 acres. Runway length NA. Altitude 28 ft. ANG military 513, full-time personnel 50. Payroll $4.4 million. Two-bed dispensary.

**Hancock Field,** N.Y. 13211-7099; 5 mi. NE of Syracuse. Phone (315) 470-6100; DSN 587-9100. 174th Fighter Wing (ANG). Base operations for Hancock ANGB. 152d Tactical Control Gp.; 108th and 113th Tactical Control Sqdns. (ANG). Area 376 acres. Runway length NA. Altitude 421 ft. Military 1,433, full-time personnel 378. Payroll $15.1 million. Dispensary.

**Harrisburg International Airport,** Pa. 17057; 10 mi. E of Harrisburg. Phone (717) 948-2201; DSN 430-9201. 193d Special Operations Gp. (ANG). ANG area 39 acres. Runway length NA. Altitude 310 ft. Military 1,134, full-time personnel 294. Payroll $18.4 million.

**Hector International Airport,** Fargo, N.D. 58105-5536. Phone (701) 237-6030; DSN 362-8110. 119th Fighter Gp. (ANG). Area 209 acres. Runway length NA. Altitude 900 ft. Military 1,154, full-time personnel 400. Payroll $18.6 million.

**Homestead ARB,** Fla. 33039; 5 mi. NNE of Homestead. Phone (305) 224-7303; DSN 791-7303. AFRES station. 482d Fighter Wing (AFRES); 301st Rescue Sqdn. (AFRES); Det. 1, 125th Fighter Gp. (Fla. ANG, NORAD). Limited billeting for official business only. No medical facilities. Area approximately 1,000 acres. Runway 11,200 ft. Altitude 11 ft. Base was devastated by Hurricane Andrew in August 1992 and is still under reconstruction.

**Hulman Regional Airport,** Ind. 47803-5000; 5 mi. E of Terre Haute. Phone (812) 877-5210; DSN 724-1210. 181st Fighter Gp. (ANG). Area 279 acres. Runway length NA. Altitude 585 ft. Military 1,170, full-time personnel 321. Payroll $13.9 million. Five-bed dispensary.

**Jacksonville International Airport,** Fla. 32229; 15 mi. NW of Jacksonville. Phone (904) 741-7150; DSN 460-7150. 125th Fighter Gp. (ANG). Area 332 acres. Runway length NA. Altitude 26 ft. Military 1,007, full-time personnel 405. Payroll $17.7 million. Five-bed dispensary.

**Joe Foss Field,** Sioux Falls, S.D. 57104; N side of Sioux Falls. Phone (605) 333-5700; DSN 939-7210. 114th Fighter Gp. (ANG). Field named for Brig. Gen. Joseph J. Foss, WW II ace, former governor of South Dakota, former AFA national president, and founder of the South Dakota ANG. Area 166 acres. Runway length NA. Altitude 1,428 ft. Military 962, full-time personnel 291. Payroll $12 million.

**Key Field,** Meridian, Miss. 39302-1825; located at municipal airport near Hwys. 20 and 59. Phone (601) 484-9000; DSN 694-9210. 186th Air Refueling Gp. (ANG); host to 238th Combat Communications Sqdn. (ANG). Area 116 acres. Runway length NA. Altitude 297 ft. Military 1,272, full-time personnel 368. Payroll $15.2 million. Dispensary.

**Klamath Falls International Airport** (Kingsley Field), Ore. 97603-0400; 5 mi. SE of Klamath Falls. Phone (503) 883-6350; DSN 830-6350. 114th Fighter Training Sqdn. (ANG); 142d OLAD (ANG). Area 425 acres. Runway length NA. Altitude 4,000 ft. Military 406, full-time personnel 375, Title 5 civilians 16. Payroll $40.1 million. Clinic.

**Lambert-St. Louis International Airport,** Bridgeton, Mo. 63145; 3 mi. W of St. Louis. Phone (314) 263-6200; DSN 693-6200. 131st Fighter Wing (ANG). Area 49 acres. Runway length NA. Altitude 589 ft. Military 1,551, full-time personnel 375. Payroll $22.8 million.

**Lincoln Municipal Airport,** Neb. 68524-1897; 1 mi. NW of Lincoln. Phone (402) 473-1326; DSN 720-1352. 155th Reconnaissance Gp. (ANG). Also hosts ARNG unit. Area 175 acres. Runway length NA. Altitude 1,207 ft. Military 1,117, full-time personnel 342. Payroll $12.9 million. Tactical clinic.

**Mansfield Lahm Airport,** Ohio 44901-5000; 3 mi. N of Mansfield. Phone (419) 521-0100; DSN 696-6210. 179th Airlift Gp. (ANG). Airport named for nearby city and aviation pioneer Brig. Gen. Frank P. Lahm. Area 224 acres. Runway length NA. Altitude 1,296 ft. Military 945, full-time personnel 259. Payroll $10.8 million. Clinic. Coast Guard exchange.

**McEntire ANGB,** S.C. 29044; 12 mi. E of Columbia. Phone (803) 776-5121; DSN 583-8201. 169th Fighter Gp. (ANG). Also host to 240th Combat Communications Sqdn. (ANG) and Army Guard aviation unit. Base named for ANG Brig. Gen. B. B. McEntire, Jr., killed in F-104 accident in 1961. Area 2,473 acres. Runway length NA. Altitude 250 ft. Military 1,356, full-time personnel 383. Payroll $14.9 million. Dispensary.

**McGhee Tyson Airport,** Tenn. 37901; 10 mi. SW of Knoxville. Phone (615) 985-3210; DSN 588-3210. Host unit is 134th Air Refueling Gp. (ANG). Tenants include 228th

Combat Communications Sqdn. and ANG's I. G. Brown Professional Military Education Center. Area 271 acres. Runway length NA. Altitude 980 ft. Military 1,162, full-time personnel 354. Payroll $16.4 million. Dispensary.

**Memphis International Airport,** Tenn. 38181-0026; within Memphis city limits. Phone (901) 369-4111; DSN 966-8111. 164th Airlift Gp. (ANG). ANG occupies 99 acres. Runway length NA. Altitude 332 ft. Military 949, full-time personnel 263. Payroll $11.7 million. Clinic.

**Minneapolis–St. Paul International Airport/ARS,** Minn. 55450-2000; in Minneapolis, near confluence of the Mississippi and Minnesota rivers. AFRES base. Runway length NA. Altitude 840 ft. ANG and AFRES have separate phones and facilities. ANG phone (612) 725-5011; DSN 825-5110. 133d Airlift Wing (ANG). ANG area 128 acres. Military 1,399, full-time personnel 315. Payroll $18.5 million. AFRES phone (612) 725-5011; DSN 825-5110. 934th Airlift Gp. (AFRES) flies C-130s. AFRES area 300 acres. Full-time personnel 138, civilians 194, Reservists 1,200. Payroll $20.5 million. Other units include 210th Engineering and Installation Sqdn. (ANG); 237th Air Traffic Control Flt. (ANG); Navy Readiness Comd., Region 16; Naval Air Reserve Center; Marine Wing Support Gp. 47, Det. A; Civil Air Patrol—USAF NCLR and CAP-USAF MNLO; Rothe Development Inc. (AFRES). Billeting and BX available.

**Nashville Metropolitan Airport,** Tenn. 37217-0267; 6 mi. SE of Nashville. Phone (615) 361-4600; DSN 446-6210. 118th Airlift Wing (ANG). Area 85 acres. Runway length NA. Altitude 597 ft. Military 1,392, full-time personnel 372. Payroll $19 million.

**Naval Air Station Dallas** (Hensley Field), Tex. 75211. Phone (214) 266-6111; DSN 874-6111. 136th Airlift Wing (ANG). Area 49 acres. Runway length NA. Altitude 495 ft. Military 961, full-time personnel 255. Payroll $13.1 million.

**Naval Air Station Moffett,** Calif. 94035; 2 mi. N of Mountain View. ANG phone (415) 404-9129; DSN 494-9129. 129th Rescue Gp. (ANG). Area 13 acres. Runway length NA. Altitude 34 ft. Military 749, full-time personnel 263. Payroll $15.4 million.

**Naval Air Station New Orleans** (Alvin Callender Field), La. 70143-5400; 15 mi. S of New Orleans. Runway length NA. Altitude 3 ft. ANG and AFRES have separate phones and facilities. ANG phone (504) 391-8618; DSN 457-8618. 159th Fighter Gp. (ANG). ANG military 1,215, full-time personnel 426. Payroll $18 million. AFRES phone (504) 393-3011; DSN 363-3011. 926th Fighter Gp. (AFRES). Military 986, full-time personnel 303. Payroll $15 million. NAS New Orleans was the first joint Air Reserve Training Facility. Field named for Alvin A. Callender, who served with the British Royal Flying Corps during WW I and was shot down over France in 1918. Area 3,245 acres (ANG 19 acres). Dispensary.

**New Castle County Airport,** Del. 19720; 5 mi. S of Wilmington. Phone (302) 323-3500; DSN 445-3360. 166th Airlift Gp. (ANG); ARNG aviation company. Area 57 acres. Runway length NA. Altitude 80 ft. Military 1,010, full-time personnel 261. Payroll $10.8 million. Two-bed dispensary.

**Niagara Falls International Airport/ARS,** N.Y. 14304-5000; 6 mi. E of Niagara Falls. Phone (716) 236-2000; DSN 238-3011. AFRES base. 914th Airlift Gp. (AFRES); 107th Fighter Gp. (ANG). Base activated Jan. 1952. Area 979 acres (ANG 104 acres). Runway length NA. Altitude 590 ft. AFRES: Reservists 1,300, civilians 314. ANG: military 943, full-time personnel 326. Total payroll $41 million.

**O'Hare International Airport/ARS,** Ill. 60666-5010; 22 mi. NW of Chicago's Loop. Phone (312) 825-6000; DSN 930-6000. AFRES base. 928th Airlift Gp. (AFRES); 126th Air Refueling Wing (ANG); Defense Contract Management District North Central, Fort Dearborn (US Army Reserve). Base activated Apr. 1946. Named for Lt. Cmdr. Edward H. "Butch" O'Hare, USN, Medal of Honor recipient, killed Nov. 26, 1943, during battle for Gilbert Islands. Area 349 acres (ANG 36 acres). Runway length NA. Altitude 643 ft. Reservists 1,559, full-time personnel and civilians (all units) 419, Illinois ANG 1,403, full-time personnel 351. Total payroll for facility $74.5 million.

**Ontario International Airport,** Ontario, Calif. 91761. Phone (714) 984-2705; DSN 947-3559. 148th Combat Communications Sqdn. (ANG); 210th Weather Flt. (ANG). Area 13 acres. Runway length NA. Altitude 900 ft. Military 154, full-time personnel 26. Payroll $1.1 million.

**Otis ANGB,** Mass. 02542-5001; 7 mi. NNE of Falmouth. Phone (508) 968-1000; DSN 557-4003. 102d Fighter Wing (ANG); 567th USAF Band (ANG); 101st and 202d Weather Flts. (ANG). Adjacent installations and organizations include Cape Cod AFS (6th Missile Warning Sqdn., 2165th Communications Sqdn.); US Coast Guard Air Station Cape Cod; Camp Edwards Army National Guard Training Site; 26th Aviation Brigade (ARNG); 1st Battalion, 25th Marines (Reserve); Massachusetts National Cemetery (VA). Base named for 1st Lt. Frank J. Otis, ANG flight surgeon and pilot killed in 1937 crash. Area 3,883 acres. Runway length NA. Altitude 132 ft. ANG military 1,149, ANG full-time personnel 417 (plus 318 Title 5 civilian employees). Payroll $27.8 million.

**Pease ANGB,** Portsmouth, N.H. 03803-6505. Phone (603) 430-2453; DSN 852-2453. 157th Air Refueling Gp. (ANG). Area 229 acres. Runway length NA. Altitude 101 ft. ANG military 1,170, ANG full-time personnel 370. Payroll $12 million.

**Pittsburgh International Airport/ARS,** Pa. 15108-4403; 15 mi. NW of Pittsburgh. Runway length NA. Altitude 1,203 ft. AFRES base. ANG and AFRES have separate phones and facilities. 171st Air Refueling Wing (ANG); phone (412) 269-8402; DSN 277-8402. 112th Air Refueling Gp. (ANG); phone (412) 269-8441; DSN 277-8441. ANG area 179 acres. Military 1,881, full-time personnel 517. Payroll $21.2 million. AFRES phone (412) 269-8000; DSN 277-8000. 911th Airlift Gp. (host unit). AFRES area 176 acres. Military 26, full-time personnel 142, civilians 222, Reservists 1,302. Payroll $20 million. Base activated 1943. Housing: 24 VOQ, 230 enlisted qtrs. Limited BX; no on-base housing.

**Portland International Airport,** Portland, Ore. 97218-2797. Phone (503) 335-4000; DSN 638-4000. 142d Fighter Gp. (ANG); 244th Combat Communications Sqdn. (ANG); 272d Combat Communications Sqdn. (ANG); 12th Special Forces Gp. (USAR); Oregon Wing, CAP. Also host to 939th Rescue Wing (AFRES) and 83d Aerial Port Sqdn. (AFRES). Area 246 acres. Runway length NA. Altitude 26 ft. Military 1,773, full-time personnel 621 (plus 100 civilians). Payroll $20.5 million.

**Puerto Rico International Airport** (Muniz ANGB), Puerto Rico 00914; E of San Juan. Phone (809) 253-5100; DSN 860-9210. 156th Fighter Gp. (ANG). Base named for Lt. Col. José A. Muniz, killed in aircraft accident July 4, 1960. Area 86 acres. Runway length NA. Altitude 9 ft. Military 969, full-time personnel 300. Payroll $15.7 million.

**Quonset State Airport,** R.I. 02852; 20 mi. S of Providence. Phone (401) 886-1200; DSN 476-3210. 143d Airlift Gp. (ANG). Area 79 acres. Runway length NA. Altitude 9 ft. Military 996, full-time personnel 270. Payroll $15.1 million.

**Reno-Cannon International Airport** (May ANGB), Nev. 89502; 5 mi. SE of Reno at 1776 ANG Way. Phone (702) 788-4500; DSN 830-4500. 152d Reconnaissance Gp. (ANG). Base named for Maj. Gen. James A. May, Nevada Adjutant General. Area 123 acres. Runway length NA. Altitude 4,411 ft. Military 1,104, full-time personnel 334. Payroll $13.5 million. Dispensary.

**Richmond International Airport** (Byrd Field), Va. 23150; 4 mi. SE of downtown Richmond. Phone (804) 222-8884; DSN 274-8884. 192d Fighter Gp. (ANG). Field named for Adm. Richard E. Byrd, famous Arctic and Antarctic explorer. Area 143 acres. Runway length NA. Altitude 167 ft. Military 1,089, full-time personnel 337. Payroll $13.9 million.

**Rickenbacker ANGB,** Ohio 43217-5887; 13 mi. SSW of Columbus. Phone (614) 492-8211; DSN 950-1110. Base transferred from SAC to ANG Apr. 1, 1980. 121st Air Refueling Wing (ANG); 907th Airlift Gp. (AFRES); 160th Air Refueling Gp. (ANG); Naval Air Reserve and Naval Construction (USNR). Base activated 1942. Formerly Lockbourne AFB; renamed May 7, 1974, in honor of Capt. Edward V. Rickenbacker, top US WW I ace and Medal of Honor recipient, who died July 23, 1973. Area 2,016 acres. Runway length NA. Altitude 744 ft. ANG military 1,940, full-time personnel 583, Title 5 civilians 299. Payroll $32.7 million. AFRES 1,176, full-time personnel 238. Payroll $11.1 million. Base was scheduled to close in Sept. 1994.

**Rosecrans Memorial Airport,** Mo. 64503; 4 mi. W of St. Joseph. Phone (816) 271-1300; DSN 720-9210. 139th Airlift Gp. (ANG). Area 207 acres. Runway length NA. Altitude 724 ft. Military 916, full-time personnel 264. Payroll $11.5 million.

**Roslyn ANG Station.** N.Y. 11576-2399; 27 mi. E of New York City. Phone (516) 299-5214; DSN 456-5201. 274th Combat Communications Sqdn. (ANG); 213th Engineering Installation Sqdn. (ANG). Also hosts two ARNG units. Area 50 acres. Runway length NA. Altitude 320 ft. Military 399, full-time personnel 42. Payroll through Stewart IAP, Newburgh, N.Y.

**Salt Lake City International Airport,** Utah 84116; 3 mi. W of Salt Lake City. Phone (801) 595-2200; DSN 790-9210. 151st Air Refueling Gp. (ANG); 169th Electronic Security Sqdn. (ANG). Also hosts ANG's 130th Engineering Installation Sqdn. and 106th and 109th Tactical Control Flts. Area 135 acres. Runway length NA. Altitude 4,220 ft. Military 1,585, full-time personnel 409 (plus 41 civilians). Payroll $20.2 million. Dispensary.

**Savannah International Airport,** Ga. 31402; 4 mi. NW of Savannah. Phone (912) 964-1941; DSN 860-8210. 165th Airlift Gp. (ANG). Also field training site. Area 20 acres. Runway length NA. Altitude 50 ft. Military 1,176, full-time personnel 330. Payroll $17.7 million. Housing: 156 officer, 736 enlisted. Three-bed dispensary.

**Schenectady Airport,** Scotia, N.Y. 12302-9752; 2 mi. N of Schenectady. Phone (518) 381-7300; DSN 974-9221. 109th Airlift Gp. (ANG). Area 106 acres. Runway length NA. Altitude 378 ft. Military 1,102, full-time personnel 258. Payroll $11.6 million. Dispensary.

**Selfridge ANGB,** Mich. 48045-5046; 3 mi. NE of Mount Clemens. Phone (313) 466-4011; DSN 273-0111. 127th Fighter Wing (ANG); 191st Fighter Gp. (ANG); 927th Air Refueling Gp. (AFRES). Also hosts Air Force, Navy Reserve, Marine Air Reserve, Army Reserve, Army units, and US Coast Guard Air Station for Detroit. Base activated July 1917; transferred to Michigan ANG July 1971. Named for 1st Lt. Thomas E. Selfridge, first Army officer to fly an airplane and first fatality of powered flight, killed Sept. 17,

1908, at Fort Myer, Va., when plane piloted by Orville Wright crashed. Area 3,070 acres. Runway length NA. Altitude 583 ft. ANG military 2,070, ANG full-time personnel 581 (plus 530 civilians). Payroll $44.6 million. Dispensary.

**Sioux Gateway Airport,** Iowa 51110; 7 mi. S of Sioux City. Phone (712) 255-3511; DSN 939-6210. 185th Fighter Gp. (ANG). Area 106 acres. Runway length NA. Altitude 1,098 ft. Military 937, full-time personnel 294. Payroll $13.4 million. Dispensary.

**Sky Harbor International Airport,** Phoenix, Ariz. 85034. Phone (602) 244-9841; DSN 853-9072. 161st Air Refueling Gp. (ANG). Area 58 acres. Runway length NA. Altitude 1,230 ft. Military 1,076, full-time personnel 342. Payroll $16.6 million.

**Springfield-Beckley Municipal Airport,** Ohio 45501-1780; 5 mi. S of Springfield. Phone (513) 323-8653; DSN 346-2311. 178th Fighter Gp. (ANG); 251st Combat Communications Gp. (ANG); 269th Combat Communications Sqdn. (ANG). Area 114 acres. Runway length NA. Altitude 1,052 ft. Military 1,205, full-time personnel 333. Payroll $15.9 million. Six-bed dispensary.

**Standiford Field,** Louisville, Ky. 40213. Phone (502) 364-9400; DSN 989-4400. 123d Airlift Wing (ANG); 223d Communications Sqdn. (ANG). Area 65 acres. Runway length NA. Altitude 497 ft. Military 1,121, full-time personnel 317. Payroll $13.5 million.

**Stewart International Airport,** Newburgh, N.Y. 12550-0031; 15 mi. N of USMA (West Point). Phone (914) 563-2000; DSN 247-2000. Hq. New York ANG; 105th Airlift Gp. (ANG); USMA subpost airport. Stewart AFB until 1969; acquired by state of New York in 1970. ANG area 272 acres. Runway length NA. Altitude 491 ft. ANG military 1,757, full-time personnel 672. Payroll $18 million. Dispensary. Most military services available through West Point or subpost.

**Toledo Express Airport,** Swanton, Ohio 43558; 14 mi. W of Toledo. Phone (419) 868-4078; DSN 580-4078. 180th Fighter Gp. (ANG). Area 84 acres. Runway length NA. Altitude 684 ft. Military 1,040, full-time personnel 297. Payroll $14.3 million. Four-bed clinic.

**Truax Field** (Dane County Regional Airport), Wis. 53704-2591; 2 mi. N of Madison. Phone (608) 241-6200; DSN 273-8210. 128th Fighter Wing (ANG). Activated June 1942 as AAF base; taken over by Wis. ANG in Apr. 1968. Named for Lt. T. L. Truax, killed in P-40 training accident in 1941. Area 155 acres. Runway length NA. Altitude 862 ft. Military 1,006, full-time personnel 310. Payroll $12.2 million. Housing: 7 transient. Dispensary.

**Tucson International Airport,** Ariz. 85734; within Tucson city limits. Phone (602) 573-2210; DSN 853-4210. 162d Fighter Gp. (ANG). Area 86 acres. Runway length NA. Altitude 2,650 ft. Military 1,583, full-time personnel 862. Payroll $24.3 million.

**Tulsa International Airport,** Okla. 74115. Phone (918) 832-8300; DSN 956-5297. 138th Fighter Gp. (ANG); 219th Electronic Installation Sqdn. Area 82 acres. Runway length NA. Altitude 676 ft. Military 1,148, full-time personnel 310. Payroll $13 million.

**Volk Field,** Wis. 54618-5001; 90 mi. NW of Madison. Phone (608) 427-1210; DSN 798-3210. ANG field training site featuring air-to-air and air-to-ground gunnery ranges and providing training for ANG flying units. Base and field named for Lt. Jerome A. Volk, first Wisconsin ANG pilot killed in the Korean War. Area 2,336 acres. Runway length NA. Altitude 910 ft. Military 74, full-time personnel 74. Payroll $2.1 million. Six-bed dispensary.

**W. K. Kellogg Airport,** Battle Creek, Mich. 49015-1291. Phone (616) 963-1596; DSN 580-3210. 110th Fighter Gp. (ANG). Area 315 acres. Runway length NA. Altitude 941 ft. Military 951, full-time personnel 254. Payroll $10.6 million.

**Westover ARB,** Mass. 01022-5000; 5 mi. NE of Chicopee. Phone (413) 557-1110; DSN 589-1110. AFRES base. 439th Airlift Wing (AFRES). Also home of Army, Navy, and Marine Corps Reserve and Massachusetts ARNG. Base dedicated Apr. 6, 1940; named for Maj. Gen. Oscar Westover, Chief of the Air Corps, killed Sept. 21, 1938, in crash near Burbank, Calif. Area 2,386 acres. Runway length NA. Altitude 244 ft. Full-time personnel (AFRES and tenant units) 526, Reservists 2,945, civilians 537. Payroll $59.8 million. Housing: 356 VAQ (500 beds), 50 VOQ (80 beds).

**Willow Grove ARS,** Pa. 19090-5203; 14 mi. N of Philadelphia. Runway length NA. Altitude 356 ft. ANG and AFRES have separate phones and facilities. ANG phone (215) 443-1500; DSN 991-1500. 111th Fighter Gp. (ANG). ANG area 39 acres. Military 1,147, full-time personnel 292. Payroll $11.2 million. AFRES phone (215) 443-1100; DSN 991-1100. 913th Airlift Gp. (AFRES). AFRES area 162 acres. Full-time personnel 140, Reservists 1,040, civilians 137. Payroll $18 million. Other units include Army, Navy, and Marine Corps Reserve. Defense Contract Administration Services Region, Philadelphia; 92d Aerial Port Sqdn. off-base tenant. Base activated Aug. 1958. Navy transient quarters available but limited.

**Will Rogers World Airport,** Okla. 73169-5000; 7 mi. SW of Oklahoma City. Phone (405) 686-5210; DSN 956-8210. 137th Airlift Wing (ANG). Area 134 acres. Runway length NA. Altitude 1,290 ft. Military 1,253, full-time personnel 254. Payroll $14.2 million.

**Yeager Airport,** W. Va. 25311-5000; 4 mi. NE of Charleston. Phone (304) 341-6210; DSN 366-9210. 130th Airlift Gp. (ANG). Airport named for Brig. Gen. Charles "Chuck" Yeager, first man to break the sound barrier. Area 236 acres. Runway length NA. Altitude 981 ft. Military 942, full-time personnel 249. Payroll $11.1 million. Dispensary, clinic.

**Youngstown Municipal Airport/ARS,** Ohio 44473-5000; 16 mi. N of Youngstown. Phone (216) 392-1000; DSN 346-1000. AFRES base. 910th Airlift Gp. (AFRES); 757th Airlift Sqdn. (AFRES). Other units include 76th Mobile Aerial Port Sqdn. (AFRES); Defense Contract Administration Services OLC; Naval Reserve, REDCOM 5; Marine Corps Reserve, H&S Co., H&S Bn., 4th FSSG; Army Corps of Engineers, Louisville District; FAA area office. Base activated 1952. Area 403 acres. Runway length NA. Altitude 1,196 ft. Full-time personnel 161, Reservists 1,053, civilians 230. Payroll $21 million.

## Appendix B

# Air University Suggested Professional Reading Guide

*An ignorant officer is a murderer. I have studied war long, earnestly and deeply, but yet I tremble at my own derelictions.*

—Sir Charles Napier

Note: The following is the most recent reading guide, released in 1990.

1. *Air Power Journal.* Professional journal of the U.S. Air Force. Published bimonthly by Government Printing Office, Washington, DC. A journal designed to stimulate professional thought concerning aerospace doctrine, strategy, tactics, and related matters.
2. Sun Tzu Wu. *The Art of War.* New York: Oxford University Press, 1971. This short military treatise written in the 6th century B.C. lays down a set of basic military principles dealing with strategy, tactics, communications, supply, etc. The basic nature of Sun Tzu's tenets gives them a lasting relevance.
3. Keegan, John. *The Face of Battle.* New York: The Viking Press, 1976. A highly readable, thoroughly researched analysis of human conduct in war based on compelling accounts of three battles fought within 100 miles of each other: Agincourt, 1415; Waterloo, 1815; the Somme, 1916. The author proposed that a study of what moves men to fight will provide the most useful lessons for the conduct of future wars.
4. Newman, Aubrey S. *Follow Me: The Human Element in Leadership.* Novato, CA: Presidio Press, 1981. This book is basic to the better understanding of military life and leadership. The author, a seasoned combat veteran, draws upon a long and rich experience, flavored with humor, to illustrate practical lessons of leadership.
5. Parton, James. *"Air Force Spoken Here": General Ira Eaker & The Command of the Air.* Bethesda: Adler and Adler, 1986. Skillfully written biography of Ira C. Eaker, aviation pioneer, wartime commander

of the Eighth Air Force, and beloved "grand old man of the Air Force," by his former military aide and close friend since 1942.

6. Taylor, Robert L., and William E. Rosenback. *Military Leadership—In Pursuit of Excellence.* Boulder, CO: Westview Press, 1984. This book of readings by noted military and civilian authors covers the concept of leadership, the dilemma of leadership and management, leadership in transition, and military leadership as a challenge and an opportunity. The readings are well chosen to reflect traditional and contemporary leadership thoughts and practices.
7. Van Creveld, Martin L. *Command in War.* Cambridge, MA: Harvard University Press, 1985. Reviews the evolution of military staffs from ancient to modern times and examines related developments that have served to strengthen the commander's planning of and control over increasingly diverse and dispersed military operations. This is virtually the only historical study of command and staff arrangements as they have developed over time. A careful study by a thoughtful Israeli military historian.
8. Frisbee, John L. *Makers of the United States Air Force.* Washington, DC: Government Printing Office, 1987. Chapter-length biographical sketches of twelve officers who helped shape and promote the modern U.S. Air Force. Includes several officers whose contributions are not well known throughout the Air Force: Hugh Knerr, Frank Andrews, William Kepner, and Benjamin Davis, Jr. Must reading on development of the USAF.
9. Liddell Hart, B. F. *Strategy.* New York: Frederick A. Praeger Inc., 1954. Provides insights into strategy, doctrine, and maxims of warfare. Stresses the indirect approach to warfighting and is the philosophical basis for current doctrinal thought. Also provides an excellent historical overview of warfare.
10. Paret, Peter, Ed. *Makers of Modern Strategy: From Machiavelli to the Nuclear Age.* Princeton, NJ: Princeton University Press, 1986. This revised edition of the classic *Makers of Modern Strategy* contains 28 essays that trace the evolution of military thought. The coverage and quality of the essays, greatly improved over the treatment provided in the original volume, make this a valuable source on military strategy.
11. Howard, Michael. *War in European History.* London, Oxford, and New York: Oxford University Press, 1976. A short survey of military history in Europe. Briefly examines some of the main trends in warfare from the Middle Ages into the nuclear age. It traces the major developments in society, politics, and technology that led from feudal to modern warfare.
12. Drew, Dennis M., and Donald M. Snow. *Making Strategy: An Introduction to National Security Processes and Problems.* Maxwell AFB, AL: Air University Press, 1988. A readable explanation of the strategy process across the entire spectrum of conflict, including the influence of military doctrine. Presents an analysis of military theory and the dilemmas facing the strategist in the nuclear, conventional, and insurgent warfare arenas.
13. Van Creveld, Martin L. *Supplying War: Logistics from Wallenstein to Patton.* New York: Cambridge University Press, 1979. Examines the practical art of moving armies and keeping them supplied. The author initially surveys the logistical practices of the 17th and 18th centuries and then closely examines six major campaigns from Napoleon against Russia to the Allies in Normandy.
14. Weigley, Russell F. *The American Way of War.* Bloomington, IN: IU Press, 1977. This is probably the most readable military history of the United States. The Weigley thesis divides our strategic thought into two categories. The first, annihila-

tion as practiced by Grant and Eisenhower in the broad-front, wear down of the enemy, is cited as "the American way." The second strategy is that of attrition, as practiced by George Washington, Winfield Scott, and Geronimo. This strategy is not "the American way" in Weigley's view but deserves more attention than it gets.

15. Krepinevich, Andrew, J., Jr. *The Army and Vietnam.* Baltimore: The Johns Hopkins University Press, 1986. Major (now lieutenant colonel) Krepinevich argues that the Army failed in Vietnam because its leaders refused to acknowledge the unconventional aspects of the war. Perfect counterpoint to Colonel Summers's *On Strategy*, demonstrating how institutional imperatives can sometimes drive strategy and policy.
16. Osgood, Robert E. *Limited War Revisited.* Boulder, CO: Westview Press, 1979. The author examines the development of limited war strategy since the end of World War II. In particular, he focuses on the impact of strategy on the Vietnam conflict and a limited war scenario in Central Europe. He also offers a comprehensive discussion on the types of conflict most likely to occur in the future.
17. Whiting, Kenneth R. *Soviet Air Power.* Boulder, CO: Westview Press, 1986. Air University's long-time professor of Russian and Soviet studies (1950–85) describes the history and present state of development of the Soviet air forces.
18. Scott, Harriet Fast, and William F. Scott. *The Armed Forces of the USSR.* 3d edition, revised and updated. Boulder, CO: Westview Press, 1984. The best one-volume treatment of Soviet military doctrine, forces, training, manpower, organization, and the role of the military in political affairs.
19. Clausewitz, Carl Von. *On War.* Edited and translated by Sir Michael Howard and Peter Paret. Princeton, NJ: Princeton University Press, 1976. The military classic on the art of waging war and the foundation of modern strategic science in warfare.
20. Brodie, Bernard. *War and Politics.* New York: The Macmillan Company, 1973. Brodie addresses an idea put forth by Clausewitz that the question of why we fight must dominate any consideration of means. Brodie first provides a general history of World War I, World War II, Korea, and Vietnam. He then discusses changing attitudes toward war and provides some theories of the causes of war.
21. Larrabee, Eric. *Commander in Chief: Franklin Delano Roosevelt. His Lieutenants and Their War.* New York: Harper and Row, 1987. Through stories of the president's "principal subordinates—their personalities, their battles (sometimes with each other), and the consequences of their decisions," Eric Larrabee tells the story of "FDR's war," "how he ran it, picked his key military leaders," and the extent and importance of Roosevelt's role in directing America's wartime strategy.
22. Builder, Carl H. *The Masks of War: American Military Styles in Strategy and Analysis.* Baltimore: Johns Hopkins University Press, 1989. This provocative study by a senior analyst for the Rand Corporation provides a detailed taxonomy of military strategies and thinking within the armed services and endeavors to strip away the "masks of war" that cover the pursuit of institutional self-interests. With a foreword by Senator Sam Nunn (GA), this is for students wanting fresh perspectives from which to view service strategic planning in the light of recent developments in superpower relations.
23. Warden, John A., III. *The Air Campaign: Planning for Combat.* Washington, DC: National Defense University Press, 1988. Written while Colonel Warden was Deputy Director for Warfighting Concepts in the Air Staff's Directorate of Plans, this book endeavors to come to grips with the theory for employing air power at the operational level. The result is thought-provoking, controversial, and should occupy a prominent place in any warfighting professional's library.

24. Clodfelter, Mark. *The Limits of Airpower: The American Bombing of North Vietnam.* New York: Free Press, 1989. The author, a professor of history at the Air Force Academy, provides a well-wrought analysis of the ways in which (and how well) air power complemented American political objectives in the Vietnam War. His most useful finding: "Doctrinal conviction established long before Vietnam colored air commanders' perceptions of bombing effectiveness." This slight tome (only 279 pages) is essential reading for any student of air power who craves a better understanding of how political necessities affect military decisions and results.
25. Hartle, Anthony E. *Moral Issues in Military Decision Making.* Lawrence, KA: University of Kansas Press, 1989. A provocative examination of critical military issues in the United States. Argues that the environment in which the military member must function poses a severe threat to morally consistent and defensible decisions. Proposes a coherent rational justification for codifying a professional military ethic. Currently the definitive book on the subject.
26. Blanchard, Kenneth, and Norman Vincent Peale. *The Power of Ethical Management.* New York: William Morrow and Company, Inc., 1988. A landmark book providing usable guidance to assist in creating "a healthy work environment where people don't have to cheat to win." Concise, readable, immensely important for developing leadership integrity.
27. Mets, David R. *Master of Air Power: General Carl A. Spaatz.* Novato, CA: Presidio Press, 1988. To read *Master of Air Power*, about General Carl A. Spaatz, is to read the history of the birth and growth of air power from its start through two world wars. It is also the story of the life of one of our greatest Air Force generals. This is an excellent textbook to teach our young people our history and the history of the development of air power.
28. Gansler, Jacques S. *Affording Defense.* Cambridge, MA: MIT Press, 1989. The United States had two compelling reasons to get more bang for the buck in military spending when this book was written. The first was the Soviet Union, which, even under the relatively benign Gorbachev, had three times the military equipment of the United States and produced new weapons at three times the rate that we did. President Ronald Reagan asked for 2 percent growth for 1990, and President George Bush lowered it to zero. So there was only one way to stay even militarily: get more defense for less money. Mr. Gansler, a private defense analyst who also teaches at Harvard University's John F. Kennedy School of Government, insisted it could be done.
29. Phillips, Thomas R. *Roots of Strategy: The Five Greatest Military Classics of All Time,* Harrisburg, PA: Stackpole Books, 1985. This collection contains the most influential military classics written prior to the nineteenth century: *The Art of War*, Sun Tzu; *The Military Institutions of the Romans*, Vegetius; *My Reveries upon the Art of War*, Marshall Maurice de Saxe; *The Instruction of Frederick the Great for His Generals*; and *The Military Maxims of Napoleon.*
30. Williamson, Porter B. *General Patton's Principles for Life and Leadership.* Tucson: Management and Systems Consultants, Inc., 1988. General George S. Patton, Jr., in addition to being one of the greatest field generals in the history of the Army, was also quite a philosopher. Mr. Williamson, who was on General Patton's staff, groups some bits of Patton's philosophy into areas such as command, management, success, life, and death. An interesting book holding many truths for today.

Appendix C

# Gallery of USAF Aircraft

F-111.

F-15 EAGLE.

F-16 FIGHTING FALCONS.

B-52 STRATOFORTRESS.

B-2.

B-1.

AC-130H HERCULES GUNSHIP.

HH-53 SUPER JOLLY.

MC-130E COMBAT TALON I.

KC-10 EXTENDER REFUELING C-5A GALAXY.

C-17.

A-10 WARTHOG.

X-29.

F-117A, THE STEALTH FIGHTER.

C-20A GULFSTREAM III.

YF-22 ADVANCED TACTICAL FIGHTER.

## Appendix D

# Selected Air Force Publications

This book contains references to the Air Force regulations, manuals, pamphlets, and forms listed below. As the *Guide* goes to press, the information below is correct. You should be aware, however, that sometimes the status of a publication will change (e.g., an AFP may become an AFR) or a publication will be renumbered or renamed.

| | |
|---|---|
| AFR 11-7 | Air Force Relations with Congress |
| AFR 12-50 | Disposition of Air Force Documents and Records |
| AFR 30-2 | Social Actions Program |
| AFR 30-9 | Meetings of Technical, Scientific, Professional or Similar Organizations |
| AFR 30-30 | Standards of Conduct |
| AFR 31-3 | Air Force Board for Correction of Military Records |
| AFR 31-11 | Correction of Officer and Airman Evaluation Reports |
| AFR 35-1 | Military Personnel Classification Policy |
| AFR 35-4 | Physical Evaluation for Retention, Retirement and Separation |
| AFR 35-7 | Service Retirement |
| AFR 35-9 | Leave and Administrative Absence Policy |
| AFR 35-10 | Dress and Personal Appearance for Air Force Personnel |
| AFR 35-11 | The Air Force Weight and Fitness Program |
| AFR 35-18 | Personal Financial Responsibility |
| AFR 35-32 | Unfavorable Information File Program |
| AFR 35-35 | Individual Newcomer Treatment and Orientation Program |
| AFR 35-54 | Appointment to and Assumption of Command |
| AFR 36-1 | Officer Classification |
| AFR 36-2 | Administrative Discharge Procedures |
| AFR 36-10 | Officer Evaluation System |
| AFR 36-12 | Administrative Separation of Commissioned Officers |
| AFR 36-20 | Officer Assignments |
| AFR 36-23 | Officer Professional Development |
| AFR 36-41 | USAF Officer Exchanges with Air Forces of Other Governments |

| | |
|---|---|
| AFR 36-51 | Active Duty Service Commitments (ADSC) |
| AFR 36-94 | Specified Period of Time Contract (SPTC) |
| AFR 45 Series | The Reserve Forces |
| AFR 45-48 | AFROTC |
| AFR 46-3 | Civil Air Patrol Cadet Program |
| AFR 50 Series | Training |
| AFR 50-5 | USAF Formal Schools |
| AFR 50-9 | Special Training |
| AFR 50-12 | Extension Course Program |
| AFR 50-14 | Drill and Ceremonies |
| AFR 50-36 | The U.S. Combat Arms Training and Maintenance Program |
| AFR 53-8 | USAF Officer Professional Military Education (PME) System |
| AFR 53-11 | Air Force Institute of Technology |
| AFR 90 Series | Housing |
| AFR 110-22 | Legal Assistance Program |
| AFR 111-1 | Military Justice Guide |
| AFR 143-1 | Mortuary Affairs |
| AFR 146 Series | Food Service |
| AFR 147-7 | Defense Department Exchange Service (General) Policies |
| AFR 170-17 | Credit Unions on Air Force Installations |
| AFR 176-1 | Basic Responsibilities, Policies and Practices (Non-Appropriated Funds—NAF) |
| AFR 190-1 | Public Affairs Policies and Procedures |
| AFR 205 Series | Intelligence and Security |
| AFR 205-1 | Information Security Program |
| AFR 206-2 | Air Base Ground Defense |
| AFR 211-1 | Air Force Aid Society (AFAS) |
| AFR 211-3 | Personal Affair (PA) Information and Assistance |
| AFR 211-11 | Red Cross Activities within the Air Force |
| AFR 211-19 | Voting Assistance and Information |
| AFR 213-1 | Operation and Administration of the Air Force Education Services Program |
| AFR 215-1 | Air Force Morale, Welfare and Recreation Programs and Activities |
| AFR 215-11 | Air Force Open Mess Program |
| AFR 265-1 | The Chaplain Service |
| AFR 900-29 | Special Trophies and Awards |
| AFR 900-48 | Individual and Unit Awards, Special Badges and Devices |
| AFM 50-2 | Instructional System Development |
| AFM 67-1 | USAF Supply Manual |
| AFM 143-2 | State, Official and Special Military Funerals |
| AFM 177-373 | Joint Uniform Military Pay System—JUMPS AFD Procedures |
| AFP 30-6 | Guide for an Air Force Dining-In |
| AFP 35-75 | Overseas Housing Allowance (OHA) |
| AFP 35-76 | Cost of Living Allowance (COLA) |
| AFP 50-34 | Promotion Fitness Examination (PFE) Study Guide |
| AFP 143-8 | Escorting Deceased Air Force Military Personnel |
| AFP 177-4 | JUMPS Pay Tips |
| AFP 208-1 | Coping with Terrorism Abroad |

| | |
|---|---|
| AFP 211-4 | Voting Assistance Guide |
| AFP 211-14 | Survivor Benefit Plan |
| AFP 211-35 | Once a Veteran |
| AFP 211-40 | Insurance |
| AFP 211-41 | Estate Planning |
| AF Form 90 | Career Assignment Worksheet |
| AF Form 475 | Education/Training Report |
| AF Form 1137 | Unfavorable Information Files Summary (LRA) |
| AF Form 1466 | Request for Family Members Medical and Education Clearance for Travel |
| DD Form 2 AF | Identification Card (ID Card) |
| DD Form 93 | Record of Emergency Data |
| DD Form 149 | Application for Correction of Military Record |
| DD Form 214 | Certificate of Release or Discharge from Active Duty |
| DD Form 397 | Claims Certification and Voucher for Death Gratuity Payment |
| DD Form 458 | Charge Sheet |
| DD Form 1173 | Identification and Privilege Card |
| DD Form 1278 | Certificate of Oversea Assignment to Support Application to File Petition for Naturalization |
| DD Form 1299 | Application for Shipment and/or Storage of Personal Property |

## Appendix E

# Selected Acronyms and Abbreviations

| | |
|---|---|
| AAM | Air Achievement Medal |
| ACE | American Council on Education |
| ACSC | Air Command and Staff College |
| ADSC | Active Duty Service Commitments |
| AFAM | Air Force Achievement Medal |
| AFC | Air Force Cross |
| AFEM | Armed Forces Expeditionary Medal |
| AFGCM | Air Force Good Conduct Medal |
| AFIT | Air Force Institute of Technology |
| AFLSA | Air Force Longevity Service Award |
| AFM | Air Force Manual |
| AFMPC | Air Force Military Personnel Center |
| AFOEA | Air Force Organizational Excellence Award |
| AFOSR | Air Force Overseas Ribbon |
| AFOUA | Air Force Outstanding Unit Award |
| AFP | Air Force Pamphlet |
| AFR | Air Force Regulation |
| AFRM | Armed Forces Reserve Medal |
| AFROTC | Air Force Reserve Officer Training Corps |
| AFRR | Air Force Recognition Ribbon |
| AFS | Air Force Specialty |
| AFSC | Air Force Specialty Code |
| AFTR | Air Force Training Ribbon |
| AFWC | Air Force Wargaming Center |
| AIS | Academic Instructor School |
| AM | Air Medal |
| AMC | Air Mobility Command |
| AmnM | Airman's Medal |
| AO | airdrome officer |

| | |
|---|---|
| APOE | Aerial Port of Embarkation |
| APZ | above the promotion zone |
| ARFMSM | Air Reserve Forces Meritorious Service Medal |
| ARI | Airpower Research Institute |
| ASM | Antarctica Service Medal |
| AWC | Air War College |
| BAQ | Basic Allowance for Quarters |
| BAS | Basic Allowance for Subsistence |
| BDU | battle dress uniform |
| BMT | Basic Military Training |
| BMTHGR | USAF Basic Military Training Honor Graduate Ribbon |
| BOQ | bachelor officers' quarters |
| BPZ | below the promotion zone |
| BSM | Bronze Star Medal |
| BX | base exchange |
| CADRE | Center for Aerospace Doctrine, Research and Education |
| CAP | Civil Air Patrol |
| CEI | Combat Employment Institute |
| CHAMPUS | Civilian Health and Medical Program of the Uniformed Services |
| COLA | cost of living allowance |
| CPOs | chief petty officers |
| CRM | Combat Readiness Medal |
| DANTES | Defense Activity for Non-Traditional Education Support |
| DDSM | Defense Distinguished Service Medal |
| DFC | Distinguished Flying Cross |
| DMSM | Defense Meritorious Service Medal |
| DOD | Department of Defense |
| DODPM | Department of Defense Military Pay and Allowances Entitlement Manual |
| DOPMA | Defense Officer Personnel Management Act |
| DOS | date of separation |
| DSM | Distinguished Service Medal |
| DSSM | Defense Superior Service Medal |
| DUC | Distinguished Unit Citation |
| DVs | Distinguished Visitors |
| EAD | extended active duty |
| ECI | Extension Course Institute |
| GOC | Ground Observer Corps |
| HSM | Humanitarian Service Medal |
| IOS | International Officer School |
| IPZ | in the promotion zone |
| IRS | indefinite reserve status |
| JOPS | Joint Operation Planning System |
| JSCM | Joint Service Commendation Medal |
| JTR | Joint Travel Regulations |
| JUMPS | Joint Uniform Military Pay System |
| LAO | legal assistance officer |
| LM | Legion of Merit |
| LPDP | Lieutenants' Professional Development Program |
| MAJCOM | Major Command |

| | |
|---|---|
| MH | Medal of Honor |
| MHA | Medal for Humane Action |
| MPO | Military Personnel Office |
| MRE | Meals Ready to Eat |
| MSM | Meritorious Service Medal |
| MWR | Morale, Welfare, and Recreation |
| NAF | non-appropriated funds |
| NCOPC | NCO Preparatory Course |
| NCOPMEGR | NCO Professional Military Education Graduate Ribbon |
| NDSM | National Defense Service Medal |
| NHSC | National Home Study Council |
| OAYR | Outstanding Airman of the Year Ribbon |
| OD | officer of the day |
| OER | officer effectiveness report (now OPR) |
| OJT | on-the-job training |
| OOD | officer of the deck |
| OPR | officer performance report (formerly OER) |
| OSI | Office of Special Investigations |
| OTS | Officer Training School |
| PCS | permanent change of station |
| PEB | Personnel Evaluation Board |
| PH | Purple Heart |
| PLS/TAFCS | Promotion List Service/Total Active Federal Commissioned Service |
| PME | Professional Military Education |
| POWM | Prisoner of War Medal |
| PT | physical training |
| PUC | Presidential Unit Citation |
| ROTC | Reserve Officer Training Corps |
| RVNCM | Republic of Vietnam Campaign Medal |
| SAEMR | Small Arms Expert Marksmanship Ribbon |
| SBP | Survivor Benefit Plan |
| SNCOA | Senior NCO Academy |
| SOPs | standing operating procedures |
| SPTC | Specified Period of Time Contract |
| SS | Silver Star |
| SWASM | Southwest Asia Service Medal |
| TDY | temporary duty |
| UCMJ | Uniform Code of Military Justice |
| UNM | United Nations Medal |
| USAF | U.S. Air Force |
| VEAP | Veterans Educational Assistance Program |
| VNSM | Vietnam Service Medal |

# Index